PLANNING
A PLURALIST CITY

A Publication of the Joint Center for Urban Studies of the
Massachusetts Institute of Technology and Harvard University

PLANNING A PLURALIST CITY

CONFLICTING REALITIES IN CIUDAD GUAYANA

Donald Appleyard

The MIT Press

Cambridge, Massachusetts, and London, England

This book was set in IBM Composer Univers by Techdata Associates, Inc. and printed and bound by Murray Printing Company in the United States of America.

Library of Congress Cataloging in Publication Data

Appleyard, Donald.
Planning a pluralist city.

(Publication of the Joint Center for Urban Studies)
Bibliography: p.
Includes index.
1. Cities and towns—Planning—Ciudad Guayana. I. Title.
II. Series: Joint Center for Urban Studies. Publications.
HT169.V42C582 309.2'62
75-40026
ISBN 0-262-01044-5

CONTENTS

ACKNOWLEDGMENTS

I was a consultant to the Joint Center Group in Caracas from the very beginning of the Guayana Project and was one of the first people from Cambridge to go down to Caracas in the summer of 1961. The ensuing three summers were spent in Venezuela.

The initial impetus for this study came from Lloyd Rodwin, then Director of the Guayana Project and Chairman of the Faculty Committee of the M.I.T.-Harvard Joint Center for Urban Studies. It could not have been carried through without the support of Dr. Juan Andrés Vegas, of the Corporación Venezolana de Guayana, and of Willo von Moltke, at the time Director of the Joint Center's Urban Design Group in Caracas. The idea for the study grew out of my years of teaching and research with Kevin Lynch.

An agency that plans a city rarely supports evaluations of its planning process. Most published city plans never tell of the debates, problems, mistakes, and corrections—information eagerly sought by other professionals, journalists, and citizens. The Guayana Project was unique in providing an opportunity for evaluation during the planning process.

Some chapters or parts of chapters have been previously published. Part of chapter 5 was originally published in *Environment and Behavior* 1, no. 2 (December 1969), under the title "Why Buildings Are Known: A Predictive Model for Architects and Planners." Part of chapter 8 was published in *Environment and Behavior* 2, no. 1 (April 1970), under the title "Styles and Methods of Structuring a City." An earlier version of chapter 10, appearing under the title "Notes on Urban Perception and Knowledge," was published in *Proceedings 1, Second Annual Environmental Design Research Association Conference* (Pittsburgh: Carnegie-Mellon University, 1970), and in R. M. Downs and D. Stea, eds., *Image and Environment: Cognitive Mapping and Spatial Behavior* (Chicago: Aldine, 1973).

I should also like to acknowledge the M.I.T.-Harvard Joint Center for Urban Studies and the Corporación Venezolana de Guayana planning teams for the preparation of the figures 1.1-1.3, 2.1-2.3, 4.4, 4.10, 4.11, 7.8, 7.19, 7.45, 7.48-7.50,

8.1, 8.32-8.34, 9.16, and 9.18.

I am indebted to those who have worked directly on the project, especially to Anna Maria Sant'Anna, who organized the interviews and processing of the data: Carl Steinitz, who conducted the field surveys and map coding; and Harriett Older, who completed the data processing. Lisa Peattie and Frank Bonilla helped to formulate the research design. Kevin Lynch, Lloyd Rodwin, Anthony Penfold, William Porter, Carl Steinitz, Gary Winkel, George McKechnie, and Kenneth Craik have all made invaluable comments on earlier drafts of the text.

The M.I.T.-Harvard Joint Center for Urban Studies provided the main support for the study. Various other sources—the Institute of Urban and Regional Development, the Farrand Research Fund of the Landscape Department, and a Humanities Fellowship, all at the University of California at Berkeley—have enabled me to complete it.

The person who has contributed more to the book's completion than anyone else—although she may not realize it—is my wife, Sheila.

INTRODUCTION

This book is about how the people and planners of Ciudad Guayana viewed the city and its plans. Its purpose is to make professionals and citizens more conscious of the bias in their own perceptions, to help them understand the perceptions of others who live in cities, and to propose some new guidelines for structuring cities for functional, social, and educational purposes.

Ciudad Guayana was many cities in one. Different people knew it in different ways. Their perceptions of its parts, their cognitive maps of the city, and their predictions of how it might grow varied from group to group and from person to person. Citizens viewed the city in different ways depending on their backgrounds, familiarity with the city, patterns of use, educational level, and methods of transportation.

Their perceptions differed, too, from those of the professional planners, architects, landscape architects, and engineers—a difference made visible in the contrasts between buildings and districts designed by professionals and those constructed by the inhabitants of the "rancho" or self-help housing areas of the city. The professional designers visualized the sites primarily from the vertical viewpoint of their plans; the inhabitant located and constructed his rancho by eye. The professional oriented his buildings to the cardinal points, while the inhabitant oriented his to existing paths or slopes, Thus, the professionally designed parts of the city took on a clear order from the air—just like Brasilia—while the indigenous settlements looked more fitting when seen from the ground. Each group produced coherent designs through different media: one of maps, the other of the real world.

The illusion that professionals are value-free technicians has been somewhat dispelled in recent years,[1] but the illusion of objective perception endures. Since the city can be mapped, measured, and physically changed, it appears to be an objective entity, but the items of analysis and the media chosen to plan cities are subjectively selected. The paradox is that as planners become more adept and sophisticated at conceptualizing the so-called objective city—through the use of aerial photographs, maps, statistics, and mathematical modeling—their conceptual distance from the inhabitant's subjective personal city usually increases. The trained person cannot see the city with an eye innocent of the concepts, vocabulary, and media of his profession or discipline.

In the planning of new cities the distance between planners and population tends to be accentuated. Frequently the planners do not live near the site, since much of the planning is carried out in the metropolitan centers where professionals concentrate. Usually there is a time gap between the planners, who are there before the city is built, and the inhabitants, who arrive after it is finished. This may explain why professionals experience such exhilarating freedom in the planning of new cities. They can experiment with linear, concentric, or gridiron plans, tree structures or semilattices, alternative densities, building types, or transportation systems. The inhabitants seldom, if ever, engage in these deliberations, and their viewpoints are rarely sought later.

Yet the planning and layout of a new city is an especially powerful kind of planning. Plans for new cities can determine where different kinds of people will live, they can control which kinds of facilities will be available to those people, and they can shape the population's urban knowledge. Of course, control is not complete. People can and do rebel against imposed environments by refusing to use them as intended. But this is difficult in new cities when choices are limited and pressures to "conform to the plan" are high.

For environmental professionals such differences in perception and production are serious matters. They can unwittingly plan aspects of the environment that have no relevance to the population, while ignoring aspects that are critical. They can put life into a straitjacket for a time. They may unknowingly destroy or damage valued places or build white elephants, empty of meaning or subsequent use. Such misperceptions occurred frequently in Ciudad Guayana despite all efforts at comprehension. Indeed, they have probably occurred in every city, for professionals are still relatively ignorant of their public clients.

Moreover, the public clients often differ as much between themselves in their perceptions of a city as they do from the professionals. Social classes can have quite opposite views of even the same building, migrants see a different city from long-time residents, those who travel by bus live in a different world from those who drive automobiles, and so on. Each personal city has idiosyncratic qualities, and people are strangely unaware of these differences. Why is this?

It seems that homogeneous groups viewing the city in similar ways reinforce each other's isolation from other groups. Environmental pluralism is not apparent because in most cases different citizen groups do not even cross each other's frontiers. They select the world they wish to live in and exclude the parts that are too strange—an isolation and ignorance that can lead to misty-eyed romanticism or outright intolerance. In Ciudad Guayana, the overlap in urban knowledge was so low that only two buildings were mentioned by more than 50 percent of our sample when they were asked to draw maps of the city.

One obvious answer to the problem of planning for such diversity is to let the people do it for themselves; encourage each population group to articulate its own viewpoint. But even when ways are developed for citizens to participate in and control planning decisions, they too must know something of the personal environments of other citizens, for, given the limited time that most citizens have for engaging in planning, most decisions have to be worked out by small groups in the absence, or only brief presence, of representatives of various population groups. Therefore, both decision makers and inhabitants have a stake in learning more about differences in urban perception and the significance of these differences in the structure and design of cities.

The first major study of urban perception appeared in 1960 when Kevin Lynch published *The Image of the City.* Since then many studies have been carried out replicating Lynch's techniques.[2] Geographers, planners, sociologists, and psychologists have become interested for various reasons in perception and cognition of the larger environment.[3] This study takes off most directly from Lynch's work, however, and we shall be more interested in the social, functional, and environmental attributes by which the city is identified and structured.

We shall pay particular attention to certain aspects of environmental *meaning* by exploring how well the city's functional and social pattern, economic base, and natural environment are communicated to and accurately interpreted by its inhabitants. We shall also describe the inhabitants' perceptions of environmental change, remembered past, perceived present, expected future, and knowledge of the city's future plans.

Perceptions cannot be understood in isolation from values or behavior. Though these are peripheral to the central theme of the study, they will be brought in where they bear on perceptions. We shall try to see how what people value relates to what they recall, and we shall also look at the city as a product of different group perceptions. Ciudad Guayana provides a unique opportunity for comparing planners' and inhabitants' perceptions through their products, because the city was a mixture of "planned" and "indigenous" development.

Behind this study lies the conviction that the citizens' comprehension of their city and its meaning over time is a worthwhile planning and educational goal. Urban knowledge can help individual citizens and social groups to function well in the world, make informed choices, and master their environments. Shared knowledge, while not ensuring shared values, permits common experience and open discussion and encourages community care for cities and their environments. Ignorance, secrecy, misperceptions, and other barriers to communication usually prevent such sharing. But the mere wish to impart knowledge is too global an aim. In the modern city we are faced with an information explosion, which makes it difficult to discriminate between the meaningful and the trivial or even to handle all the meaningful information that is available. Many kinds of information can be significant to the inhabitants of a city, from operational information for survival and emergency, for using the city efficiently, and for finding amenities, to general information about the social and economic structure of the city, its natural substructure, its past and present, and its future plans. Different population groups value one kind of information more than another. Some are more interested or adept at gaining information; others are information-deprived.

In existing cities some operational information is available to the public in the form of maps, historical guides, and telephone directories. However, much of the general information—if not picked up from the ephemeral news media—requires significant search, and even then it is often fragmented in single channels not easily related to spatial locations. It is rarely available as a person travels around the city.

The city environment itself, the direct experience, serves as an essential information source. The city environment can be viewed as a vast collection of verbal and nonverbal signs containing messages that are read, ignored, or misread by its population. The inhabitant's comprehension of a city is limited by the level of attention that he reserves for that activity, his experience and skill, and by the scope of his travels.

The inhabitant's comprehension of the city is also limited by the *communicability* of the urban environment. The city environment communicates what is going on through many kinds of cues: the presence of people; their dress, manner, means of locomotion, and various activities; explicit verbal signs labeling establishments, streets, and neighborhoods; the transparency of buildings, which reveals the processes, products, and accoutrements of their housed functions; architectural style, composition, and conformance of buildings with known stereotypes; tree-filled parks; gas stations; high-rise office buildings; or church steeples. Much depends on which items are visible.

In planning a new or rapidly growing city, those responsible for the spatial allocation of land uses and the design of the transportation system have the opportunity to increase and order the information available to inhabitants and to allow many groups to enter the arena of communication. By learning what cues inhabitants select in their perceptions of the city, we can discover the environmental language by which messages are conveyed. For example, commercial enterprises consciously try to sell their products and services through the use of billboards and other symbols, but few modern planners have attended to this information system.

The educational structure of a city can have an aesthetic quality too. Learning occurs through the actions, senses, and images. A communications system takes on aesthetic quality when the form of the message is treated as an end in itself (Jacobson 1960). In this sense the city is analogous to movies, drama, and poetry: arts that depend for their aesthetic effect on the power and vividness of their forms of communication.

This book will concentrate, then, on the ways in which various kinds of information can be structured through the urban environment. Structuring the city as a communications medium is, of course, not the only purpose of structuring cities. The provision of access, related to but distinct from communication; the avoidance or reduction of hazards, nuisance, discomfort, and pollution; the maintenance of privacy and social relations; the preservation and care of the natural environment; and pure aesthetic qualities must also be accounted for. These are subjects of discussion here, but only as much as information about them affects city structure. Hence, some of the policies proposed may be in conflict with other urban purposes. Revealing information about facets of the city may intrude on group privacy, may expose "undesirable" facets of the city's environment, and may not solve problems of transportation or pollution. But information should be considered with other factors at moments of decision.

We shall begin with a background description of Ciudad Guayana, its planning team, and the research methods (chapter 1). Following this will be chapters on the inhabitants' general perceptions of the city and its surrounding landscape (chapter 2), the spatial extent and complexity of the inhabitants' knowledge (chapter 3), the perceptions and meaning of settlements and barrios (chapter 4), the perceived attributes of buildings and places (chapters 5 and 6) and the communication of their social and functional meanings (chapter 7), the spatial structuring of the city (chapter 8), and perceptions of plans and structural change (chapter 9).

Each chapter compares the ways in which the planners set about conceptualizing and planning the city, with the perceptions of the population and differences within the population samples. Chapters conclude with policy implications for the planning of other cities. Because of the loose relation between evidence and policy, the recommendations at the end of each chapter are often couched in qualifying language. Since prediction is precarious, actions taken on such recommendations will require monitoring and management.

The reader should be aware of the distinction between evidence and policy. The accumulation of evidence—in this case of the inhabitants' knowledge of cities and their evaluations of it—produces no overriding mandate to carry out one policy or another. We only know better the existing state of affairs. Policy makers may decide not to satisfy expressed preferences if it can be argued that people do not know what is best for them, like those living in flood plains, or that other groups might suffer, or that resources do not allow such satisfaction. Similarly, in the case of perceptions, policy makers may or may not decide to change perceptions or reduce ignorance for any of several reasons.

Evidence in these cases will, however, help to inform policy makers of possible consequences. It may show how far inhabitants are being "stretched" from their existing life-styles and thoughtways, and signal possible problems. Without evidence, decisions are made in a vacuum. In many cases throughout this book there will be instances of environmental proposals that were carried through without prior knowledge of perceptions and values, where the citizens eventually rejected proposals and even rejected built projects. An early warning system could have avoided many of these problems.

The two concluding chapters summarize the two themes of the book. Chapter 10 attempts to characterize different perceptions of the city and concludes with some strategies for structuring the plural city. Chapter 11 focuses on public environments as the principal arena for structuring knowledge of cities.

Lest the unwary reader take the criticisms in this book as faults solely of the Guayana Project, let me dispel that notion at the beginning. The staff of the Guayana Project was of exceptional quality, and its members were valued colleagues. The book questions primarily the media and methods available then and now to the planning and design professions. The plans of other cities, both new and old, do not appear to be any more conscious of inhabitants' perceptions than do the early plans of Ciudad Guayana.

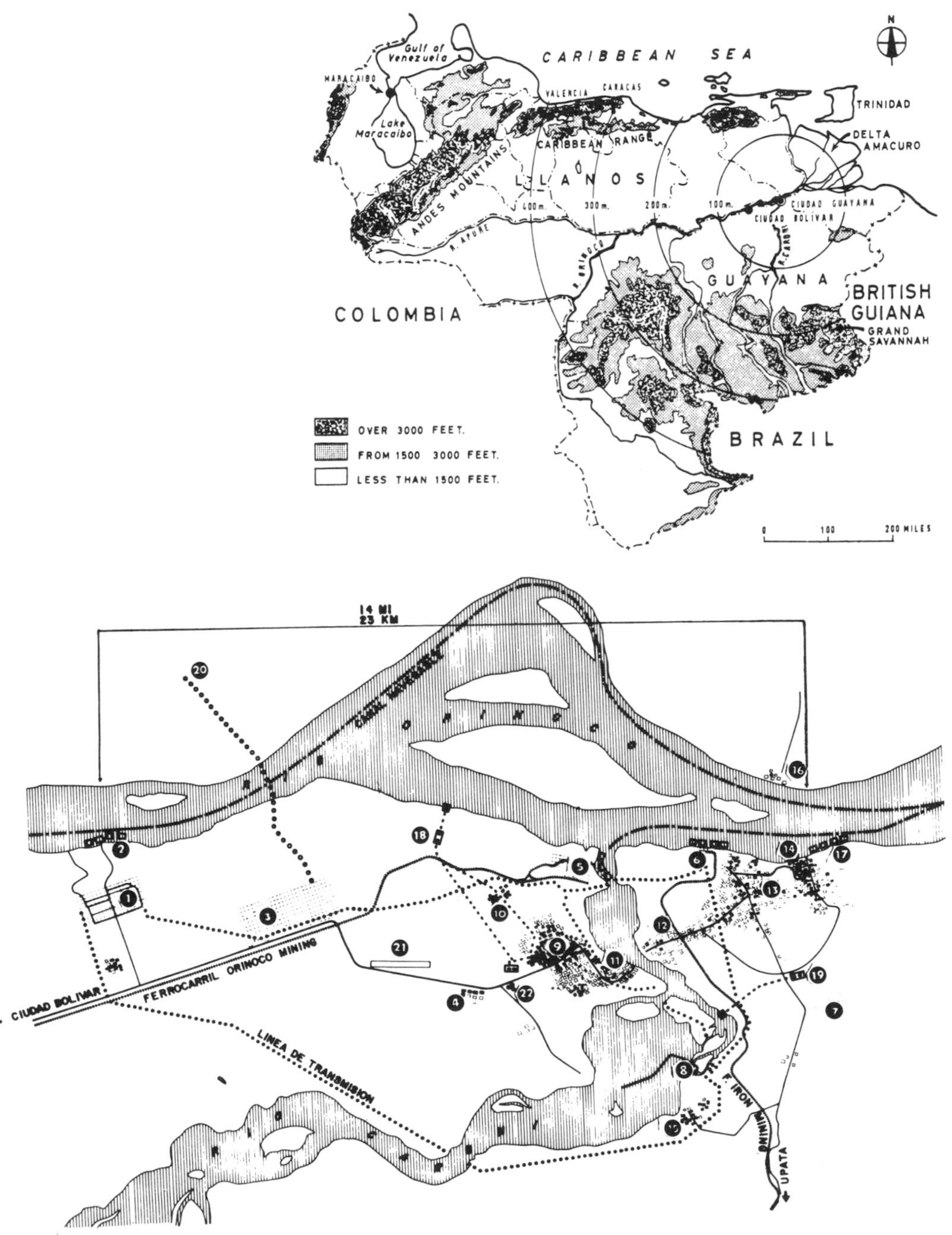
N
CARIBBEAN SEA
Gulf of Venezuela
MARACAIBO
Lake Maracaibo
VALENCIA
CARACAS
TRINIDAD
DELTA AMACURO
CARIBBEAN RANGE
ANDES MOUNTAINS
LLANOS
400m.
300m.
200m.
100m.
CIUDAD GUAYANA
CIUDAD BOLIVAR
R. APURE
R. ORINOCO
R. CARONI
GUAYANA
BRITISH GUIANA
GRAND SAVANNAH
COLOMBIA
BRAZIL
OVER 3000 FEET.
FROM 1500 3000 FEET.
LESS THAN 1500 FEET.
0 100 200 MILES
14 MI
23 KM
CIUDAD BOLIVAR
FERROCARRIL ORINOCO MINING
LINEA DE TRANSMISION
UPATA

1 THE GUAYANA PROJECT

The Guayana Project

In the early 1960s, the Joint Center for Urban Studies of the Massachusetts Institute of Technology and Harvard University was asked by the Corporación Venezolana de Guayana (CVG) to act as resident consultant for the development of the resource-rich Guayana region of Venezuela, and particularly for the planning of Ciudad Guayana, the new industrial city growing on the banks of the Orinoco River at the expanding center of that region (figure 1.1).

Figure 1.1 Guayana region of Venezuela.

Figure 1.2 Man-made site conditions of Ciudad Guayana, 1963: (1) Matanzas Steel Mill; (2) port; (3) industrial estate; (4) small industries; (5) Orinoco Mining Company port installations; (6) Iron Mines Company—port installation; (7) light industrial estate; (8) Macagua Dam; (9) Puerto Ordaz; (10) Orinoco Mining Company—Country Club; (11) Castillito; (12) Dalla Costa; (13) El Roble; (14) San Félix; (15) Macagua Dam—housing; (16) Los Barrancos; (17) San Félix—general port; (18) and (19) water treatment plants; (20) oil pipeline; (21) airport; (22) microwave transmission tower.

At that time, some 30,000 people were living near the confluence of the Orinoco and Caroní rivers, about 300 miles to the east of Caracas (figure 1.2). For nearly four centuries a small population had inhabited San Félix, a fishing village below the confluence, but the region witnessed little change until extensive deposits of iron ore were discovered in the 1940s (Orinoco Mining Company 1959). In the late 1940s, two North American steel companies began to extract ore from the iron mountains at Cerro Bolívar (the Orinoco Mining Company, a subsidiary of U.S. Steel) to the west of the Caroní River and at El Pao (the Iron Mines Company, a subsidiary of Bethlehem Steel) to the east. Both companies constructed railroads from these mines to ports west (Puerto Ordaz) and east (Palúa) of the Orinoco-Caroní confluence.

The Orinoco Mining Company planned Puerto Ordaz as an open city for about 6,000 people, with neighborhood units called "camps" for different levels of personnel and a separate country club for the predominantly North American executives. Many of those who could not afford a house in Puerto Ordaz began to settle in Castillito on the main road, at the entrance to the company property, and by 1961 Castillito included a few hundred ranchos, shops of all sorts, bars, cinemas, churches, and schools.

The construction of Puerto Ordaz and its airport was followed by the Macagua Hydroelectric Dam built above the Caroní Falls during the late 1950s, and the mammoth steel mill at Matanzas, which started production in 1962. These projects attracted new populations to the area, most of whom settled in and around the old town of San Félix, which grew from 1,500 persons to 24,000 within a few years, especially after the policing of illegal squatters was relaxed when the Pérez Jiménez dictatorship fell in 1958. A scattered suburban community called El Roble began to grow along the main road to the west of San Félix, followed by a small commercial center named Dalla Costa at the ferry crossing over the fast-flowing Caroní River.

The Corporación Venezolana de Guayana was formed some six months before the Joint Center planning group began to arrive in Caracas. Before this, the planning of the new city had been in the hands of the Ministerio de Obras Públicas. The CVG was given jurisdiction over the whole Caroní District—a large area of land surrounding the river confluence—with extensive ownership of the land and powers to plan and develop the new city of Ciudad Guayana, as well as the larger region.

The Planners and Designers

The representatives of the Joint Center for Urban Studies were to work in conjunction with counterparts in the CVG. Since the CVG itself was a new entity, all members of the team were new to the project. The urban planning and design group consisted of city and transportation planners, urban designers, architects, landscape architects, and engineers. This small group—working in close contact with economists, housing experts, lawyers, sociologists, anthropologists, natural resource planners, and others—was given responsibility for developing the plans for the city.[1]

The goals of the CVG were high. They were to develop not only an efficient and economically viable city but also a beautiful one. For the first year of the project, 1961-1962, while the economists were gathering data for estimating the industrial potential of that particular combination of natural resources, hydroelectricity, and a steel mill, the physical planning group possessed only the haziest image of what growth to expect. Early guesses at an eventual population level of 150,000 to 250,000 were later raised to 600,000 people by 1980 and continued to fluctuate throughout the project. However, the designers were kept occupied by more urgent needs. A hospital, a technical school, and an aluminum smelter were among a dozen or more major facilities that required immediate locations, plan or no plan. The Caroní Bridge crossing had already been located, but its detailed design was still in question. These design problems suited the talents of the early Joint Center group, and it was a year before serious thought was given to the development of a coherent planning procedure for large-scale and long-term planning. In the interim the design team asked for a moratorium on development in certain parts of the city.

In the second year, as the economists began to project estimates of employment, population size, and future family expenditure patterns, they predicted alternative programs of growth, in figures that were more precise than they should have been. They estimated the areas required for industrial, commercial, residential, and other facilities and developed a land-use-and-transportation model (Penfold 1969).

While the long-term forecasting was under way, two members of the Joint Center group, an anthropologist and an urban designer, took up residence in the city. They immediately reported frustration among the population due to the "freeze" that had been placed on development (Peattie 1962). Contrary to the planning group's assumption that it might be difficult to stimulate private industrial development, one or two small industries desirous of locating in the city were being prevented from doing so. Such misperceptions began to make the planning team feel uneasy about their understanding of the situation. From that time on, the need for surveys and the question whether the planning group should be nearer to the population—in the city itself—than to the seat of decision making in Caracas were frequently mentioned. There were sensible arguments for staying in Caracas in the early stages of planning when plans had to be worked out with other agencies in the capital, but as the new city grew and local problems became more complex, arguments to move to the site became indisputable.

During the second year the designers studied the terrain, flood levels, soils, vegetation, and microclimate with the help of some natural scientists. They constructed models of the terrain, identified visual regions, and plotted the visibility of important facilities and prominent features. Although the landscape was complex, the designers made great efforts to understand it.

Also in the second year, the planning team split into groups to analyze and program industrial, housing, commercial, recreational, transportation, and institutional needs. During this period, several attempts were made to rationalize the planning process, and several sets of objectives were formulated.

Economic objectives were considered paramount. High priority was given to an economic scale of facilities, an efficient use and transportation pattern, and adaptability in the face of future uncertainty. But economic development could not be achieved without a satisfied population, and the shortage of skilled personnel, executives, and professionals became a major issue.

There was much debate about what would attract this elite population. Good services and economic opportunities were essential, but which were more needed, and what kind of environment would this group desire? Would they prefer high- or low-density housing, urban or outdoor recreation, order or diversity? Without any clear knowledge of such preferences, the planners and designers all argued from the perspective of their own values and experience. Urbanity was proposed as a major goal, but interpretations of urbanity ranged from high-density enclosed spaces to a rich mix of uses. Others suggested that the desired personnel, mostly engineers, might have very different values from design professionals and might prefer low-density development, with facilities for outdoor recreation, to high-density urban surroundings.

Discussions between the "order" and "diversity" poles of the planning-design spectrum were frequently the most heated. Those who saw the current development as chaotic and formless were concerned more with unity and order—the "completion" of Puerto Ordaz, the "reorganization" of El Roble. Others were more willing to tolerate diversity, open-endedness, and flexibility and were prepared to accept a less complete form of development.

Those with social concerns focused initially on providing minimal services for low-income migrants and on building stable, preferably mixed-income communities—goals that were based both on equitable grounds and on a concern for minimizing the social conflict dramatized at the time by terrorism in other parts of Venezuela. As the difficulties of attracting skilled personnel became more apparent, the planning group began to see this low-income population as an essential human resource to man the future industry. Thus the education and social mobility of this population became a high-priority goal. (McGinn and Davis 1969)

Attention was also given to the political problems inherent in the trend toward a split city, with upper-income groups to the west of the Caroní and lower-income groups to the east. This bore particularly on the issue of locating the city center.

Many of these concerns were crystallized into a loose set of objectives for the city that, although couched in general terms, were useful when some of the more important locational decisions had to be made (Appleyard 1962; Fawcett and Kise 1962). As the project developed, however, it became evident that different members of the planning team were not only emphasizing different sets of values but also projecting quite different images of the future city.

Experts selected their aspect of the environment as the most critical. Planners concentrated on land uses; social scientists on institutions. Architects focused on buildings and searched for sculptural solutions; landscape architects were dismayed to find that the population gave the landscape so little attention; engineers waited impatiently to detail and construct the road system. The subjective nature of these viewpoints meant that unless a policy gained the personal support of a team member, it might be acknowledged by all as important, but no sharp and enduring arguments would be made on its behalf. Thus, until a specialist in transportation planning became part of the group, transportation concerns were given only lip service.

Images of the future varied in clarity and in form. Those working in Caracas on the transportation model were conceptually at home in the plan for 1980; those living on the site responded to immediate happenings. Such groupings also cut across professional lines. The urban designers, anthropologists, and engineers living in the city sometimes had more similar viewpoints than their long-term planning colleagues in Caracas.

All members of the group brought their own images of other cities to bear on the planning of this city. Some had European cities in mind and would talk eloquently of boulevards, sidewalk cafes, museums, and an opera house. Others referred to Brasilia, with its formal clarity, symbolism, and monumentality. The latest English New Towns and even Philadelphia row houses were brought into the discussions. Other members of the team drew on the qualities of existing Venezuelan cities, with their Spanish cuadras and plazas, and some imagined modified versions of the rancho areas or the California-like auto-oriented commercial developments of the Caracas suburbs.

Planners and designers frequently work through analogy; this is the stuff of the planning culture. But personal perceptions and values were often claimed to be congruent with those of the present population of Ciudad Guayana, and evidence of conversations with inhabitants of the city was occasionally produced in their support. Were these claims true? How did the people see the city; how much did they understand; what did they consider important; and what were their values? The decisions to be made would be meaningless and fragile if they were imposed on an ignorant, apathetic, or even hostile population. Moreover, without the evidence of popular opinion and concern, the more intangible social and environmental goals might carry less weight in the CVG planning process than the more quantifiable, though socially no more valid, engineering and economic criteria.

Therefore, in the second and third year of the planning operations, three surveys of the population were carried out, one on political and social perceptions, one on housing needs and preferences, and the one reported here on urban and environmental perceptions.

The Interviews and Field Surveys

The environmental interview began as a small-scale test of urban perception carried out by an anthropologist. It was subsequently expanded into a large-scale interview of over 300 subjects from four representative parts of the city, including the model "North American" community of Puerto Ordaz, the indigenous rancho area of Castillito, the partly self-help and low-density area of El Roble, and the old village of San Félix. This was a sample large enough to give us reliable information about the population differences in urban perception (see appendix B).

The interview itself (see appendix C) covered a wide range of material beginning with an assortment of questions probing the environmental knowledge of the respondents. It gave them open tasks like naming the city, mapping it, recounting a journey along the main road, and describing selected buildings and districts. They were asked to identify places of social, political, functional, and natural significance and were questioned about their knowledge of existing and future change. Finally, their opinions were asked on current needs and preferences, and they were asked to compare Ciudad Guayana with imagined ideal and worst cities, as well as with the national capital, Caracas, and the state capital, Ciudad Bolívar.

The interview elicited information on several aspects of each inhabitant's background. In addition to his or her age, sex, marital status, education, occupation, and income, the respondent was questioned concerning his or her origin, present and previous use of the city, modes of travel, and knowledge of maps. Most of the interview, then, was directed toward urban perception and knowledge; only one section dealt with preferences.

Simultaneously with the interviews, field surveys of the city environment were carried out, and data were collected on the functional, social, and political patterns of the city. The environmental surveys identified outstanding features and made judgments on the degree to which the city was structured. Panoramic photographs, time-lapse movies, and descriptive tape recordings were collected along the main roads, and photographs were taken of over 200 buildings and of typical streets in all the districts. These surveys were to be correlated with the interview results.

Without a detailed census it was impossible to survey accurately the use of buildings or the location of social groups. Land-use surveys located the types of building and the more important community facilities, and some economic surveys gave employment figures in major industrial and commercial facilities. For the rest, we were forced to rely on the consensus of experts. Some estimate of the news being disseminated to the population was made by studying the editions of the local newspaper for three months before the time of the interviews. Elements mentioned in interview responses were assumed to be present partly because of this publicity.

One purpose of the interviews and field surveys was to serve the immediate needs of the project. The second was to advance basic knowledge in the field of urban perception and to draw conclusions for the benefit of planners in general.

While this book attempts to fulfill the second purpose, the initial purpose was only partly achieved. Many of the planning implications cited in this volume were conveyed to the planning team within six months of the interviews, and decisions that were influenced by these findings will be mentioned in later chapters. But the conclusions were not easy for the designers to absorb. This was due mainly to the difficulty of converting behavioral research findings into policy recommendations. Even more serious was the problem of changing the ways in which the planners and designers planned the city. For instance, it is one thing to report that the population knows what is visible in the city. It is quite another to change the planning media to incorporate visibility as a variable. The difficulty of bringing the planners' vocabulary closer to everyday life is a real obstacle to progress in user-orientated planning. Meanwhile, planners and designers continue to spend time solving the wrong problems.

Time of Interviews

At the time of the interviews in the spring of 1964 and after three years of planning under the CVG, Ciudad Guayana was in a state of transformation. (See figure 1.2.) The government steel mill was finally in production and employing over 2,000 workers. New steelworkers' housing was being built in Puerto Ordaz and outside Castillito, and a self-help housing program, new roads, and utilities had opened up *unidades vecinales* (neighborhood units) in El Roble and San Félix. The streets in San Félix had been blacktopped, more substantial buildings (some three stories high) were under construction, and concrete-block buildings and glass shop fronts were beginning to appear in Castillito. The commercial area that had grown up along the road into Puerto Ordaz was flourishing. Educational, medical, and other facilities were under construction. An industrial area was being laid out on the road to the steel mill, and the CVG engineers had built themselves a small camp, Campo Caroní, by the Macagua Dam.

However, the most dramatic change, scheduled to take place at the time of the interviews, was the opening of the first bridge across the Caroní to supplant the old ferry and the connection of that bridge to a new *autopista*, the Avenida Guayana, bypassing Puerto Ordaz.

The first schematic plans for the whole city had also been made (figure 1.3). The city was due to grow in a westerly direction toward the steel mill, with residential areas located along the upper Caroní. A new commercial and governmental center was to be constructed on Alta Vista, the ridge to the west of Puerto Ordaz. The Avenida Guayana was to act as a spinal link between all the major centers of the city, from the steel mill in the west, through a heavy industrial complex, the airport, the Alta Vista center, a proposed cultural and hotel center on Punta Vista, across the Caroní to a hospital complex on the eastern San Félix ridge, and on into San Félix itself.

Thus, the interviews were carried out at a time when the city was changing from a number of small settlements, mostly indigenous, to a planned large-scale development. This should be held in mind by the reader. This is a study in the perception not of a purely planned city but of a city in evolution from spontaneous to planned growth, a confusing yet rich mixture of several kinds of development encompassed in one site.

New Cities

New cities like Brasilia, Chandigarh, or Ciudad Guayana capture the imaginations of the citizens of their countries. Their very newness opens the possibility of breaking with the traditional weight of old cities; they become symbols of national aspiration, pride, and achievement. They attract dedicated groups of administrators and professionals and are announced with fanfare and high promises.

Yet this focus of attention also breeds controversy. New cities almost always enter the gauntlet of criticism as soon as they begin to emerge from the ground. Things always go wrong. No one can anticipate all the problems, conflicts, and discoveries that can occur in the development of anything as complex as a city. Visitors are disappointed, inhabitants complain, and the critics sharpen their pencils.

New cities have a raw, chunky quality.[2] Site clearance and construction are crude processes, the sequencing of development is spatially discontinuous, and trees and vegetation take time to grow. It often takes twenty or thirty years for inhabitants to change and modify them according to their own living

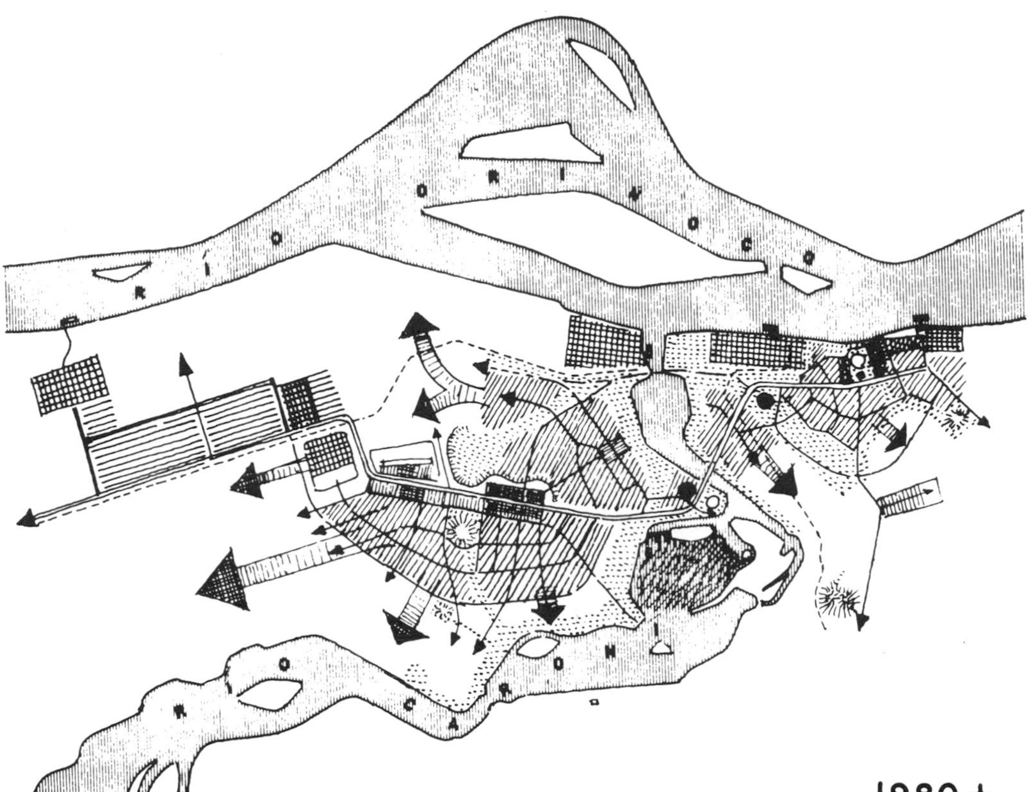

Figure 1.3 Outline of planned development, 1964, showing the proposed westward thrust of the city toward the heavy industrial areas.

habits. Only then does the work of professionals and people begin to fuse and take on life and depth, for small groups of professionals find it difficult to visualize how the inhabitants will view and use their designs. The history of new cities is replete with later-discovered misconceptions.

Ciudad Guayana was planned in a different way from most new cities. It was not planned by any single personality, or even by one profession, although we shall refer to the group as planners. It was probably the first attempt to bring a multidisciplinary team of economists, social scientists, lawyers, planners, architects, engineers, and others together in the planning of a new city. It was also one of the first attempts, albeit in too limited a way, to incorporate the attitudes and viewpoints of a city's population into the plan.[3] Yet, it will no doubt receive as much criticism as its fellows.

2 THE CITY AND ITS LANDSCAPE

The Planners' City

Flying from Caracas to the new city—the land journey across the Llanos even in the dry season took eleven hours—the first signs of the site were some white patches in the undifferentiated landscape, which signaled the Orinoco River, majestically wide, mud-colored, flanked by green jungle and yellow swamps. As the plane flew downriver, there would suddenly appear through a voluminous smokescreen the elegant and extensive complex of the Matanzas steel mill startling and dramatic in its incongruity. The plane circled once around the airport, giving the passengers a panoramic view of the Caroní River, its rapids, and scattered urban development, before setting down on the airstrip to the west of the city (figures 2.1-2.3). Visitors were then taken along the main east-west road to all the outstanding features of the site (figure 2.4): the spectacular Caroní Rapids rushing through heavily forested islands to plunge over the Llovisna Falls; Macagua Dam, representing the first tapping of the Caroní River's great power reserve; the belching Matanzas steel mill; new housing areas; and recently built schools and facilities, some still under construction. The unique features of the setting—the Guayana highlands (the legendary El Dorado) to the south, the Llanos stretching like a featureless sea to the north, the misty heat, and the massive afternoon cloud formations in the rainy season—impress the first-time visitor. Thus began the visitors' learning sequence: from the panoramic overview to the detailed inspection of new facilities. Maps and project reports were available, but a common problem of the visiting expert was to match this information with that of firsthand experiences on the site. There were many disoriented consultants.

With just this kind of introduction, the urban designers began their work with systematic surveys of the natural terrain around the city to assess its development potential. By trudging and jeeping along the tracks of the Savannah, by boating up and down the rivers, and by viewing the site from helicopters and small planes, they were able, with the help of excellent maps and aerial photographs, to gain a thorough knowledge of the landscape. Every turn in the riverbanks was

Figure 2.1 Matanzas Steel Mill, looking east.

Figure 2.2 Caroní-Orinoco confluence with Caroní Bridge and falls in the background; Puerto Ordaz on right.

Figure 2.3 Caroní Falls.

Mobil
CHEVROLET
LICORES
TOSTADA EL ROBLE
cauchos
GENERAL
Cauchos
Firestone
LIBERAL

Figure 2.4 Views from the main road. This series of 180-degree photographs was taken along the main east-west road as part of the photographic record of the character of the city at that time.

Entering the city from the west, the traveler first passed the steel mill. The road continued across featureless terrain, with no views of the rivers on either side, for about five miles before the airport (1) was reached. Soon after this the road suddenly turned and descended toward the Caroní River, opening up a dramatic view of the valley filled with scattered development. Very little of Puerto Ordaz was seen, since the civic center was located off the road, but the General Electric warehouse (2) (center) and the Mobile gas station (far right) at the main intersection were among the best-recalled buildings in the city. From Puerto Ordaz the road, deteriorating in quality, turned right into the rancho settlement of Castillito (3), usually crowded with people and traffic, to arrive finally at the ferry (4), which crossed the Caroní to the other ferry landing at Dalla Costa (5). At the El Roble intersection (6) stood the Phillips gas station (left), a building that received more attention than any one of the three new community schools, placed off the road, in El Roble. Continuing its devious path through El Roble, the road approached the entrance to San Félix, marked by the well-known Firestone billboard (7) and the only close view of the Orinoco River, and carried on through the market area (8) to the Plaza Bolívar (9) (center). At this stage in the city's development practically no planned part of the city could be seen from this road.

learned; geological and geographical features were surveyed and labeled from aerial photographs; the alignments of roads, railroads, and shipping channels were noted; vegetation, soils, and special views were recorded. The designers became practiced at drawing accurate sketch maps of the area, sketches on which the rivers stood out above all other features as a framework for locating roads, settlements, and bridges (see figures 1.2, 1.3).

The landscape, an exotic one to most of the planners, quickly took on significance. The falls and rapids were seen as unique resources, a "world of fantasy" to some, and the hills of the ancient and unexplored Guayana Highlands on the skyline were viewed with a certain awe. Perhaps the hills possessed meanings similar to those invested in landscapes by primitive peoples or the ancient Greeks. Several were named in the aerial photographs.

The tropical climate was regarded as a special problem. Reports of "breezy" and "hot" areas were recorded, and a rigorous survey of the microclimate in various parts of the city was proposed, but the planners' knowledge of the climate rested on questionable interpretations of visible evidence. The climate of an enclosed valley to the west of Puerto Ordaz was for a long time rated poor because the valley sides were eroded and "looked arid." Hence, it was not considered as a housing site until closer investigation showed that it had breezes comparable to the other sites.

The emphasis on the future city and the pressure to make plans for it led to some neglect of the existing city. A land-use survey made at the very beginning of the project was never used and subsequently lost. In consequence, all available maps were either of the existing landscape or of the future city, and it was difficult to tell from them exactly how much of the city had been constructed at any one time. The planners' knowledge, though extensive, placed more emphasis on the landscape than on the existing settlements.

How much did the population know of the urban and natural environment; how much meaning did it have for them; and how did they like the city? Since the industry was remote and invisible, would they know much about it? The possible meanings of the landscape were speculated on, and there were questions about whether the city would be seen as two separate entities split by the Caroní River, or one unified place.

The Inhabitants' City

The inhabitants did in fact see things very differently from the planners. When asked to name the city, more than one-half (54 percent) of the inhabitants named their own settlement. When specifically asked to describe the urbanized area between the steel mill and San Félix, only one-third could name it correctly, and more than one-quarter could not name the city at all. Sixteen percent still gave the name of their own settlement. Since the planners were accustomed to calling the city by a single name (either Santo Tomé or Ciudad Guayana) the parochialism of these responses was surprising.

Differences between residence groups were also significant (at the .01 level). Only in El Roble, the least distinct settlement in our field surveys, with a confusing road system and no visible boundaries, did a majority call the city by its overall name. As local identity weakened, identity with the city seemed to grow. The priority given to local area identity is generally noted as a characteristic of urban "villagers" in larger cities, but in Ciudad Guayana it appeared to be true for the upper-class groups as well. Despite a ceremony in 1961 in which the then President of Venezuela, Rómulo Betancourt, laid the foundation stone for the city, a majority of the city's inhabitants thought of the area as composed of several small towns rather than as a single city. Some thought that the new city was to be a separate development. This conceptual reluctance to aggregate small units into a larger one could be a bad omen for the future political unity of the area.

The Inhabitants' Landscape

Although it would have taken too long to establish the boundaries of our respondents' knowledge, we were able to see where their attention was concentrated.

Respondents were asked to draw a map of the city and its surroundings as they recalled them. This was an open question, and they were free to draw anything and in any style that they wished. In addition they were asked to describe the features that they most vividly recalled and to describe a trip along the main road through the city (see appendix C). Composites of the subject maps (figures 2.5-2.7) together with a survey sketch of features visible from the main road illustrate the results.

Here there was another sharp contrast with the planners' perceptions of the environment, for the inhabitants' maps confined their attention in the main to the urbanized areas. In a city whose pattern of development was fundamentally influenced by two great rivers, both vital to its economy as transportation routes and sources of power, these rivers were virtually ignored. The Caroní River was usually noted only at the ferry and bridge crossings, the Orinoco River only where it passed San Félix. Elsewhere, they were seldom included. The responses had some justification. The banks of both rivers were swampy and lined with impenetrable forest, public travel on them was low, and industry had preempted much of the Orinoco shoreline except for the site of San Félix.

In another question asking the subjects to name the hills in the city, only El Gallo (a hill visible from San Félix, the location of an important new housing development, and historically the scene of a battle between the Spaniards and the Indians) was mentioned. One-third of the respondents did not mention or give names of any hills, despite the presence of several dominant rock outcrops like San Joaquin and the Isla Fajardo, which were clearly labeled on the planner's maps.

The surrounding landscape, therefore, seemed to have little meaning to the inhabitants of Ciudad Guayana. They appeared to see the city as an outpost in an unknown territory, rather than as one embedded in its surroundings—an attitude more typical of the frontier city that it was than of a market center, which was its minor function. Only when the natural form was useful as part of an urban activity, as a source of economic riches, as a name for a barrio, or as a recreational setting did it appear to enter their environmental schema. With this lack of interest they were not likely to value conservation or to care deeply about destruction of the natural landscape.

Respondents were, however, sensitive to the comforts offered by a fresh breeze, for climate was given as one of the major assets of Ciudad Guayana when they compared it with neighboring Ciudad Bolívar. But climatic perception was unreliable. When asked to rank various parts of the city for the quality of their climate, each residential group claimed the climate in its own area was superior. In reality, locations on windward-facing slopes such as Puerto Ordaz received perceptibly more breeze than those on leeward slopes such as El Roble. They may have been judging out of ignorance; they may have adapted to particular conditions; or they may simply have been justifying their own locational decisions. In any case, this might be an illusion worth maintaining.

In sum, while the inhabitants' interest in the surrounding landscape was low, their knowledge of the urban area turned out to be reasonably extensive. The major industrial facilities, the steel mill, and the iron ore ports—all in remote locations—received high attention, though Macagua Dam and a new port to the east of San Félix, both beyond the urban area and not intensely used, were for most beyond the frontier of attention.

The inhabitants' knowledge of the city was therefore the very converse of the planners' knowledge. In perceptual terms, the inhabitants saw the "figure," and the planners saw the "ground."

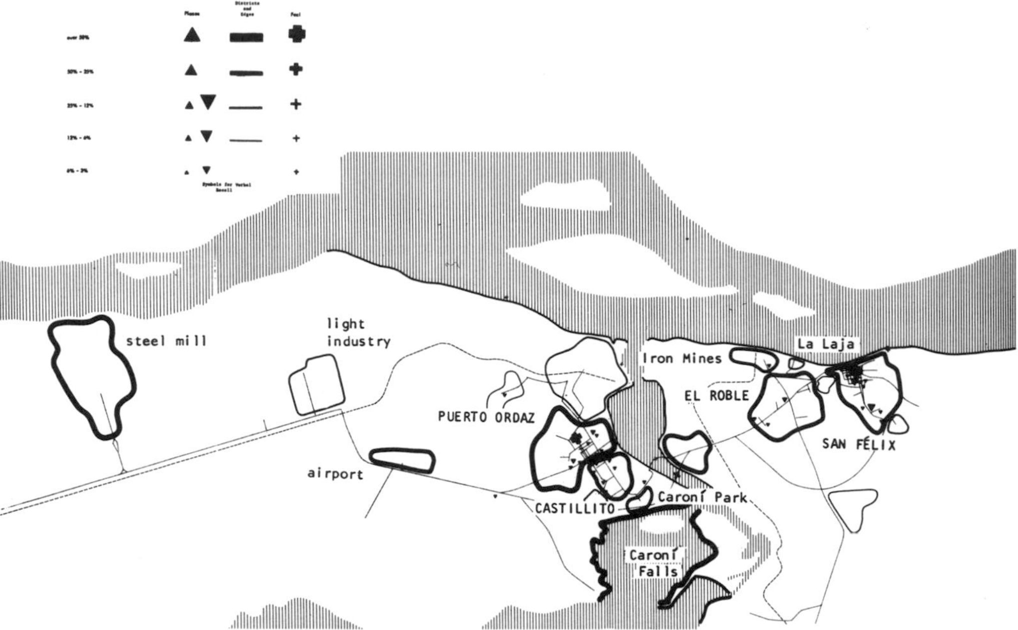

Figure 2.5 Free verbal recall of districts and places. The major settlements, the steel mill, the Caroní Falls, the airport, and the Iron Mines Company are the best-remembered areas in the city. The Centro Cívico and the plaza in San Félix with several other significant buildings were also well recalled.

Figure 2.7 Free trip recall. The places and districts are predictably confined to those that are encountered along or visible from the east-west road. Nearly all the same districts as those recalled in general are mentioned, with the exception of the Macagua Dam, the Centro Cívico in Puerto Ordaz, and the Seguros Sociales in San Félix. The remarkable similarity between the two maps shows how much of significance lay on the main road and how influential the main road was in the inhabitants' general image of the city.

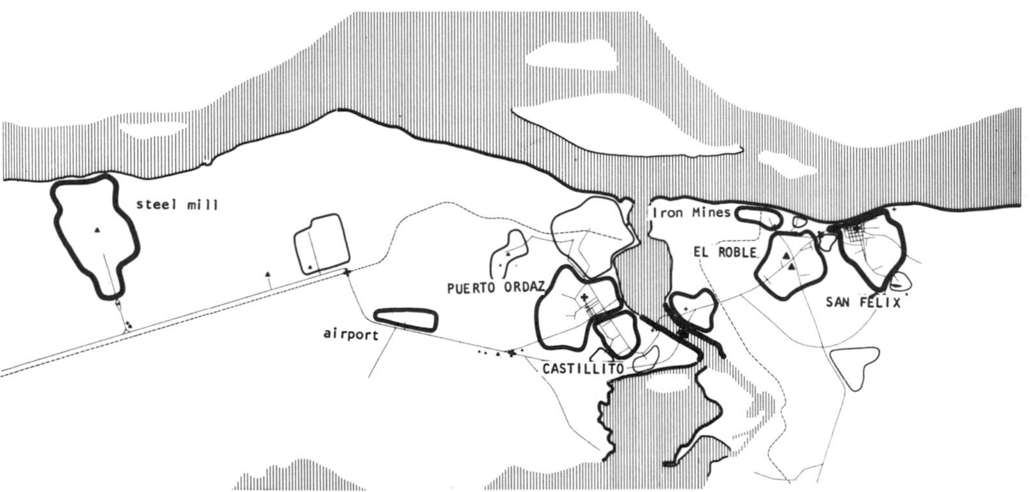

Figure 2.6 Free map recall (general map). When subjects were asked to draw a general map of the city, their responses lay somewhere between the free verbal and free trip responses: the rivers were mentioned in quantity only at the crossing of the Caroní and along the edge of the Orinoco above the confluence. The main districts, the steel mill, and the airport all received attention, but other facilities that were on the edge of development and hidden from view, however important, were relatively ignored. The largest triangles are gas stations. Note the larger crosses, which mark frequently mentioned bridges and traffic circles.

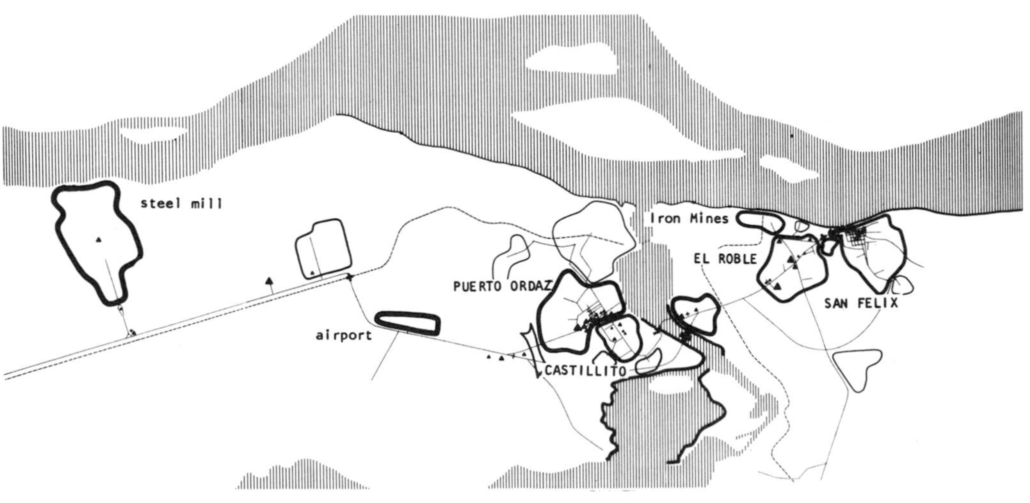

Rating Ciudad Guayana on a Self-Anchored Scale

The planners saw Ciudad Guayana as a place to be planned. They noted the problems of existing development and the potentials of the natural site. Though parts of the city were interesting for their bustling activity and occasional picturesqueness, the existing city was thought of primarily as a place to be improved. We did not expect, then, to find that 80 percent of our sample were satisfied with the city and only 10 percent were not. Moreover, when asked if they thought the city was getting better or worse, 97.8 percent thought it was getting better.

Then we used a technique developed by Kilpatrick and Cantril (1960) for probing cross-cultural goals and values. A self-anchoring scale is "simply one in which each respondent is asked to describe, in terms of his own perceptions, goals, and values, the top and bottom, or anchoring points of the dimension in which the scale measurement is desired, and then to employ this self-defined continuum as a measuring device." In this case, the respondents were asked to define the characteristics of their ideal and worst imagined cities (see chapter 7), and then to rate Ciudad Guayana on a ten-point scale between these two extremes. Most people were now rather cautious in their assessments and concentrated on the middle area of the scale. (See table 2.1; see appendix A for all tables.) Their mean vote was still positive (5.51) but not extremely so.

There were significant differences between residence groups and between education groups. Surprisingly, the most satisfied settlement groups were those in the poorer areas; San Félix (5.91), El Roble (5.65), and Castillito (5.55) The least enthusiastic were the engineers and others in the Campo Caroní (4.0) and the executives in the Country Club (4.25). Similarly, those with only a primary education placed Ciudad Guayana higher (5.73) on their scale; those with a university education placed it lower (4.46). The higher satisfaction of bus travelers (5.88) may also be attributed to class differences. The dissatisfaction of the educated may have been due to their broader experience of other cities or to their regret at the passing of the smaller, conceptually more manageable city they had previously dominated and the destruction of the natural environment. Conceivably, the engineers were comparing the present city with the city of the future.

Differences between other groups were not statistically significant, but there were discernible trends. The city was given a higher value by the young (5.93) than by the older groups (5.28 and 5.30) and by females (5.61) than by males (5.44). Among occupations the professionals (4.64) and business executives (4.50) placed the city slightly lower than did the unemployed (4.83), while small businessmen (6.05) and students (5.91) were much more positive.

The newly arrived were cautious in their judgments (5.27), but those who had been residents for between six months and one year were the most enthusiastic (6.04). This period coincided with high-complexity maps and supports the notion that the enthusiasm resulted from the newcomers' intense interest in the city. Enthusiasm dropped in the groups more familiar with the city (5.24 and 5.65) but remained positive. The physically mobile (6.13) who were not the most affluent in this city, placed the city higher on their scale than did the locals (5.60).

Comparing Ciudad Guayana with Other Cities

When respondents were asked to compare Ciudad Guayana with Caracas and Ciudad Bolívar, Caracas, preferred by 52 percent, was favored for its better economic situation (12 percent), although opinion was divided on this issue; for its urban character (11 percent); and for its beauty, better climate, recreational facilities, social environment, educational opportunities, living costs, housing, and planning, in that order. Ciudad Guayana was preferred by 37 percent, primarily for its tranquillity and its economic security. Expressions such as "a quiet town," "rest," "meditation," "spiritual enjoyment," lack of "street brawls" and "fights" were interpreted as desires for tranquillity.

Ciudad Bolívar, the old capital of the state of Bolívar, being rapidly overtaken in population by the newer industrial city, was favored by only 19 percent, while Ciudad Guayana was favored by 47 percent for its employment opportunities, industry, dynamism, and economic potential, as well as for its climate; 28 percent adjudged the two cities equal. Opinion was split on which city had the better recreational and entertainment facilities and social environment, but Ciudad Bolívar came out slightly ahead on the issue of urban character and security. Ciudad Bolívar was the traditional center of the region's social life, since it contained some prestigious facilities, two large hospitals, a branch of the Universidad del Oriente, and a historic colonial environment. The climate was given as a superior quality of Ciudad Guayana by 12 percent despite the geographic proximity of the two cities. Most housing in Ciudad Bolívar lies on the leeward side of the hill on which the city is built, creating an unpleasantly hot air pocket.

In their choices between the two pairs of cities, employment (28 percent) was the key factor, followed by the climate (11.5 percent), tranquillity (11 percent), and the social environment (6 percent). While the factors mentioned in the "ideal" and "worst" cities were mostly essential services like utility systems, schools, and medical facilities, the priorities in the comparative questions shift to more general concerns for employment, pleasantness of climate, and the state of the social environment. These apparently would be the crucial issues in the decisions that migrants would have to make. However, people do not always end up in the city they prefer. Although 52 percent preferred Caracas, there was very little contemplated migration out of Ciudad Guayana (MacDonald 1969).

Local versus City Identity

The inhabitants' parochial emphasis on local areas suggested a problem for the future social and political unification of the city. A more coherent structuring of the city, as proposed in chapter 8, might alleviate this problem. The news media might also communicate the concept of the whole city as being more significant than the individual settlements. At the time, the CVG information office was situated in the main hotel and oriented only to incoming tourists. But the inhabitants needed these services just as much. Information about the location of new facilities could be periodically referred to in the news media. Detailed sign systems, including public display maps, could be installed throughout the city.

Since there was evidence from El Roble that local settlement identity varied inversely with citywide identity, parochialism might be reduced by emphasizing citywide elements and playing down the identity of local areas. An emphasis on the spinal road system could provide sufficient citywide coherence in the future to allow a simultaneous enhancement of local character in areas like El Roble.

Awareness of Nature

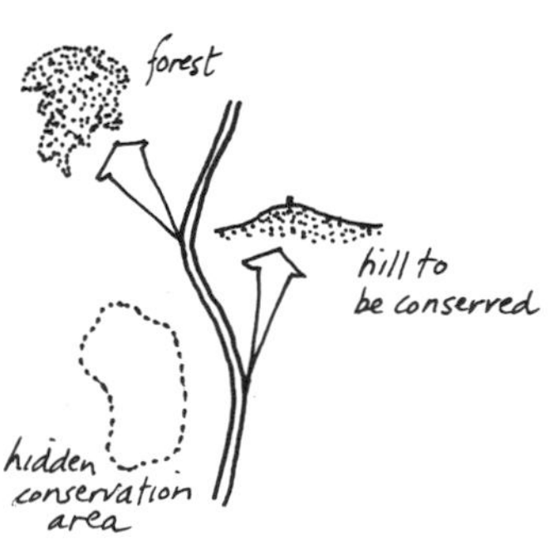

Figure 2.8

Ignorance of the landscape might also be a premonition of upcoming problems. If not protected, riverbanks, *quebradas*, hilltops, forests, and future scenic and recreational resources could all too easily be overlaid with development, leaving Ciudad Guayana with the same legacy of polluted and inaccessible rivers as other industrial cities. Indeed, the industries had already preempted the banks of the Orinoco. Several strategies could be developed to remedy this blindness. Urban facilities, recreation places, important roads, and highly used centers could be placed at strategic points where the best landscape features could be seen—but not destroyed (figure 2.8). The scheduling of events at these places might also enhance their symbolic value to the population. On the other hand, some policies should intentionally limit public access and knowledge of the landscape. "Hidden" areas should be staked out for conservation and reservation.

Maintaining Satisfaction

While satisfaction with Ciudad Guayana was remarkably high, when compared with a personal ideal city or with Caracas or Ciudad Bolívar, it did not always hold its own. The attributes mentioned by the population as strengths or weaknesses would obviously be critical in the future evolution of the city. Many of these—its climate; its tranquillity, its relative lack of urbanity, beauty, recreational facilities, social environment, and educational opportunities; and its high living costs—could be influenced to a degree by the plans.

Besides the provision of good housing and medical and educational services, the city's layout could enhance or ruin the climate, for the city was potentially subject to air pollution from the several industries. The location of residential areas and local centers to catch the best breezes would enable the city to hold its present edge over neighboring Ciudad Bolívar. Tranquillity, although predominantly a social attribute, might be affected by orderly "planning"—a quality often mentioned by inhabitants as an attractive aspect of new United States towns (Lansing, Marans, and Zehner 1970). Urbanity might be achieved by providing cultural, entertainment, and recreational facilities and by clustering them in high-density centers (see chapter 3).

The enthusiasm of the lower-income groups and the young was as unexpected as the dissatisfaction of the executives, the more affluent, and the middle-aged. Both pointed up problems. Clearly the flood of low-income migrants was likely to continue as long as optimism was high. On the other hand, the more rare and needed professional and executive personnel were not to be satisfied so easily. Analysis of their particular desires and problems evidenced in the ideal and worst city responses (see chapter 7) would be a priority.

3 THE SPATIAL DISTRIBUTION OF URBAN KNOWLEDGE

Complexity, Density, and Urbanity

Urbanity is one of the qualities that are frequently quoted as desirable or lacking in contemporary cities. Yet, there are several interpretations of urbanity: some think of physical forms, others of crowded streets or cultural diversity. And there have been no explicit measures of its presence.

We computed from the inhabitants' maps the total number of facilities mentioned in each settlement by all respondents, as a measure of the *perceived complexity* of each settlement (see table 3.1). By this measure San Félix (108 perceived facilities) was by far the most complex settlement, with Puerto Ordaz (60) trailing some way behind and El Roble (35) and Castillito (33) less than one-third the complexity of San Félix. Since San Félix had the largest population and Puerto Ordaz was a major center, these scores fit our expectations, but Castillito gave the appearance of being a far richer and more lively settlement than El Roble, for in El Roble the key facilities were spread out and hidden.

When complexities were divided by the areas of the settlements, *perceived densities* were more in line with the impression they made. San Félix (.31 perceived facilities per hectare) was the most densely packed, Castillito (.27) rose to second place past Puerto Ordaz (.20), and El Roble (.10) revealed the lowest perceived density.

But do diversity of use types or variety of forms create complexity? In field surveys, two observers rated all the buildings and objects mentioned for the relative intensity and singularity of their use and the relative distinctness and singularity of their forms (table 3.1). The rules for these measures are described in chapter 5.

San Félix, rated highest in complexity and density on the subject maps, contained the largest numbers of singular activities (79) and unique building forms (47). Puerto Ordaz, with considerably lower complexity and density scores, contained fewer singular facilities but greater numbers of intensely used or distinctive-looking buildings. Therefore, singularity of either use or form was a major factor in the perception of a settlement's complexity, its density, and, probably, its sense of urbanity. A community may not need high intensities of use, or even large and prominent buildings, to achieve richness. An increase in the number of unique elements, even if small in size, should increase its perceived diversity.

Complexity Differences

The free-recall maps of different population groups (figures 3.1-3.6) showed significant variations in the distribution and quantity of their urban knowledge (see tables 3.2 and 3.3). *Group complexity* measures (C_f, C_d, C_r) for each population group were derived from the mean number of elements mentioned per person in each group. They were calculated by dividing the total number of times that elements (facilities, districts, and road units) were mentioned by each group by the number of respondents in that group.

Figures 3.1-3.6 Free recall maps of resident groups. (Recalled rivers and surrounding districts have not been shown on these maps.) The Country Club sample (only 10) produced rich and detailed maps of Puerto Ordaz but virtually nothing across the Caroní River. The Puerto Ordaz composite map shows more recognition of the facilities in El Roble and San Félix, but very little in comparison with the Castillito sample, who drew maps of all four settlements. They were the only group interviewed while the Caroní ferry was still in operation. The El Roble sample drew rich maps of San Félix and their own settlement, but showed only moderate knowledge of the west side of the Caroní. Those in San Félix showed a similar level of cross-river knowledge. The engineers and others in the Campo Caroní demonstrated a broad comprehension of the city, especially of the road system.

Residence Groups and Spatial Familiarity

Those living in Castillito (figure 3.3), the settlement with the lowest number of perceived elements, surprisingly had the highest citywide complexity scores (C_{df} = 10.0). They perceived San Félix and Puerto Ordaz in as complex a way as the inhabitants of those settlements. The suburban nature of Castillito, placed between the two centers of San Félix and Puerto Ordaz, apparently stimulated mobility and therefore complexity of knowledge. Those living in Castillito used San Félix as their major shopping and community center, as did lower-income groups from all over the city. They also had to travel all the way to the Seguros Sociales in San Félix for medical treatment, to the Liceo for school, to the Consejo for affairs of the municipality, and possibly to church, since there were none in Castillito. Many Castillito residents were employed in neighboring Puerto Ordaz and also used its civic center.

Since independent measures of mobility were based solely on work trips—travel for shopping and other services was not recorded—the dependence of complexity on mobility is not clearly established, but the tendency is evident. Another reason may also have boosted their complexity scores. One-fifth of the Castillito sample had previously lived in San Félix, but they moved on to Castillito to be nearer employment sources and a more affluent market.

San Félix residents (figure 3.5) achieved the next-highest complexity scores (C_{df} = 8.87), and they achieved higher scores in neighboring El Roble than did its own inhabitants. But their knowledge faded rapidly across the Caroní River. The citywide complexity scores of those in El Roble (figure 3.4) were low (C_{df} = 6.7). Their urban center was San Félix, and they mentioned little across the river. Complexity of

Figure 3.1 Free recall map: Country Club.

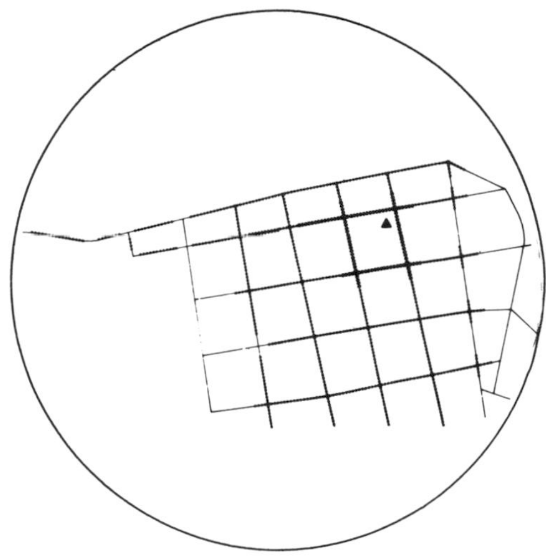

Figure 3.2 Free recall map: Puerto Ordaz.

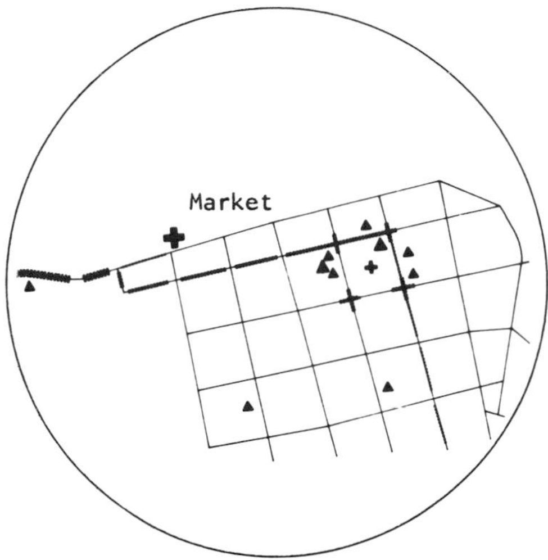

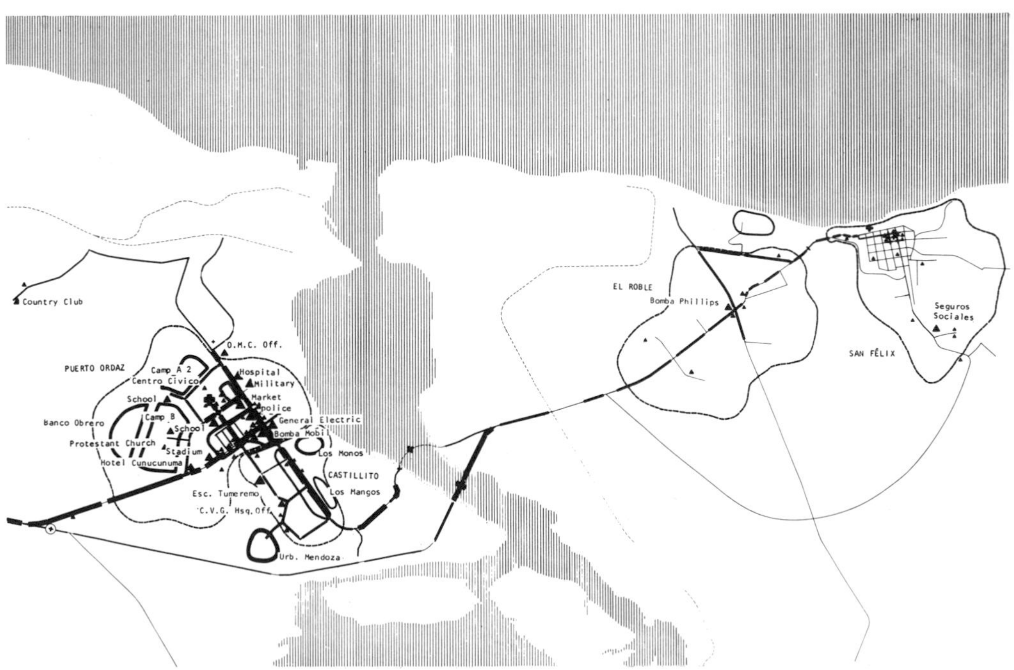

Figure 3.3 Free recall map: Castillito.

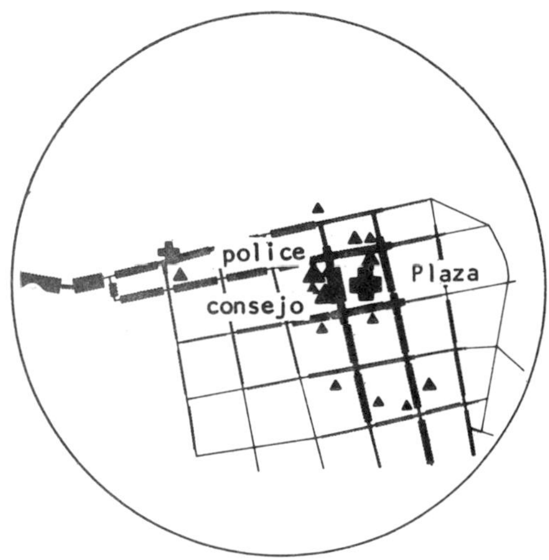

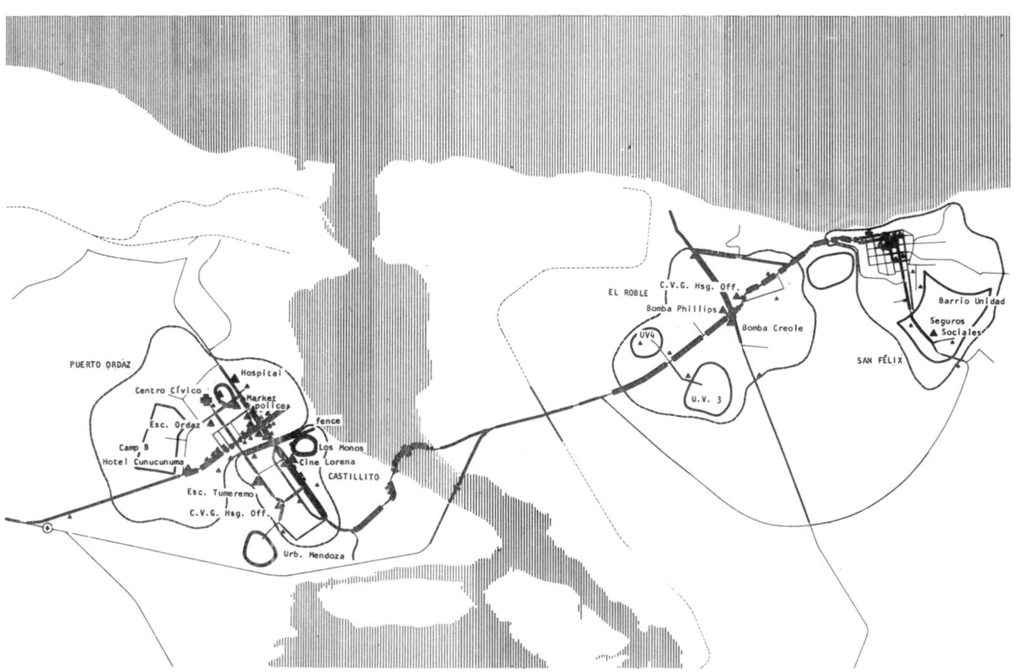

Figure 3.4 Free recall map: El Roble.

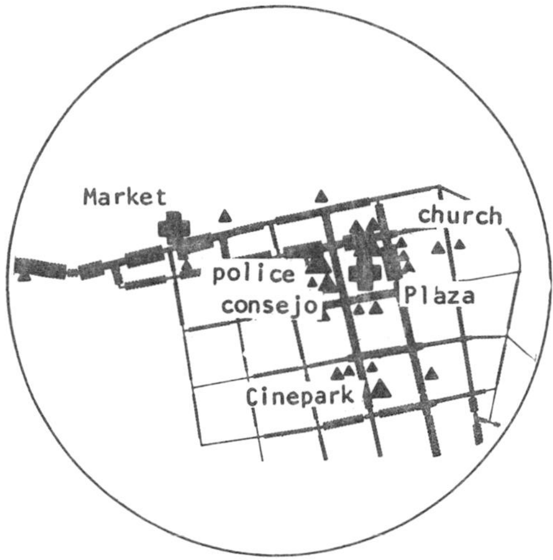

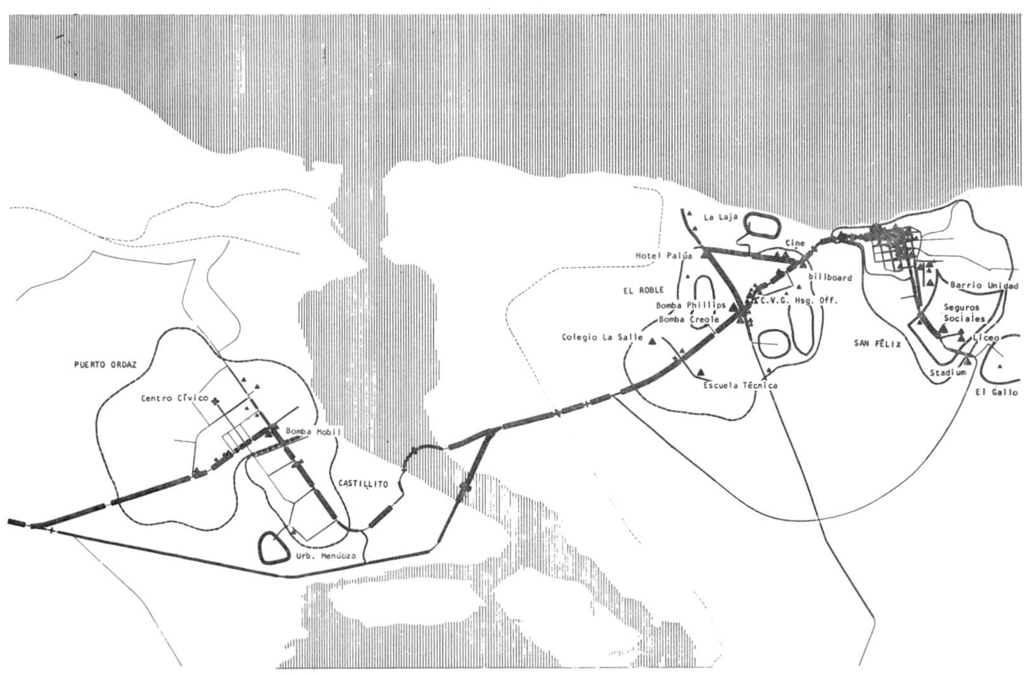

Figure 3.5 Free recall map: San Félix.

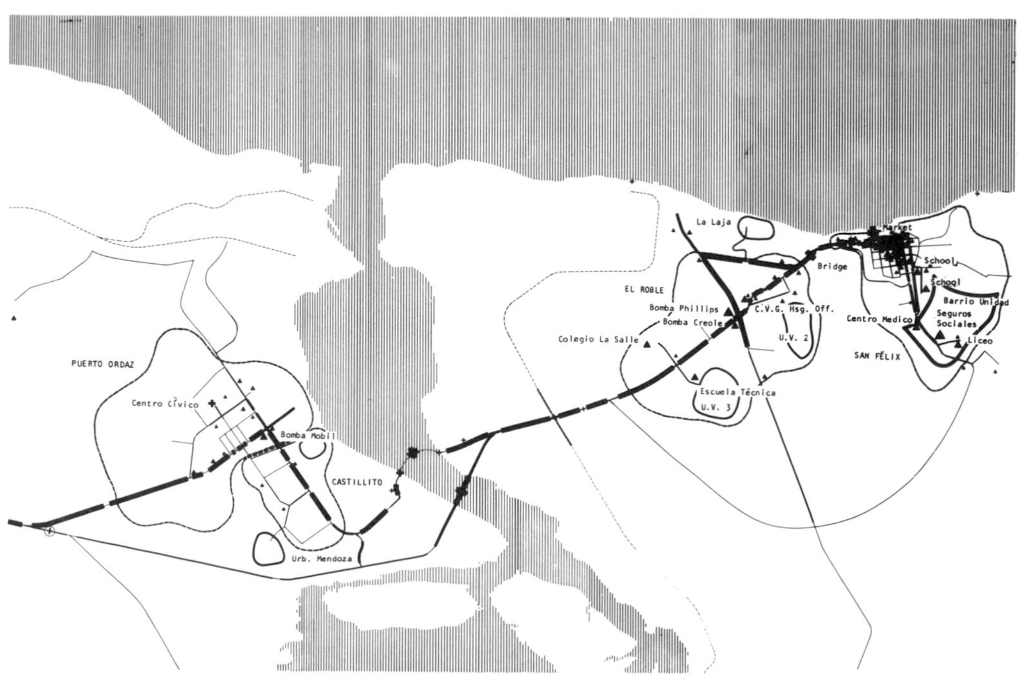

Figure 3.6 Free recall map: Campo Caroní.

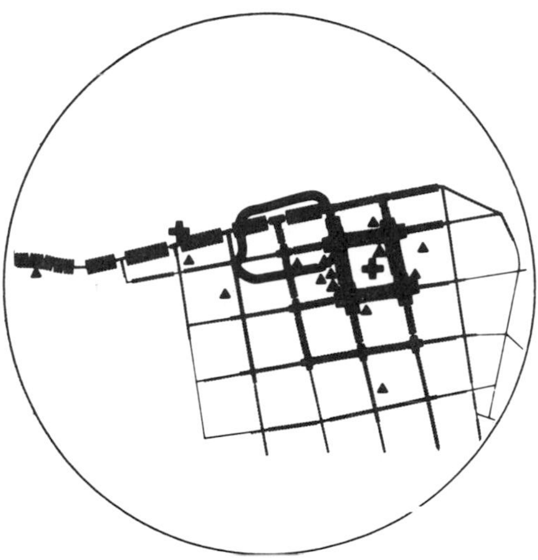

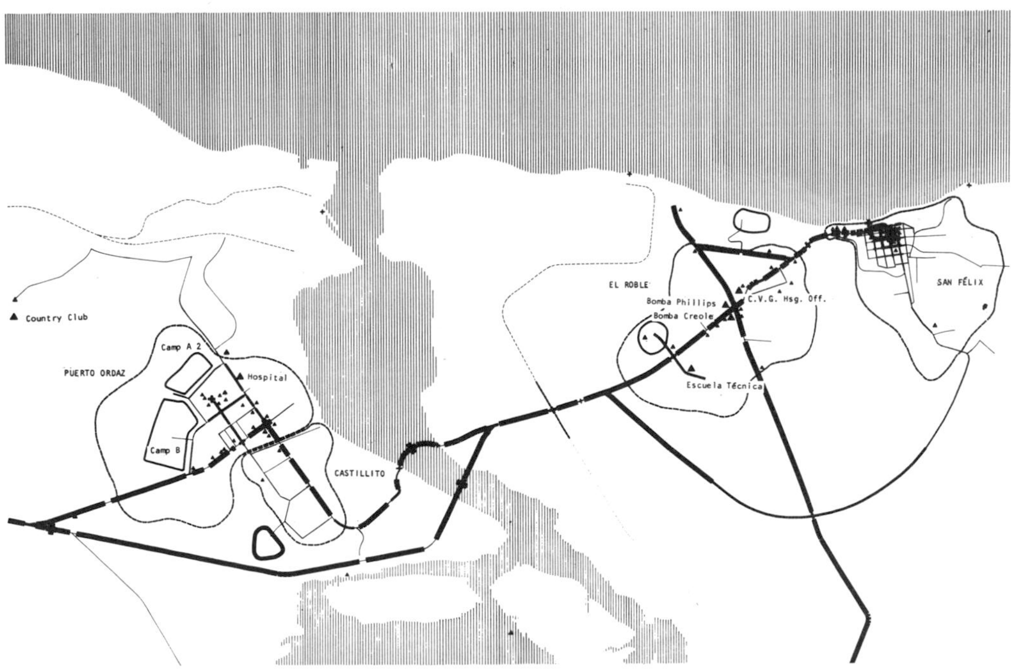

knowledge related therefore more to the centers used than to distance.

The middle- and upper-income residents of Puerto Ordaz (C_{df} = 6.6) (figure 3.2) drew more restricted and simpler maps of the whole city than any of the lower-income groups of Castillito (C_{df} = 10.0), San Félix (C_{df} = 8.8), or El Roble (C_{df} = 6.7). Although complexities were not calculated for the small Country Club sample, scrutiny of their composite map (figure 3.1) indicates a confinement even more restricted than those in Puerto Ordaz, with no attention to the east side of the Caroní River.

The relation between the locations of residence groups and the facilities they used appeared to affect the scope of their knowledge more than anything else. When all facilities were provided within the local area, as in Puerto Ordaz, there was no inclination or need to travel beyond its borders, but when facilities were spread, as for Castillito, inhabitants were carried through to other islands of knowledge. In Ciudad Guayana, the better-educated middle- and upper-income groups displayed more limited knowledge, partly because the professional classes usually insisted on a house and a job as a precondition to their settlement in the city and were, therefore, relieved of the search tasks common to the ordinary migrant, and partly because they lived in their own self-contained town. This was an unexpected finding, since the better-educated groups had greater mobility by virtue of their higher automobile use. In larger U.S. cities, where the middle and upper social majority have more facilities available to them, and the lower-income minorities are more frequently ghettoized and immobile, the relative knowledge of income groups is usually reversed (Orleans 1967). Our evidence also reveals a tendency toward "one-way visibility," a bias toward looking up the social scale and a reluctance to look down the scale, part of a common inclination to perceive urban spatial patterns "directionally"—toward the higher-income areas—in ways that are distorted by the relative social status of surrounding areas.[1] The civil engineers, who were responsible for the layout of the city and lived in Campo Caroní (figure 3.6) were the exceptions. They demonstrate broad knowledge of the city, evidence of their high mobility and extensive data sources.

It also appeared that those living in the denser indigenous settlements, namely those in Castillito and San Félix, possessed generally higher levels of interest in or knowledge of the city than those in lower-density El Roble or Puerto Ordaz. Density and complexity themselves may attract or stimulate those with higher curiosity levels.

Temporal Familiarity

Facility complexities rose to a peak for the six-month residents (C_f = 14.2) and thereafter declined for the longer-term inhabitants (C_f = 11.1, 10.7). At the same time, the newest migrants achieved the highest scores on the larger district units, and the longer-term residents scored higher on road complexities. These differences were not statistically significant, but this was probably due to the small numbers in some of the groups.

All this suggests that newcomers conceptualized the city at a gross level on first arrival but quickly engaged in an exploratory burst of attention to detail after about the first six months. During the first year, travel about the city is likely to be extensive—searching for a job, meeting new people, sampling various commercial and recreational establishments. With familiarity, the city dweller's world becomes more routine and limited. Initial explorations are remembered but fade into the background as work, residence, friends, and recreation begin to assume the dominant pattern.

The length of this first period of search must have varied appreciably. In a later survey of twenty newcomers, one-half of the sample felt they knew the city three months after their arrival, while the other half said that they were still getting to know it at six months. A few said that they knew it within two weeks. There is at present no measure of when a person knows a city, but these individuals seemed able to mark identifiable moments in their learning sequence.

The decline in facility complexity scores of residents of over five years standing may have been due either to the routinization of their knowledge or to their lessened interest in the city after years of contact. Their emphasis on the road system supports the former theory, since it suggests that they know that system in detail.

Mobility and Travel Mode

Facility complexity scores for localists and for those who traveled across the Caroní River to work were both high (C_f = 11.4, 11.7), while scores for the middle group were lower (C_f = 9.9). District complexities were definitely higher for locals (C_d = 2.3, compared with 1.9, 1.8), while road complexities were substantially higher for the more mobile, (C_r = 4.9, compared with 4.2 for the less mobile, although these differences were not statistically significant.

The higher facility and road complexities for the more mobile might be expected from their broader knowledge of the city. The high facility complexities for the locals suggest that immobility is compensated for by intensity of knowledge within the more limited domain; their high district complexities show that they perceive most of the city at a coarser grain.

Por puesto and bus travelers achieved higher facility and district complexities than did automobile riders, although the latter were as cognizant of the road system. Travel by these modes was certainly more difficult than private car travel and involved much more walking.

Age, Sex, and Education

There was no progression of complexity from youth to middle age. The under-twenties and over-thirties registered higher complexity scores than those in the twenties to thirties. The higher interest levels of the young and the greater experience of the older group might explain their scores.

The lower facility and road complexities of the college-educated group could be due to their more confined knowledge of the city or their greater ability to abstract the environment into larger units. Since their complexity scores for districts were no higher than the other groups, lack of mobility appears to be the main reason.

Males achieved significantly higher road complexities than did females. The explanation is likely to be found in physical mobility differences since sex and physical mobility characteristics were significantly correlated in our sample ($r = 0.23$).

Selected Occupations

The skilled workers, mostly employed in the steel mill and the Orinoco Mining Company, produced the most complex facility and road scores ($C_f = 13.7$, $C_r = 5.4$). Since more than one-half of the skilled workers in our sample lived on the eastern side of the Caroní and traveled to work on the western side, the journey to work may well have been a factor in their higher complexities.

Other high scorers were students ($C_f = 12.6$, $C_r = 4.6$), whose interest levels were probably high and who also had to travel long distances to get to the few secondary schools in the city. Office workers ($C_f = 12.4$) would also have to traverse the city to work at the limited number of facilities. Those with locally oriented occupations, such as housewives ($C_f = 10.7$) and small businessmen ($C_f = 8.9$), were medium scorers.

The most impoverished maps were produced by the business executives ($C_f = 5.0$, $C_r = 2.7$), the professionals ($C_f = 8.5$), and the unemployed ($C_f = 8.2$). Each occupation, however, exhibited a unique configuration. The businessmen's maps displayed a general impoverishment both of facilities and roads. The professionals' maps, on the other hand, though limited in facilities, were among the highest scorers on roads and districts ($C_f = 5.0$, $C_d = 3.0$). They were apparently quite conversant with the highway system, but for some reason displayed less interest in or knowledge of individual facilities. The unemployed followed a similar pattern, with reasonably high mentions of road units and districts but a limited mention of facilities. Their relative ignorance could constrain their chances for jobs.

Summary

1. Those living in the densest settlements, Castillito and San Félix, achieved the highest citywide complexity scores, a finding that suggests that they either attracted those with higher cognitive complexities or stimulated their inhabitants to take a higher interest in the city.

2. Complexity of knowledge was home based, fading with distance for those living in central settlements but peaking away from home in the main centers for those living in satellite or suburban type settlements.

3. Social class appeared to influence the directions in which people viewed the city ("one-way visibility"), which resulted in the confinement of upper-class knowledge to the affluent "ghetto" areas. The impoverished knowledge of the better-educated and business executives supports this contention.

4. Mobility produced high complexity scores, but so did lack of mobility. Localists appeared to compensate for lack of travel by developing an intensely complex knowledge of their local area. The influence of mobility was therefore only a partial one.

5. The peaking of knowledge with the young and middle-aged may be due to the interest levels of the young and the experience of the older groups.

6. Travel mode was expected to affect complexity levels, but the public transport modes involving more pedestrian movement and slower contact with the city produced only slightly more complex maps. The automobile's speed and directness of movement did not significantly reduce complexity.

7. Interest in the city during initial encounter phases apparently encouraged higher complexity levels among the newcomers and the young; these groups were also among those most satisfied with the city (chapter 2). The declining complexity of familiar inhabitants could be due to routinization, increased abilities in cognitive economizing, and loss of interest.

8. Cognitive skills may have reduced the complexity of detail in the maps of the college students and professionals.

9. Occupational differences might be explained primarily by mobility in the city and social, educational, and interest differences among occupational groups.

Although the causal variables of perceived complexity will not be clear until other cross-validational studies are carried out, a number have been identified; the environmental variables include singularity of use and function; the social variables include social class, physical mobility, level of interest, experience, and education level.

Reducing Ignorance

Certain groups were relatively more ignorant of the city than others. The chosen ignorance of the elite has already been explained. What we see here is an almost deliberate turning away from the rest of the city. But is that a problem? On social grounds it appears to be. The blindness of the elite leaves the poor invisible and the elite in isolation, thus encouraging prejudice and intolerance. One could see, even in this embryonic city, the elite already living introspectively in their isolated island, with a growing political and social split between the two sides of the Caroní River. It would not be easy to break down this self-imposed isolation in a society where the elite have virtually free choice. They were needed to run the industry, and if they felt threatened by forced mixing, they would presumably leave. There are, however, a number of spatial strategies that might increase knowledge of and contact with the rest of the population.

Knowledge through Access

Strategies for increasing urban knowledge depend very much on the quality of the transportation system. The opening of the Caroní Bridge was bound to increase such knowledge, but it remains to be seen whether the elite groups use the bridge to travel to the east side.

Facility Location

The kinds of facilities and environments a group ordinarily uses or benefits from could be located outside the group's territory beyond their usual reach. This would encourage them to enter neutral territories or cross other territories, thus meeting other groups and seeing other parts of the city. At the same time such a locational strategy would bring facilities usually located in the more affluent areas within reach of other groups. In locating hospitals, schools, cultural centers, movie houses, recreational facilities, and so on, the population groups

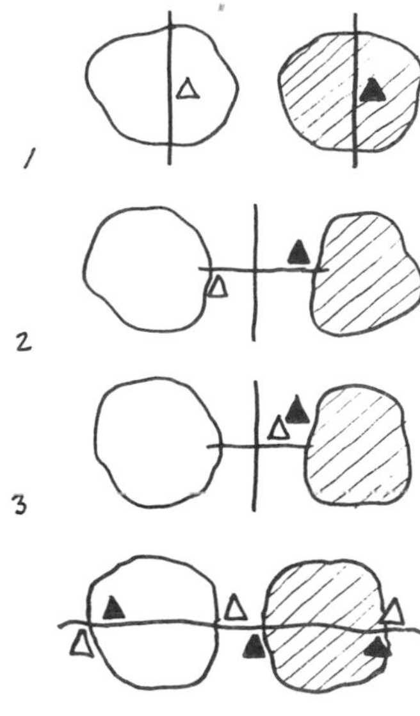

Figure 3.7 Alternative facility locations: (1) present segregation; (2) at community entrances; (3) shared facilities; (4) stretching community travel patterns.

that will have conceptual and real access to them should be kept in mind (figure 3.7). Access may have to be along amenable routes that do not threaten the upper group. In Ciudad Guayana, the new hospital was placed on the east side of the Caroní River, and the new hotel was located by the bridge. However, the new city center to the west of the city (see chapter 9) might well remain a higher-income facility unless more low-income housing is allowed to locate in that area.

Other ways of reducing isolation will be suggested in chapter 7. The segregation of social groups in Ciudad Guayana is likely to continue and sharpen unless such strategies are adopted. Higher groups will tolerate only so much of such "stretching," however, before they back off from using a distant facility, as the U.S. experience of forced busing has demonstrated.[2] Monitoring these different strategies through subsequent surveys would be revealing.

For the unemployed, whose ignorance was probably unelected, and the immobile, whose knowledge was intensive but local, restricted knowledge could limit job, educational, and life-style choices. Keller (1968) considers overdependence on the neighborhood to be a sign of deprivation, and this is partly true. For the inhabitant who has the psychological and financial resources to make alternative choices, a broad knowledge of the city should increase actual choice.

On the other hand, extensive knowledge can mean a loss in intensity of local awareness—an important factor in the current revival of localism. Those who travel extensively cannot participate as much in the local scene; thus there is a decrease in the strength of local communities and care for their environments. Extensive and complex knowledge can also be overwhelming and irrelevant. The knowledge explosion is a major contemporary problem (Toffler 1970), and in many respects ways of coping with complexity are more seriously needed than ways of increasing it. We need to balance local and nonlocal exposure in varying ratios among population types, some benefiting from broad horizons, others from intense and local interests. For deprived groups, cheap and easy transportation is a prime means for extending awareness. The construction of the bridge was a service to this group. Spreading similar-level populations throughout a city could also help to prevent the feeling of "strangeness" about the rest of the city that often confines lower-income groups to their local areas (Goering and Kalachek 1973).

4 THE SETTLEMENTS AND RESIDENTIAL AREAS

The Four Settlements

Puerto Ordaz, Castillito, El Roble, and San Félix, the home territories of our respondent groups, each possessed a distinctive character for the newcomer to the city. To the planners, Puerto Ordaz looked disturbingly like an American suburb. San Félix (figures 4.7-4.9) was viewed as a bustling overgrown village, El Roble (figure 4.6) as a semirural rancho settlement, and Castillito as a dense urban squatter community.

Puerto Ordaz (figures 4.1-4.4), a planned community located high on the western slopes of the Caroní Valley, was laid out as a number of camps, each containing a different housing type and social group. The houses were regularly spaced, with well-kept gardens, fronting on wide grass-verged streets equipped with streetlamps and trees. The narrow "green belts" between these camps gave the settlement an open quality, and views out of the community were frequent, but the openness added to the fragmentation of the settlement. Puerto Ordaz had two focuses: (1) The Centro Civico, constructed originally as the core of future commercial development, with a small plaza enclosed by a church, movie house, club, supermarket, and other small commercial facilities; and (2) a new unplanned commercial center built down on the main road. Community facilities, schools, the hospital, the union building, and others were scattered throughout the community in the spaces between the camps, often hidden from view.

The road system, although running along or across the contours, had no structural clarity. The boundaries of the settlement were mostly unseen or, if seen, were unclear. Only the tattered fence defining the Orinoco Mining property formed a clear break from the ranchos of Castillito, which crowded up to this border line apparently posed for invasion. A no-man's-land was left on the Puerto Ordaz side of the boundary before the clean new buildings began. Puerto Ordaz was clearly seen in the distance across the Caroní Valley from the east but, except for the roadside stores, disappeared on approach, since the Centro Civico and residential areas lay off the main road.

Castillito (figure 4.5), a dense settlement of ranchos, straddled the main road outside the Puerto Ordaz fence. At the time of the interviews the road was still unpaved and subject to frequent flooding. Through traffic, delivery trucks, pedestrians, and parked cars filled the street, which was lined with open shops and shacks displaying goods and signs. One or two shop fronts were newly glazed. The impression was lively but chaotic, enough for some planners to propose "cleaning the whole area out."

Castillito, nevertheless, gained considerable identity through the intensity of movement, signs, and other activity in its long main street. Outside the main street, ranchos on the eastern side (Los Monos) invaded the swampy shores of the Caroní and on the west broke through into land being prepared for the next new Banco Obrero housing area. To the south the Caroní Park fenced off expansion, and to the north Puerto Ordaz defined the limits. The community was bursting its seams, but the boundaries on either side were so obscure and unseen that this was not easily apparent.

El Roble (figure 4.6) was the least distinctive settlement, though perhaps the most private. As a suburb of San Félix outside the small mining camp of Palúa (Iron Mines), it straddled the main road but did not clearly focus on it. Less dense than Castillito, El Roble blended into the landscape with houses scattered among the trees and mud streets following their natural bent. Much of El Roble had a rural character, although new housing was occasionally to be found at the edges. The self-help housing areas of UV3 and UV4 (*unidades vecinales*) were often more formless than the indigenous rancho areas, for the streets were not built to a clear system and new houses were scattered. But these areas did not have such a jarring effect on the texture of development as the *urbanizaciónes*.

The main road divided into two routes through El Roble, creating a great deal of confusion (chapter 9). The secondary path system was also unclear. A number of small focuses occurred at points on the main road, but, except for the two gas stations at the junction, these were unimportant. Other community facilities, the new Escuela Técnica, the INCE school for adult education, and the La Salle School were located in apparently random positions, adding to the confusion.

With its already obscure character, El Roble had no clearly defined or visible edges. Only the lagoon separating it from San Félix acted as a definite entrance or edge to the community. El Roble was invisible from the outside and, given its lack of focus and unclear road system, made no impact on a passing traveler despite its exposure to the main road.

San Félix (figures 4.7-4.9) was both the largest and the old-

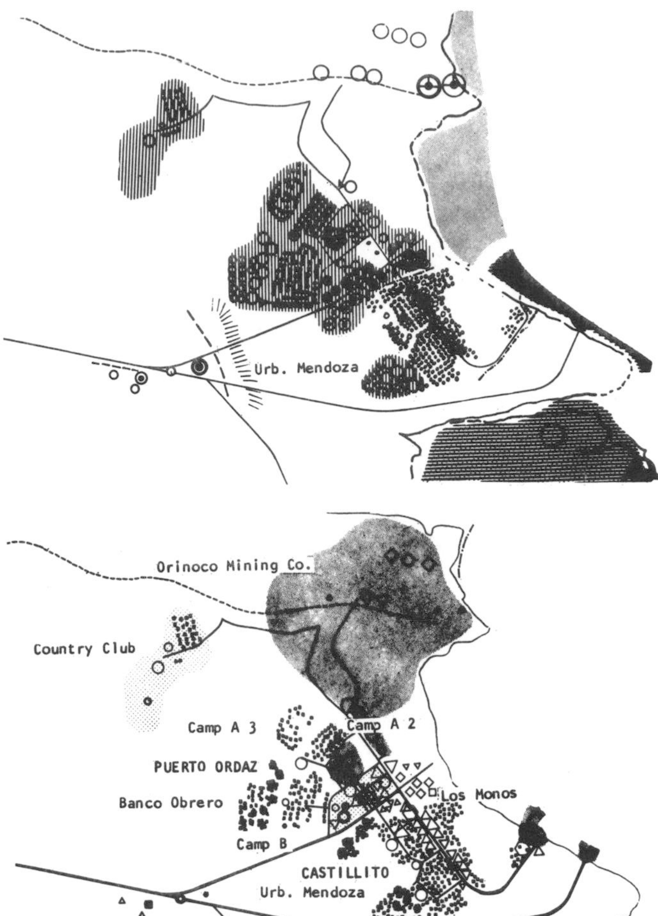

Figure 4.1 Form diagram, Puerto Ordaz and Castillito, showing the large isolated structures as large circles—apartment buildings, schools, the hospital, Centro Cívico, and small industrial buildings on the west road. Buildings with signs and activity are to be found along the east-west road entering Puerto Ordaz, and on its way through Castillito. The hatched areas are those with professionally designed structures; the rest are not. Note the incongruity of the Urbanización Mendoza in Castillito.

Figure 4.2 Use diagram, Puerto Ordaz and Castillito. The triangles illustrate the layout of commerce along the main roads; the circles isolate the larger number of institutions in Puerto Ordaz.

Figure 4.3 Original plan for Puerto Ordaz ca. 1940, with the Centro Cívico, top center, and no commercial development projected along the main east-west road at bottom, although this has now become the main commercial center. Other high-density housing around the Centro Cívico had not been constructed in 1964. The plan shows (1) Centro Cívico; (2) bachelor's quarters; (3) junior sector; (4) workers' sector; (5) service sector; (6) hospital; (7) barracks.

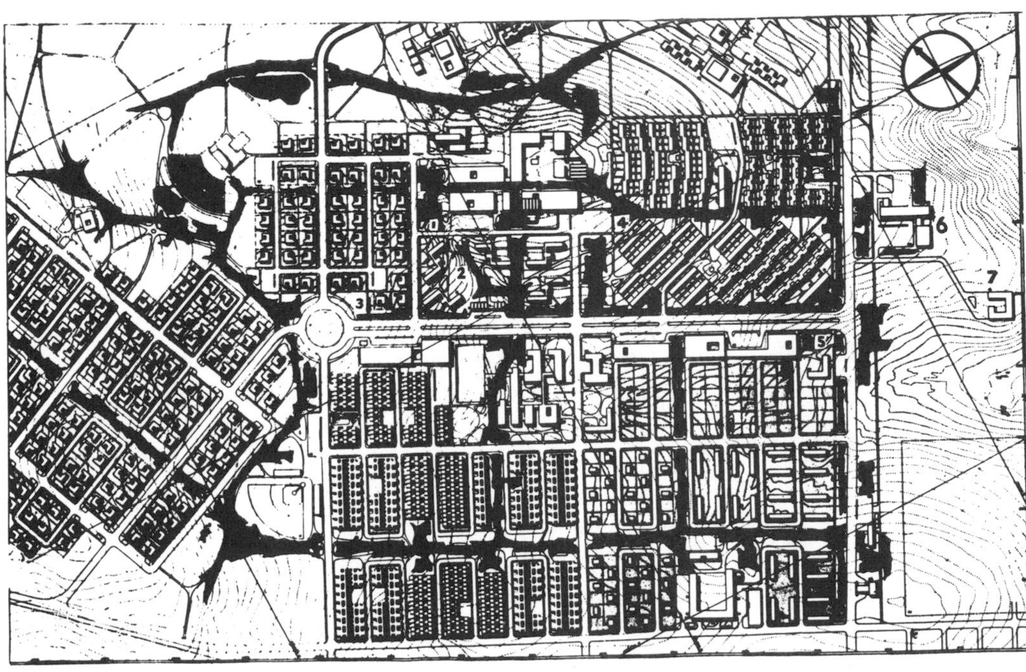

Figure 4.4 Puerto Ordaz and Castillito one year after the interviews were taken with a new housing project to the right of Castillito and a new hotel in the Centro Cívico.

Figure 4.5 Castillito, looking southwest, with the flooded and afforested banks of the Caroní in the foreground, Los Monos, right foreground, the main street running from left to right across the center of the photograph, the Caroní Rapids, left background, Urbanización Mendoza, center distance, and the upper Caroní River in the background.

Figure 4.6 El Roble with its scattered ranchos, looking north, with the main intersection and gas stations center right; the road to Dalla Costa passing left across the middle ground.

Figure 4.7 Form diagram of Dalla Costa, El Roble, and San Félix showing significantly fewer large structures, with the exception of the schools in El Roble, the industrial structures in Palúa, the small institutional group to the southeast of San Félix, and its port to the east.

Figure 4.8a Use diagram of Dalla Costa, El Roble, and San Félix showing commercial development scattered along the main road at various points in El Roble and clustered intensively in the central Casco of San Félix.

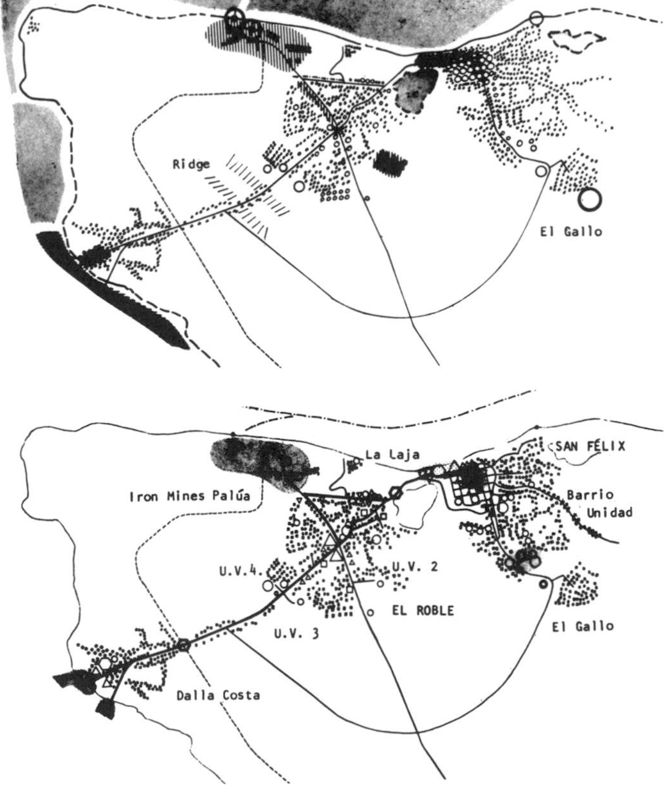

Figure 4.8b San Félix, looking west along the Orinoco.

Figure 4.9 San Félix, looking east along the waterfront.

est settlement. Its center, the Casco, laid out in the sixteenth century in a square-block pattern, retained its dominant role in the image of the community since it was near the edge of the water and received the single main road that entered along the waterfront. The Casco was the only extensive area with a clear geometrical pattern and continuous buildings. Although most of its buildings were only single-story, *bajareque* ranchos, the activity and traffic confirmed its role as a center, especially at the gathering points of the Plaza Bolívar, the open market on the waterfront, and the corner of the Calle Bolívar near the Cine Park.

The housing spread more thinly toward the edge of San Félix where the rectilinear pattern of the roads loosened into alignments that malleably responded to the landscape. The area outside the Casco was called the Barrio Unidad, an expansion area built after the 1958 revolution that merged into smaller indistinguishable barrios: San Raphael, La Esperanza, Los Palmitos, San Antonio de Berrio.

San Félix was bounded by the Orinoco to the north and the Laguna Las Delicias to the west. Both edges were visible, the first because it faced the main road traveling along the waterfront, the second because it flanked the lagoon. To the south and east expansion rendered the boundaries fluid and ambiguous. San Félix as a whole was visible from the outside, but the sharply defined forms of its streets were submerged by the trees that grew in the centers of the blocks and a water tower that dominated the skyline.

Inhabitants' Views of Settlements

Of the four settlements, Puerto Ordaz was the most praised by our respondents. It was described as "rich suburban," "a model town," and "American camp," with the "aspect of a city." Castillito was heavily criticized for "the quantity of bars and poverty," "ranchos and flooded streets," "movement of traffic," and "proliferation of vice," but it was "getting to be a big place." El Roble, the partially planned self-help community, elicited less colorful comments: "nothing here," "most people are moderate," "has little water and the roads are badly planned"; while San Félix was noted for "the movement of workers," "poverty," "dirt," for its "view of the Orinoco," and, by a foreigner, as "a little old Venezuelan town."

Although the Caroní Falls (63 percent) and Caroní Park (22 percent) were the most popular places to visit in the city, Puerto Ordaz (43 percent) and its Centro Civico (38 percent) were also primary places of attraction, with San Félix (33 percent) and its Plaza Bolívar (18 percent) following. The only other place of major interest was the steel mill (31 percent).

The popularity of Puerto Ordaz was probably due to its social status and affluence. This is what people would be curious to see. Indeed, its "American" characteristics, exotic to the populace though uninteresting to the American planners, may have been part of its attraction.

Descriptions of Settlements

When asked to describe the typical characteristics of the four main settlements, respondents found the task more difficult than that of describing individual buildings (chapter 6). Their responses were much less rich, relying frequently on specific features and parts of the settlement to exemplify character, or resorting to descriptions of general functions (see table 4.1).

Thirty-seven percent of the responses described settlements by facilities, such as parks, plazas, entertainment, housing, commerce. Eleven percent of all responses related to questions of environmental quality, and only 4 percent referred clearly to social characteristics. The plazas, parks, and other recreational facilities received the most responses (10.8 percent), followed by housing (10.3 percent); commerce (6.3 percent); transportation and utilities; and medical, educational, and community services.

This ranking related directly to the visibility and prominence of commerce, housing, and streets in these settlements. Plazas and commerce were considered dominant in Puerto Ordaz and San Félix, the main commercial centers, while in the more locally oriented Castillito and El Roble, housing was ranked as a primary characteristic. Where improvements were badly needed or where they had recently been carried out, as in Castillito and San Félix, transportation and utilities were mentioned, either for their presence or absence. Social status was noted when it was either high, as in Puerto Ordaz, or low, as in Castillito, where the lack of "morality" was mentioned.

Environmental qualities were not well articulated. Lack of cleanliness was noted in Castillito and San Félix. The "planned" character of Puerto Ordaz and El Roble was contrasted with the "unplanned" Castillito and San Félix. In San Félix, which received the most environmental responses, its view of the Orinoco, its new street paving, and its age were mentioned.

The richest responses came from those in Puerto Ordaz, Castillito, and San Félix, although one-half of those for Castillito were negative. El Roble received 50 percent fewer responses than any other settlement, more evidence of its weak image. San Félix, Puerto Ordaz, and Castillito also received equal attention on inhabitants' maps from about one-half the sample, while El Roble was mentioned only by one-third. In free verbal recall, however, Puerto Ordaz was mentioned twice as frequently as the other settlements. The factors that appeared to capture most attention were the social status and significance of Puerto Ordaz, the centralized focal structure of Puerto Ordaz and San Félix, and the perceived densities of San Félix and Castillito (chapter 3), El Roble's scattered development, lack of a center, and confusing street pattern resulted in the weakest identity of all.

The following characteristics appeared to influence settlement recall.

Settlement Form

Size The larger settlements and the rivers were well known; although the larger valleys remained unmentioned.

Texture The textural "sharpness" of the new camps and *urbanizaciónes* with their clean-cut houses and apartments, regular spacings, organized street patterns, curbs, and sidewalks, distinguished them from the softer irregular indigenous areas.

Isolation Isolated districts like the Country Club, the Steel Mill, and La Laja were frequently mentioned; but the narrow "green belts" in Puerto Ordaz did not appear to create sufficient buffer to set off the camps conceptually from each other.

Structural Simplicity Settlements with a central focus consisting of prominent landmarks, or nodal points such as plazas, and a simple street pattern—a grid as in San Félix, or a linear center as in Castillito—were recalled more frequently than the structurally confusing El Roble.

Visible Activity San Félix, Castillito, and Dalla Costa were crowded active centers, with high perceived densities.

Quality The better-quality areas were usually well known, but so were some of the worst. Quality correlated with social status.

Visibility

Internal Visibility When the main road passed through a settlement's center, as in Castillito and Dalla Costa, the settlement was internally visible and well recalled, providing that its form qualities were sufficiently distinctive.

External Visibility Only in the case of the Urbanización Mendoza, seen from the passing Avenida Guayana, did external visibility appear to be a factor in recall. Usually settlements were not seen from the outside unless at a distance across a valley.

Use and Significance

Use The most intensely used centers, San Félix and Puerto Ordaz, were well known.

Social Status Districts at the top and bottom of the social scale, such as the Country Club and Castillito, received particular attention.

Names Districts with names were recalled, while those without names, including clearly distinguishable units, such as the valleys and bowls, were not discussed.

Publicity Prominence in the news media due to a recent police raid was clearly the reason that Los Monos was recalled.

Perceived Functions

When inhabitants were directly asked to describe the activities of each settlement, their ratings were again affected by the form and visibility of facilities (see tables 4.2A, B, C). Commerce, nearly always in the foreground on the main road, was the most frequently noted function of every settlement except Puerto Ordaz, where the dominance of the Orinoco Mining Company, which owned the settlement, raised "mining" to the top of the list. Housing, in response to this question received no mention, perhaps because it was taken for granted.

Education was usually ranked according to the relative visibility of schools. In Puerto Ordaz, where the schools were hidden in the residential areas, education was ranked low (3 percent). In El Roble, where the Escuela Técnica, a citywide educational facility, was located on the main road, education was mentioned by 7 percent. In San Félix, although the city's only liceo was located in a remote part of the settlement, education was also mentioned by 8 percent. Although medical facilities were not ranked as principal activities, individual facilities were frequently mentioned despite their hidden locations.

Administrative offices (2 percent) were rarely mentioned as activities of San Félix, the seat of the Consejo Municipal. The building, though located on the plaza, was small and obscure in form. But the CVG offices in El Roble and the planned *unidades vecinales* (UV2 and 3) were acknowledged by 7 percent. Sports too were mentioned more in Puerto Ordaz, where the stadium was visible (7 percent), than in San Félix, where it was relatively remote (3 percent).

Functions that were widely and regularly used were less affected by lack of exposure than others of community significance that, when hidden, remained unknown or known by only a few. Poor access and poor exposure were characteristic of many public services in the city. It must have been only the absolute necessity for using them that caused them to be known at all. Other important facilities, subject to more voluntary use, such as the INCE adult training school, were scarcely mentioned.

Insiders and Outsiders

When inhabitants were asked to draw local maps showing schools, hospitals and clinics, churches, markets and shopping centers, meeting places, the police station, sports fields, offices of the CVG, and political parties, the insider's image was usually different from the outsider's image. Tables 4.2A, B, and C compare the rankings in each settlement of functions recalled by the whole population and by the local inhabitants.

In San Félix, the plaza, market, church, Seguros Sociales, and police station (all facilities of citywide use) were ranked in the same order by locals and outsiders. On lesser-mentioned buildings the groups began to differ, with the outsiders concentrating on the cinema, stadium, and liceo (all of citywide importance), and the locals paying more attention to the Consejo Municipal and two local primary schools.

In the other settlements, there was a wider split between outsiders and locals, with the outsiders again concentrating on the visible and citywide facilities and the locals on a wider choice including local and hidden facilities. In El Roble, although both groups mentioned the Bomba Phillips gas station, several outsiders noted the slaughterhouse, for which the community was apparently well known, while the locals, naturally, suppressed mention of this facility.

These facts emphasize the split between the insider's and outsider's concept of a settlement. San Félix, like many pre-automobile cities, placed all its major buildings—the church, administration, police, and hotel—in the central plaza. The stranger penetrated to the heart of the community and learned quickly how it was organized. In Puerto Ordaz the Centro Cívico was more distant from the main road and the entrance to the community, so the stranger was, as it were, kept at the gates, seeing only the hotels, gas stations, and commercial foreground, while the community maintained its privacy. Strangers there gained only a partial impression of the community.

Perception of Social Characteristics

The demographic data from our interviews distinguished the Puerto Ordaz community from all others by its higher income and education levels. El Roble possessed the lowest income and educational levels, while Castillito and San Félix had comparable proportions of each category. Nationality was quite mixed. The foreign born, including those of Latin American, British Caribbean, European, North American, and Middle Eastern origin, made up over one-quarter of our sample. The largest foreign groups were Italians and Spanish from the Mediterranean. These foreign populations were distributed over all income levels and throughout the city, with a slight preponderance in Puerto Ordaz, where most of the North Americans were concentrated.

When direct questions were asked about the kinds of people who lived in each settlement, judgments were based almost exclusively on social rank, by either income, education, or occupation. The highest proportion of replies identified areas as generally "heterogeneous" or "middle class," a socially noncommittal response. Nevertheless, Puerto Ordaz received the highest proportion of high-rank responses (18.7 percent) and the lowest proportion of the low-rank responses (3.7 percent). San Félix received the highest number of mixed or heterogeneous answers. Castillito was generally ranked lower than El Roble, although incomes were actually higher in Castillito. This misperception may have been due to the higher perceived densities and unkempt commercial image of Castillito. Nationality was seldom mentioned, except in the case of the North Americans in the Country Club, the only ethnic ghetto in the city. These responses in general avoided precise social descriptions of settlements and, in the case of Castillito and El Roble mistakenly correlated higher incomes with lower densities.

Residential Areas

The chief concern of the planners was to provide housing that would fit the needs and self-perceptions of each population group, minimize social conflicts, and be economical. A range of housing types had to be provided, from the planned communities for the executives and workers in the heavy industry to areas where low-income migrants could construct their own housing.

Some misinterpretations were made during this process. Early efforts to plan "sites and services" projects for the low-income population relied on inferences that areas like El Roble with its semirural ranchos were "reception areas" for new migrants, because they were on the outskirts of San Félix. Accordingly, the first "sites and services" project was laid out in El Roble, with large plots around culs-de-sac. It was later found in a housing survey that a majority of those living in El Roble had lived in the city for some time. The common pattern was for young men to arrive in San Félix, stay in small hotels or other accommodations, and only later, if they had a family and sufficient income, move out to a suburban location. New migrants needed good access to jobs more than anything else.

The new "sites and services" neighborhoods in El Roble

(figure 4.10), fitted more closely the residential needs of longer-term inhabitants and, unexpectedly, middle-class residents, who were also short of housing. It was embarrassing to find that several middle-income families managed to get plots in these first neighborhoods, a phenomenon that has occurred in such projects in other developing countries unless strict controls of allocations are enforced. The "sites and services" effort to incorporate the construction energies of the low-income migrants into the city's plan was both innovative and realistic from a resources viewpoint. It took time and much research, however, to learn the real needs and desires of this lower-income population (Corrada 1969).

In the field of middle-income housing for the steel mill executives and professionals, the urban design group opted for medium-density row housing as a way of saving on services and roads and of creating a more urbane environment (figure 4.11). This type of housing was one of the ideas imported by the American consultants. Modern brick row housing was popular on the U.S. east coast at the time and seemed an attractive and familiar image for the new city. A similar effort to build row housing and apartments was made in the original design of Puerto Ordaz (see figure 7.3), though later modified under the pressure of those who wanted single-family housing. Financing for the rather unconventional row houses proposed for UV4 was delayed for several years, while other single-family neighborhoods went ahead. The difficulty of changing the desirable image of housing was greater than expected.

Camps, Urbanizaciónes, Self-Help Neighborhoods, and Barrios

Respondents were asked to describe and differentiate eight smaller residential units—barrios, camps, *unidades vecinales* (neighborhood units), and *urbanizaciónes* (subdivisions)—from various parts of the city (see table 4.3). Emphasis on environmental qualities (25 percent) was now much higher than in settlements, while attention to functional facilities (13 percent) was much less. Only 8 percent were explicitly social in nature.

The commonest distinctions were between housing or building types (17 percent) and between the administrative agencies involved (5 percent). Social status, level of "morality," and house size were other differentiating qualities, followed by contrasts in cleanliness, community services, rates of change, transportation and utilities, housing comfort, and view.

As the functional contrasts between settlements diminish, environmental and then social characteristics become the distinguishing features. Again explicit social descriptions may

Figure 4.10 Unidade Vecinale 2, El Roble.

Figure 4.11 Site Plan, Unidade Vecinale 4, Puerto Ordaz.

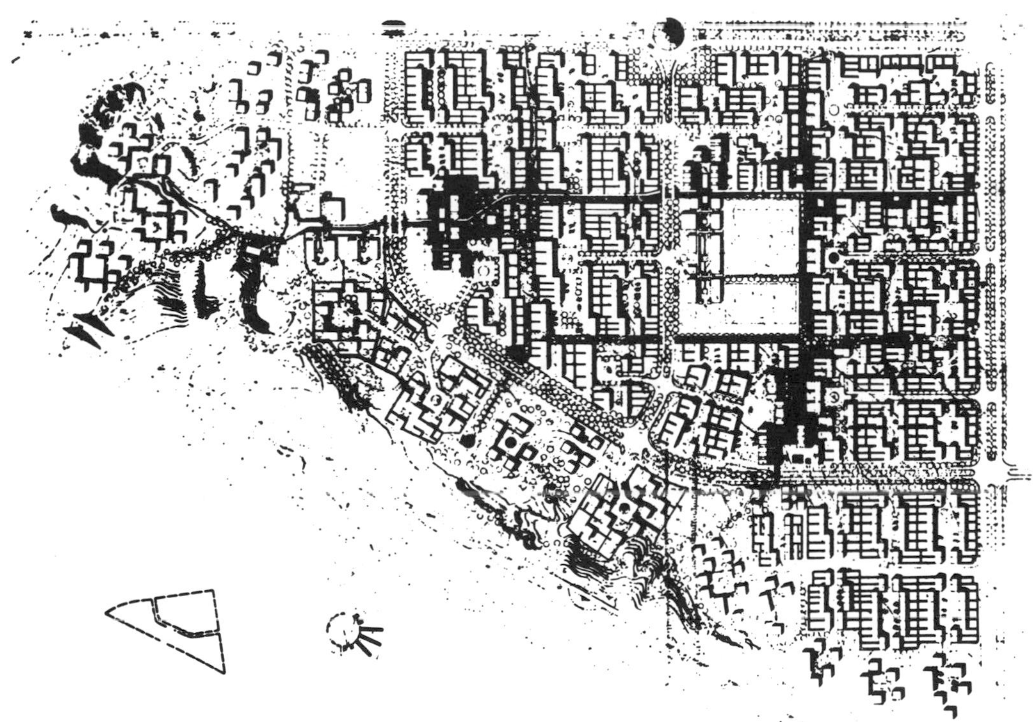

have been suppressed because of their sensitivity. It is easier to talk of environmental qualities. The importance of the administrative agency involved, for example, Banco Obrero, or FUNVICA, highlights the institutional dominance over housing in the city. Probably, as settlements grow older, their origins will be forgotten, and these areas will be seen as belonging more to the inhabitants.

Urbanización versus Barrio

The sharpest perceived differences occurred between the Urbanización Mendoza (figure 4.12), a planned new middle-income community, and Los Monos (figure 4.13), a dense low-income rancho area in swampy land by the Caroní. Housing types, the degree of "planning," and population character were the principal distinctions, followed by differences in rate of change—the urbanización was constructed all at one time, the barrio grew by increments—cleanliness, beauty, status, age, density, and infrastructure. Urbanización Mendoza received more attention and was always regarded in a positive sense, while Los Monos was looked upon negatively.

Two Barrios

When the two identical-looking indigenous barrios (La Unidad, figure 4.14, and La Esperanza) were compared, only local people could distinguish between them. The distinctions depended on housing quality—"more beautiful houses in La Unidad," "fewer ranchos," "better construction"—infrastructure—"La Unidad has many asphalted roads, and they have been named" —the presence of community services, and social status—"the people of La Esperanza are 'lower' than in La Unidad." These differences would be very difficult for a stranger, or planner, to detect.

Two Planned Neighborhoods

When two planned developments in Puerto Ordaz were compared (the Banco Obrero housing and Camp A, figure 4.20), housing type and quality were again the principal differences: "duplexes in Camp A, row housing and apartments in the Banco Obrero." Distinctions in social status came next (the existence of Americans in Camp B was noted by many), followed by comparisons of house quality, "the houses in Camp B are more spacious, individual, and better ventilated than Camp A or the Banco Obrero." With the clear social stratification of these neighborhoods, differences like these would be apparent to an outsider.

Figure 4.12 Urbanización Mendoza, Castillito.

Figure 4.13 Los Monos, Castillito.

Figure 4.14 Barrio La Unidad, San Félix.

Figure 4.15 UV 4. Typical street, El Roble.

Two Self-Help Neighborhoods

Two newly planned self-help neighborhoods in El Roble (UV4 [figure 4.15] and UV3) were the most difficult to distinguish, partly because their characters were scarcely formed. They both received the lowest attribute scores, sharing both positive and negative evaluations. The presence or absence of community schools in these neighborhoods was taken as a more distinguishing characteristic than differences in housing types. A few subjects noted differences in the slope of the ground and surfacing of the streets.

The greater emphasis on social distinctions in the camps of Puerto Ordaz than in the indigenous and self-help settlements was indicative of the trend toward separation of social groups in the new middle-income developments.

Environmental Cues to Social Perception

Perception of social rank and nationality can be made through the appearance, dress, and mannerisms of people themselves,[1] through environmental cues gained from reading their houses and neighborhoods, or from locational cues. In Ciudad Guayana, immigrants from the British West Indies were identified by their felt hats, Americans and North Europeans by their light complexions. But, while such perceptions of social rank can be accurate in one's own locality, in other parts of the city the social perception of neighborhoods depends more on environmental cues such as the size, style, and quality of buildings or the presence of automobiles, paved streets, landscaping, signs, and maintenance. Sensitivity to these indicators of social status was usually accompanied by strongly evaluative overtones. Materials like concrete blocks were admired; others like *bajareque* were disdained.

Interpretations of social rank, particularly by foreigners, were often stereotyped and tenuous. For one respondent, the people in a certain barrio were "nice" because it was kept tidy, while another suggested that the "signs on the walls show that they have no community spirit." The signs were, in fact, sensitive indicators of community feeling. Current social attitudes were made quite clear through messages like "Viva Fidel" and "Cuba Si, Yanqui No" at the time of the Cuban missile crisis, and later "Abajo los terroristas" and "Viva Leone" during the 1964 elections.

The population appeared to be quite aware of these cues of social rank and adopted them to achieve status in their homes, even at the cost of other needs. In the indigenous areas, status seemed to depend on the degree to which one's house resembled a *quinta* (figure 4.16)—a suburban villa of permanent construction, with concrete-block, plastered walls; concrete roof, porch, and walled garden; and ornamental railings, flowers, and lamps—rather than the simple *bajareque* rancho (figure 4.17). In the self-help areas, where prospective home builders were offered a choice of house types, a house made to appear larger by a high parapet wall in the front had a similar social status appeal.

There was as yet no clear system of locational cues to the social structure, for the community had not yet worked out a clear spatial pattern of social groups. The old tradition of elite families living on or near the Plaza,[2] in the center of the town, had virtually disappeared, except for some instances in San Félix, where the store owners lived behind their stores. But only in El Roble had a small suburban group of upper-class families built a row of *quintas* on the main road.

On the other hand, in the newer parts of the city planned by the Orinoco Mining Company, especially Puerto Ordaz, social status was clearly articulated by the company. Districts of homogeneous housing type denoted the rather precise social status of the executives, professionals, and technicians who worked in the companies. The top-rank houses were North American in style (figure 4.18), differing from the *quinta* type in that they had lawns and shrubs rather than flowers and were usually without boundary walls. The camps (figures 4.19, 4.20) differed in prestige according to housing type, isolation, and altitude, where better views, breezes, and "tranquillity" could be found. The exclusive Country Club was isolated on a separate hill. But this pattern of the company town was beginning to disintegrate as new housing areas of varying social levels were constructed in scattered locations. It was one of the aims of the planners to try to keep this social pattern fairly ambiguous.

The Planned and the Indigenous Areas

The elements of construction in the indigenous areas were similar to one another. Building materials and styles were similar whatever their use. Streets were of similar width. Barrios looked alike, yet there were always a few individual variations between buildings. Streets in barrios responded to the peculiarities of the terrain. There were few sharp changes, and seldom did any individual building stand out. Barrios were not named until the demand arose or names were imposed on them. The names generated for the barrios referred either to particularities of location (such as Las Palmas, or Dalla Costa), to national heroes (like Antonio de Berrio), or to someone's aspirations (such as La Esperanza). There was none of the pessimism found in Puerto Rican barrio names like "Sale si Puede."

Figure 4.16 Home resembling a *quinta.*

Figure 4.17 Simple *bajareque* rancho.

Figure 4.18 Country Club house for executives.

These areas were built incrementally and individually and probably worked well for the local user, although for the stranger they were labyrinthine.

The planned areas, on the other hand, consciously articulated the environment both physically and verbally. Individual houses and other buildings conformed more narrowly to their use categories, with less individual variation between houses. Community buildings were set off from their surroundings, streets were laid out and named in consistent systems, neighborhoods were separated and articulated by open spaces.

The components of the planned residential areas were more easily distinguished from each other than those in the indigenous settlements, but they were laid out with little "feel" for the actual travel and visibility patterns of the public. Public facilities were frequently hidden, and even the civic commercial center in Puerto Ordaz was distant from the main traffic artery. Since commerce is highly sensitive to visibility patterns, it began to grow—in contradiction to the earlier plan—along the main artery, a witness to the struggle between planners' and market orientations.

A few years ago many planners and architects would like to have seen the whole population housed in bright, clean new housing areas. Planning authorities in many developing countries still feel this way. But to many of the planners on this project the indigenous and planned self-help developments possessed the attractive qualities of individuality, small scale, class anonymity, and harmony with the landscape, while the planned neighborhoods stratified social groups, set up barriers between residential areas, standardized the houses, emphasized larger-scale house-to-street and street-system relationships, and often ignored the natural environment.

The inhabitants, however, held the latter areas in high esteem. Their choices of housing in the self-help areas and the kinds of alterations made to their own houses clearly indicated the desire of many to live in *quintas.* Rejection of traditional forms of housing and neighborhood and adoption of imported forms can be seen everywhere in developing cities. The residents lose confidence in old buildings like the church in the Plaza Bolívar or in the brightly painted housing, and the American-type or middle-class Venezuelan houses become symbols of aspiration. This may well be a phase of eclectic adoption that people must live through before rediscovering their own identities. But imposing professional images without consultation is not the way. At least in the "sites and services" areas people were given the choice of different house styles, which they then built themselves.[3]

Figure 4.19 Camp B houses for skilled workers.

Figure 4.20 Camp A row houses for lower-rank workers.

Figure 4.23 Uprooting of vegetation for the new urbanizaciónes.

Achieving Settlement Identity

The perceived character of the settlements was affected in several ways by the configuration of the environment. The need for identity is often discussed in the planning literature, but more important than mere identity is the need to have the "right" identity, an identity of which people can be proud. If an area takes on an identity that puts its inhabitants to shame, they will wish to change it or keep it quiet, just as those in El Roble played down its identification with the slaughterhouse. If settlements wish to improve and clarify their public image, however, a number of strategies are suggested by the evidence.

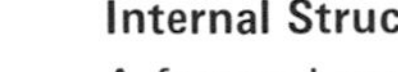

Internal Structuring

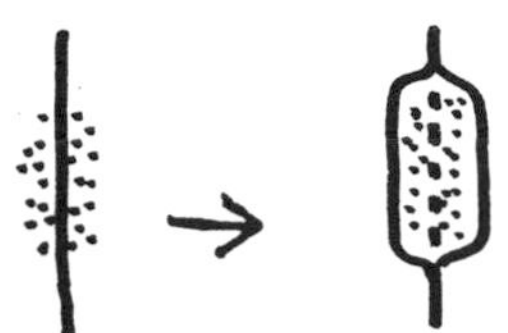

Figure 4.21

A focused road system, a single center of activity on that road system, with a high density and variety of establishments will encourage a clear identity much more directly than defined boundaries if each settlement is somehow unique in its structure and facilities. A settlement planned next to Los Olivos on the west side of the Caroní was placed with its center on the through road rather than in the geometric center as in Puerto Ordaz. Then when traffic increased, a bypass service route was planned on each side to leave the old road as a pedestrian mall (figure 4.21). Hence the community would retain its center throughout its growth.

Exposure of Facilities

Figure 4.22

Exposure and prominence on the main circulation structure (figure 4.22) is a powerful means of establishing the presence of facilities a settlement wishes to emphasize. Plazas, parks, commercial facilities, schools, medical facilities, or housing offices could play such prominent roles in a community's image.

Preserving Natural Identity

The indigenous barrios provided some good lessons in site planning and landscape preservation. They maintained the topographic and ecological character of a site, while the new *urbanizaciónes* generally uprooted all vegetation and carved out flat sites (figure 4.23).

Breaking Stereotypes

Social stereotypes might be broken down by the diversification of physical cues to social class. Since intergroup perception depended mostly on perception of group habitats, the diversification and use of housing types across social class, the cleaning of main streets in the poorer areas, and the placing of better units in more visible locations might help to transform the stereotype that lower-income areas were always "chaotic" and "dirty."

The multiplication of housing types and their use by different social ranks were already complicating the identification of social status. If the new row housing for the professional personnel in the steel mill supplanted the American single-family house and *quinta* as prestige housing types, a diversification in the residential cues of social status could be achieved. The culs-de-sac designed for self-help housing could have lent prestige to lower-income housing if these groups had been able to occupy them.

Transition Units

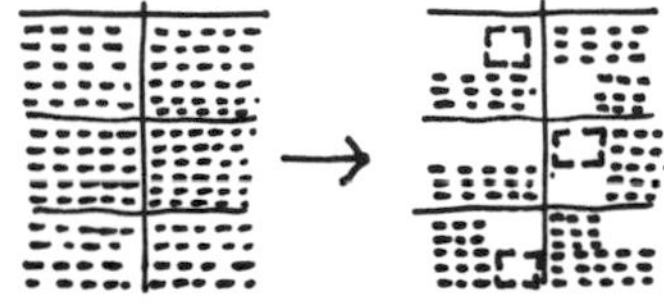

Figure 4.24

Scattering units of better housing (figure 4.24) might alleviate the monolithic qualities of large rancho areas while not wholly disguising their presence. These transition units could also act as development models for the rancho areas in schemes of *Mejoramiento Progresivo.*[4] Through the diversification of size, character, and visibility, these areas could therefore strike a balance between a high visibility of a rancho settlement like Castillito and the formlessness of lower-density El Roble. Such a prototype development was proposed for Dalla Costa.

This area in Dalla Costa was to include a range of income groups representative of the city as a whole in both the short and the long term. It was to be developed for a low percentage occupancy at first. Growth would take place at the edges of the area and in its interstices by filling vacant lots and by opening new streets and adjacent land. The streets to be built later were to have the best access and highest visibility in the area, and the larger lots among them would provide places where those who wished to stay in the community could build larger homes or businesses. We believed that most new areas would increase both in per capita income and in density over time, and we felt that these new streets and adjacent properties could take advantage of the increase in social and economic values. Some spaces in the development pattern were to be kept open—some permanently, others until their use was decided on later by the people living in the area (Porter 1969).

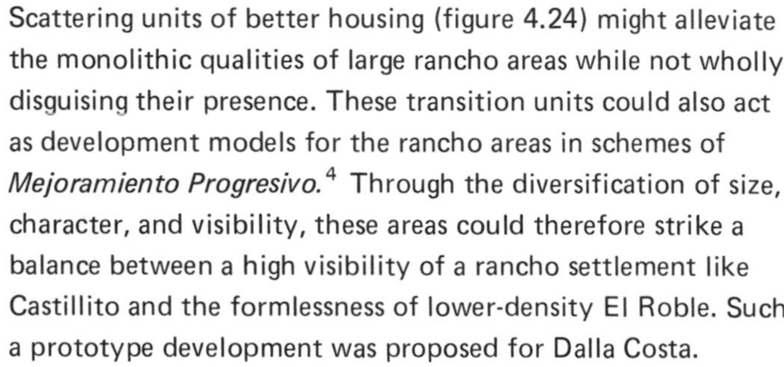

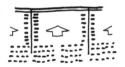

Figure 4.25

There were risks of diseconomies in construction and of losing social balance, either from a takeover by the affluent groups or through illegal squatting, but it was an experiment worth trying.

At a larger scale, an "outside-in" growth strategy (figure 4.25) was proposed for the western side of the Caroní. The main intent of the outside-in strategy was to develop corridors away from the spinal highway through Alta Vista, preserving future high-priced land between corridors for later development, thus avoiding urban renewal (Downs 1969). Hence a crust of good-quality development would reach out to the hidden self-help housing areas. While this compromise did allow planned squatter development west of the Caroní, the site was isolated by poor access to the main transportation. Considerable incentives and controls would be needed to tempt low-income families out there and keep squatters off the highly accessible land.

Smaller Residential Units

The scale of residential areas was another issue. Recent efforts at structuring cities have attempted to "dissolve" neighborhoods into the fabric of cities (Milton Keynes Development Corp. 1970; Alexander 1965) because they have been seen as a socially constraining form. However, there is no empirical evidence that neighborhood units actually constrain life-styles in any way.

The newly planned areas of Ciudad Guayana were called neighborhood units (*unidades vecinales*), and they usually followed the form of the "camps" in Puerto Ordaz, but no claims of social integration were made for these units. They were seen as convenient building blocks for the city. However, since they were each designated for a relatively homogeneous population group, their structure and groupings could lead to large homogeneous areas of population and consequent social segregation.

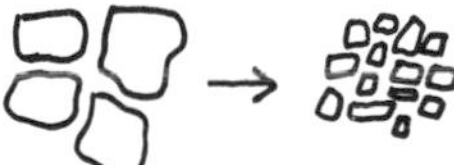

Figure 4.26

The success of the indigenous areas in allowing a degree of social mix suggests that the use of residential units smaller than those presently under construction could keep this possibility more open in the future planned areas. The later plan for Dalla Costa proposed scattered units (figure 4.26) as small as five to ten acres to be designed and developed under single control.[5]

These devices for achieving desired community identity depend on what a community wants. Interviews give an idea of how people in settlements see themselves and others, but closer cooperation will be needed to find out exactly what kind of images inhabitants wish to have, for in a planned city with a severe housing shortage, the consumer does not have a wide array of neighborhood choices.

5 WHY PLACES WERE KNOWN

The Planners' Media

The spatial language employed by the environmental professionals to describe and plan Ciudad Guayana was based on traditional modes of simulating cities. For the large-scale plans of the city, land-use maps allocated zones of use by gross categories, such as residential, industrial, and commercial, and showed a limited number of public and quasi-public facilities, such as schools, hospitals, community centers, stadia, and churches (see figure 8.34). Each land-use zone was of even density and distinctly bounded, whether occupied by houses, stores, or trees. These maps emphasized use, density, and public facilities but suppressed and distorted social, economic, and environmental factors in the planning process. Social and environmental information might be inferred, but often incorrectly, from these maps.

To describe the physical form of planning proposals, maps were drawn showing an aerial view of the plans of buildings and vegetation with their projected shadows, the layout of roads, and the patterns of various floor surfaces (see, for example, figure 4.11). These plans were more specific about the form of the physical environment than the land-use maps, but even so roofscape, contours, and floor patterns shown in such aerial views are distant from the ground-level city experience, with its people, traffic, signs, lighting, and other details. Moreover, the rendered site plan now widely used in urban design details both visible and unseen parts of the city with equal attention, failing to distinguish between public and private or city and local environments. It perpetuates the fallacy that the urban designer can engage in the "total" design of a city.

Although the planners of Ciudad Guayana were aware of many social and environmental issues, and the limitations of their media, their perceptions and proposals were still subtly screened and distorted by their simulations. Even the form of the data they received contributed to the distortion. The aerial photographs, already mentioned, indicated several features of the landscape, especially hills, that were assumed to be well known. They were not.

How did this planning language relate to the inhabitants'

perceptions of the city? Did the inhabitants see the city as a pattern of social affiliations, a kind of mental layout of the census data; as a pattern of activities and movement; or as a physical environment of sights, sounds, smells, colors, textures, and materials?

The Inhabitants' Language

In this chapter we shall concentrate on perceptions of buildings and structures. We asked our respondents to describe a few selected buildings (chapter 6) to gain insight into their verbal environmental vocabulary. Then we examined the responses to three questions that tapped their freely chosen recall of various elements in the city.

The three questions (translated from the original Spanish) were:

1. Free verbal recall: Can you tell me which points or places in the city and its environs you remember best? (122 building elements mentioned.)

2. Free map recall: Please draw . . . a map indicating the points and places in the city that you have just mentioned. After that add any other important features that come to mind. (188 building elements mentioned.)

3. Free trip recall: Would you please describe the road that goes between Matanzas (steel mill) and San Félix, mentioning the appearance, the changes in direction, the views, and all the important or the interesting features of the city you can see on this trip? (104 building elements mentioned.)

We recorded and photographed all buildings, establishments, and landmarks that were recalled in response to these three questions and then scaled a number of attributes that we predicted might be the reasons for their recall. Most of the buildings other than houses, ranchos, and smaller stores received some attention and were included in the analysis. They included every type of element from factories to stores, from hills to statues, from schools to bridges. The attribute scalings[1] were then correlated with the frequencies of element recall in each of the three sets of responses to assess which attributes captured greater attention.

The Attributes of Buildings

Three principal attributes were selected as likely predictors of recall:

1. Distinctiveness of form (see tables 5.1, 5.2)
2. Visibility (see table 5.3)
3. Use and symbolic significance (see table 5.4)

Distinctive Form

Distinctiveness of form is similar to the quality of "image-

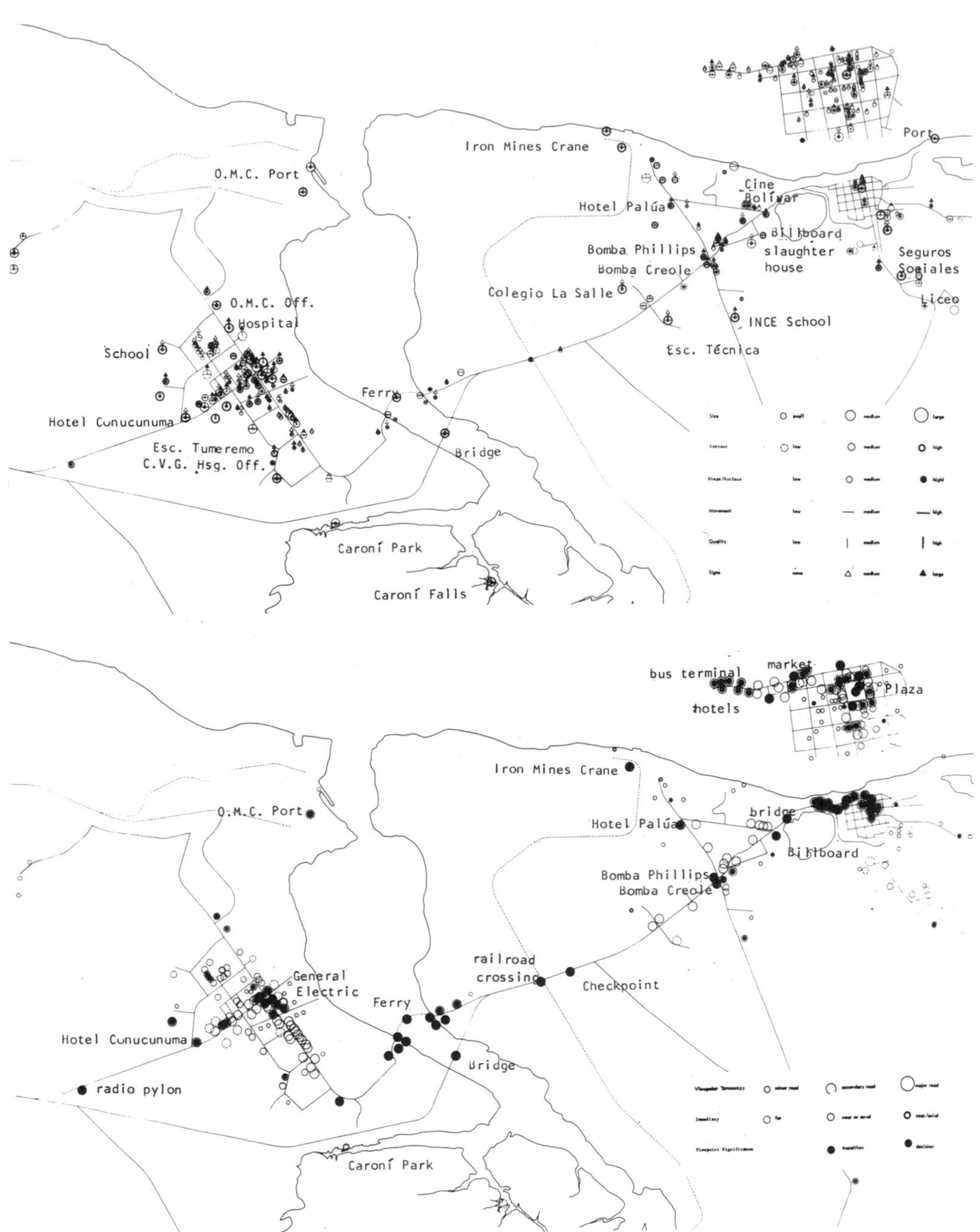
Iron Mines Crane
Port
O.M.C. Port
Cine
Bolívar
Hotel Palúa
Billboard
Bomba Phillips
slaughter
house
Seguros
Sociales
Bomba Creole
Colegio La Salle
Liceo
O.M.C. Off.
Hospital
INCE School
School
Esc. Técnica
Ferry
Hotel Cunucunuma
Esc. Tumeremo
C.V.G. Hsg. Off.
Bridge
Caroní Park
Caroní Falls
bus terminal
market
Plaza
hotels
Iron Mines Crane
O.M.C. Port
bridge
Hotel Palúa
Billboard
Bomba Phillips
Bomba Creole
railroad
crossing
General
Electric
Checkpoint
Ferry
Hotel Cunucunuma
Bridge
radio pylon
Caroní Park

Figure 5.1 Form of buildings. The diagram describes by a graphic symbol the form of each building mentioned by the inhabitants (see legend). Some patterns emerge from visual inspection. More buildings in Puerto Ordaz, the model American type of community, have strong contours, are larger, and have dominant signs than in San Félix, the indigenous settlement where buildings are smaller, joined to each other, and less prominently advertised. Many of the more distinctive buildings are distant from the main road.

Figure 5.2 Visibility of buildings. Buildings and places seen from viewpoints of high intensity cluster along the major circulation spine and in the intensive pedestrian center of San Félix. Those seen at decision or transition points cluster around main intersections in Puerto Ordaz and El Roble, the entry to San Félix, and the ferry crossing on the Caroní.

ability" except that Lynch's definition appeared to cover also the visibility of buildings. The *distinctive form* of each facility (figure 5.1) was assessed as viewed from in front of its main entrance or from the most common approach. Any noticeable qualities that might make the building stand out were rated, both on the basis of their absolute *intensity* within the city and for their *singularity* in the local surroundings, in the neighborhood, or in the city as a whole. The two measurements were made to test whether the relative distinctness of a facility might be more important than any absolute characteristic.

Movement, contour, size, shape, surface, quality, and signs (see tables 5.1, 5.2) were the attributes selected to assess the distinctiveness of each building. The *intensity* of each attribute was an absolute measure of its presence on a scale that was calibrated to Ciudad Guayana. Hence, three-story or higher buildings were given a high rating for size because they were among the largest buildings in this particular city. The *singularity* of attributes was a relative dimension measured by the scale at which they were deemed unique,[2] that is, whether they were singular on the scene, in the neighborhood, or in the city. Attributes of a house that were singular only at the scale of the local scene would receive a low score on the singularity scale. Attributes, like those of a primary school, that were singular at the neighborhood scale received a higher score, and those that were singular in the whole city—for example, the steel mill—received the highest singularity rating. Neither the intensity nor the singularity of attributes alone was predicted as sufficient to capture attention; for a singular building could be uniquely small, or a prominent sign could be lost in a sea of prominent signs.

Visibility

Unless a building is seen, it cannot project an image. Visibility is therefore a necessary component for recall (figure 5.2). It depends on the location of a facility and on the focus of the inhabitants' actions and vision. It is the visual counterpart of a building's accessibility. Many buildings that were distinct in both form and significance, like the INCE adult education school, were seldom mentioned because they were off the main routes. Only those who used such a building might know of it. The visibility of each building was measured by three component attributes (see table 5.3): (1) *viewpoint intensity*, an estimate of the number of people who might regularly see it from its most commonly used viewpoints; (2) *viewpoint significance,* its presence at important decision points or transition points on the city's circulation system; and (3) *imme-*

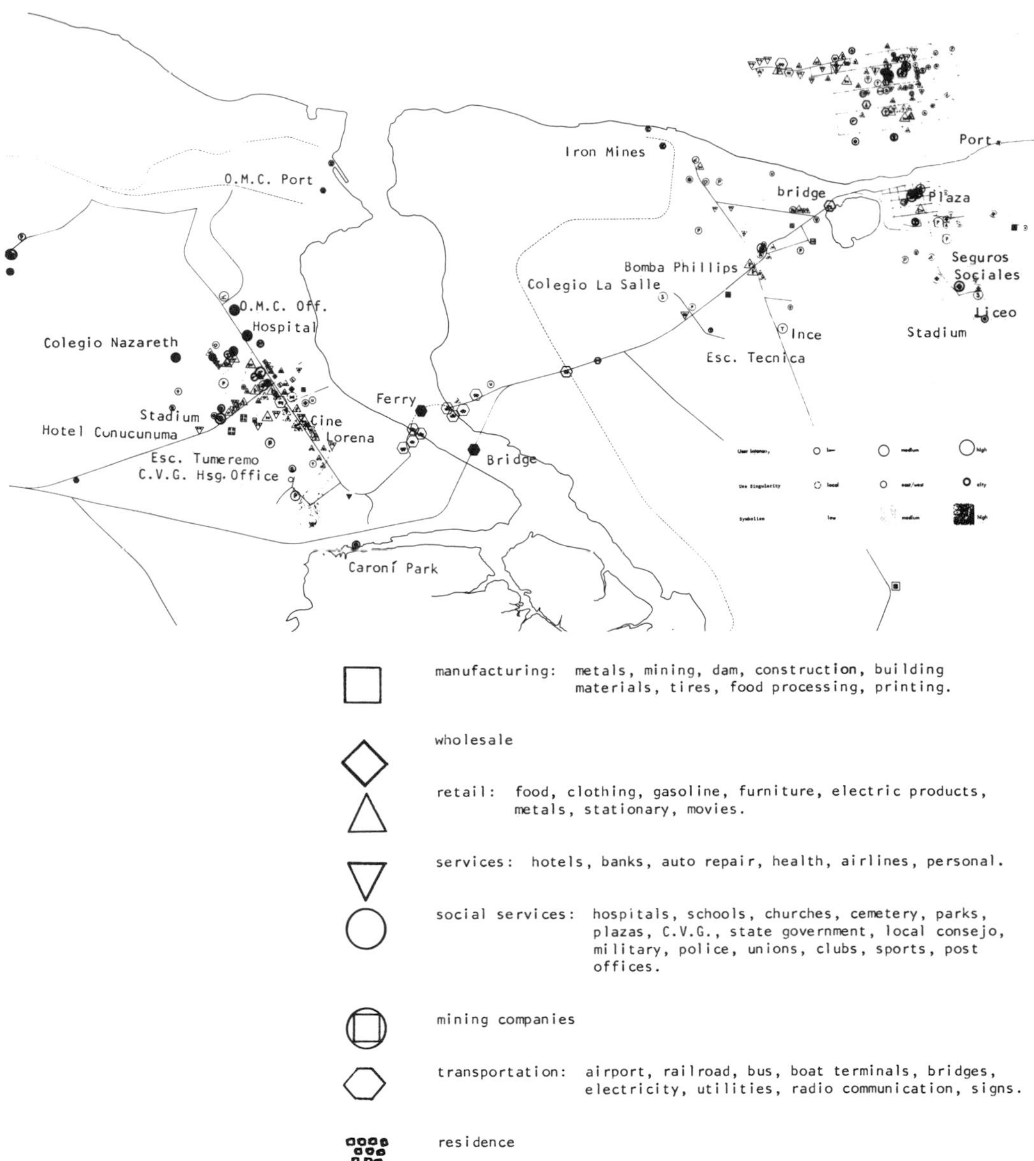

Iron Mines
Port
O.M.C. Port
bridge
Plaza
Seguros
Sociales
Bomba Phillips
Colegio La Salle
Liceo
O.M.C. Off.
Hospital
Colegio Nazareth
Ince
Stadium
Esc. Tecnica
Ferry
Stadium
Cine
Hotel Conucunuma
Lorena
Esc. Tumeremo
Bridge
C.V.G. Hsg. Office
Caroní Park
manufacturing: metals, mining, dam, construction, building materials, tires, food processing, printing.
wholesale
retail: food, clothing, gasoline, furniture, electric products, metals, stationary, movies.
services: hotels, banks, auto repair, health, airlines, personal.
social services: hospitals, schools, churches, cemetery, parks, plazas, C.V.G., state government, local consejo, military, police, unions, clubs, sports, post offices.
mining companies
transportation: airport, railroad, bus, boat terminals, bridges, electricity, utilities, radio communication, signs.
residence

diacy, a measure of its distance and centrality in the line of public view.

The measure of viewpoint significance was introduced because many small and functionally insignificant buildings at major decision points, bus terminals, and entrances to settlements were frequently recalled. This could be attributed either to the high attention levels of travelers at these points or to their need to identify such points with associated buildings for purposes of social communication or personal recall. The latter was a likely reason, since few of the intersections possessed names. Both the viewpoint significance and immediacy scales took viewpoint intensity into account. Hence, an important decision point or a location of high immediacy on a minor road would be rated lower on these scales than one on a major road. Only the highest immediacy and decision points on the minor road systems were scored, however, so that the scales were only partially composite.

Figure 5.3 Use intensity, singularity, and symbolism of buildings. More buildings in Puerto Ordaz are heavily used, but more in San Félix are unique in function, even though not highly used. The latter include the city's only telegraph office, the cemetery, the Consejo Municipal, the police station, and the plaza.

Use and Significance

Finally, the use and significance of each facility was assessed by its *use intensity*, its *use singularity*, and its social, political, economic, aesthetic, or historic *significance* (see table 5.4 and figure 5.3). The first two measures were relatively objective and easy to take. The measure of singularity attempted to account for those facilities that had a wide realm of users. When functions were highly singular but catered to a narrow realm of users, the ratings were adjusted downward.

The most elusive measure was that of significance. An assessment of social, economic, and historical significance was made for every building after consultation with two professionals who had lived in or had contact with the city for some years. The scaling was applied only to those symbolic facilities that were not already accorded a high use intensity rating. Hence, a school, although of symbolic importance to the community, would not receive a high score on significance because it had been counted as a building of high use intensity. The hydroelectric plant, which was relatively unused, received a high score on the significance scale.

Intercorrelations between Attributes

When the buildings mentioned on the maps ($N = 188$) were rated and their attributes intercorrelated, there were some significant intercorrelations within the major attributes (see table 5.5).[3] The singularity and intensity of each of the form attributes were moderately intercorrelated (between .39 and .68). Larger buildings tended to be isolated, to have unique shapes and high quality (size intensity to contour singularity

$r = .44$; to shape singularity, $r = .49$; to quality intensity, $r = .47$). Uniquely shaped buildings also tended to have unique surface colors, textures, or materials (shape singularity to surface singularity, $r = .43$).

Among visibility components, viewpoint significance and immediacy correlated ($r = .47$), probably because buildings tend to cluster around decision points, which lie on the axis of vision. These components correlated less with viewpoint intensity. Correlations were also low between the attributes of use and significance.

Most significantly, there were few correlations across components of form, visibility, and significance, with the exception of use singularity and size ($r = .38$), use intensity and movement ($r = .32$). The attributes of form, visibility, and significance were seldom equally present in any one building. Indeed, correlations between the significance of buildings and their visibility were mostly negative, a key indicator of low communication.

Correlations with Recall

The wide array of attributes that appeared to affect inhabitants' recollections, and their varying influence in the three different response situations were remarkable (see tables 5.6, 5.7). Significant, though not high, correlations occurred between most of the attributes and recall frequencies, the only exceptions being signs (highest $r = .06$) and recency (highest $r = .08$). The generally low level of correlations was to be expected since the buildings were spread across fifteen miles of development, and individual inhabitants mentioned only a portion of them. When local inhabitants recalled local buildings (table 5.8), correlations rose.

Form

Movement, contour, size, shape, and surface (highest r's = .35, .36, .38, .41, .43) rivaled each other for the highest correlations in the three different response situations, while signs (highest $r = .06$) and quality (highest $r = .16$), appeared to have relatively low influence over recall. The most powerful identifying qualities in the map responses were those of movement ($r_{int} = .34$, $r_{sing} = .29$) and contour ($r_{int} = .26$, $r_{sing} = .30$), both being more influential than the apparent size of buildings ($r_{int} = .25$, $r_{sing} = .24$). In free verbal recall, however, size and shape rose in importance while contour diminished. When simulating the more concrete task of imagining a journey through the city, respondents must have focused on these more sensorial attributes, either because the task emphasized them or because the buildings situated along the road system possessed these attributes more than others.

Movement Most of the movement associated with buildings had to do with people—for example, people clustering around bars, people lining up outside the cinema, and children playing in the school playground. Parked cars were treated in our ratings as potential activity, and other kinds of motion—smoke, flags, trees, and water—were recognized. The fluctuating nature of this phenomenon, however, made it difficult to measure. A school would be empty for a good part of the time and would appear empty when the children were in classes; a stadium might be used heavily just once a week. Scores were usually measured by the peak periods of apparent movement. Intensity of movement was slightly correlated ($r = .32$) with the estimated numbers of people using a building, the differences being accounted for by buildings that displayed different levels of external and internal movement. A school with a hidden playground would appear to be less used than a store or a heavily trafficked street corner.

Contour Sharpness of boundary defines a building from its ground, making it stand out, even (according to these correlations) if it is a small building.[4] But an isolated house in a field of isolated houses may be less noticeable than the end house on the row. Singularity therefore adds to contour visibility, a proposition that seemed to be borne out by its usually higher correlations. Many of the more important buildings in the city, particularly the newer ones, such as the steel mill, several schools, the medical facilities, and the churches, were isolated and received their due attention, but in the older indigenous parts, important public buildings like the Consejo Municipal were joined to others, making them difficult to identify.

Size Building size was measured by the apparent height and bulk of a building as seen from its approach view. These qualities were not always perceptible, however, in the densely built-up areas of town such as the center of San Félix. Clear perception of size frequently depended on isolation. Size singularity was also influential. In the planned parts of Puerto Ordaz, large buildings like schools and industrial sheds stood out more in residential areas, where their sizes were more distinctive. Size, like movement, correlated highly ($r = .38$) with use singularity, because buildings housing unique functions, such as the hospital, were often large.

Shape In the first scalings, simplicity of shape was thought to be an imageable characteristic;[5] but when it received low correlations, the scale was inverted, and complexity was taken as the high measure with slightly more success. Each end of the simplicity-complexity spectrum seemed to catch some attention. Simplicity allows for quicker perception in a time-constraining situation—one possible reason for wide recognition of the General Electric warehouse at the main intersection in Puerto Ordaz, where an equally visible but more complex building was virtually ignored. In other contexts, complexity captured attention. The Hotel Cunucunuma and various schools that were externally articulated into blocks and complex industrial structures, like the steel mill and the smaller cement plant, may have been noticed because of their complexity in simpler contexts. Unique shapes were especially striking to the visitor. The arches of the Protestant Church (figure 6.4), the barrel-vaulted roofs of the steelworkers' Syndaco in Puerto Ordaz, and the La Salle School in El Roble (figure 7.13) stood out in a city dominated by rectangular buildings. The dominant influence of shape singularity in the trip responses ($r = .41$) may well dismay those who condemn the search for novel forms in buildings, for it shows that they did succeed in attracting attention.

Surface Brightness, coarseness, and complexity of surface can be salient characteristics of a building, but the buildings of Ciudad Guayana were predominantly white, while the landscape was green and brown. This made it difficult to establish a single calibrating system for urban and rural situations. The higher singularity correlations confirmed that relative rather than absolute brightness was the more distinctive characteristic. The brown and rocky dike of the Macagua Dam dissolved into the landscape, but it would have been noticeable against a white housing area; green trees, which would ordinarily have dissolved into the landscape, were dominant in the white environment of the San Félix Plaza.

Quality Quality was a catchall category that included expensive materials, careful landscaping, cleanliness, and good condition. It usually correlated with social status, but since buildings of the same quality were grouped together in areas, quality seemed to be a noticeable characteristic only when it occurred at the boundary between areas of different social level or where individual improvements were being carried out in an older environment. The Puerto Ordaz supermarket near the Castillito boundary was used by those from Castillito and was quite well known, as were the new banks in San Félix. These instances were not sufficient to make quality in general an important differentiating characteristic of buildings in the city, although it certainly distinguished residential areas from each other.

Signs Verbal signs were the primary means whereby shopkeepers, gas stations, and advertisers hoped to attract the customer's attention. Doctors, lawyers, architects, and public facility managers placed signs outside their offices, too, but they were usually quiet in form and modest in size. The low correlations received by signs were unexpected. The names of many buildings must have been learned through their signs, yet the signs themselves did not appear to influence attention patterns. The reason perhaps was that the more significant and larger community buildings did not have large signs on them. The churches were unsigned, schools and hospitals were dignified by discreet lettering over their entrances (often invisible from the street), and the steel mill was announced by no sign at all: it did not need one. The smaller commercial buildings displayed the largest signs, but only those that were well located gained attention.[6]

Intensity and Singularity When regression analyses were made of the intensity and singularity components, the multiple correlation coefficients (singularity R = .43, and intensity R = .44) were comparable (table 5.7). This strongly suggests that the recall of a building depends as much on its relation to the context as on any absolute qualities. However, correlations with recall frequencies varied considerably among components. For instance, singularity of shape and surface appeared to be more important than their respective intensities, while in other attributes, intensity and singularity held comparable correlations.

Visibility

Of the three components of visibility, *viewpoint significance* and *immediacy* achieved the most significant correlations both in map (r = .39, .38) and trip recall (r = .38, .37), while *viewpoint intensity* was significant in the maps (r = .20) (tables 5.3, 5.6, 5.7). No visibility index correlated significantly with verbal recall responses.

Viewpoint Intensity The number of people (both auto and pedestrian travelers) likely to pass the most prominent viewpoint of the building during a typical day was an approximate measure, since accurate flow data did not exist.[7] Although most of the frequently mentioned buildings were situated either on main roads or in intensely used centers, viewpoint intensity received a relatively low correlation, because of the numbers of insignificant and indistinct buildings lining the main roads of the city, which received only small attention.

Viewpoint Significance The readiness of travelers to see buildings at decision points in the city, whether at intersections, bus stops, bends, or ferry crossings, was confirmed by this high correlation. Many quite diminutive and insignificant buildings situated around these points—for example, the small Hotel Palúa at an acute bend in the main road, the gas stations at the intersections in Puerto Ordaz and in El Roble, the Firestone billboard at the turn before San Félix—received high frequencies on the subject maps, while similar and sometimes identical-looking buildings in other locations went unmentioned.

The travelers' need to identify decision points or to describe them to others when giving directions appeared to be so strong that they were forced to search for distinctive features, even when there were no obvious ones.[8] If intersections were unnamed, as in Ciudad Guayana, then the nearest namable feature became the commonly used symbol for that intersection, for example, "the turning by the Hotel Palúa."

Immediacy The immediacy of a building to the viewing or circulation system, defined by its closeness and centrality in the cone of vision, was also an attention-drawing attribute. With the automobile traveler focused on the road ahead, buildings that happened to be in front of his line of vision stood a high probability of being seen, as long as they were minimally differentiated and not too far away. No buildings in Ciudad Guayana at this time were consciously placed on view lines, but some were placed there by chance. The radio pylon on the Ciudad Bolívar road, the Hotel Palúa in El Roble, and General Electric in Puerto Ordaz were all on the axis of vision or crossed the axis while the traveler was turning and, consequently, received high attention.

Use and Significance

The relatively high correlations of use intensity (r = .32, .36, .35) and use singularity (r = .22, .31, .37) were to be expected (see tables 5.4, 5.6, 5.7). The low correlations of significance can be explained because the rating was conceived as a boost given only to significant elements that had not already received a high score for use intensity. Had the significance score incorporated use intensity and singularity scores, it would have achieved a higher correlation.

Use Intensity Like assessments of viewpoint intensity, measurements of use intensity were approximate. Information was gained from a survey of industrial and commercial establishments, but in most cases customer use had to be projected from expert opinion. There were difficulties in assessing daily and weekly use similar to those affecting the scaling of movement, and similar scoring rules were employed. Indirectly used features like water towers were also rated, although at a reduced level. This measure of user intensity received high correlations, although no higher than some of the visibility attributes. Clearly, many respondents were looking at the environment as a setting for activity, but this was not the only or dominant environmental attitude.

Use Singularity The measure of singularity partially described the range of users and the realm of a facility. As there was only one hospital, for instance, it was important to the whole community. However, certain unique facilities, like the Protestant Church or the Country Club, were open only to limited groups. The measurement of singularity also depended on the level of categorization. Schools were not unique, but a high school was. To be meaningful, then, singularity required a fine level of categorization. The correlations suggest that singularity was slightly less important than intensity as a functional attribute, perhaps because many of the singular functions like the cemetery, the brick kiln, or the cock-fighting ring were not sufficiently dominant or visible to be noticed.

Significance The measure of significance included buildings of economic significance like the political party headquarters and landmarks of historical significance like the statue of Simon Bolívar in the main plaza. The significance measure received very low correlations under these rating rules, confirming the dominance of use intensity but not clearly refuting the importance of significance due to the limitations of the boost score.

Other Attributes

Three other attributes were considered influential: recency, publicity, and nomenclature. Of these, only recency was scaled and correlated. The correlations were insignificant.

Recency was scaled by the age of buildings, newness achieving a high rating. The publicity scale depended on whether a building had been mentioned recently in the local newspaper, and nomenclature was rated high when the name was unique rather than duplicated or common. In most cities the newer buildings are outstanding and well recalled, but in Ciudad Guayana this was not the case. Since most buildings were new, a recent building or activity was distinguished only if it was imageable, visible, or significant—hence the low correlations.

To measure publicity for three months before the interviews, we scanned clippings from the local newspaper, the *Bolivarense*, and noted the places mentioned in the news. The more important new buildings and events were mentioned, suggesting some correlation between publicity and selection. Specific and unique names were more identifiable than those that were duplicated or similar, like the *bombas* (gas stations) or, at the district level, the *unidades vecinales* (neighborhood units). Singularity of nomenclature might therefore have achieved some correlation with recall frequencies.

Map, Trip, and Verbal Recall as Indicators of Operational and General Knowledge

The multiple correlation coefficients of the three groups of component attributes with recall frequencies were positive and comparable (see table 5.7), particularly with the frequencies from the map and trip recall responses (form, R = .50 and .63; visibility, R = .47 and .48; significance, R = .44 and .45).[9] The role of visibility (R = .15) dropped in the verbal recall correlations to an insignificant level.[10]

Attention to environmental attributes varied with the question asked or the task simulated. The maps appeared to describe the inhabitants' *operational knowledge* of the city, that is, their commonly used routes and destinations and the elements they encountered on their journeys. Thus they generally selected attributes similar to those selected in their trip recall task, except that form attributes were more dominant on the trip responses. The map responses in Ciudad Guayana may also have been a purer expression of this operating knowledge than is usual in subjective city maps, since there was no public map to assist or interfere with their direct recall of urban experience.

The low multiple correlation of visibility attributes with verbal recall frequencies suggests that in this task the inhabitants were employing more *general knowledge* of the city; that is, they were depending more on general use and significance than on personal travel and visibility. This distinction is an important one for environmental cognition and will be used in chapter 7 to differentiate operational and general significance.

Levels of Ignorance

In Ciudad Guayana, where the physical, visual, and significance patterns were incongruent, the inhabitants' knowledge was incongruent with the pattern of public significance (the R's between significance and recall, although they were relatively high, were never more than .45), and their operating knowledge and general knowledge were also revealed as incongruent. Hence, a person's immediate experience of the city differed from what he knew in general about the city, and this in turn differed from the objective physical, social, and functional city. Such levels of ignorance may be especially troublesome to those who depend most on the environment for urban knowledge: migrants, youngsters, visitors, and those learning about the city for the first time.

Differences in Building Perception

In our interpretation of group differences in correlations, we shall also consider group differences in the descriptions of buildings, the subject of chapter 6.

Residence Groups

In low-density, planned Puerto Ordaz, locals appeared to depend more on the physical form qualities of buildings and on use intensity, but, with the exception of contour ($r = .49$), individual correlations were low. Individual visibility correlations were not significant. Several of the more important functional buildings, such as the schools, hospital, and market, were isolated, as is common in planned neighborhoods, yet invisible from the main road. For outsiders, the visibility, movement, and shape of buildings became much more important. Strangers were therefore using different attributes and different buildings.

In Castillito, built up mostly along the main road, with a few important buildings on hidden streets, locals used a much wider range of attributes and achieved much higher correlations than the Puerto Ordaz population for more attributes. They were more conversant with the local functional pattern (significance $R = .72$ compared with $R = .49$ for Puerto Ordaz locals) than any other group. The building form attributes they responded to were those of movement ($r = .55$), contour ($r = .57$), size ($r = .60$) and shape ($r = .51$). Strangers to Castillito used a similar pattern of attributes but with less emphasis on functional qualities and more on visibility.

In El Roble, locals responded very little to form qualities except to surface colors and textures ($r = .69$), probably because of the influence of the brightly colored gas stations and the movie house. Their high score for use singularity ($r = .54$) indicates the attention they gave to the few unique citywide facilities such as the Escuela Técnica and the La Salle high school. Since most of the important facilities were situated on the main roads in El Roble, even locals responded to the visible buildings. Strangers to El Roble followed a similar pattern, but they were less aware of the singular uses that were somewhat hidden from the main road.

San Félix, where, apart from the plaza, all major buildings were located within the rectangular block plan or invisibly outside the settlement, the inhabitants and strangers relied very little on visibility or form. Local frequencies correlated significantly only with movement ($r = .37$), that is the activity of people around buildings, such as the marketplace, the main ***areparias***, or the Consejo Municipal. Strangers also relied heavily on movement ($r = .38$) but also on size ($r = .27$) and contour (r = .42). The singular use buildings were better known by the strangers (r = .45).

The important differences between the settlements appeared to depend on whether the significant, highly used, or singular facilities were isolated in form as they were in Puerto Ordaz, El Roble, and to a lesser extent in Castillito, and on whether such buildings were visible from the main circulation system as they were in El Roble but not in Puerto Ordaz.

In San Félix, the rectangular block settlement, the form and visibility of buildings counted for less in the correlations than in other settlements, and facilities of unique significance were not heralded by locals. In Puerto Ordaz, while form received high attention from locals, visibility did not. Only in El Roble, with its major facilities on the main roads, did form, visibility, and significance receive high attention from locals. For a settlement that appeared to be confused and formless, this paradoxical achievement shows that the clarity of functionally significant facilities is insufficient by itself to create a clearly structured settlement.

Spatial Familiarity: Locals versus Outsiders

In all cases, local inhabitants achieved higher correlations with the form attributes of buildings in their local settlements than did outsiders from other settlements (see table 5.8). The correlation appears to mean that local inhabitants were responding to the form of local buildings whatever their visibility, while outsiders' attention was restricted to those that were visible. This did not seem to hold, however, for El Roble and San Félix, probably because there appeared to be a greater congruence between form and visibility among buildings in those areas than in Puerto Ordaz and Castillito, where many of the most imposing buildings were not visible.

We expected local inhabitants to be more aware of significant activities in their local area. This proved to be true in Puerto Ordaz (locals R = .49, all R = .40) and in Castillitos (locals R = .72, all R = .41), but not in San Félix and El Roble. In these areas the outsiders were more aware of the citywide functions, while the locals paid more attention to what was locally significant. In Puerto Ordaz, the locals were more aware of citywide facilities than outsiders because some facilities, like the hospital and the police station, were relatively invisible. In other words, where the significant buildings were imposing in form and highly visible—that is, where there was a congruence between form, visibility and significance—the differences between local people and strangers tended to converge. Where the attributes failed to correlate (a more usual occurrence in present-day cities), group images diverged.

Mobility

The more mobile inhabitants, looking at the whole array of buildings in the city, depended slightly more on visibility (whole city R = .50, local R = .45) and less on form and significance than the locally oriented group. The mobile inhabitants' view was broader but not deeper than those who stayed at home.

Temporal Familiarity

Form attributes rose steadily in importance with increased familiarity (R = .30, .40, .49, .50). The influence of visibility also grew with time (R = .17, .31, .44, .48), a result that can be explained by increased use of the city. Although the correlations were not significant, signs received their highest correlation during the early search period (r = .04, .13, .04, .08).

Preconceptions of the city seemed to guide the newcomers' selection. Those who had been in the city for only three months paid high attention to buildings that were socially significant or were highly singular, but they displayed little knowledge of the intensively used places. Of twenty newcomers asked in a separate interview what they expected to find when they arrived in the city, 75 percent mentioned employment and industry, the principal motive for immigrating. But their first impressions, which all remembered, focused first on the unique and unexpected features of the city, such as rivers, the new bridge, and Puerto Ordaz, and only secondarily on the already known steel mill. This shift from prior concerns about employment and industry to uniquely visual impressions was followed by increasing interest among the long-time inhabitants in the most intensely used parts of the city.

We can trace an evolutionary relationship with the city environment from the time when the newcomer arrives with his preconceptions about economic matters, through his unique first images at the time of arrival, to his growing knowledge of its activity pattern and detailed environmental form. The multiple coefficients of all attributes showed use of an increasingly wide range of attributes by the more experienced inhabitants.

A pattern similar to the preceding was evident in subject descriptions of buildings (chapter 6), where efficiency and location grew in usage with increasing familiarity, while formal attributes like color and architectural style were used less over time.

Age

Age groups showed slightly increasing dependence on form and significance as they grew older (form *R* = .46, .50, .50; significance *R* = .39, .41, .46). The under-twenties identified buildings more by their visibility (*r* = .21, .40, .40), especially for their immediacy and their presence at decision points, than did the over-thirties (*r* = .17, .32, .32).

Since new immigrants were from all age groups, age was not always an indication of familiarity with this city. The correlations do suggest how the style of looking at a city develops with age. The older inhabitants, with their somewhat greater dependence on form and greater awareness of community use and significance, seem to have learned more thoroughly the locational rules of the city's functional and social structure. As for their descriptions of buildings, rank correlations among all age groups were high.

Education

Figure 5.4

The more-educated university group concentrated their attention on buildings with more skeletal form attributes, such as contour (*r* = .30), size (*r* = .20), and shape (*r* = .26), while the less-educated more often recalled those with pronounced surface (*r* = .29), and movement qualities (*r* = .29) (figure 5.4). The highly educated were less dependent on the visibility (university *R* = .20, primary *R* = .47) and the significance pattern (university *R* = .38, primary *R* = .43) but more aware of political and economic significance (university *r* = .32, primary *r* = .01). Contrary to expectations, quality was not noticed more by the poor.

These findings, although not very differentiated, do substantiate the hypothesis that the highly educated were better able or more inclined to conceptualize and abstract the environment through their greater emphasis on significance and skeletal form characteristics. Their lower correlations for use intensity, visibility, and all other form attributes suggest that the upper social groups to which the educated belong were using fewer cues to identify buildings and therefore might have a more impoverished relationship with the environment. Their insignificant use intensity correlations suggest that they knew considerably less about the use pattern of the city than the less-educated groups.

When buildings were described, a revealing pattern of evaluation emerged. Both the most-educated and the least-educated groups evaluated buildings more in terms of beauty, while those with secondary education emphasized efficiency. Perhaps the latter were busy absorbing the instrumental values of an industrializing culture, while the university-trained group was more relaxed about it, and the less-educated had not yet encountered it.

Residents of Puerto Ordaz, the educated middle- and upper-income community, correlated the least (r_s = between .60 and .67) with other major (and less-educated) residential groups. The engineers of the Campo Caroní correlated the least with all groups (r_s = between .44 and .71) emphasizing beauty, architectural style, age, and maintenance more than other groups. Perhaps this was due to their professional involvement in the planning and construction of the city.

Travel Mode

Those traveling primarily by car and ***por puesto*** depended more on visibility (car R = .46, bus R = .35), a scale determined principally by measurements of views from the road system, while the bus travelers were more oriented to buildings of functional significance. These scores confirm again that the slower-moving transit travelers possessed a deeper knowledge of the city's functional pattern than the automobile travelers, who "skimmed" over its surface.

Sex

Males gave slightly more emphasis to form attributes in the correlations. In their descriptions of buildings, males referred to them slightly more by location (18 percent), activity (16 percent), size (12 percent), and efficiency (11 percent) than did females. Females gave some emphasis to beauty (18 percent) and color (9 percent) as well as to location, with less attention to efficiency and size. Nevertheless, rank correlations between the sexes were high (r_s = .91).[11]

Summary

The data on group differences are rather complex, and many of the differences are only tendencies, but they do suggest the following general hypotheses:

1. The configuration of the *local environment*—its physical, visible and functional pattern—affects the ways in which groups recall buildings within it. In environments where there was a high degree of congruence between form, visibility, and significance, strangers and locals held a similar image of the settlement. Where there was incongruence, their images diverged.

2. A person's *familiarity* with the city will affect his knowledge of it. The response pattern was not simple. In terms

of spatial familiarity, there was a clear tendency for the unfamiliar to depend on visibility. The close relation of visibility to travel patterns is the probable reason for its importance. At the same time there was evidence that the unfamiliar were searching for the more significant facilities and in some cases knew them better than the locals. Visibility was also a slightly more important factor for the younger groups, although for the newer migrants it was less important than expected. We might characterize the less familiar as encountering a new environment with a mental set searching for the significant, selecting only from the visible, and attracted to the unique and distinctive.

3. Educational differences may be explained by distinctions in *cognitive skills or styles*, such as the greater emphasis by the educated on more abstract skeletal characteristics and by the less-educated on concrete surface attributes. Other differences appeared to be due to social values and tastes. Still others, such as the educated group's poor knowledge of the use pattern seemed to be caused by the way they used the city as a social group, selecting only certain facilities and ignoring others.

Distinctions between the Campo Caroní engineers and other residential groups may well have been due to the contrast between professional and lay interests.

4. *Travel mode* data revealed distinct differences between automobile travelers' greater dependence on visibility and the bus travelers' greater emphasis on use and significance.

The Prominence of Buildings: Design or Control?

Some of the questions raised at the beginning of this chapter have been answered. Inhabitants directed their attention to all kinds of buildings: those with dominant and imageable forms, those at decision points on the transportation system, those that were highly used, and those of community significance. No single level of interpretation or mode of viewing dominated.

Perhaps the most important finding, however, was the role that visibility—the exposure of buildings to the main transportation routes—played in perception of the city. Access, affected by the location of uses and the structure of transportation systems, is already a primary variable in city plans. Visibility is of comparable importance in the real city.

The coordination of building forms or uses with visible locations can create a legible urban structure. The coordination of building forms and significant uses with exposed locations can create a more meaningful city (chapter 7). Coordination can also help foster more commonly held urban knowledge between "locals" and "outsiders."

Furthermore, the exposure of certain uses, buildings, and attributes can influence the character and sense of pride in a community. The old church in San Félix, the gas stations in El Roble, and the Cine Lorena in Castillito played key roles in the structure of these settlements, but neither the church nor the Cine Lorena was looked on as a positive status symbol (chapter 6). Exposure of historic buildings can help maintain the status quo; the exposure of new buildings may encourage an image of change. The selection of buildings for exposure depends on the value system of the community (chapter 7). Alternative policies are possible.

Directing Public Attention

It is first necessary to ascertain levels of public and group knowledge. This could be done by making a survey of all major facilities and by assessing their levels of distinctness, visibility, use, and significance, using professional judgment, field surveys, available data, and polls. Questionnaires would be similar to public opinion polls or television rating systems and could be part of a regular urban monitoring system. Such surveys would identify incongruences between the attributes wherever they occurred and would provide the basis for incentive, corrective, or preventive policies. From the surveys planners could develop a *predictive model of public attention* similar to that illustrated in this chapter. The probabilities of recognition for each new building could then be predicted from its measured attributes. The attributes might be similar to those used in Ciudad Guayana but with modifications for the local situation.

Levels of *appropriate public attention* could then be established in relation to all major facilities in a city, which would set performance standards closer to public response than present billboard or building height controls. The planners could use such a model to survey all existing and proposed facilities of public significance so that proponent agencies and their architects could locate and shape their facilities to gain the level of public attention appropriate to their use, the nature of their user population, and their symbolic significance.

In the case of public control over private development, individual architects, agencies, or developers could locate and shape their buildings according to their own discretion as long as they also captured no more than an appropriate level of public attention. The building could be noticed regularly by its potential clientele, but it should not intrude unduly on the

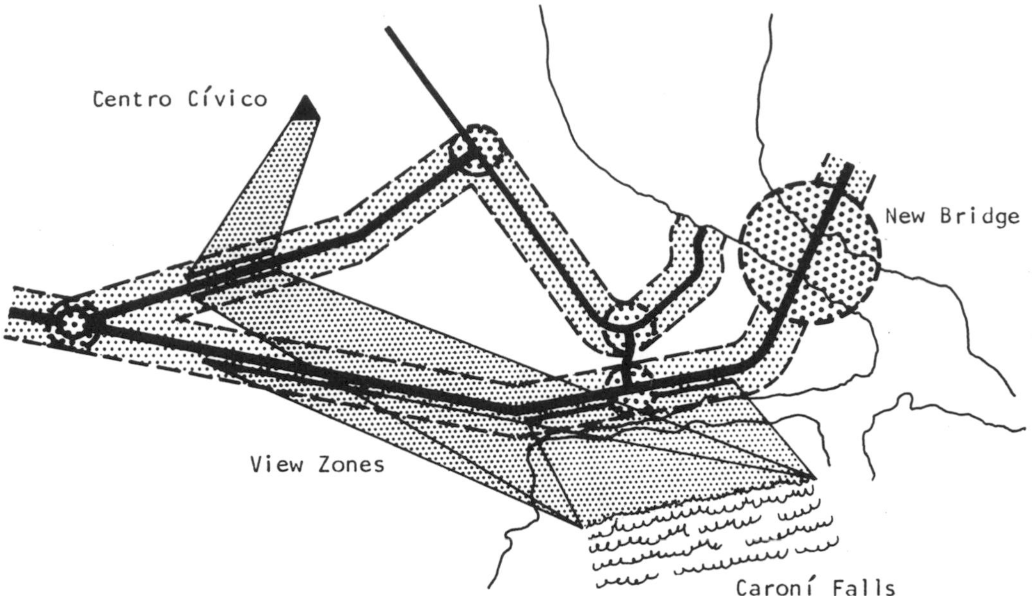

Figure 5.5 Example of view zoning as applied to Puerto Ordaz. The intersections are the most vulnerable points in the public's urban environment. The significance of buildings and information in these zones might be subject to public selection. The sites might be publicly owned, and the quality and design of these areas might be specified by the public or be under specific form controls. Zones along the main roads could be much less controlled. Areas visible but more distant from the road system might be under minimum control. Views of important elements from the road system could be preserved: views of two elements, the Caroní Falls and the Centro Cívico, are shown as examples in this diagram.

Zones where the significance, form, or visibility range of buildings might be publicly owned, designed, or controlled.

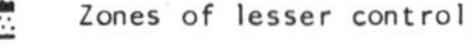

Zones of lesser control.

Zones where views of designated landmarks and other features should be preserved.

public vision. Perhaps no single private building should attract greater attention than any other.

Such a predictive model for building recognition could also be of use to individual architects or developers, for they might wish to know what impact their design or investment would have on the general public and on particular population groups.

Visibility Zones

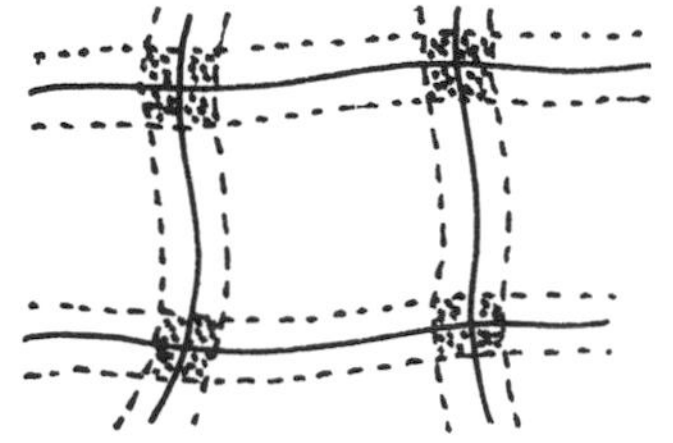

Figure 5.6

A simpler but less participatory method would be to designate zones of high visibility where stricter controls would be enforced. Visibility would be highest around decision points on the main transportation system and at major activity centers, next highest along the edges and on the axes of the traveler's vision, down to the sites visible only from the secondary and tertiary system, or invisible from any circulation flow. High visibility zones could be designated as the "visible public environment" (chapter 11) and could be highly controlled in terms of kinds of facilities, their significance and form, and their designed quality (figures 5.5, 5.6). All buildings in high visibility zones might respect certain form considerations and might be architect designed or subject to a review board. In less visible areas, more freedom could be allowed.

Figure 5.7

In the design of new circulation systems, the creation of visibility zones could be more carefully predicted. The paths of vision could be directed to select significant existing and potential landmarks, centers, and districts, while elements of low public significance could be played down (figure 5.7). Skylines could be scanned, and attention could be focused on high points (Appleyard, Lynch, and Myer 1964).

In the new settlement of Los Olivos, design controls of this nature were planned: "The special areas selected [for control] were the most publicly visible and accessible in the district; they contained the greatest intensity of activities and many of the public buildings and parks over which the CVG would have considerable control." (Porter 1969)

Form Controls

If more public control over the form of buildings was desirable or available, direct form controls might be implemented. These could be stated as a general form index, such as the appropriate level of form singularity, or, if the community wished to go further, the presence of specific attributes. The isolation of a building, or its brightness and shape, for instance, might be easier attributes to adjust than size, which is usually geared to function. Hence, a public agency could direct that no building in a certain zone be isolated from others or have surfaces contrasting with surrounding buildings. The individuality of build-

Figure 5.8

Figure 5.9

ings could thus be suppressed to encourage a more homogeneous zonal character or to foster compatibility in a historical zone (figure 5.8). They could also be clustered to emphasize focuses and attract commercial development. In other cases, individuality could be exaggerated to break or fragment an isolated homogeneous zone in the interest of dissolving its "monolithic" quality (figure 5.9). Each of these devices would have some effect on how the spatial structure of the city is perceived. However, the critical attributes must be covered. Cities like San Francisco, with its height controls, and Jerusalem, with its insistence on facing stone for all buildings, have been unable to prevent dominance of their cities by buildings through other attributes, such as shape or color.

Significance Zoning

The control of form and visibility to communicate an appropriate level of significance is the most obvious way of using this knowledge, but significance could also be controlled to support a certain level of form and visibility. If the building is to be located on a highly prominent and visible site, then it would have to be of high public significance or provide some public service.

Changing the Media

The evidence suggests that the planning and design vocabulary of architects and urban designers, while it may serve some purposes, is in fact substantially incongruent with the public's urban vocabulary. For buildings alone, the site plan's emphasis on size and shape and its inattention to the location and behavior of users, as well as to visibility, contour, and social significance, are blind spots. It may be argued that experienced designers can read a site plan and infer what it will be like in reality. This may be so for the "designer's reality," but the population's perception can hardly be predicted so easily. Moreover, should new and inexperienced professionals be trained in a vocabulary that fails to describe a large part of the impact of their plans and designs?

To increase the relevance of the planning and design language, we need more realistic simulations of the urban environment. Changes in the graphics of design are an economic way of doing this, although notation systems tend to be so idiosyncratic that they fail to communicate. Multiple perspective drawings, perhaps generated by computer, can give cartoonlike impressions of environments, but three-dimensional models viewed through periscopes may produce the most realistic simulations. These promise to be media that can also be understood by the layman, whose interest in such issues is increasing.

6 DESCRIPTIONS OF BUILDINGS

Sixteen Buildings

In chapter 5 the "identification" of buildings through free recall was a means of discovering the attributes used by the population to identify these buildings. In this chapter we shall report the responses of inhabitants who were asked to describe their recollections of specific buildings (table 6.1).

In a free recall situation, like the drawing of a map, respondents freely select buildings from an imagined context, but when buildings are preselected by the interviewers, context plays a less important role. Also, in the free recall of elements, no direct description of identifiable attributes is required, whereas in asking inhabitants to describe buildings, only namable attributes would be mentioned. But the most important contrast in response is in the implied criteria operating in the inhabitants' selection of elements or attributes. In drawing maps, the criteria for selection were primarily those of significance, distinctness, or visibility. In a preselected situation, the criteria for selection can relate more to other qualities such as functional or aesthetic considerations.

Four buildings from each of the four main settlements were selected for their varying form, visibility, use, and significance (figures 6.1-6.16). Since few buildings possessed high form, visibility, and significance, selections were made that would emphasize one attribute at a time. Thus some of the buildings selected were of high significance but low visible form, like the post office in Puerto Ordaz, of high significance and form but low visibility, like the primary schools (invisible from any road), or of low significance and form but high visibility, for example, the Materiales Bolívar (a builders' supply store). The instructions to the respondents can be found in Appendix B, questions 49, 50, 52, and 53. Although photographs of the buildings are shown in figures 6.1 to 6.16, the respondents were not presented with any such stimulus. They were asked to describe the buildings from memory. There was no interference with their direct recall except that the name of each building was presented to them, which explains the somewhat high proportion of nonresponses.

Responses were coded under the main headings of "form,"

"location," "use," and "significance" (see table 6.1). External and internal attributes of building form were coded separately. References to the building's role in orientation and visibility were clustered under the heading "location"; references to function or social use were grouped under the headings "use" and "significance."

Since respondents were asked to describe buildings rather than their functions, the form qualities received the most attention (57.9 percent), with significance attributes (14.8 percent) and locational attributes (10 percent) following. The most frequently mentioned individual attributes were those of location (10 percent), beauty (9.4 percent), size (7.4 percent), activity type (7.1 percent), and efficiency (6.2 percent).

There were two notable results from the survey. First a large number of qualities, particularly the physical, received attention, while no single attribute received more than 10 percent of the responses over the whole array of buildings. Second, the responses evinced a strongly evaluative quality. Although asked only to describe the buildings, respondents frequently evaluated them, particularly in terms of their aesthetic or functional qualities.

External Form

Beauty This mode of descriptive evaluation, more common in Latin than northern countries, was a predominant way of describing buildings. Several buildings were called "beautiful": the Seguros Sociales, Escuela Técnica, the schools, the Hotel Cunucunuma, the Protestant Church, General Electric, and the Bomba Phillips. But the old church in the Plaza of San Félix, the two movie houses, and the Medicatura Rural were condemned as "ugly." Following inspection of these buildings, preference seemed to depend more on newness, cleanliness, brightness, and order than on style or proportion. Disliked buildings were criticized for being old, poorly maintained, or dirty.

Size Size was a frequent way of describing larger buildings like schools, General Electric, and the Seguros Sociales. Although they were all only two stories high, they stood out in a city of single-story dwellings. Small but important buildings like the Consejo Municipal ("It must have a more ample building"), the church in San Félix ("It needs a larger and more modern building"), and the Medicatura Rural ("A small building insufficient for the enormous population") were noted for their lack of size.

Shape Shape usually ranked high when the buildings described were very simple—simplicity was usually favored—or when they were complex and broken in form, as, for example, the Escuela Tumeremo and the Hotel Cunucunuma, two buildings with many blocklike forms. But complexity alone was not always of sufficient note to mention. The Bomba Phillips was complex enough but gained no mention on grounds of external shape. Much depended on contrast with the surroundings.

Surface Color Color as a distinguishing feature gained high mention in certain cases. A building like the Consejo Municipal, whose form merged with the continuous facade surrounding the plaza, could be distinguished only by its color. Other buildings like the Cine Bolívar and the Grupo Escolar in San Félix stood out because of their bright coloring, but even in low-keyed buildings like the Seguros Sociales (green) and the Escuela Técnica (gray), the color was recalled. The vivid yellows, blues, and greens to be seen on houses throughout the city confirmed that color was a highly valued quality.

Construction Materials Materials were noticed and used frequently in the evaluative sense. Well-constructed buildings of good materials were praised; those with poor or impermanent materials were held in low esteem. The church in San Félix was criticized severely for its *bajareque* (mud and wattle) construction, for a concrete block structure was valued much more than a *bajareque* house. The difference would be noted immediately by the locals, although to a stranger these wall materials, when plastered, were difficult to distinguish.

Height Height was distinguishing only for the higher buildings. In a survey of San Félix in 1961 only fifteen buildings were over one story. Three-story buildings were even rarer. Hence, height was still a distinctive feature, and buildings of two floors were described as such. A number of high buildings have recently been constructed in Puerto Ordaz, and this will undoubtedly alter many assessments.

Style The building's style, usually "modern" but sometimes "old," was mentioned in describing the Bomba Phillips building, the unique arched facade of the Protestant Church in Puerto Ordaz, and the simple dignified warehouse of General Electric. This term seems broad enough to encompass several personal assessments, depending on a building's simplicity, uniqueness of shape, or other traits.

External Furniture Some attention was given to the wide variety of unique adjuncts to buildings, from gas pumps to the church campanile in San Félix, the pillar of the Ten Commandments by the Protestant Church in Puerto Ordaz to the signs outside the Cine Bolívar in El Roble.

Open Space Open space around buildings was usually noted when it was present. In San Félix, where open space was rare, it was the second most distinctive feature of the Seguros Sociales. In other places it was mentioned only if some special attention had been given to features such as the playground or landscaping, as with the Hotel Cunucunuma.

Other Attributes Of the attributes receiving 2 percent or less of the responses, age was mentioned in the case of the old church in San Félix and other *bajareque* buildings. Since all the other buildings were relatively new, newness did not attract attention. Maintenance was usually noted when it was poor. There was pride in well-kept buildings, however temporary or poor their construction. The church in San Félix was especially criticized for its poor condition; so was the Escuela Tumeremo, a new building whose broken playground equipment could be seen from the street outside. Entrances were probably noted for their functional role. Signs were noticed in a few commercial facilities, but even there they ranked low. Buildings with glass windows were mentioned in several instances. Parking in front of gas stations, the hotel, and the Seguro Sociales was recalled by a few. It is interesting to note aspects that were not mentioned. For example, roofs were recalled only in their absence, when the open-air movie houses were described. Night lighting was scarcely mentioned, even though the movie houses were usually open at night.

Internal Form

Respondents who had presumably used the buildings at some time described their interiors as well. The number of rooms (2.5 percent) was the most general way of describing the interior of a building. In the Hotel Cunucunuma, the number may have been inferred from the outside, where they were clearly expressed as a series of boxes. The General Electric warehouse and Cine Caroní were described by many as containing only a single room. Furniture was a noted feature of the church in San Félix, where the seating was of unique character, and another infrequent attribute, the presence of air-conditioning, was noted in the Seguros Sociales and the Hotel Cunucunuma. Functional elements like stairs, floors, and corridors received some attention.

Location

The most frequently described quality of buildings was their location, particularly the less distinctive buildings, which were described as near or within more dominant elements. The church and the Consejo Municipal in San Félix were "in the plaza," and the Bomba Phillips was at the "intersection of the

El Pao and Dalla Costa roads." This use of context as the most important attribute of a building reiterates the dominance of location, visibility, and orientation in the city. In many cases, a building was not clearly recalled as an image, but people knew where it was. Buildings were often described as being well sited or well located, and there were few criticisms of location even though many important buildings like the Seguros Sociales were not centrally located.

Significance

The identification of the functional qualities of buildings depends more on inference than on the perception of visible features and is subject to greater inaccuracies. In describing function most people identified the buildings by their activity type (7.1 percent). Since in every case the function of the buildings was implied in the question, many of these responses were gratuitous, but it did point up concern with functional identification. We do not know whether the respondents were actually thinking of the activities that took place in the building or were merely describing the building as a stereotype, since in Spanish and English the words for the activity and the building that houses the activity are generally the same (Whorf 1956). But many clearly saw the buildings as service facilities and described the personnel or people who used them and the kind of service offered.

The efficiency of buildings was frequently mentioned (6.2 percent), although perception of efficiency was seldom objective or accurate. The Escuela Técnica, a building not yet completed and therefore untested for its operational merits, was already deemed "efficient" by several of the respondents. A cleanly designed building "looks" efficient, and this makes a good impression unless or until particular malfunctions are discovered. Even this judgment is usually made on the basis of personal experience rather than objective knowledge. Certain buildings were evaluated more in terms of efficiency than others, and concern for efficiency often arose when it was absent. The two cinemas and the Medicatura Rural were all criticized for their inefficiency, while opinion was divided in the case of the Consejo Municipal and the post office, a universal victim of criticism. Inefficiency and ugliness were applied with equal fervor to the cinemas and the Medicatura Rural. The church in San Félix was often labeled ugly but seldom inefficient. The Consejo and the post office were sometimes called inefficient but seldom ugly.

References to intensity of use were made by a few respondents, for instance, in the case of the Consejo Municipal, which was noticeably crowded. The social status of users was occasionally referred to in high-status buildings like the Hotel Cunucunuma and in low-status facilities like the Cine Lorena. Status was probably a more important qualifying characteristic than people would admit to in an interview.

Building Evaluation

The evaluative manner in which buildings were described emphasizes the influence of values and expectations on reactions to buildings.[1] Studies by Michelson have described how people react to different dwelling types with varying values.[2] The same is apparently true for all building types. The churches were evaluated primarily for their beauty, while public buildings like the Consejo Municipal and the post office were evaluated more on the basis of their efficiency. Houses were evaluated on both dimensions. The inhabitants also criticized several buildings for being too small. This may have been simply because they functioned inadequately or, in the case of important buildings like the church, because they were not sufficiently imposing. Many inhabitants had a very definite idea about the appropriate or necessary size of buildings to serve the growing region.

A comparison of the rankings of the buildings by their identifiability and by positive-negative evaluations was revealing (see table 6.2). The old church in San Félix was ranked as the most widely recalled of the sixteen buildings but received the lowest evaluative score. It was considered "old," "poorly managed," and "too small." In other words, a building can be clearly recalled and yet disliked. Visibility, or distinctness, is only one among many desirable qualities of the environment, and sometimes it may actually be undesirable.

The positive-negative evaluations of buildings revealed some other interesting reactions. High in the ranking of preferred buildings, mostly architect designed, was a gas station, the Bomba Phillips, member of a despised class of buildings in the United States. The popularity of this building may have arisen for any number of reasons: its central location at a major intersection, its identifiability at that point, its role as a social meeting place, its bright newness, or its efficiency of service. Perhaps it was seen as a symbol of the affluent automobile society. Another commercial building, the General Electric warehouse and sales facility, received the highest praise of the group. This building also marked a major intersection. It was clean and simple in form, and relatively unused.

Public buildings like schools, churches, and the health center gained positive but generally less enthusiastic responses than did the commercial buildings mentioned earlier. The sharper reactions to private buildings may well have been due to their greater prominence or to their commercial nature. Investigations in other cities will be needed before these questions can be answered.

For most buildings there was a remarkable unanimity of reaction whether positive or negative. Only a few buildings such as the Escuela Tumeremo produced differences in viewpoint. In this case the few upper-income English-speaking respondents were far more critical of its condition than the bulk of the Venezuelans.

Rank correlations between responses to the four schools were high with an emphasis on their size, shape, beauty, color, surrounding open spaces, efficiency, and in some cases architectural style, which was usually clean and modern. But buildings like the Hotel Cunucunuma, the Seguros Sociales, and the General Electric warehouse were also highly correlated with these. Most of the indigenous nonprofessional buildings with the exception of the Bomba Phillips received lower evaluations than did the professionally designed buildings.

Descriptions versus Free Recall

In an effort to compare the attributes of building descriptions with those used in identification from the free recall responses, the described physical attributes were grouped into similar categories (see table 6.3). Size and height frequencies were grouped under size; references to materials, landscaping, and style were combined under quality; color was categorized as surface; and open space as contour (since it usually set a building off from its surroundings). Such groupings may be subject to error, but they did produce some interesting and credible contrasts. There was zero rank correlation between map recall and descriptive responses (r_s = .00) but higher correlations between the descriptions and verbal (r_s = .46) and trip recall (r_s = .88), both of which were verbal response situations; even here certain attributes received very different emphasis.

Size, shape, and surface rose above movement and contour in the description of buildings. The instruction to describe buildings by emphasizing permanent features may have suppressed normal perceptions of movement. If not, the high correlations of movement in building identification may have been inflated more by the use of the building than by perception of its form. The decreased importance of a clear contour in the descriptions of buildings was to be expected, because relation to context would be less important in describing a preselected building and because contour is not an easily namable attribute. Quality received very high mention as a described attribute even though it was not a primary means of identifying buildings. This is an indication that social status aspects of environmental quality were of dominant concern to residents. As suggested before, its low rank in identification attributes may have been because buildings of similar quality tended to cluster together in the city.

Building Perception

This chapter, by concentrating more on the inhabitants' conscious descriptions and attitudes toward buildings than on their knowledge has revealed some useful insights about building perception.

1. Buildings were usually viewed in an evaluative manner, beauty and efficiency being the two primary criteria of importance, with newness, size, cleanliness, and brightness of some importance. Different building types were also evaluated by different criteria.

2. The most visible and distinct buildings—the General Electric warehouse and the Bomba Phillips at major intersections and the church in the Plaza at San Félix—elicited the strongest reactions: positive in the former case, negative in the latter.

3. Many of the most popular buildings were not used much by the general public. Heavily used buildings such as the Seguros Sociales, the Consejo, and the schools were evaluated on a more functional basis, with more sober and critical comments.

4. Smaller buildings received more negative reactions.

5. The locational attributes of buildings turned out to be extremely important. Since location is closely related to access and visibility, this is in line with the earlier discovery that visibility is a major contributor to our knowledge of buildings.

6. Planned and designed buildings received a different set of response rankings from indigenous buildings. Not only were they evaluated more positively, but also different attributes were used.

7. Private buildings received sharper, more vivid responses than did public buildings, which may have been due to the public buildings' lack of visibility, their generally quieter forms, or the public character of their activities, which are also usually quieter.

8. The attributes of buildings receiving attention were prominent visually—their size, color, shape, signs, and landscaping—but, while the actual use of the buildings was seldom mentioned, rooms, entrances, windows, and stairs were probably recalled for functional reasons. Other elements such as wall materials, landscaping, maintenance, and architectural style may also have acted as status indicators beyond their utilitarian or aesthetic value.

9. Buildings that were new, clean, brightly colored, and commercially oriented received most praise. Modern public institutions such as schools, a church, and public health facilities were next. Small commercial buildings, movie houses, and small public service facilities were criticized.

Buildings and the City Image

The coding of these responses begins to formulate a richer lexicon of meaningful building descriptors than that proposed in chapter 5. We also have some idea about which attributes and building types were preferred. These suggest policies beyond those discussed in the last chapter.

Primary Attributes

Whether preferred or disliked, the primary attributes of the building descriptions—location, size, color, shape, materials, height, style, and so on—should be considered primary attributes in the design of buildings within the city of Ciudad Guayana and could be the characteristics by which the public might wish to monitor their form.

Building Criteria

The knowledge that some buildings are evaluated on the basis of their beauty, others on efficiency, and others on some combination of these and other criteria could be very helpful to architects and planners. It also suggests that the public prefers different external attributes in different building types. These hypotheses need more substantiation.

New Buildings

Since the public favored clean, modern, bright buildings (except for the diminutive post office), the equitable distribution of new facilities and their effective exposure would be sound planning policies. Replacement of the old church in San Félix with a modern building would therefore be a popular act at this time, for almost any evidence of the "new" city emerging from the old was greeted positively.

Locating Buildings

Since the most visible and distinct buildings evoked the strongest public reactions, the selection and design of such buildings will be crucial in the public's reaction to the city. But we do not have sufficiently clear evidence to propose firm policies about which buildings should be placed in these locations. Had modern public buildings been located at intersections, they might have elicited more positive reactions than they received or more guarded responses than the commercial buildings that were actually there.

Figures 6.1-6.4 Selected buildings: Puerto Ordaz.

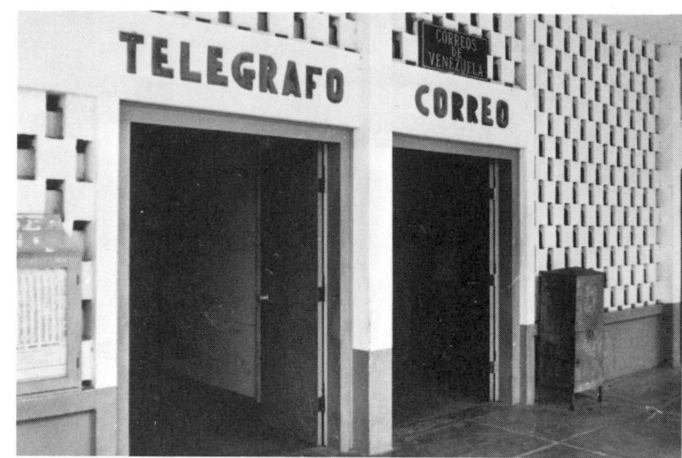

Figure 6.1 Post office. "In the Centro Cívico, northside, by the side of the telegraph office and pharmacy, with a metal grille in front"; "Old and ugly"; "Service is *pessimal*"; "Untidy"; "Very small, and very badly constructed"; "Well located"; "Poor appearance, it should be larger and more modern"; "Difficult to get stamps"; "Very beautiful."

Figure 6.2 Hotel Cunucunuma. "A tourist hotel at the entrance to Puerto Ordaz"; "Three floors, block construction, glass doors, garden in front"; "Very beautiful, large and has a garden"; "Simple, modern, in accord with the rest of the buildings"; "Has air conditioning, central telephone, swimming pool, good service; it is two blocks on the main road from Matanzas to Puerto Ordaz"; "It is the most elegant in Puerto Ordaz and in the region."

Figure 6.3 General Electric. "In front of the Bomba in Puerto Ordaz"; "Very luxurious"; "*Muy bien apresentado*"; "Beautiful"; "Modern"; "Magnificent service"; "Blocks, asbestos roof, two floors, large glass windows"; "Air-conditioned, it has electrical apparatus, and a large sign which says General Electric."

Figure 6.4 Protestant church. "Situated in Camp B, red roof, block construction, bell tower in the patio"; "Yellow, of blocks, asbestos roof, benches inside and a cross on the altar"; "Very beautiful and simple"; "Very pretty, structure looks like a church"; "Marvelous"; "It has enough seats, but it is small"; "It has a large cross and is very modern"; "Never open or used (looks that way) they say the inside is nice!"; "Simple yet functional."

Figures 6.5-6.8 Selected buildings: Castillito.

Figure 6.5 Cine Lorena. "Main street in Castillito, in a hole"; "Old, ugly building"; "Poorly constructed, few seats"; "Recreational place"; "It does not meet the conditions for a movie house"; "A large screen, block walls"; "It is a bad cinema, with much disturbance"; "There is no other place to go at night"; "Block construction, gallery in front, medium roof, cream and brown with posters."

Figure 6.6 Materiales Bolívar. "It is a small building with two doors, painted blue, and with all the necessary supplies and many employees"; "Situated by the Agencia Plymouth, where construction materials are sold"; "It is a fairly well-known store"; "Newly established and well supplied"; "A rancho"; "It is not something definite, only provisional, inadequate"; "Useful for now."

Figure 6.7 Escuela Tumeremo. "Next to Urbanización Mendoza, white building, with windows broken out, fence, badly kept"; "Functional and well-located"; "Good teachers"; "Large, beautiful"; "Gray color, with an old look"; "They tell me it is large, I have not seen it"; "It is somewhat abandoned, fault of the paint, has few trees in the yard"; *"Es antihigiénico"*; "Built one side open; in rainy season children get wet"; "From the viewpoint of capacity, furniture, and teaching, it is good."

Figure 6.8 Medicatura Rural. "Block construction, steel protection blinds, entrance hall for visitors, office at the right, consultation on the left"; "Block building, small, tiles inside, modest"; "Poor and deficient in assistants"; "Clean, fresh and large"; "Small building insufficient for the enormous population"; "Very ugly"; "Undesirable appearance for its situation and destination"; "Depressing"; "Typical"; "Deficient."

Figures 6.9-6.12 Selected buildings: El Roble.

Figure 6.9 Escuela Técnica. "A large building with many trees on the road between El Roble and Dalla Costa"; "Well built and well situated"; "A gray building"; "A beautiful institution with ample space"; "Is very beautiful and well equipped (you can tell when you see it)!"; "Situated in its own grounds with all the conditions needed for a modern educational institute"; "A building in keeping with the aspirations of future technicians."

Figure 6.10 Escuela J. A. Ruiz. "Modern building with dining hall, surrounded by trees with all necessary educational and sanitary conditions"; "A low building divided into departments"; "Simple yet adequate"; "Acceptable"; "Well ventilated, walls of colored blocks."

Figure 6.11 Bomba Phillips. "At the intersection of the El Pao and Dalla Costa roads"; "Well-located"; "It is located a little way from the village; many people go there"; "Parking, gas pumps, glass windows, washing, and lubrication service"; "Between the road, block construction, gas pumps outside with a sign in front"; "Beautiful with a bar in front"; "It has a bar and sells *arepas*"; "Very small building, very good repair service"; "It has all the modern exigencies of a gas station."

Figure 6.12 Cine Bolívar. "It is located in the district office of the AD (Acción Democrática) Party, on the rise of the hill"; "It has no roof, and benches for sitting on"; "Its screen is small, it has furniture and block walls"; "Black and white"; "Where people go to enjoy themselves!"; "I don't believe it is very good"; "Poor appearance."

Figures 6.13-6.16 Selected buildings: San Félix.

Figure 6.13 Seguros Sociales. "Block construction, air-conditioned, two floors, parking for vehicles, consulting offices, pharmacy, beds"; "Large, clean and ventilated"; "The patio has plants and trees, it is a high building, colored yellow, the entrance has a gate and to enter it has a staircase"; "Glass windows, of blocks, it has a staircase and trees in front"; "Fairly advanced in comparison with other cities, small for the zone"; "Well located and has a good appearance"; "It is small for the population, inefficient."

Figure 6.14 Church. "Situated at the side of the Plaza Bolívar a fairly old building"; "A building with three doors, two at the side and one in front, it is poorly managed and does not have the conditions of a modern church"; "Many seats and an altar with many saints"; "Of *bajareque* (wattle and daub), zinc roof, altar, seats, saints"; "Esthetically poor, very small for the importance of the region"; "An old building that needs to be replaced by a larger and more modern building"; "Too old, still it has not yet fallen down."

Figure 6.15 Consejo Municipal. "Block construction fronting on the plaza by the prefectura"; "Brown and white building"; "Inadequate for the importance of the Distrito Caroní"; "It must have a larger building"; "Granite floors, painted walls"; "It has very competent personnel"; "A new building, well painted."

Figure 6.16 Grupo Escolar San Félix. "Two floors, near the warehouse of Cerveza Caracas (a beer company) and the bus garage of the CVG"; "It has small trees in the patio, a dining hall, two floors, venetian blinds"; "Pleasant"; "Modern and simple"; "Good appearance externally although inside the writing desks and tables are nearly all in bad condition."

7 THE INFORMATION STRUCTURE

Planners, Designers, and Symbolism

Designers like to talk of functional expression, meaningful form, and symbolism, but their intentions are often far from clear.[1] For whom are the functions to be expressed? What is the form to mean? What is to be symbolized? "Expression," spoken of as some manifestation of structural or functional integrity, offers no guidance about which elements to select. "Symbolism" and "meaning" imply limitless depths of interpretation, take on a mystical aura, and often become simply a pretext for monumentality.

In Ciudad Guayana, some of the planners talked of making the whole city symbolize "the gateway to the Guayana." With this in mind, one plan was to emphasize the axis of the Caroní River with pylons (Von Moltke 1969). For symbolic reasons, too, special attention was to be given to certain facilities and complexes: the heavy industrial complex, the new commercial and government center on the western ridge, the cultural center on the banks of the Caroní, and the new hospital on the eastern ridge. Other facilities, such as the new CVG headquarters, the new Consejo Municipal, the technical school, markets, stadia, and museums, were also proposed as focal points in the city. But there was always debate about which buildings or parts of the city should be considered important. Later, there were other questions. Would such facilities be important to the population, and would they be noticed, in any event? Was there any justification for emphasizing symbolic form? Had Ciudad Guayana been a capital city like Brasilia or Chandigarh, there might have been less doubt about the role of symbolism. Also, the most obvious symbol of the new city, the steel mill, was already located and built.

There do seem to be some powerful, pragmatic reasons for communicating various aspects of the functional and social structure of a city through its outward environmental form. As a city grows more complex, the inhabitants depend increasingly on cues from the environment—as well as from the mass media—to tell them what is going on. The communicability of the city's information structure can contribute to or hinder operational, educational, social, economic, and political goals.

At an operational level, the communicability of a facility can be as important as its spatial accessibility, and, on an educational plane, a general knowledge of urban functions has social and political as well as educational value. The emphasis in this chapter will be on communication rather than expression, on what the public learns from the city rather than what some designer wishes to express.

In the preceding chapters, we have examined the reasons why certain elements of the city were recalled, but we did not test the relation of this knowledge either to the actual functional and social structure of the city or to the inhabitants' value systems. We do not know yet whether the resulting knowledge of the city was "true" or "false," significant or trivial. In this chapter we shall examine the three main issues in communicating the city's functional and social pattern through its visible environment: What should be communicated, to whom, and how?

Determining Significant Information

Valued Functions

A number of questions in the interview provided clues as to which aspects of the city the population deemed significant.

In the first of these questions respondents were asked, "Imagine an ideal city in which you would like to live. What would be the characteristics of this ideal city?" (See table 7.1.) This was followed by asking, "Imagine a city in which it would be very disagreeable to live. What are the characteristics that would make it bad?" (See table 7.2.)

Recreational facilities, parks, sports fields, and plazas were given by 41 percent as their preferred characteristics, but these were almost equaled by demands for utilities (39 percent). Educational facilities (25 percent), economic security (24 percent), transportation (23 percent), and medical services (21 percent) were each mentioned by about one-quarter of the sample as components of their ideal city, followed by commerce (14 percent) and culture (10 percent).

Housing (10 percent) was lower in the ranking than expected. Either it stood in the background of city perception, or it was seen more as a private than as a public concern. Communications media (8 percent) rated next. In 1964 the city had one intermittent newspaper, a radio station, and very poor telephone service. Television was expected at the time but had not yet arrived. The importance of good communications with the rest of the country and within the city was frequently mentioned in project memoranda. Low on the list of desired facilities were churches, a sign of the small role that religion appeared to play in the lives of the inhabitants. The importance of industry, although not directly mentioned by any significant number of respondents, was indicated through the high ranking of "economic security."

Social and environmental qualities were ranked lower than functional establishments probably because they were less concrete than specific facilities. Climate (8 percent) was the most frequent environmental quality mentioned. Very few responses cited general qualities like beauty, cleanliness, and the natural context of the city or social attributes such as friendliness, morality, and tranquillity.

When asked to describe the worst city they could imagine, the lack of the desired facilities and the negative aspects of the preferred qualities were mentioned, but attention shifted toward basic needs. In describing their worst city, the lack of utilities (sanitation, water, electricity, and gas) was cumulatively mentioned by 78 percent of the sample—three times more than any other facility. This was an emphatic response and a sharp rise from 39 percent on the ideal city question. Many areas of the city were still without sewage systems, water was provided in many barrios only through communal water spigots, and electricity still did not reach many houses. Concern for recreational facilities dropped from 41 on the "ideal" question to 15 percent, while the absence of transportation (28 percent), medical facilities (23 percent), and economic security (20 percent) were considered more serious. Lack of educational facilities, housing, and cleanliness (11 percent) were also seen as concerns.

Value Differences

Education and Residence The better educated and those in the Country Club differed sharply in their value ratings from the lower educational groups. In response to the ideal city question, those in the Country Club had low correlations with the other residential groups ($r_s = .32$). The college-educated group, correlating from .43 to .58 with the other groups, placed more emphasis on education, climate, open space, and commerce as essential components of their ideal city and paid slightly less attention to the problems of cleanliness and social morality in their worst imaginable city. The less-educated groups emphasized the need for utilities and employment, medical and educational services. Those with a secondary education placed high value on recreation and on open space.

Judgments were made according to the immediacy of problems, standards derived from past experiences, and the respondents' degree of adaptation. The lower-income groups were more concerned with the problems created by lack of sanitation and other services. More people of lower-income Castillito wished to avoid problems of crime and immorality than those who were in more distant and comfortable locations. The preferences of the upper groups for good climate, open space, and places of natural beauty were in accord with the usual suburban standards of upper- and middle-income residential developments. The less educated placed a higher value on visits to urban focuses, like the Centro Cívico in Puerto Ordaz or the plaza in San Félix. This was supported by their slightly higher preference for visiting and urban beauty and their greater dislike of low morality. The educated group emphasized the natural environment and lack of cleanliness.

Age and Sex While all age groups emphasized good utility systems in their ideal city, the under-twenties showed more interest in medical services and commercial facilities and somewhat less concern with education, employment, or recreation than those over thirty. Males emphasized economic security, parks and squares, and a good climate; females valued educational, transportation, and medical facilities somewhat more. But rank correlations between age groups and between sex groups (all between r_s = .73 and .83) were higher than those between the more extreme education and residence groups.

Information for the Migrant

A second question asked which facilities a newcomer would need to know and which places of interest he should visit (see table 7.3). The facilities mentioned as most important in these responses were the housing offices of the CVG (where applications for housing accommodations were made), the major industries, the police headquarters, and the movie houses. The Caroní Falls and the new Caroní Bridge were cited as places of interest for the newcomer. Educational and medical facilities, high on the ranking of general values and intensive use, were not considered important in this context. Unfortunately, the interview did not seek the information needs of some other groups, like housewives, professionals, and steelworkers.

Intensity of Use

Independent measures of the intensity of use of facilities were taken as another indicator of significance. The facilities measured as significant on our use intensity and singularity indices (chapter 5) were the steel mill and larger industries, schools, hospitals, stadia, the two main churches, the Consejo, cinemas, the largest hotels, banks, bus terminals, and the ferry. In many facility types only the largest ones were recorded as intensively used. No rankings of use intensity were calculated, since precise figures were not available.

We cannot be sure that these facilities were considered significant by the population. Constrained choices due to limited time, budget, or knowledge may have imposed a pattern of use and knowledge that was incongruent with the pattern of public desire or esteem. Poorer people could not afford to use certain kinds of recreational facilities, and many may have remained unaware of facilities that could have been important to them.

Perceptions of Valued Functions

Having measures of operational significance through our objective field surveys and of general and operational significance through response, we then asked ourselves how well the population recalled these valued activities. (See table 7.4.) Measurement of public attention to various facilities was derived primarily from the map responses and secondarily from verbal and trip recall. These responses were evidence of the salient operational and general knowledge of the respondents.

Two types of ranking were made, one by facility type, the other by individual facilities. When the frequencies of all individual facilities on subject maps were totaled by function, the bridges received the most attention, followed by gas stations, hospitals, cinemas, schools, public squares, hotels, the ferry, churches, wholesale facilities, stadia, and drugstores. Since there were more of some facilities than others, this ranking is biased in favor of the more numerous facilities. When the rankings of individual establishments on the maps were surveyed, some individual facilities missing from the above list (for example, the steel mill, the airport, one of the mining ports, a market, and a quarry) gained higher mention, while others (the hospitals, cinemas, and schools) dropped in the rankings.

If the general rankings of functional types are compared with the facilities valued in the ideal city responses, the gas stations, cinemas, hotels, churches, wholesale facilities, and advertising signs received more attention than the value question appeared to warrant, and recreational and industrial facilities, utilities, and banks appeared to receive less attention. The police, CVG housing office, and the banks, all deemed important for incoming migrants, were not high on this list, although their whereabouts may still have been known.

Comparing the rankings of individual facilities with the verbal map and trip recall responses, the verbal recall rankings bore the greatest similarity to the value rankings. The most commonly mentioned school, hospital, stadium, and plaza were relatively higher in the verbal rankings than they were in the map responses. Verbal recall responses again depended more on significance, while map and trip responses depended more on distinctness and visibility.

The difference in the rankings of facilities in map recall (closest to people's operational knowledge of the city) from the rankings of valued facilities reveals a considerable distortion in the city's pattern of communicability at that time. That many of the facilities deemed important for newcomers received so little attention in a city where migrants dominated the population also raises some questions. This is not to say that facilities should always be known at levels equivalent to their desirability, for some require communication more than others, but ignorance about important urban facilities can have serious consequences.

Differences in Functional Perception

Education

Those with primary education or less responded more to public welfare services, like the CVG housing office and medical facilities, and law enforcement agencies, like the police and the military. They also paid more attention to the public meeting places, churches, banks, and hotels. Those with a secondary education emphasized the Consejo Municipal and the schools, suggesting a more active concern with education and government. They were also much more interested in recreation facilities like cinemas and stadia and commercial facilities like supermarkets and gas stations. They gave equal attention to banks, churches, hospitals, and police. Their interest in recreational and commercial facilities is presumably a sign of their relative affluence and more leisure time. The college-educated groups generally gave lower responses to facility types, with the single exception of parks.

The less-educated groups' knowledge of public welfare and protection services probably resulted from their higher contacts with these services. We have no evidence, except in their concerns about crime and vice, of whether they saw the police and military outposts in a friendly or a hostile light. Their attention to hotels and banks cannot be clearly interpreted, since both were highly visible; but the small hotels catered to new immigrants, and one of the banks issued the paychecks for the steel mill.

The lower-income groups' poor knowledge of the INCE vocational training school revealed a serious gap between need and attention, for this was a facility specifically aimed at improving their job-seeking capabilities.

Age

The maps of teenage respondents emphasized social, recreational, entertainment, and commercial facilities: the plazas, stadia, cinemas, gas stations, supermarkets, and advertising signs. They also paid some attention to schools and the police. The over-thirties, more sober in their selections, focused on hospitals, schools, churches, banks, the CVG housing offices, hotels, and the military. The only facilities noted more by the twenty to thirties group were the bridges and parks. Here is a sharp contrast between age groups, the young attending to the more striking and visible facilities and the public meeting places, and the middle-aged "seeing through" the foreground screen to the quieter, more secluded establishments.

Sex

Males paid relatively more attention to nearly all facilities than did females with the exception of the churches, Consejo Municipal, military, plazas, and supermarkets. Female attention to churches and supermarkets is easily understood. Their emphasis on the plazas and the Consejo may have been due to their extreme familiarity. No explanation for their attention to the military comes to mind.

Travel Mode

Differences in attention that could be attributed to travel mode were few. The relatively high attention of bus riders to facilities visible on the road, like hotels, advertising signs, and gas stations, is surprising since these are usually thought of as auto-oriented facilities. However, these facilities did cluster around major intersections and the entries to settlements, as did the bus stops and terminals, partly to catch the attention of bus travelers. The attention of automobile travelers to the parks, schools, Consejo, and military appears to be more of a class difference than one due to travel mode.

Temporal Familiarity

Although data for this group were processed only on knowledge outside their own areas, it indicates again the emphasis of newcomers on the more "showy" facilities like the gas stations, hotels, stadia, parks, and bridges, rather than, for instance, the hospitals or the police stations, which were considered important for a newcomer to know (table 7.2). However, newcomers did show some knowledge of the CVG housing offices despite their relative obscurity. One surprise was the attention that longer-term inhabitants gave to advertising signs. Since billboards usually change, they must continue to capture the attention of the familiar inhabitants.

Exposure of Functions in Ciudad Guayana

A detailed examination of the form, visibility, and significance (figure 7.1) of various facility types should be revealing. We shall take the facilities in the order of value expressed in the ideal city responses.

Open Spaces and Recreational Facilities

Open spaces and recreational facilities were mentioned several times as desirable constituents of an ideal city. The two best-known urban spaces were the Centro Cívico (map recall 32 percent; figures 7.2, 7.3) and the Plaza Bolívar (map recall 33 percent; figures 7.4, 7.5). Both were popular places to visit, the sites of many meetings, and among the top facilities reported in subject maps. Other outdoor spaces of importance were the Caroní Park and the Caroní Falls (map recall 17 percent). A picnic area had been laid out at the falls and was ranked as the most popular of all places to visit. The rivers, where people still washed their clothes and their cars, were being transformed into recreation places (figure 7.6).

The Caroní Park, occupying the peninsula called "Punta Vista" by the planning group, was marked by a clear sign on the old east-west road, but the falls were unseen. The new Avenida Guyana (figure 7.7), however, passes right by the falls (figure 7.8) and deliberately brings them into a highly visible location, though cutting the park in two. Just over one-half of our respondents were for increasing access to the falls; but one-third, a sizeable minority, were against it, the classic dilemma between retaining natural areas free from intrusion and making them available to large numbers of people.

The two stadia were marked by high lamps shining at night and by the crowds of players and spectators at events, but during most of the day they were empty. Their varying locations—right on the main road in Puerto Ordaz (map recall 13 percent; figure 7.9), in a remote location in San Félix (map recall 9 percent)—and consequently their relative visibility appeared to influence recall. The plazas and parks and the Puerto Ordaz stadium were sufficiently visible and accessible to the city's population. The stadium in San Félix was remote for those who lived outside San Félix.

Other recreational activities such as bocce ball and cock fighting (figure 7.10) occurred in the barrios, and a great deal of recreation took place in the streets (figure 7.11), countryside, and marketplace, blending in with other uses in the indigenous areas. But some formal playgrounds were under way, the first signs of an apparently inevitable trend toward formalization of play into designated play areas (figure 7.12).

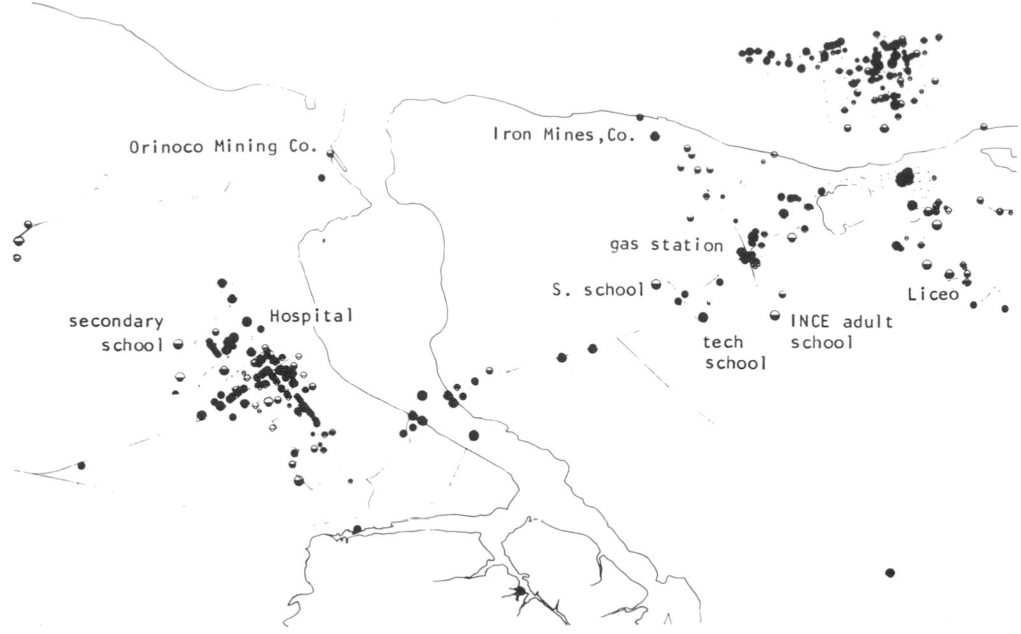

Figure 7.1 Communication of significance. A detailed survey of the buildings identified by the interviewed respondents rated each building for distinctness of form, visibility, and functional significance. This particular diagram describes the mismatches between the visible form of buildings and the significance of their function. When the upper semicircle is larger, form and visibility combined are too important for the function, for example, a gas station at a major intersection; when the upper semicircle is smaller, the form and visibility are insufficiently important for the function, for example, the adult training school located on an obscure byroad. This was one measure of how well functions were being communicated.

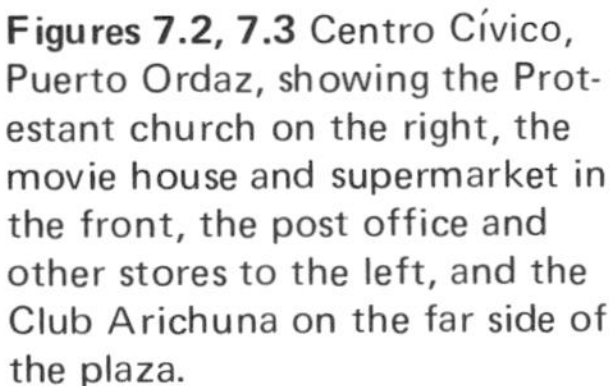

Figures 7.2, 7.3 Centro Cívico, Puerto Ordaz, showing the Protestant church on the right, the movie house and supermarket in the front, the post office and other stores to the left, and the Club Arichuna on the far side of the plaza.

Figures 7.4, 7.5 The Plaza, San Félix, with the church on the left, the Banco Venezuela on the right near corner, with police and Consejo Municipal on the right-hand side of the plaza. At lower left center is the old Hotel Bolívar, with a school to its right. At top left is the Club Español, and on the far side are shops and a clinic. The plaza, well treed, with a statue of Simon Bolívar in the center, is typical of the central plazas in Venezuelan towns.

Figure 7.6 People washing their clothes in the river, a traditional use.

Figure 7.7 The new Avenida Guayana.

Figure 7.8 The falls located in Caroní Park.

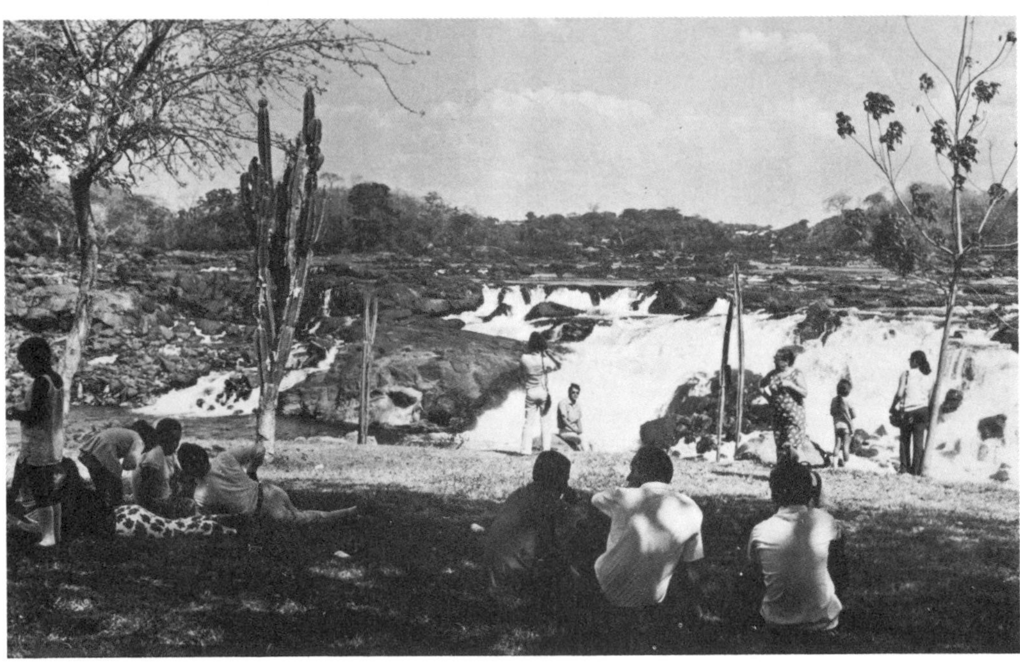

Figure 7.9 Stadium on the main road in Puerto Ordaz.

Figure 7.10 Cock-fighting ring.

Figure 7.11 Children playing in street.

Figure 7.12 Modern playground.

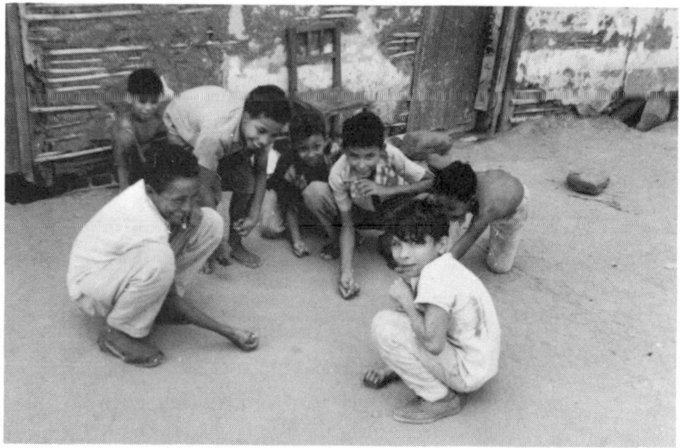

Many of these new playgrounds looked like the elegant exports from Caracas that they were.

Utilities

Utilities were the most urgently needed facilities in the city, but they are facilities that people do not necessarily wish to see. They prefer their sewers and electrical, gas, and telephone services to be invisible since they directly use only the terminal facilities. On the other hand, certain major facilities, such as dams, sewage plants, reservoirs, and aqueducts, may have sufficient symbolic status to merit exposure. As public concern for use of resources and waste disposal rises, the symbolic and educational value of exposing these facilities may also increase.

In Ciudad Guayana, the utility lines were visible in the usual haphazard manner of U.S. cities. Electrical and telephone lines were strung along the main road, and main electrical power lines crossed the natural landscape from the hydroelectric plant to the steel mill. As for drainage and sewage lines, their absence was more visible. In Castillito, flooding of the main road was common, and at the time of the interviews it was being dug up for a new sewage system, one reason that utilities and transportation were referred to as the second most typical characteristic of that settlement. Water towers, some brightly colored (map recall, 4 percent), were prominent and occasionally mentioned. A delightful plan to cascade open storm-water channels through hillside residential areas promised to take advantage of the ample water resources and emphasize their abundance.

Educational Facilities

Educational facilities, considered as top priorities by the population, were not well displayed in Ciudad Guayana. The public liceo in San Félix (map recall 7 percent) and the private Colegio Nazaret (map recall 3 percent) in Puerto Ordaz were both more than a mile from the main road—although the liceo was at the terminal of the main bus route. The Colegio La Salle (map recall 10 percent; figure 7.13) in El Roble was closer to the road but still unseen. The new Escuela Técnica (map recall 17 percent; figure 6.9) was partly visible from the main road and achieved a higher rating than any other school in the city. But the INCE school for adult training suffered from a very poor location and was reported by almost no respondents (map recall 0 percent; figure 7.14). Its program was having difficulty getting off the ground (McGinn and Davis 1969), and the location did not help. With the new Avenida Guayana completed in its planned location north of El Roble, these important citywide buildings will recede even further into the background.

The locally oriented primary schools were sited on minor roads in the geometrical centers of their communities, following rules of safe pedestrian access for the children. One would expect these local schools to be locally exposed, and, appropriately, they received small attention from the citywide sample of respondents. They were more evident in the maps of their local inhabitants (chapter 4) but did not rank very high in relation to other facilities. In El Roble (figure 7.15), for instance, the hidden school ranked below the two gas stations, the cinema, the CVG training office, and the citywide technical school. By a coincidence of timing, the Escuela Tumeremo in Castillito was located on a detoured major route during the interviews and for this reason received a higher rating than any other primary school (map recall 7 percent).

The almost random way in which some schools were known and others were unknown was to be expected given the uncoordinated state of education and of the city's layout. Some of the primary schools were private, and some public; some of the public schools were run by the federal government, others by the state. The first school census in Ciudad Guayana was taken at about the same time that our interviews were done (McGinn and Davis 1969).

The location of school facilities was clearly instrumental in giving them visibility. Whether or how this affected enrollment we do not know, nor do we know the subtler effects that the visibility of certain schools and the obscurity of most will have on attitudes toward education in the city.

As for libraries, a correspondent from the city in 1971 was "distressed to see the concrete skeleton of a projected library out near the old ring road . . . the location in effect, inaccessible to anyone without a motor car" (Peattie 1971).

Industry

The raison d'être for Ciudad Guayana is the presence of water power for cheap electricity and available iron ore to be transformed into steel through the new steel mill. The industrial facilities were therefore highly significant to the city and, in the cases of the steel mill (5,000 employees) and the Orinoco Mining Company (1,200 employees), employed large numbers of people and received frequent visitors.

The steel mill (figure 7.16) itself was a large and monumental complex of elegantly designed industrial sheds with a high office building, located some seven miles west of Puerto Ordaz and the main urban development. It was, however, located on

Figure 7.13 The Colegio La Salle in El Roble.

Figure 7.14 Hidden INCE school for adult training.

Figure 7.15 Aerial view of primary school.

low ground near the Orinoco River. From the main road only the twelve-story office building and the upper skyline of chimneys and smoke could be seen, and then only if the traveler searched for them. The Macagua Dam (figure 7.17), catching part of the Caroní River above the falls with a long earth dike, also "sank" into the landscape; the dike, which guided the river through the white concrete power plant, although visible from the city, blended with its surroundings. It was noticeable only at night, when its street lamps staked out a dotted line against the southern darkness. The iron ore ports of Puerto Ordaz and Palúa, both marked by gantries, docking facilities, railroad cars, and ships, were, with the exception of the Palúa gantry, also hidden and inaccessible from the city.

The hidden nature of the major industrial facilities led to an expectation that they would not be well known. The population, however, was well aware of the main industrial base of the city. When asked why the city was growing, more than one-half of our respondents referred directly to the industrial base, one-third referred to jobs, and only one-sixth attributed it merely to immigration. So the main causes of growth were clear, but awareness of industrial facilities varied with their exposure. Although the steel mill (map recall 83 percent) ranked third among the best-remembered places in the city, the dam (map recall 8 percent) ranked sixteenth, below the best-known movie theater; and the Orinoco Mining Company (map recall 6 percent; figure 2.2) received much less response than the smaller but more visible Iron Mines Company at Palúa (map recall 39 percent; figure 4.8). The new, well-designed, but distant sheds of the industrial park beyond the airport (map recall 7 percent) also received less attention than the dusty but prominent tangle of the cement quarry and plant on the same road (map recall 25 percent). Thus, while attention was directed toward industrial facilities through use and value, they were also perceived differentially according to their form and visibility.

Transportation Facilities

The form of a street gives a clue to its importance. In 1964, the main road in Ciudad Guayana was a narrow two-lane highway with ranchos and billboards scattered along either side, while the new streets under construction in the housing areas were in many cases wider, with median strips. This anomaly, resulting from the transformation of the small-scale old city to the new scale, illustrates the ever-present disruption of the information structure in a rapidly developing city. When the new Avenida Guayana, a limited-access highway, replaces the

Figure 7.16 Matanzas Steel Mill from the main road, with the administration building visible and the higher chimney stacks barely peering above the skyline.

Figure 7.17 Macagua Dam, from Puerto Ordaz, lies hidden below the dike, which is discernible only in a sketch of this kind.

old main road, it will restore a clearer hierarchical structure to the form of the system.

Nevertheless, the interview maps reflected circulation use rather than channel dimensions. The main east-west road received the most attention, and even in the grid pattern of San Félix the roads with higher traffic flows were more distinguished than those with less traffic.

Intersections and decision nodes, however, were not so well correlated with use. The distinctive ferry crossing (map recall 34 percent; figure 7.18) and the new bridge (map recall 62 percent; figure 7.19), floodlit at night, gained high attention. The relatively imageless major intersection in Puerto Ordaz received less attention than a minor bridge (map recall 30 percent; figure 7.20) at the entrance to San Félix. The new traffic circle west of Puerto Ordaz was well recorded, but the bus terminal (map recall 5 percent; figure 7.21), an area of waste ground with buses occasionally parked on it, was noted by only a few. Thus, for recall, the decision nodes seemed to depend more on their formal definition than on their use. As the road system develops, the recall of each part will depend more and more on formal distinctions, since levels of use will become more evenly spread.

Connections with the outside world were fairly visible. The airport (map recall 46 percent; figure 2.4) was situated close to the main road west of Puerto Ordaz, and shipping could be seen on the Orinoco from San Félix.

Medical Facilities

The hospital in Puerto Ordaz (map recall 15 percent; figure 4.4) and the Seguros Sociales in San Félix (map recall 18 percent; figure 6.13), although distinctive as buildings, were both hidden from the community on minor roads. The Seguros Sociales was also inaccessible. A quiet location for a medical facility is appropriate, but good access is essential. Despite this obscurity, the medical facilities received relatively high attention. Their high value and intense use compensated for their poor communicability.

Commerce

Within the commercial areas, the cinemas, banks, and hotels stood out because of their size and height, while bars, *areparias*, and gas stations were prominent because of their corner locations; but most retail facilities formed groups.

Markets The markets needed only the bustle of activity and the goods themselves to attract attention. The market in San Félix (map recall 32 percent; figure 7.22), for instance, was on

Figure 7.18 Old ferry crossing.

Figure 7.19 New bridge, floodlit at night.

Figure 7.20 Minor bridge at the entrance to San Félix.

Figure 7.21 Bus terminal. An area of waste ground with buses occasionally parked on it.

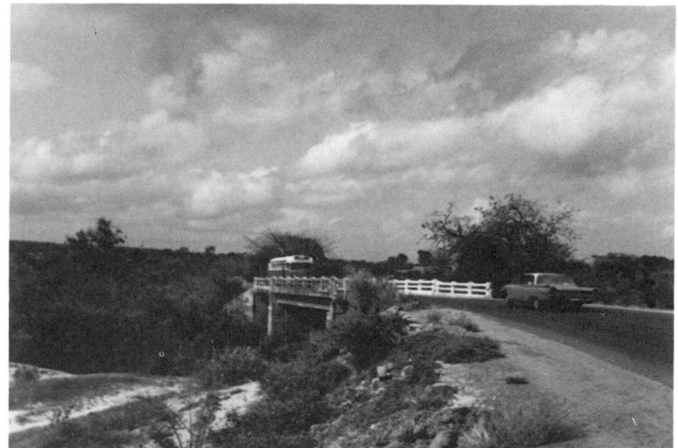

a lively street at a perfect location near the entrance to the community, and it received more attention than almost any other single facility. It also caused a major traffic problem. The free market in Puerto Ordaz (map recall 13 percent; figure 7.23) was much less visible and displayed few external signs of its activity.

Stores Grocery stores were moving from the traditional *abastos* toward more modern types of supermarkets, with their large signs, closed facades, carrying carts, and parking lots. Other stores were also changing from an older unsigned and unpretentious form, through the phase of large and personal signs, to the more controlled forms of self-presentation complete with sharp modern details and glaring, simple, impersonal lettering.

Hotels Out to capture the attention of strangers and visitors, hotels were usually placed at prominent locations, and the better ones capitalized on some adjacent amenity, like a view, the plaza, or their own garden. Many immigrants used the hotels as transient residences before they found a place to live. The old Hotel Bolívar (map recall 4 percent; figure 7.4) was located on the plaza in the center of San Félix, but the newer hotels stood at highly visible points on the main road, usually at the entrances into settlements. The Hotel Cunucunuma (map recall 20 percent; figure 6.2) stood prominently above Puerto Ordaz, the modest Hotel Palúa (map recall 14 percent; figure 7.24) by the entrance to Palúa, and a whole group of small hotels were clustered at the entrance to San Félix. The extraordinarily high attention given to the diminutive Hotel Palúa can be attributed only to its visibility at a unique intersection in the city.

Gas Stations Gas stations did not rank high on the value responses, but they were regularly used by anyone with a motorized vehicle and vied for the most visible locations on the road system outside the commercial centers. Some had already preempted the key intersections on the system, an astuteness that was rewarded by their capture of more attention than any other type of bulding in the city. (Bomba Phillips [figure 6.11], map recall 33 percent; Bomba Mobil, map recall 27 percent; Bomba Creole, map recall 27 percent.) The Bomba Phillips incorporated a bar and was something of a social center in El Roble, but the others were just ordinary gas stations at important intersections.

Banks Banks were luxury buildings in Ciudad Guayana, especially the Banco Union (map recall 8 percent), where the steelworkers' paychecks were handed out, and the Banco de Venezuela (figure 7.25), the highest building in San Félix at

Figure 7.22 The market in San Félix.

Figure 7.23 The free market in Puerto Ordaz.

the time. They were large buildings of expensive materials and on corner locations, but they received only modest attention, less than cinemas, schools, hotels, or sports stadia. This was a surprise. Perhaps they were too little used.

Areparias and Bars *Areparias* and bars were mentioned in general but seldom as individual places. The Areparia Las Quatro Esquinas (The Four Corners) (map recall 1 percent; figure 7.26), a popular day and night meeting place in San Félix, was specifically mentioned by only a few. Bars, too, although highly used, received little mention. Bars with "girls" (figure 7.27) had been exiled to secluded locations at the fringes of town. Familiarity with bars may have been suppressed in our interviews because they were looked on as centers of vice.

Wholesale Facilities The major automobile and appliance warehouses were located to the east of the Puerto Ordaz intersection, with the General Electric sales office (map recall 17 percent; figure 6.3) ostensibly in the foreground. These were unique facilities in the city, mainly serving the middle- and upper-income groups. Few received attention, however, except for the highly visible General Electric building.

Cinemas Perhaps the principal agents bringing "culture" from the outside world to Ciudad Guayana, the cinemas were large, identifiable, and well-known buildings, although they were not always well sited. The upper-income groups, for instance, traveled six miles to the auditorium at the steel mill to see movies. The most visibly located cinema in town, the Cine Lorena (map recall 11 percent; figure 6.5), was held in low esteem by those who knew it (table 5.2). Equally known was the less visible Cine Park (map recall 11 percent; figure 7.28) in San Félix, perhaps because of its superior quality and its air conditioning.

Churches

Churches did not receive a strong vote as components of the ideal city, yet the two principal churches held important locations in the Centro Civico of Puerto Ordaz and in the plaza of San Félix. The Centro Civico, however, was itself a highly noticed landmark, and this seemingly subsumed some of the church's attention (map recall 4 percent; figure 7.29); but the Plaza Bolívar, with more reticent buildings around it, allowed its church to stand out and receive much more notice (map recall 18 percent; figure 6.14). Other churches serving smaller sects—the Protestant in Puerto Ordaz (map recall 3 percent; figure 6.4), the Baptist in San Félix (map recall 2 percent), and a little corrugated aluminum chapel in Castillito (figure

Figure 7.24 Hotel Palúa by the entrance to Palúa.

Figure 7.25 Banco de Venezuela, San Félix.

Figure 7.26 Areparia Las Quatro Esquinas.

Figure 7.27 Bars with "girls" were located in secluded locations at the fringes of the town.

Figure 7.28 Cine Park in San Félix.

Figure 7.29 Church in the Centro Cívico.

Figure 7.30 Corrugated aluminum chapel in Castillito.

7.30)—were located on less-visible sites and were less known, despite their efforts to compensate with flamboyant shapes and signs. The cemetery (figure 7.31), hidden in the residential area of San Félix, was rarely mentioned.

Clubs

Clubs were important in Ciudad Guayana for certain special groups. The Club Caronoco (map recall 8 percent; figure 7.32), which was situated in the secluded Country Club and had a guarded entrance, received the most attention. It was visibly located on the ridge line and could be seen across the valley from Puerto Ordaz, but its high status may have been the chief reason for its ranking. Two other clubs, the Club Arichuna (map recall 1 percent) and the Centro Español (map recall 3 percent) were well positioned in the main plazas but received only limited attention.

Communications Facilities

Communications facilities ranked fairly high on the list of needed and desired facilities. But the post offices (map recall 0 percent), unlike their imposing counterparts in the United States, were small and obscure buildings (see figure 6.1) seldom mentioned by our subjects. The Radio Caroní (map recall 0 percent) and the newspaper offices were seldom mentioned either. Their location remained unknown, although their influence may have been widespread. Only the high microwave pylon (map recall 4 percent, figure 7.33) on the ridge above Puerto Ordaz was noted, and that much less than its prominence had led us to expect.

Administrative and Political Centers

When the inhabitants were asked where they thought the major political decisions with respect to the region were made, 62 percent mentioned the CVG. The labor unions, which have frequently been involved in strikes, were rightly considered another power; and other agencies like the police force, the state government, and the national government were accorded some influence. Just over one-half of our respondents thought that the major political decisions were made in Ciudad Guayana, and nearly one-third located them in Caracas. Scarcely anyone considered them to be made in Ciudad Bolívar, the state capital. Few thought that the local municipality made significant decisions for the city.

The CVG was in fact the most powerful agency in the city—entrusted with the management of the steel mill, the Macagua Dam, and urban development—and many decisions were made

Figure 7.31 Cemetery hidden in the residential area of San Félix.

Figure 7.32 Club Caronoco situated in the Country Club.

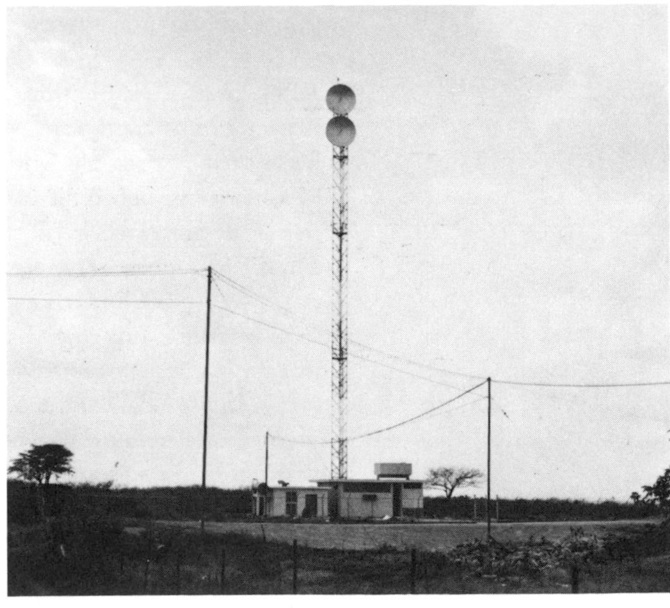

Figure 7.33 Microwave pylon on the ridge above Puerto Ordaz.

in Caracas. The urban plans were developed in Caracas, and their execution was supervised from a small office (map recall 0 percent) obscurely placed on the El Pao road. The two corporation housing offices in El Roble (map recall 13 percent; figure 7.34), and Castillito (map recall 5 percent) received much more notice than the planning office. Although housed in small buildings, they were located on the secondary roads in those settlements; this, with their significance and use, was sufficient to rank them among the better-known facilities in their communities.

The Orinoco Mining Workers had a modern arch-roofed union headquarters, but it drew little attention from the people interviewed. The steelworkers union met in the steel mill.

Local government was in the hands of the Consejo Municipal (map recall 6 percent; figure 6.15). Although in 1964 it was not seen as a seat of political decision making, it nevertheless was nominally responsible for the collection of taxes in Ciudad Guayana. Located on the plaza in San Félix in a small building too insignificant to reflect its representative function, the Consejo Municipal was still a fairly well known facility, but it received less attention than the neighboring and equally diminutive police headquarters, a fact that must be some indication of the relative importance of the police in San Félix. Plans were under way to construct a new and more imposing building for local administration.

The political parties in the area were not reticent about their headquarters. Acción Democrática (AD), the government party at that time and the strongest in Ciudad Guayana, displayed brightly colored buildings in both San Félix and El Roble (map recall 1 percent). The other political parties, COPEI and URD, also had prominently signed facilities. Many of these buildings were not used all the time, however, and received very low attention in the interviews. All political party headquarters were located in or near San Félix, within reasonable distance of the Consejo Municipal.

Police stations, considered important for newcomers to know, were inconsequential-looking buildings, but the one in San Félix (map recall 17 percent; figure 7.35), was well located on the plaza and received much higher mention than the Consejo. Even the police station in Puerto Ordaz (map recall 7 percent), hidden behind the commercial strip, received a degree of attention. The army barracks (figure 7.36) in Puerto Ordaz, discreetly hidden behind foliage, with an overhead sign, were rarely recalled.

Figure 7.34 CVG housing office in El Roble.

Figure 7.35 Police station in San Félix.

Figure 7.36 Army barracks in Puerto Ordaz.

Meaningful or Trivial Cities?

The marked incongruencies between the significance, distinctness, and exposure of facilities affected and distorted public knowledge of the city. The most obvious contrasts were between commercial facilities, trying to maximize their clientele, and planned public facilities, deeming it unnecessary to attract their clientele.

There were some limits to the effect of such incongruencies. When a facility was highly significant and where use was often mandatory, like the steel mill or the Seguros Sociales, it was visible to those who used it even if its location was remote. In other cases, like the INCE adult education school, significance was apparently not powerful enough to override the effects of obscurity. People select facilities partly because they use them or might use them, and partly because of their exposure and form. People frequently search for the facilities that they would potentially use, but, confronted with an environmental configuration that obscures some and exposes others, they make concessions to physical reality.

The relative invisibility of the more significant facilities in the city and the high exposure of commercial facilities—a situation that is becoming more and more typical of cities around the world—raises some important policy questions for urban communities and their planners. Should public facilities remain in the background of the modern city, or should they be exposed? Is there and should there be a hierarchy of significance in the city, and should it be communicated through form? These are debatable and often political questions, though, while people probably do not want "trivial" cities, neither do they want overbearingly "meaningful" ones.

Criteria for Selecting Information

If significance was deemed a desirable quality for a city's environment, in designing a new city or improving an old one the public could set criteria for determining how the information structure of a city should be organized. This section proposes a method for determining significance and illustrates it with a set of proposed communication levels for facilities in Ciudad Guayana.

To determine how well a facility should be communicated to the public, its significance and the nature of the public who use it would have to be established. In chapter 5 we identified two kinds of significance, operational and general. The first is the importance of a facility in the public's use of the city; the second is its general importance in the population's value system. Many kinds of information can be useful for the urban dweller.

Operational Information

Survival and Emergency Information Migrants need to know where to find food, shelter, and employment. Travelers should know dangerous parts of the transportation system, and strangers should know the danger spots in the nighttime city. Residents should know if their air or water is polluted or if their climate is unhealthy. They should be able to find emergency services like hospitals, police, and fire services at a moment's notice.

Efficiency Information Inhabitants should be able to find their way around a city with reasonable ease, use the transportation system, and find the essential services of everyday life: industries, offices, retail stores, churches, and personal services.

Amenity Information Information about choices and amenities, access to opportunities, should also be a goal. People should have the chance of knowing the locations of the most valuable amenities, such as recreation areas, scenic beauty, and restaurants, and, in many cases, such as shorelines and unique locations, should have public access to them.

General Knowledge

Socioeconomic Significance It might be useful for the public to know the social, political, and economic structure of a city. Dictatorships, oligarchies, and many corporations enjoy the demonstration and exposure of their power and prestige, although some prefer a low profile; the affluent, for example, usually reside in secluded suburbs. The public interest might best be served by exposure of all assets. Fascinated tourists in the more expressive ethnic quarters, Sunday afternoon sightseers driving by the houses of the rich, and "straights" curious to see counterculture habitats are all evidence of the interest people have in learning about other subcultures in the city.

Historic Significance A city's past can be quickly obscured by new development, yet history can teach many lessons about the reasons for a city's existence and can encourage a sense of common value in joint inheritance. It depends on which aspects are interpreted. Remembrance of bitter conflicts may simply stir up antagonism. The recent past with which inhabitants can identify and the locus of particular population groups, events, and used places will have more immediate meaning to them (Lynch 1972).

Topical and Future Information The lack of information about plans for the future city and of places that are likely to change through tearing down or new development has often been the cause of citizen protests when the builders or wreckers have suddenly arrived on the scene. Knowledge about future plans can relieve anxiety and provide more chance for public debate. The eagerness with which most people listen to the latest news illustrates the significance they give to this kind of information.

Educational Information Comprehension of how a city works can be of general educational benefit. Citizens can better understand their city if they have at least some knowledge of its economic base, its industrial processes, the forces behind its spatial structure, and the ecological substructure on which it stands.

Operational Significance

The operational significance of a facility will depend not only on the intensity of its use but also on the social and spatial realm of its users,[2] and on the respective communications requirements of operators and users.

The intensity of facility use has already been discussed. The realm of a facility can be described socially and spatially. It can service either a narrow specific group or a wide range of the population, a local or a citywide area. A school can service a narrow population group, but a school can be primary and local or secondary and citywide. City facilities that serve a wide range of the population may require more extensive communication than the others. Each type would need a different kind of communication to reach its specific or potential population group, in terms of both the type of communication and its spatial range.

When we look at the communication requirements of the owners and users of facilities, we frequently find conflicts. Consider the gas station. The customer needs clear visual access to gas stations, but this need is usually not so great as that of the gas station owners to sell their gas. In consequence they intrude on public perception more than is necessary for the public's efficient use of the city. Retail facilities more than any others actively wish to communicate their wares to the public. Other institutions do so in subtler ways: churches through campaniles and domes, office buildings through height, and some institutions through custom design. Public agencies have on the whole paid scant attention to the communication aspects of their buildings.

The users' familiarity with a facility will determine if they need to be informed of its location. The steel mill, with its 5,000 employees, would benefit by being easily accessible from all points of the city. However, since its employees commute to the mill every day, its presence needn't be highly communicable to them. Only job seekers, visitors, and tourists require that it be visibly easy to locate. Most facilities have these two user populations with conflicting communication requirements. In the case of labor-intensive industries, the familiar population is in the majority; in publicly oriented and retail facilities (except at a local level), the unfamiliar client is the important user.

Priority should be given to emergency information about hospitals, doctors, police, and fire stations. Travelers need to find the most direct and important routes through the city, to become oriented to decision points and bus stops, and to receive assistance from service and gas stations, as well as the police.

Anyone searching for the unfamiliar requires visual access. Certain population groups—particularly immigrants, visitors, and children— are more in need of clear communication about the city than other groups. Facilities that serve these groups should have communications priority.

General Significance

The general significance of various activities can best be determined by the different value systems of those involved with the city. Evidence from the ideal city questions is useful for this determination, but the inhabitants' assessments of what is significant cannot be the only criterion of value. Their responses were personal rather than societal and were taken at only one point in the city's development. Thus the national role of Ciudad Guayana to produce economical steel, electricity, and other industrial products was at least as important as its role as employer for the local population.

Both local and societal valuations must therefore be taken into account. Rankings of community significance can be determined by the population's perceptions of significance, but they might also take into account the value estimations of political leaders, those in public agencies, even economists, planners, and historians.

In addition, values can change with time.[3] Within the existing population the lower-income groups' concern for basic needs such as utilities shifted to an interest in recreation and culture among the more affluent. Education, prosperity, and social mobility will, no doubt, encourage value change over time. Those who plan cities must therefore be concerned with potential as well as present significance; here the plans play a role in broadening interests and raising aspirations. If the natural environment is presently unappreciated, the spatial layout might promote increased awareness of it in the city.

There can also be political, social, or other reasons for wishing to communicate or suppress community information. The CVG was interested in developing a competent local government. Since buildings can be read as symbols of the power of their owners and the ways in which they are wielding it, there was some argument for making the new local municipal building more prominent than the new CVG urban headquarters even though the latter was a more powerful agency. Ultimately, however, this did not happen. A large, new CVG headquarters was constructed on the western skyline of Alta Vista.

A City Information Chart

Since there are several criteria for determining operational and general significance, no single, precise, or stable ranking of significance seems possible. It would require the weighting of several diverse criteria that would shift over time. In figure 7.37 each facility has been rated with respect to its operational significance, based on the intensity of its use, the familiarity and realms of its users, and its general significance in the eyes of the CVG planners and the local population. The ratings are no more than suggestions used to illustrate the method. No attempt has been made to add them or to rank the facilities in any way, except for the priority placement of emergency and travelers' facilities. Ratings of this kind should, in fact, be the subject of public decisions and will vary from city to city.

Strategies for Environmental Communication

Once the relative significance of a facility has been established, it may be possible to adjust the perceptible significance of any function in accord with its communication requirements. There appear to be several strategies for achieving this.

Equivalent Prominence

At the simplest level, if the rank of a building in the perceptual pattern were equivalent to its rank in the pattern of significance, it would receive the appropriate amount of attention.[4] But the issue is more complicated than this, since there is no single ranking of significance. There are different audiences, and form and visibility exert different influences.

Adjusting Form

The manipulation of physical form alone can be of use in communicating significance. The forms of certain buildings like the steel mill, the mining ports, Macagua Dam, certain cultural and administrative facilitites, the Consejo Municipal, the housing agencies, and the police station can be accentuated, while the forms of other facilities could be played down. A school, for instance, can be designed to look large and monumental, to have a unique shape, or to be brightly colored and set off from

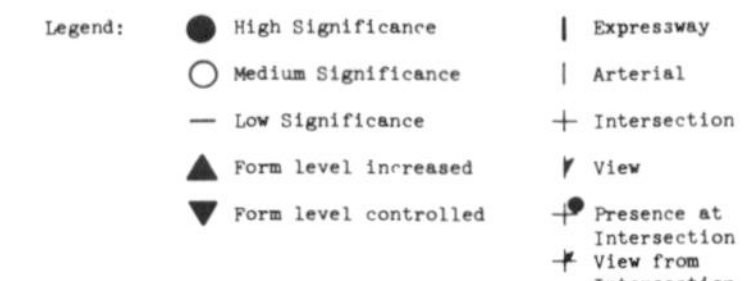

Facility Types		Significance: Operational: User Types: Familiar	Unfamiliar	Realm of Users: Social	Spatial	General: Societal Significance	Local Significance	Communication Levels: Form Level	Visibility Level	Access Levels
Emergency	Hospitals	—	●	●	●	●	●	▲	View; Presence at Intersection	●
	Police	—	●	●	●	—	●	▲	View from Intersection; Presence at Intersection	●
Traveler	Hotels	—	●	○	●	—	—	▲	View; Presence at Intersection	○
	Bus Stops	●	●	○	●	—	—		View; Presence at Intersection	●
	Gas Stations	○	●	○	○	—	—	▼	View; Presence at Intersection	●
Industrial	Steel Mill	●	○	●	●	●	●	▲	View; Presence at Intersection	●
	Mining Ports	○	—	●	●	●	●	▲	View	●
	Dam	—	—	—	●	●	●	▲	View	—
	Light Industry	○	—	○	○	○	●		View from Intersection	○
Utilities Terminals	Electricity	○	—	—	—	—	●		View	—
	Water	○	—	—	—	—	●		View	—
	Sewage	○	—	—	—	—	●		View	—
Educational	Adult	○	○	○	○	—	●		View; Presence at Intersection	○
	Secondary	●	—	●	●	—	●	▲	View from Intersection; Presence at Intersection	○
	Primary	●	—	○	○	—	○		View from Intersection	○
Recreational, Cultural, Religious	Cinemas	●	●	●	●	—	●		Presence at Intersection	○
	Stadia	●	●	●	●	—	○	▲	View; Presence at Intersection	○
	Open Spaces	●	●	●	●	—	○		View	—
	Churches	●	○	○	○	—	○	▲	Presence at Intersection	○
Administrative	CVG headquarters	—	●	○	○	●	●	▼	View; View from Intersection (?)	○
	CVG housing office	—	○	○	○	—	○		Presence at Intersection	○
	Consejo	—	●	●	●	—	●	▲	View; Presence at Intersection	○
	Unions	○	—	○	○	—	○		View	—
Commercial	Retail	●	●	○ ●	○ ●	—	○		View; Presence at Intersection	○ ●
	Banks	○	—	○	○	—	○		Presence at Intersection (?)	○
Professional		—	○	○	○ ●	—	—	—	View	—
Wholesale		—	—	○	○ ●	—	—		View	—
Communications towers		—	—	●	●	●	○	▲	View	—

Note: Two symbols side by side denote alternatives or a range.

Figure 7.37 City information chart.

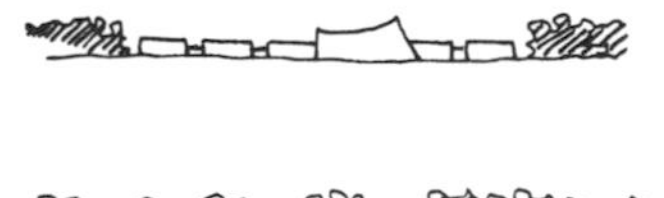

Figure 7.38

its surroundings, or it can be blended into the environment by surrounding it with trees (figure 7.38). If the form of the building cannot be altered, signs can be used to make it more visible (Venturi, Brown, and Izenour 1972). Although building shapes did not seem to have a strong effect on recall in Ciudad Guayana, their role in identification may be much more important. Distinctive shapes are particularly useful in conveying information about buildings seen from a distance.

But there are several constraints on the degree to which form can be manipulated to serve communication. Buildings usually must be economical and must fit the functions they enclose. There are limits, therefore, to how large one can make a local Consejo or how small an office building can appear to be. A building's shape is also constrained by the need to communicate the type of activity that takes place in it. Although the stereotypes of building forms are in a state of transition, a church may not be easily identified as a church if it is covered with signs. Nor will a factory be identifiable if it is made to look like a row of houses.

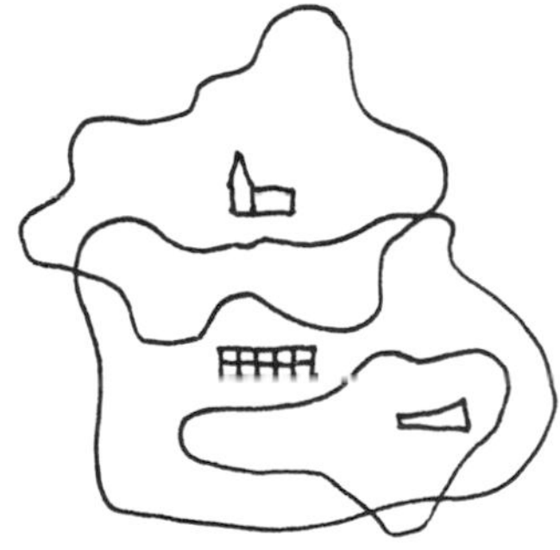

Figure 7.39

Visibility and Location

Many constraints on communication can be ameliorated by adjusting a building's visibility through its location or by the design of the circulation system.

It would be intriguing to design a city where each activity was visible from an area equivalent to its potential spatial realm (figure 7.39), each primary school could be seen from the house of every child who went to it, and each church was visible to everyone in its parish. But in Ciudad Guayana the steel mill would have to be seen from the whole city. Confusion would result from overextending the number of visible facilities, and very soon the views would become obscured. More realistically, each facility could be visible from various critical points within the city's spatial domain (figure 7.40) say from the more distant boundaries and from the most highly used centers. During the design of Ciudad Guayana surveys were made to measure the visible domain of several major facilities: the steel mill, the projected heavy industrial complex, the airport, Alta Vista, Punta Vista, the Macagua Dam, and San Félix (chapter 8). The visibility of these buildings was found to be unnecessarily limited. Diagrams derived from the survey later influenced the location of major new centers, like Alta Vista and the hospital, and were instrumental in the locational planning of the major road system (figure 8.20).

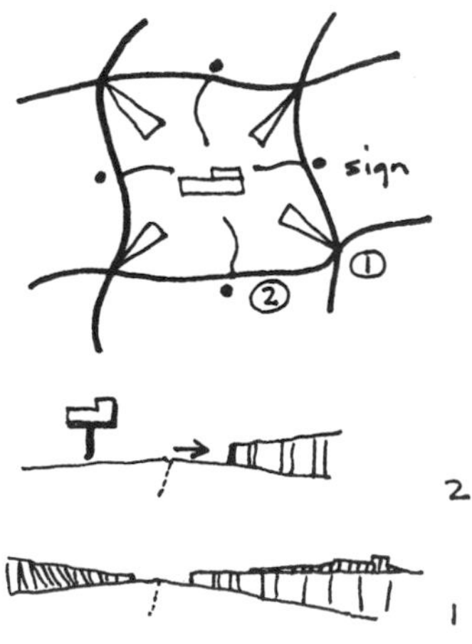

Figure 7.40

To make facilities visible to their social realm would be more difficult, but selective attention can be encouraged. Facilities that serve a narrow but citywide population group might be located along the major viewing system but with quieter forms than the facilities serving a wider range of the population. They could also be placed at special locations, for example, at the entries to parts of the city or at major intersections, and they might be coded in verbal or graphic language that would be noticeable only to their particular client group.

Visibility Zones

Locating significant buildings in appropriately high zones of visibility would be another means of obtaining adequate communication levels. Zones of visibility can be determined primarily by the level of traffic flow on the particular road, the presence of decision points, and the field of vision.

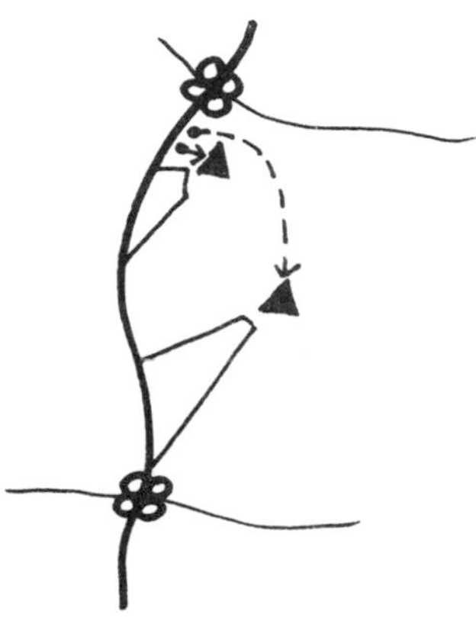

Figure 7.41

At the level of the expressway system, real accessibility radiates from the intersections and off ramps, since no facilities have direct access from the expressway itself. These, too, should be the zones of highest visibility for signs and views of upcoming destinations (figure 7.41). The most intensely used and valued citywide activities served by an intersection should be visible from its approach zone, but since there are usually too many of these to be seen, views of the more-valued but less-used facilities might be spread along whole sections between off ramps, where the traveler is usually freer to look around. For the many buildings that cannot be seen from the expressway, symbols or signs of their presence may have to suffice.

As with most American cities, the foreground scene on arterial streets in Ciudad Guayana was devoted to travelers' facilities like gas stations, bus stops, billboards, and commercial drive-ins. The traveler needs easy access to these services, but they need little more notice than that already provided by their location. From the traveler's point of view, their forms could well be quiet, appropriate to the minor and irregular service that they offer. If, as in the case of the Bomba Phillips in El Roble, they also serve as social meeting places, they might appropriately take on a different communications role, but this would not be usual. The intersections in the arterial system are also important decision points and should be geared to convey information about significant facilities in the vicinity by sign, view, or actual presence.

For newcomers and visitors to the city, the entrances are especially visible and memorable points. Travelers by plane or motor vehicle into Ciudad Guayana from Caracas and Ciudad Bolívar pass the steel mill first and arrive at the oldest part of the city last, while the roads from the hinterland to the south

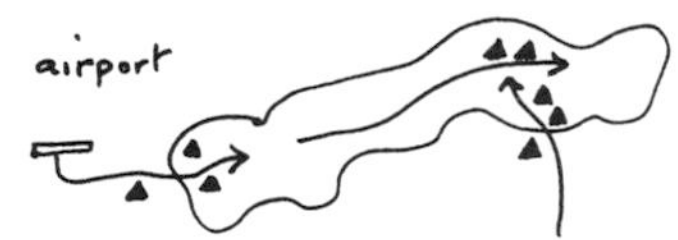

Figure 7.42

Figure 7.43

enter at the other end of the city (figure 7.42). To some extent, then, the entrances already related operationally to the particular kinds of newcomer, the higher-quality sectors being closer to the entrance from Caracas and the lower-income sectors nearer the entry from the hinterland. Such entrances, however, can lead to limited knowledge and segregation. Particular facilities like employment offices, housing agencies, information centers, and police stations should be thoughtfully located in relation to these entry points. In general, there is strong argument for confronting newcomers with a wide choice of opportunities, as long as they are not overwhelmed or disoriented by too much information.

There are several constraints on the realization of appropriate visibility patterns. Visibility is constrained when locations are fixed by other forces. For example, heavy industrial facilities, ports, dams, and bridges are located for reasons other than urban accessibility and cannot be moved for reasons of communications alone. In these cases, the urban structure has to be adapted to bring the facilities within visual compass of the population (figure 7.43). Other factors—such as noise, danger, and nuisance—may keep sensitive facilities such as schools away from high-visibility points like traffic intersections and keep significant but noxious facilities like industry or utility terminals away from residential areas. Signs and high landmarks would then be more prevalent modes of communication.

Some Communication Proposals

Given these techniques of adjusting form and visibility, how could facilities in Ciudad Guayana be shaped and exposed? The second part of figure 7.37 proposes form and visibility levels for each of the facilities listed.

Emergency facilities like hospitals and other medical services and police and fire stations could be located either at or within sight of major intersections on the expressway and arterial street system, and they should be visible from adjacent intersections. The new hospital on the San Félix ridge (figure 7.44) begins to achieve this. It will be accessible from a nearby intersection of the Avenida Guayana, and it is visible on the skyline from the Caroní Valley. Were it also visible from San Félix, its location would be ideal.

Travelers' facilities, such as hotels, gas stations, drive-in services, and bus terminals and stops, have a high proportion of irregular users. As individual facilities, they usually serve a narrow social but extensive spatial realm. Except for one large government hotel, hotels and gas stations were not considered very important by either the planners or the public. Hotels

Figure 7.44 New hospital on the San Félix ridge.

Figure 7.45 Avenida Guayana, with traffic circles at major complexes.

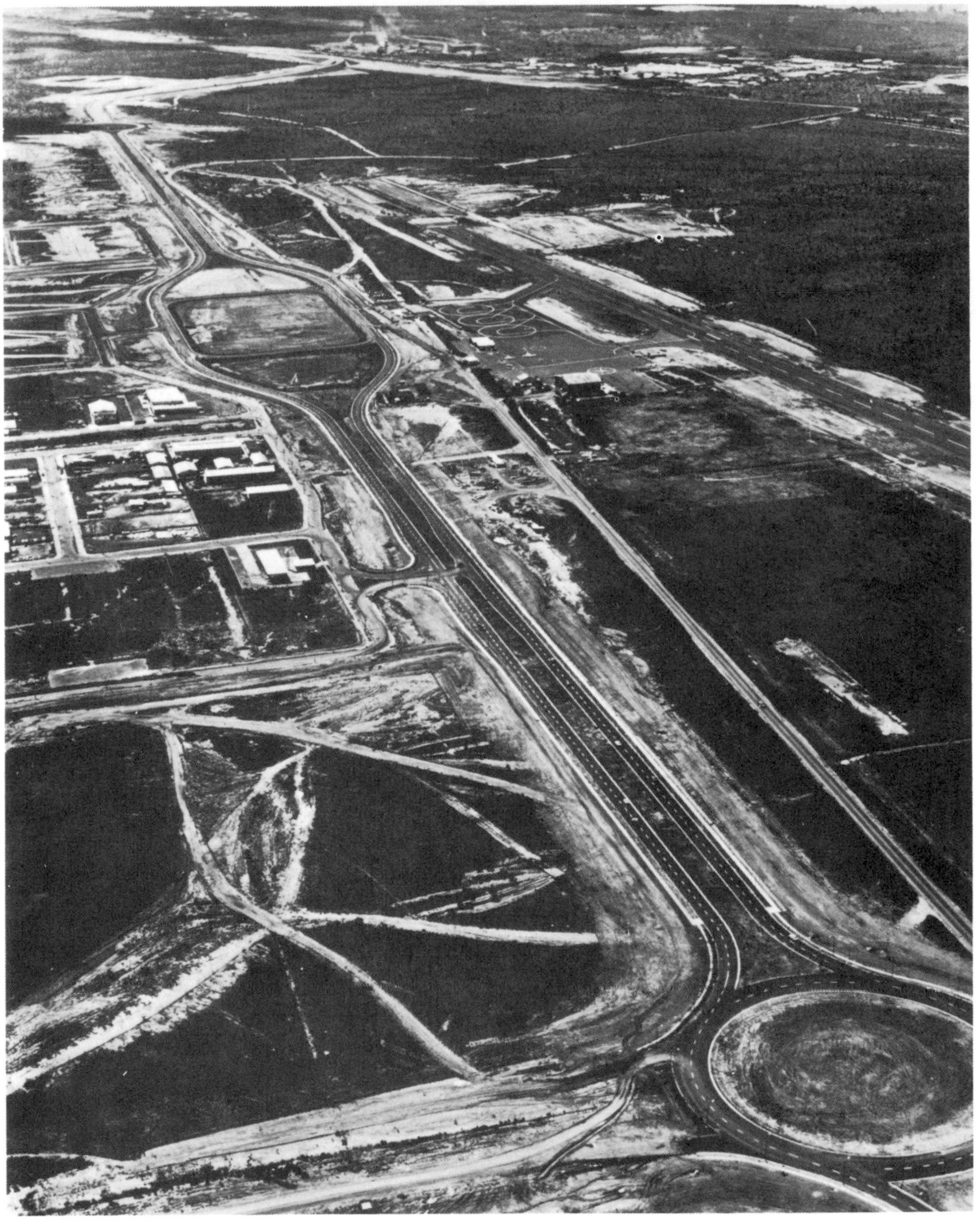

might be emphasized in form and location for the benefit of newcomers and visitors, and bus terminals could also be physically emphasized and exposed. Gas stations, necessarily visible by their location on major routes, might be more subdued in form.

The major industrial facilities are intensively used by regular and irregular populations and are of great significance to the city. They are, however, fixed in their locations, so their visual impact could be raised only by directing views from the road system toward them, accentuating their forms, and defining entrances and marking them with signs. In the current axial approach to the steel mill, for instance, the mill is masked by the office building that stands in front of it. More impressive intersections with the Avenida Guayana would later begin to emphasize the national importance of this complex, the airport (figure 7.45), and the entrance to Puerto Ordaz.

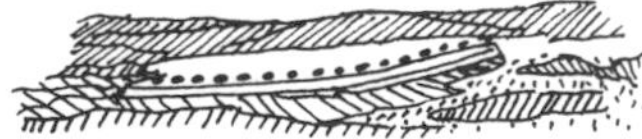

Figure 7.46

The Macagua Dam, economically important but requiring little direct access, could be accentuated in form. The dike (figure 7.46), which is visible from the main road system, could be painted white to set it off against the natural background, or a white parapet wall could line the top of its presently blurred outline. Light industry is well located on the major road system, since it is significant and requires major road access.

Public concern for *utility systems* demands some evidence of their presence. The channeling of storm water drainage in open cascades displayed that system in an attractive way, and plans were made in some of the newer residential areas to continue this system. The exposure of pipes and electric lines, however, threatens more clutter than their information value is worth. The exposure and accentuation of terminal and nodal equipment might be considered. Water towers and storage tanks already occupy skyline locations, signaling the abundance of water. New ones might be built to double as viewing towers (figure 7.47). Sewage facilities and outlets might be compulsorily exposed to inform the inhabitants of their location and quality. Such exposure may well become a source of public controversy, but the city ignores its distasteful aspects at the risk of more-disturbing later revelations. Street lighting, transformers, substations, street faucets, and manholes could be exposed if of uncluttered design.

Figure 7.47

Educational buildings of citywide significance, especially adult and secondary schools, could be located within view of the major east-west road system near major intersections. Their significance also warrants wide visibility and distinctive forms. Local primary schools require similar locations with respect to the local street systems, but their visibility from the road system should not interfere with safe access for children, and the buildings could still be surrounded by trees, as long as distinctive and identifiable parts were exposed.

Recreational and cultural facilities like churches and movie houses could be located at focal points on the arterial system, probably clustered with commercial and administrative facilities but accorded significant locations. Stadia and other citywide recreation facilities might be made visible and accessible from the major expressway system. In the case of outdoor recreation facilities that might benefit from seclusion and obscurity, directional signs might be more appropriate indicators of their presence.

Administrative facilities, heavily invested with symbolism, often require high accessibility to the public, although they do not depend on it so much as commercial establishments. In the particular circumstances of Ciudad Guayana, where there was agitation for the local government to gain some power from the strong CVG, it was proposed that the CVG headquarters be subdued in form though visible in location and that the local government accentuate its enclosing form in a similar if not adjacent location.

The plan to locate the CVG headquarters and the new Consejo Municipal in the Alta Vista center (figures 7.48-7.50) to the west of current development may succeed in directing the attention of the whole population to the westward direction of growth. But since seats of government are usually near the center of their realms, the government center may appear inaccessible to the inhabitants on the eastern side of the Caroní. The move to the new location was originally to be delayed until sufficient weight of population had gathered on the western side. However, the need for new facilities forced it to be made earlier, at the risk of temporary isolation, and in 1971

> the new CVG building in Alta Vista dominated the landscape, a great brick ziggurat against the skyline. It stands out more clearly because nothing else has come to join it in the "center" laid out by the planners. A shopping center, a building, and a drive-in movie are projected or represented by holes in the earth, but so far the rest of the center is a tract of curbing, street lights and raw red earth (Peattie 1971).

The Consejo had "refused to move to the other side" of the Caroní, and the CVG was about to remodel their old headquarters in the plaza in San Félix, another instance of the difficulty of moving the city westward (see chapter 9).

Commercial facilities require visibility from the major arterial system, with citywide commercial groups visible and near intersections of the expressway system. Since few individual facilities are significant enough to stand out, they might be clustered either in pedestrian areas or along drive-in strips like the increasingly prevalent shopping malls in north American cities.

Professional and wholesale facilities might normally merit visibility from major streets. Communications towers, symbolic links with the outside world, could be located in visible relation to the downtown area of the city.

These suggestions are particular to Ciudad Guayana and are certainly subject to debate. But some of the critical variables have been identified. The measures of operational and general significance could be quantified to achieve more exact assessments than these general descriptions. The use intensity, social and spatial realms, and values of the different publics, could also be measured, and desired levels of communicability could be more precisely set.

A chart similar to figure 7.37 could be proposed as a set of guidelines for public and private agencies in structuring any city and locating individual facilities. Guidelines should be based on public assessments of the value of each facility type and its communication requirements in that particular city. Communications guidelines for individual cities would vary according to their character and the desires of their population. A city could communicate loudly and capriciously like Las Vegas or softly like older cities; it might wish to display its commerce rather than its public facilities, its parks rather than its industry.

Identification of Functional Types

Although the relative significance of functions in a city may be apparent, the nature of the activities themselves can remain unclear. This was not a very difficult problem for most citizens in Ciudad Guayana once the facilities were recognized. The only evidence of misinterpretation of function was at the district scale, where the functions of districts were sometimes misunderstood through uneven visibility of the various facilities. However, the identification of facility types was a problem for foreign visitors, especially in the indigenous parts of the city. Several methods were used to identify functions in Ciudad Guayana.

Activity and Accoutrements

The climate allowed many activities and their accoutrements to be visibly apparent either in open structures or in buildings with open doors, especially in the indigenous parts of the city where closed air-conditioned buildings were seldom found.

Figure 7.48 Model of the new CVG headquarters.

Figure 7.49 Aerial view of the CVG headquarters building.

Figure 7.50 Aerial view of the Alta Vista center.

The market in San Félix (figure 7.51), with its throng of buyers and sellers, and the hammocks, hardware, furniture, pots, and pans hanging outside the shops in other parts of San Félix (figure 7.52) left no doubt about what activities were taking place. The docks, cement plants, gas stations, auto-repair yards, school playgrounds, restaurants, and sports fields all displayed the goods, tools, and furniture of their functions. In some of the more modern buildings, too, glass windows displayed goods and activities. Despite these attempts at transparency, the trend was toward a "closing off" of functions from view, and the substitution of signs for exposure (figure 7.53).

The most effective way of communicating an activity at first seems to be to expose it, but most activities take place for limited lengths of time, and many activities, especially nonmanual ones, are indecipherable from a distance. The use of accoutrements, products, and traces of behavior can create more permanent signs than the activity itself.

Stereotyped Buildings

From accumulated experience people build up mental models of different kinds of facilities that become their criteria for what buildings should look like. Many activities could be recognized, especially from a distance, by the stereotyped forms of the buildings that enclosed them. As in the descriptions of buildings, people noticed when a building was large or small, divided into blocks, or one unit. This method did not work well in the indigenous parts of the city, because houses, stores, kindergartens, and furniture factories all used the same kind of building. Their functions could be identified only by close inspection, by a small sign, or by a view of the activity through an open doorway. Modern buildings were articulated more distinctly by functions. Asbestos sheds were built for industries, and schools were usually single-story buildings broken into several classroom blocks. Even so, confusion still occurred (figure 7.54). It was difficult, for instance, to tell a secondary school from a primary school, and on a trip through the city one of our assistants mistook a light industrial shed for the steel mill. These building types therefore distinguished only between general types of function (schools from churches, factories from stores), which is useful at the gross recognition scale of car travel but not for more specific identification.

In the transition from indigenous to designed buildings, functional stereotypes were likely to be disrupted, yet we found some evidence that our subjects already had well-developed rules for learning the meaning of the new stereotypes. Several, for example, commented that the old church in the

Plaza Bolívar did not look like a church, while the new Protestant Church was accepted as such.

The only part of our interview that inquired about the inhabitants' stereotypes was a question that asked them to describe "a plaza." It was interesting to learn that the presence of "trees," rather than "space" or "people," was the most common characteristic mentioned. More investigation of building stereotypes would inform architects and planners of public criteria for building recognition.

Stereotyped building forms can unnecessarily restrict the detailed design of buildings unless they are confined to the exposure of typical aspects or details, like classrooms, meeting halls, shop display fronts, or repetitive office spaces. But architects should know which features are critical, even if they wish to change the stereotype.

Typical Locations

Stereotyped locations were scarcely to be found in Ciudad Guayana. There were some banks and bars on the corners, gas stations at intersections (figure 7.55), and hotels at entrances to settlements, but even these regularities were disrupted by banks that were not on corners and so forth. Public facilities like schools and housing offices were often in quite unpredictable locations.

The development of typical locations into a kind of locational symbolism (Crane 1960) for each building type could offer more flexibility in building design. Table 7.3 in effect proposes such typical locations. Schools, for instance, could always be near major local intersections, and focal points in the city could always contain certain facilities.

Signs

As a city grows, people cannot be so familiar with each establishment, and so more formal and explicit means of communication must be relied on; signs take on more importance.[5] There were no signs in the market in San Félix or on many of the small *abastos* throughout the city where the activity was apparent, but handpainted and iconic signs were becoming common in San Félix. The Eiffel Tower atop the Almacén Paris and the baby chick on Comercial Tiuna (figure 7.56) illustrate the imagination and humor going into these signs. But the modern commercial establishments in Puerto Ordaz and the gas stations had erected very large verbal signs (sometimes larger than the establishments themselves) to convey detailed information about the names of their owners, agencies, or buildings. Commercial establishments were becom-

Figure 7.51 Open market.

Figure 7.52 Semienclosed shops with external display.

Figure 7.53 Enclosed shop with name sign on top.

Figure 7.54 Factory or school? (Escuela Técnica.)

Figure 7.55 Gas stations were usually but not always located at intersections.

ing recognized more through the well-known trade symbols of the mass suppliers than by individual signs. Coca-Cola and other soft-drink signs were to be seen on nearly every bar and grocery store. Kodak and Ferrania signaled the photography shops. The Polar Beer company had given every bar a large signpost with a small space for the name of that bar (figure 7.57), often encouraging the owner to name his establishment for the first time.

The most elaborate and brilliant noncommercial signs were painted by the various political parties on their offices. Gigantic flags, portraits of leaders, party symbols, and mascots covered their facades even between elections, when the buildings were frequently empty. Community buildings like the hospital, the schools, the Consejo Municipal, and the post office all displayed signs, but they were much more reticent and frequently hidden from the road—one reason why confusion over the names sometimes occurred. The churches displayed only iconic signs—crosses, tablets, and campaniles—but given the small number of churches, these were sufficient for identification.

Unrooted off-premises signs, still uncommon in Ciudad Guayana, were not yet a cause of confusion.[6] Billboards were, however, beginning to appear. The Coca-Cola Company has a sign that welcomes travelers to every city in Venezuela. "Bienvenido a San Félix," by permission of this ubiquitous company (figure 7.58), in association with the Firestone billboard, marred the interesting entry view of San Félix. The only other unrooted signs were political slogans sprayed and scrawled on any available surface.

The informational value of signs for the more specific identification of function, significance, ownership, and name has traditionally been underemphasized in city planning. The great value of signs is their economy in conveying information and their locational flexibility. Diffusion of information about a particular facility can be dramatically increased through signs at major decision points, entrances to the city, and approaches to facilities.

In Ciudad Guayana, signs could be an important educational aid. The difficulties that our respondents experienced in trying to map urban facilities and spell their names indicated how impoverished and obscure the environmental information system was. Many of the commercial signs belonged to American firms, whose names the population could neither spell nor understand. Bomba Phillips was spelled "Filus," for instance, by a respondent who clearly could not read the enormous sign but had heard of the name. If graphic and verbal symbols for

Figure 7.56 The popular hand-painted and iconic signs show imagination and humor.

Figure 7.57 Polar Bear Company signpost, an imposed identity.

Figure 7.58 Coca-Cola sign welcomes you to San Félix.

activities were coordinated with other information about the facility, even in languages other than Spanish, a contribution could be made to general problems of literacy as well as orientation. Guidelines for the content of signs, rarely subject to scrutiny, could identify the most relevant audiences, increase the amount of information conveyed, and improve communicability (M.I.T. Students 1963; Appleyard 1969; Carr 1971). Some control of the more scattered, rootless signs and billboards was also becoming necessary.

Connotative Character

Finally, building forms can connote the character of the activity taking place within them. In Ciudad Guayana, as in other cities, banks attempted to look stable, affluent, and serious; cinemas tried to look entertaining; light industry strove to appear clean and efficient. Although our subjects used adjectives like these in their descriptions of buildings, we made no systematic questioning of these connotative meanings. Research using adjective checklists should be able to enlighten us on this subject.

The connotative impact of a facility's form may well be as communicable as its conformity to the particular stereotype. Although the meaning of forms can become a matter of disagreement, there is some psychological evidence that consensus on meanings is possible.[7] Designation by the city of the desired character of facilities and areas could certainly allow individual firms and agencies the freedom in which to interpret character.[8] For instance, if planners wanted public buildings to be open and welcoming in character, designs could be shown to groups of citizens to test whether they viewed them as welcoming.

8 THE SPATIAL STRUCTURE

Planners' Methods of Structuring the City

Ciudad Guayana at the time of our interviews was not a well-structured city. It consisted of several scattered settlements, dissimilar in character, poorly connected by an incrementally developed street system, divided into two parts by the Caroní River with only a ferry crossing, and sited on a hilly terrain cut by deeply forested *quebradas.*

From the beginning of the project, there was a general desire in the planning group to unite the diverse elements of the city. The reasons given were economy of compactness, social and political coherence, and the wish to convey the impression of as large a city as possible to promote its industrial development and attract the professional elite. Underlying these expressed aims lay the common desire of planners and designers to solve a given problem in a coherent way.

Whether or not unity would be helpful to these goals, the urban designers' methods of structuring cities turned out to be rather limited. The first methods employed were primarily "plan" techniques. The development of a large-scale geometric order in the manner of beaux arts planning was proposed. At the time, the city center was to be located on Punta Vista, a peninsula jutting into the Caroní River next to the new bridge, and a street pattern was developed symmetrically about the axis of the Caroní River. It was discovered that the main road through Castillito and Puerto Ordaz angled at sixty degrees to this axis (figure 8.1). On this base it was proposed that four boulevards extend out from this axis, each at the same angle, with the city expanding out from these boulevards. The axis on the Caroní and a perpendicular axis through the city center were to be marked by high pylons on the Isla Fajardo, above the Caroní Falls, and on the two ridges to the east and west of the center.[1]

The drama of this scheme, similar to that of Brasilia, would have been more apparent from 30,000 feet than from ground level. The terrain in Ciudad Guayana is so complex that each straight boulevard would have to negotiate hills and valleys to arrive at its goal. While the pylons would have provided a context related to the natural form, they would not have clarified the urban system. The scheme was ultimately shelved because of the impracticality of developing a city symmetrically in four directions, and the proposed center was relocated on the western ridge. A vestige of the scheme remains, however, in the long, straight-angled stretches of the Avenida Guayana.

A relic of another geometrical scheme was the semicircular road to the south of San Félix, constructed according to the plans of an earlier agency to pass the first planned center located on the San Félix ridge. This road traced out a long semicircular arc that crossed diagonally over the ridge. Not one of our subjects who drew this road on their maps recognized that its alignment was circular. There was, in fact, no evidence that our subjects could perceive any geometrical street pattern other than a grid system. So much for geometrical schemes, which in some circumstances can be useful, but which in Ciudad Guayana were difficult to fit to a complex terrain.

Another attempt at unifying the settlements was by planning for continuous urban development. This too would have to combat the topography. Barriers like the Caroní River, the park on Punta Vista, the Caroní Falls, and the several ridges, spurs, and *quebradas* that interrupted the continuity of the landscape would preclude what might appear coherent from a plan view.

Meanwhile, some of the professional plans unwittingly furthered the disruption of the city. Street widths and alignments in the new subdivisions, regularly laid out with uniformly spaced houses according to the highest engineering and site-planning standards, clashed in scale with the winding adaptive mud paths of the barrios. The planned parts of the city, frequently oriented to cardinal points or to generalized contours, were poorly connected with the indigenous communities laid out by eye on the ground.

Structural Perceptions

The ways in which the inhabitants structured the city were most clearly revealed through their interview maps. Without assistance from a preconceptualized public map, many respondents could not even draw a map, but those who were able gave many clues about their structural visualization of the real city. These maps were coded according to the types of elements that were dominant, and the types of relationships between elements (table 8.1). The various errors—faults, reversals, mislocations, and distortions—were also recorded from each map (table 8.2).[2] Rules for scanning map types and error types were developed by two researchers and were coded by one, with separate checks by the other. Differences were resolved through discussion.

The maps predominantly used sequential elements (roads) or spatial elements (individual buildings, landmarks, or districts), the most accomplished maps employing combinations of both elements. In the sequential maps, the parts were more obviously connected, and the connections were dominant. In the spatial element maps, parts were quite often scattered over the map, and connections were apparently incidental.

Within each of these map types, four subtypes were identified. Within the sequential type, there was a fairly clear gradation from the most primitive looking, which contained *fragments* of sequences, through *chains* and *branch and loop* maps, to more complex and usually more accurate *network* maps. The spatial maps were more difficult to place neatly on any gradient. A number were *scatter* and *cluster* maps of dots, points, or names, and these appeared to be the most primitive. Another set were *mosaic* in form; still others were *linked.* The final group, the more accurately *patterned*, was the only spatial group that stood out definitely as more sophisticated and assured. Figure 8.2 diagrammatically illustrates the dominant types, and figure 8.3 reproduces one example of each type from either a local or a citywide subject map. Table 8.1 shows how frequently each map type was mentioned by several of the respondent groups. Seventy percent of local and 78 percent of citywide maps concentrated primarily on the circulation system and were coded as sequentially dominant maps; only 28 percent local and 23 percent citywide maps were spatially dominant maps.

Sequentially Dominant Maps

Fragment

The most primitive kind of sequential element maps consisted of fragments of paths or lists of elements unconnected to each other and frequently out of serial order. Five percent of local maps and 8 percent of whole-city maps were of this type.

Chain

An equally simple but more schematic type of map treated the major east-west road as a straight line in spite of all its intersections, right-angle turns, and other bends. Some of these maps were no more than lists of places encountered on this route; others swept the line around in a curve, a small concession to the complex curves and bends of reality. Seventeen percent of local maps and 13 percent of citywide maps belonged to this category. Another 17 percent of the local and 21 percent of the citywide were more accurate chain-type maps attempting to show all major bends but undeveloped laterally. Some of

INDUSTRIAL AREA
THE CENTER
ARTIFICIAL LAKE

Figure 8.1 Early geometric plan for the city.

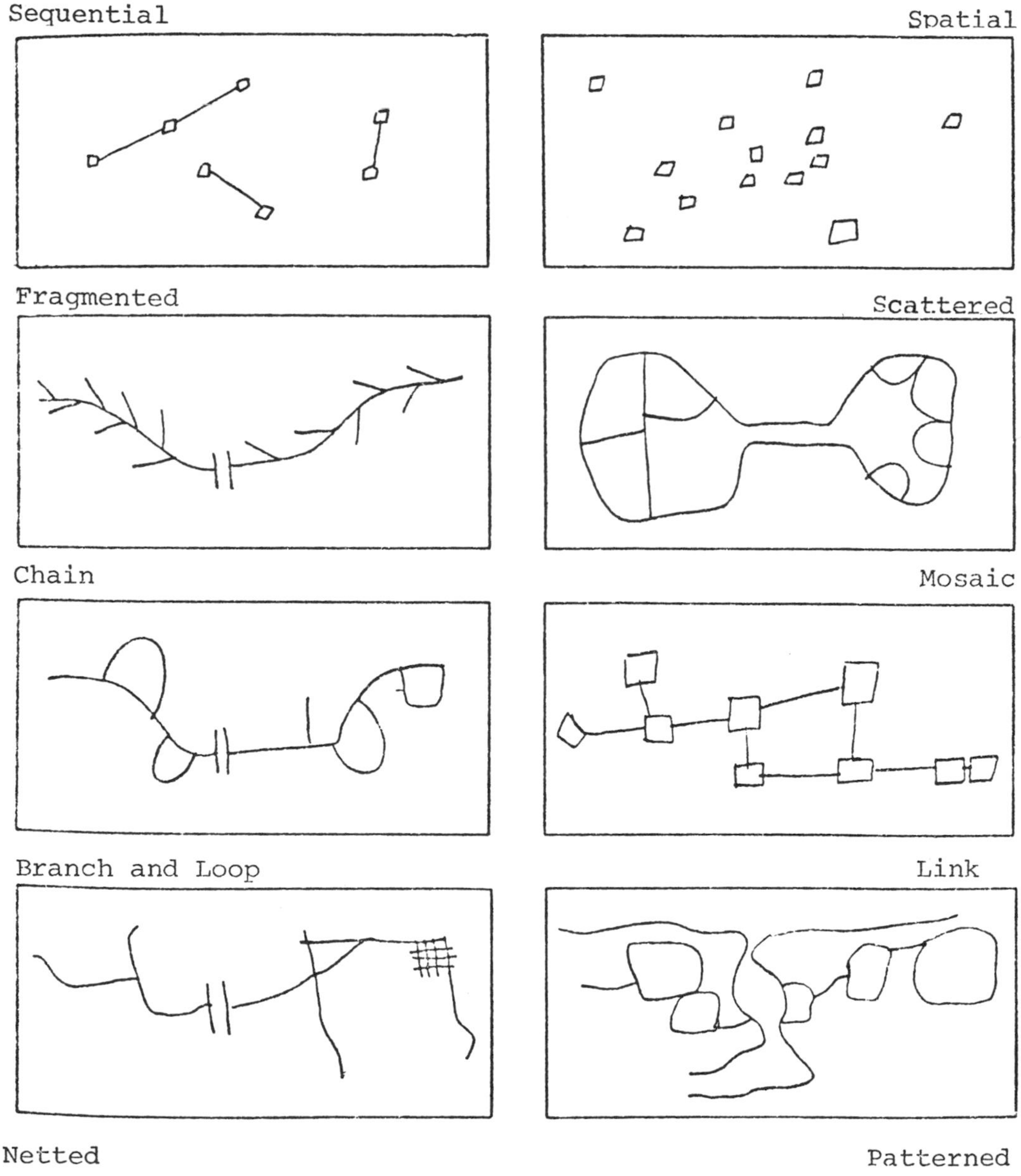

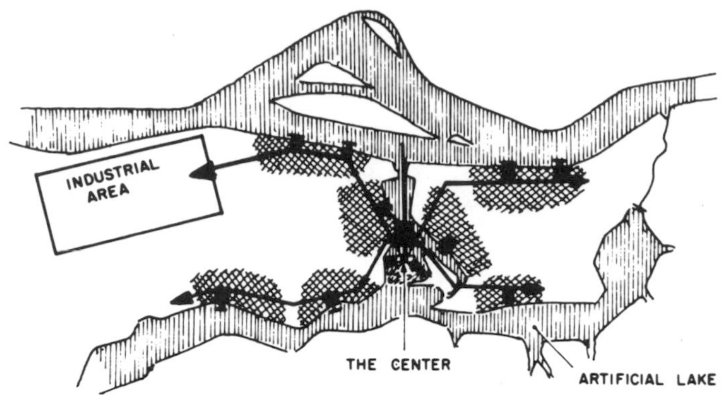

Sequential
Spatial
Fragmented
Scattered
Chain
Mosaic
Branch and Loop
Link
Netted
Patterned

Figure 8.2 Structural styles (diagrammatic).

Figure 8.3 Structural styles (examples).

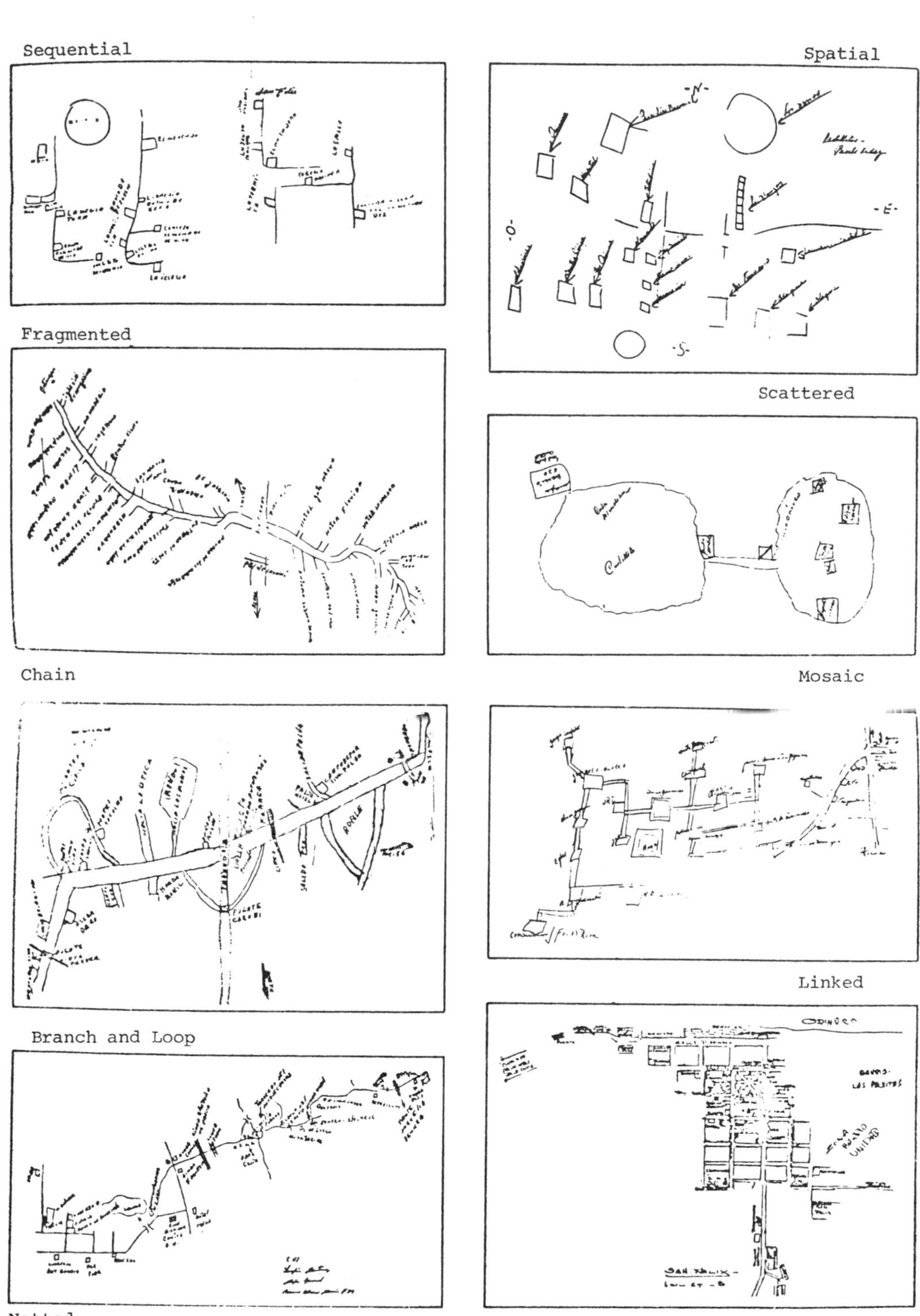

these showed impressionistic bends, merely to indicate that the road contained them somewhere.

Branch and Loop

More laterally developed maps contained loops and branches as common outcrops from the basic linear system. The loops were often drastically simplified versions of circuitous routes, as in the case of the route to the Centro Cívico in Puerto Ordaz. Nineteen percent of the local and 21 percent of the citywide maps belonged to this type.

Network

More complete road systems, often incrementally and laboriously constructed, and in many cases accurate representations of the true city, made up only about 12 percent of the local maps and 15 percent of the citywide maps. A few of these maps were schematically laid out, with the rivers outlined and the roads correctly located. These must have been drawn by the few subjects familiar with a map of the city.

Spatially Dominant Maps

Cluster and Scatter

The most primitive spatial maps contained elements like individual buildings or establishments that would be grouped together freely without any drawn connections. Frequently just the names were distributed over the sheet. Not all of these maps were primitive in their positional accuracy. Some distributed the elements more or less in their correct spatial positions. As many as 10 to 11 percent of the respondents constructed scatter maps; 6 to 8 percent clustered the elements.

Mosaic

The enclosure of districts by schematic boundaries and their division into subdistricts, like shopping centers or residential neighborhoods, created maps that were less specific or accurate than the scatter maps, yet plotted out major zonal relationships like a planner's land-use map. Only 4 percent of local and city maps belonged to this group.

Link

Places or districts were connected with schematic linkages, which occasionally stood for parts of the road system. In any case, the spatial units were dominant. In maps of the whole city, only 1 percent were found to employ this method, but in their local maps 5 percent used this method.

Pattern

Like the linear network maps, these were the more complete

and the most accurate spatial maps, with the outlines of areas and rivers as dominant features. Like the network maps, they demonstrated a subject's ability to handle and draw maps, but comprised a mere 1 percent of both local and citywide maps.

Summary

Differences between local and citywide maps were not very great. It must be remembered, however, that local maps were made both of the inhabitant's own settlement and of those distant from his home (questions 48 and 51), so that familiarity differences would be balanced out.

The most common maps were the sequential chain type, the branch and loop, and the network, followed by the spatial type scatter map. The dominance of sequential maps confirms the importance of the path system as a structural organizer of the city, perhaps more because the paths are lines of personal movement than because they are physical channels.

We do not gain a complete understanding of city structuring from this survey. The task of drawing a map can tell us a great deal about some structuring methods but little about structuring through visual imagery, association, or symbolism, since maps usually abstract elements and emphasize their spatial location. What the maps do emphasize is the extraordinary variety of methods people use to conceptualize cities.

Structuring Differences

In addition to the typological coding of table 8.1, twenty maps from each subgroup were collected and examined in detail.

Education

Many of the structuring differences between the educational levels can be explained by varying abilities to conceptualize. Few of the uneducated had ever been asked to draw a map before, and several, especially the females, required some persuasion before embarking on the task. The fact that many of the uneducated used only the bus system did not help matters, but this was not the sole contribution to their difficulties.

The less-educated respondents employed no common method of structuring, although it was dominantly sequential. As with other educational groups, they commonly drew either starkly simple or very complex maps, with a tendency toward complexity (chapter 3). A common trait of their maps was that the parts were inaccurately related. A very low percentage were able to draw coherent network or pattern maps. The most common maps of those with some primary education were of the chain or bent-chain type (37 percent of local maps; 38 percent of citywide maps). Errors of all kinds, faults, bends, reversals, mislocations, and distortions diminished with education although differences were not significant ($P < .30$). Those with primary education committed an average of 4.3 errors per zone, those with college education committed only 1.7 errors.

Many would build up their maps along the paths of movement, hesitating at intersections as if mentally traveling the journey. This incremental piecing together inevitably led to errors in the larger context. They seemed to use no extra check to adjust relationships to the map as a whole. Parts of the city would be misplaced or reversed in relation to the road. The steel mill would be located south instead of north, and in some cases the whole map was drawn in a mirror image. Many of these errors were of minor consequence as long as the main relationships were accurately established, but the lack of spatial accuracy often led to severe distortions. A difficult intersection or a forgotten curve could throw the whole map askew. The steel mill might end up near Caroní Falls, or San Félix might be found to the north of El Roble. Frequently, their drawings would run off the sheet or be distorted or skewed to keep within the confines of the paper.

Assembling concepts was another difficulty. In the map shown here as figure 8.4, the rectilinear street system of San Félix is seen as a series of separate turnoffs with no interconnection, a phenomenon that was also common in the maps of El Roble. Mismatches between visual and verbal information were discovered. In one case, the Escuela Fe Y Alegría in Castillito was located on the site of another school in Puerto Ordaz. Evidently, the individual had heard of the Fe Y Alegría, seen the other school, and made the wrong association. Mismatches like these can occur in anyone's experience, but they were more prevalent among the less-educated group. The nesting of small elements within large ones was also found to be difficult, a problem already noticed in the reluctance to place the settlements within the concept of one city (chapter 2). Frequently, the settlements through which the main road traveled would be seen as separate from rather than embracing the road. Their maps tended also to be noninferential, predicting very little beyond direct experience. Several subjects drew zigzag paths through San Félix without extending them to form the gridiron system. The river edges too would be drawn only where they were actually seen from the road.

The maps of the less educated conveyed a strong sense of subjective experience. Most of them were flow dominant, describing their own journeys rather than the physical form of the transportation system (figure 8.5). Even the people who distributed points in a scatter pattern seemed to be placing them in relation to their position at the time of the interview. As expected, their maps were less accurate than those of the college educated and were usually of the chain type.

The more-educated groups were able to draw the city more objectively, fitting their maps together more coherently and inferring more about the city, even from limited experience. Nineteen percent of the college educated drew network local maps and 23 percent network city maps, while only 6 and 11 percent of primary educated drew network maps. The educated would sketch out the rivers and lay out the rectangular street pattern of San Félix as schematic concepts, and the maps would be well fitted to the sheet. They seemed better able to fit perceptual experience to plan concepts. Rank correlations between primary and secondary were high (r_s = .81, .81), but correlations between university and primary were insignificant (r_s = .24, .43).

Inference did not always lead to accuracy. After three months in the city, a newly arrived European engineer drew in three railroad lines instead of the actual two. His logic told him to expect a railroad link between the steel mill and the Orinoco Mining port, a connection that did not yet exist. While abstraction and inference are not without problems, they enable an inhabitant to cope with larger areas and more complex environments more rapidly and with greater mastery, but he may miss the detail in his skimming of "the information given" (Bruner 1957a).

Temporal Familiarity

The newcomers were a widely diversified group; so we expected very different degrees of structuring in their first year. Mobility would affect the rate at which they came into contact with the city, conceptual abilities would affect their speed of acquiring knowledge, and travel mode would influence their method of acquiring knowledge.

Nevertheless, there were some consistent variations along the dimension of familiarity. There were low correlations between the newcomers and longer-term migrants in their local maps (r_s = .45). In the citywide maps correlations were high (r_s = .88) for these groups but low between the six-month to one-year migrants and the older ones (r_s = .44). The differences were in general as expected. With increasing familiarity, the use of spatial elements became slightly more common. Newcomers produced overwhelmingly sequential maps (86 and 78 percent local; 85 and 78 percent citywide). Older residents did

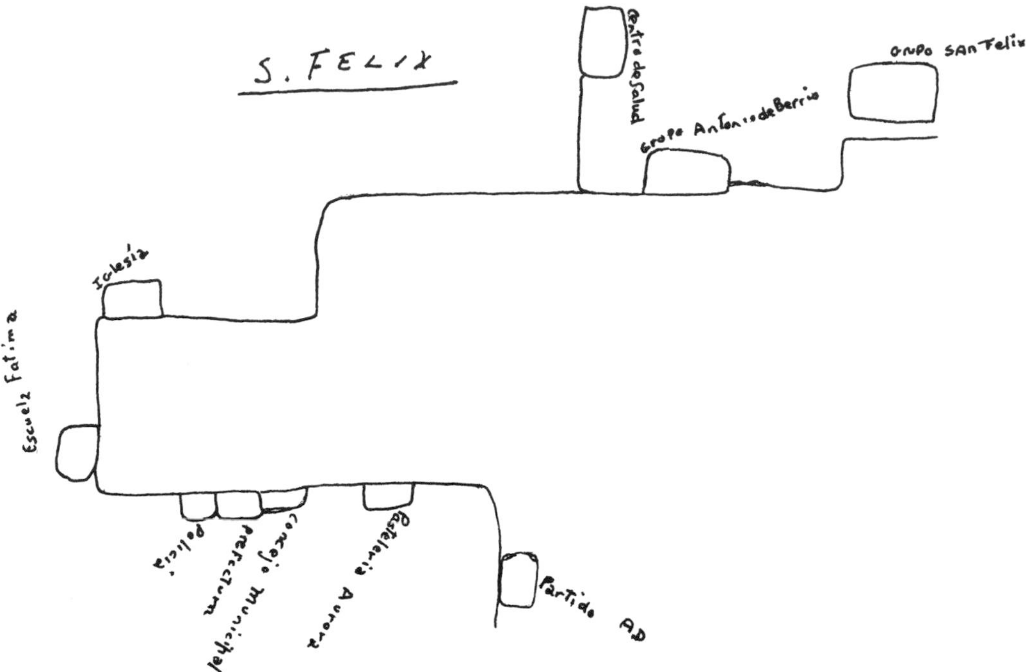

Figure 8.4 Subject map of rectilinear street system of San Félix.

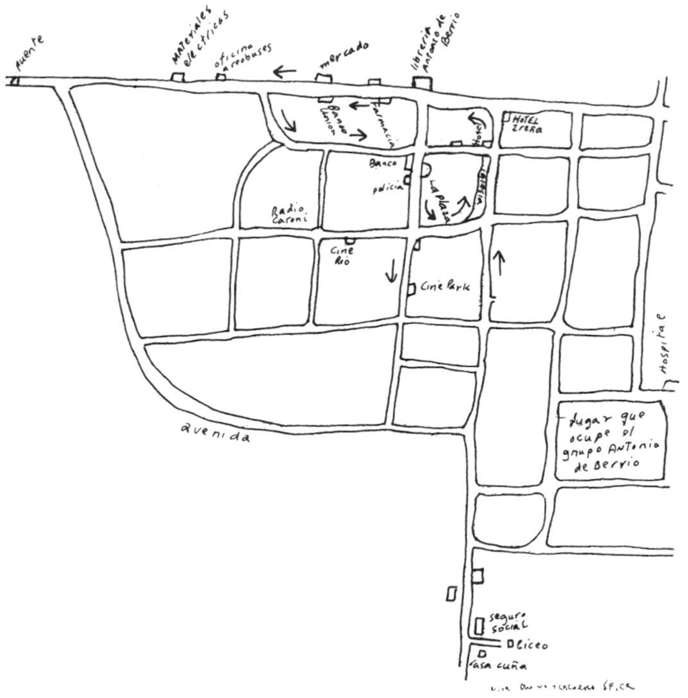

Figure 8.5 Flow dominant map of a person's own travels.

the same but to a lesser extent (61 percent local, 72 percent citywide). First-year subjects produced more restricted maps. One-half could draw only their own side of the Caroní River. However, when the bridge had been opened, a later group of newcomers were mostly able to sketch the areas on both sides of the river.

Age

There were no striking differences between age groups (r_s = .87 to .98) except for a tendency of the under-twenties to emphasize sequential elements.

Spatial Familiarity

As already discussed, local maps were drawn of familiar and unfamiliar areas. Spatial elements were very slightly more predominant in maps of local areas than the whole city. Even so, both were drawn in predominantly sequential style. More spatial element local maps were drawn by San Félix (46 percent) and Puerto Ordaz (32 percent) residents than by other groups. This may have been due to the spatial character of the San Félix gridiron plan and the confusing street system of Puerto Ordaz, which obfuscated any coherent sequential structuring. The most distinct group was the Country Club sample, whose rank correlations with all other groups were very low. Those in the Campo Caroní were also different.

Travel Mode

Variations in travel mode seemed profoundly to influence structuring. About one-half of our sample used buses as their dominant form of transportation, while one-quarter each used cars or ***por puestos.*** There were, however, problems in distinguishing their influence, because most people used more than one travel mode. For the purposes of more precise analysis, we sorted out those that traveled solely by bus and solely by car.

Of the subjects who traveled only by bus, 80 percent were unable to draw a coherent map of the urban road system. All the maps found in this group were either scatter or fragment. Although these subjects were low in education, they differed from an equivalently educated set who used ***por puestos*** or traveled by car. Analyses of several structural errors (table 8.2) including mislocations, reversals, and faults between zones, showed that the bus riders committed a slightly higher percentage of road distortions but slightly fewer zonal errors than those traveling predominantly by car. ***Por puesto*** riders committed more errors than any group. Differences were significant ($P < .10$).

There were several bus services in the city. For bus riders, the eastern terminal, located to the south of San Félix at the Seguros Sociales, was the end of the city. This explains why the buildings around this terminal were well known although they were distant from the main road system. In 1964 the buses traveled from this point along an indirect route through several barrios before reaching the plaza in San Félix. They continued along the old route in El Roble rather than along the new shortcut, then directly across the river and through Castillito following another circuitous path through the camps of Puerto Ordaz. The sign "Circunvolución" on the front of many of the buses aptly described the journey. Add to this the difficulty of seeing through the front window of a crowded bus, the agonizing slowness of the ride, the absence of announcements at each stop, and one can easily understand the defects in the bus riders' maps. The bus-riding experience seemed inevitably to lead to fragmentation and creation of islands of knowledge with only schematic, vague, or unknown links between.

All the maps drawn by the selected group of car-only travelers presented a coherent and continuous system. In the total sample of those who drew maps, distinctions between the groups were not as sharp (r_s's were all significant except between automobile and ***por puesto*** riders). This was probably because each group was to some degree mixed (see appendix A). For both car and bus groups, sequential maps were more common, but between the citywide maps 16 percent more car travelers drew spatial element maps, and 13 percent more bus travelers drew sequential element maps. Automobile travelers developed their citywide maps more broadly, relying less on the individual routes, while bus travelers kept very much to repeated sequential journeys.

Sex

Females had been expected to rely more on spatial structuring, given their supposed predilection for security and containment (Erikson 1950). Their local maps showed this predilection slightly more than males (33 to 24 percent), but there was little difference in their citywide maps ($\mathbf{r_s}$ = .74, .84). Females also made more errors in their maps ($P < .10$). These differences were probably due to their relative immobility in the city, though there was also some reluctance among many female respondents to demonstrate knowledge they were later found to have. It seemed to be taken by some as an unfeminine quality.

Selected Occupations

The maps of the small group of business executives were the most distinct (r_s = .42 to .10) from any other group. They used spatial elements, and many were fragment or cluster maps without sequential connections. However, their numbers were too small to make this a very reliable finding. Skilled workers' maps were overwhelmingly sequential, with a high proportion of branch and loop or network maps. This fits with the fact that many traveled the length of the city daily to reach the steel mill. Professionals and students produced similar map-type rankings to those of the skilled workers (r_s = .76, .88 local; .66, .69 citywide). Their maps were sequentially dominant, mostly of the more developed chain types. Housewives' map types tended to be the more primitive chain type at the local level. Their patterns of map types were similar to those of small businessmen (r_s = .76 local, .53 citywide), those in personal services (r_s = .60 local, .82 citywide) and office workers (r_s = .76 local, .56 citywide).

Three Methods of Structuring a City

At this point it will be useful to step back from the map data, which is only one method of understanding how people structure cities, and try to visualize, with the experience gained from the field surveys, how people actually relate the various parts of cities. There appear to be three principal methods of structuring cities: an *associational method*, depending on the differentiation, association, and patterning of images and character; a *topological method*, stressing continuity and juncture; and a *positional method*, emphasizing spatial placement, direction, and distance.[3] The relation of these methods to the typology of maps will be explained in the conclusion.

Associational Structuring: Differentiation, Association, and Patterning

Associational structuring depends on the ability to differentiate parts of the city and associate them in groups or patterns. This kind of structuring need not depend on any knowledge of continuities or sequences in the city, or on a sense of position or direction. If a person comes out of a subway, or if a passenger in a car wakes up from a reverie, each will rely on recognizing and differentiating the character of the place where he is. He may not know how to move from there to somewhere else, and he may have no idea in which direction to go. In its most developed form, associational structuring enables a person to "place" himself in the urban pattern. His success at this will depend on his previous experience, on the systematic patterning of the city he is in, and on the conformity of its pattern to the patterns of other cities (Bruner, Wallach, and Galanter 1959).

Consider the patterning of one sequential element in Ciudad Guayana, the old east-west road (figure 8.6). Movement along this road was highly differentiated as it zigzagged from right to left, each bend differing in its sharpness; but the movements did not group into any consistent rhythm or pattern. Vertical movement, however, into and out of the Caroní Valley and then down into San Félix, began to set up a simple hill-valley-hill-valley rhythm that helped to organize the large-scale pattern.

The activity centers along the route (Puerto Ordaz, Castillito, Dalla Costa, El Roble, and San Félix) were well distinguished from each other but formed no consistent relationship, except by their gradient of age, from west to east. The organization of decision points could also have been more systematic. Intersections were of all kinds, and the bus stops were not clearly meshed with them.

While the centers of Puerto Ordaz, Castillito, and San Félix were distinctly different, there were few regularities within the pattern of spatial elements (figures 8.7, 8.8). The residential districts did have certain similarities. The barrios in San Félix, El Roble, and Castillito were all of one kind: ranchos on mud streets. The planned districts of Puerto Ordaz, Mendoza in Castillito, and the Fondación De Vivienda Popular in El Roble were of another pattern, but each set failed to form regular structures. Had the planned residential areas been consistently near the focuses or on the fringes of each community, a more comprehensible pattern would have been perceived. A side benefit of the confusion was to leave the sociospatial structure of the city open and unpredictable.

At the larger scale, however, the terrain, with its rivers, valleys, and bowls, provided a set of landscape units that were distinctively different although difficult to perceive as wholes. The Orinoco River was wider than the Caroní, and the Llanos gave it a distinctive character. Even so, the rivers seen from a distance were often very similar in appearance, and at least one visiting consultant avowed that he was always confused by them.

Facilities such as schools, churches, and movie houses were potentially cohesive urban features, for various facility types bore a likeness to each other. But their locations were too irregular to be understood. If schools or churches could have been in specific locations in each community, as proposed in chapter 7, or on one kind of road on the street system, more order would have been apparent. The presence of gas stations

Figure 8.6 Associational pattern of the east-west road before 1964. The figure emphasizes the characteristics of movement, enclosure, views, terrain, rivers, and urban development as they were imagined along the route.

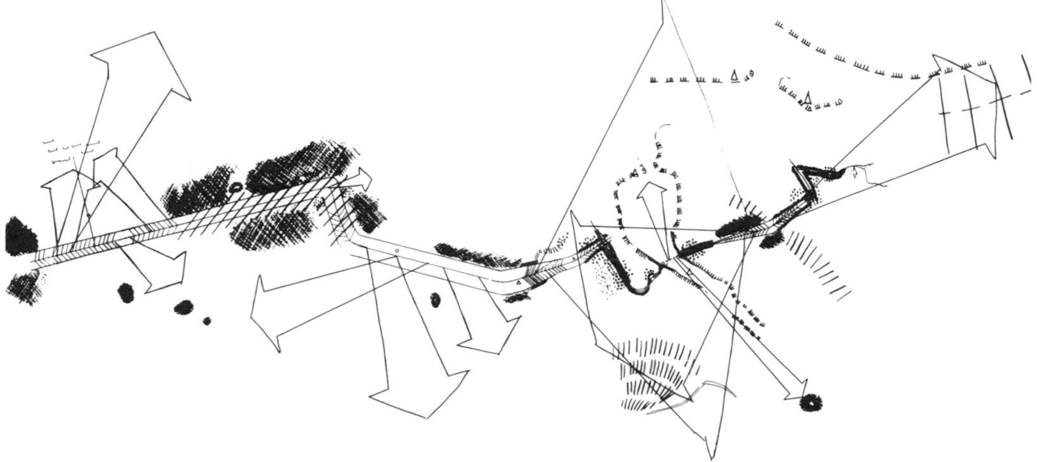

Figures 8.7, 8.8 Associational structure of spatial elements.

Figure 8.7 Form patterns. The map describes the form qualities of the main urban elements, their level of intensity, singularity, or significance. The more distinctive form elements of the city usually coincided with intensive activity, with the exception of the natural features. The areas of unique physical character are the Caroní Falls, the narrows of the river, the planned housing areas of the Country Club, and Puerto Ordaz, the Urbanización Mendoza, and El Roble. The map shows the distinction between Puerto Ordaz and the other settlements and how new planned residential units (vertical hatching) were being added to the periphery of every settlement. The Caroní rapids and river below form an associative unit, but the rest of the Caroní looks very similar to the Orinoco.

Figure 8.8 Activity patterns. The map describes the distribution of activity centers, the steel mill, some utilities, the bridge, the ferry, and various commercial and public facilities in the settlements. The most singular activity areas were those of the steel mill, the Orinoco Mining Company, the Iron Mines Company, and the hydroelectric dam. The diagram brings out the association of industry with the Orinoco River, and other complexes of high significance—the commercial and institutional centers of Puerto Ordaz and San Félix and the river crossings.

Figure 8.9

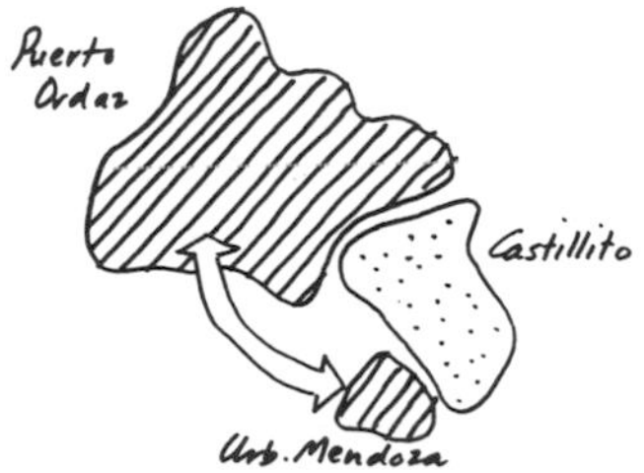

Figure 8.10

at the main intersections of Puerto Ordaz and El Roble made a useful contribution to the city's structure in this respect (figure 8.9), perhaps another reason why they were noticed so frequently in the interviews.

Structuring through social linkages may often be more important for urban residents than structuring directly through the form of the environment. No extensive questioning was carried out on this subject, but the attitude of one of our interviewers was significant. She insisted that the Urbanización Mendoza (physically adjacent to Castillito) was part of Puerto Ordaz (some distance away but an area of similar social class) (figure 8.10). Perceptual distance from a similar social area is apparently less than actual distance, while perceptual distance from a lower social group is greater than actual distance.[4]

Names failed to pattern the environment in Ciudad Guayana, for most names did not denote location. Either they referred to the owner of the organization involved (for example, Bomba Phillips, General Electric, or Urbanización Mendoza), or they adopted some stereotypical name (for example, the Hotel Embajador and the Cine Rex). In some cases, names of national heroes and saints were employed, as in the barrios San Raphael and Antonio de Berrio. Locational names like Hotel Guayaña and Seguros Orinoco were too general, and some, like Supermercado Los Alpes were too exotic, to be of any locational use in structuring the city. Only a few (Las Palmitas, Los Monos, and Dalla Costa) referred specifically to the characteristics of their location. In the planned areas, things were worse. Camps A, B, and C were designated by social level, and the *unidades vecinales* were numbered by their sequence of construction rather than by their spatial pattern.

Naming systems are given too little thought in new city design. When large areas are rapidly constructed, there are usually few ways of distinguishing parts by geographical location, but naming streets after countries and states, as was done in Puerto Ordaz, is little better than using numbers and letters. Had some care been taken to look carefully at the characteristics of areas and streets before christening them, or had the inhabitants been given the opportunity to choose the names themselves, more distinctive names might have been selected.

Ciudad Guayana did not conform to the regular model of a city, for it had neither a dominant center nor any obvious character gradients. It came closest to being a linear string of settlements, although even this was undergoing transformation. The new Avenida Guayana and the general influence of vehicular travel were shifting the focuses from the old centers to the more accessible entrances of the settlements (figure

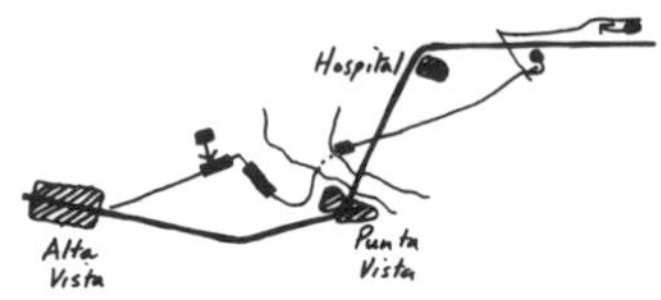

Figure 8.11

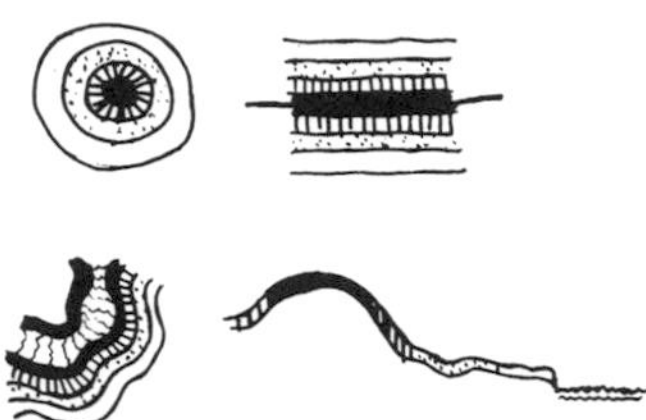
Figure 8.12

8.11). Any stranger coming to the city would find it extremely difficult to predict the locations and relationships of parts of the city.

In sum, a highly patterned city in which associational structuring is easy will be differentiated by parts in some systematic way. These parts may be sequential or spatial elements, and differentiation can be by physical character, functional type, or social group. It can be more easily structured if the pattern conforms to that of other known and structured cities.

A city can be well differentiated and patterned in many ways. Social, functional, and physical characteristics can be graded in intensity from the outside to the center, outward from a central spine, or, as in Ciudad Guayana, from the rivers (figure 8.12).

In many cities certain income groups have lived in typical locations—in the hills, by the rivers, or near active centers—and certain functions gravitate to certain types of terrain. Such techniques can aid in structuring a new city, but they will be too abstract if they are not related to the particular nature of the different parts of the city, and they may set up too rigid a social or functional pattern. Furthermore, if they are to be innovative and distinct from other cities, they will have to be easily understood.

Topological Structuring: Continuity and Connection

Structuring the city as a continuity depends heavily on the organization of sequential elements and their habitual use, on continuous movement and form, visible connections, or continuous symbol systems.

However confused and disruptive in character routes may be, habitual journeys give them a minimal structural coherence; if movement is direct, continuous, and fast, mental continuity will be more easily achieved. Hence, the replacement of the Caroní ferry by the new bridge was a major structural act, for it established continuous movement between the two sides of the river and reduced the time gap by as much as half an hour. Indirectness and breaks in the continuity of movement are disruptive. The circuitous stop-go nature of the bus trips led to fragmented concepts of the city, and even those traveling by automobile were confused by the several abrupt changes in direction on the street systems of Puerto Ordaz and El Roble. Since continuity in recall depends to a great extent on familiarity with routes, if flow patterns are not personally experienced, they are not likely to be recalled as continuous.

Besides continuities of movement, the character of a route can facilitate or hinder the traveler's ability to structure the

Figure 8.13 Topological structure. The varied and broken terrain made for dependence on topological structuring, but the sharp changes in character and direction of the main roads impaired even topological continuity. For automobile travelers, continuity of the road system was disrupted by changes of travel mode, like the ferry, abrupt changes in direction, lack of forward visibility, changes in character, hidden entrances, and the occasional dead end. For bus travelers, continuity was further curtailed by the stop-go nature of bus travel and the meandering route system.

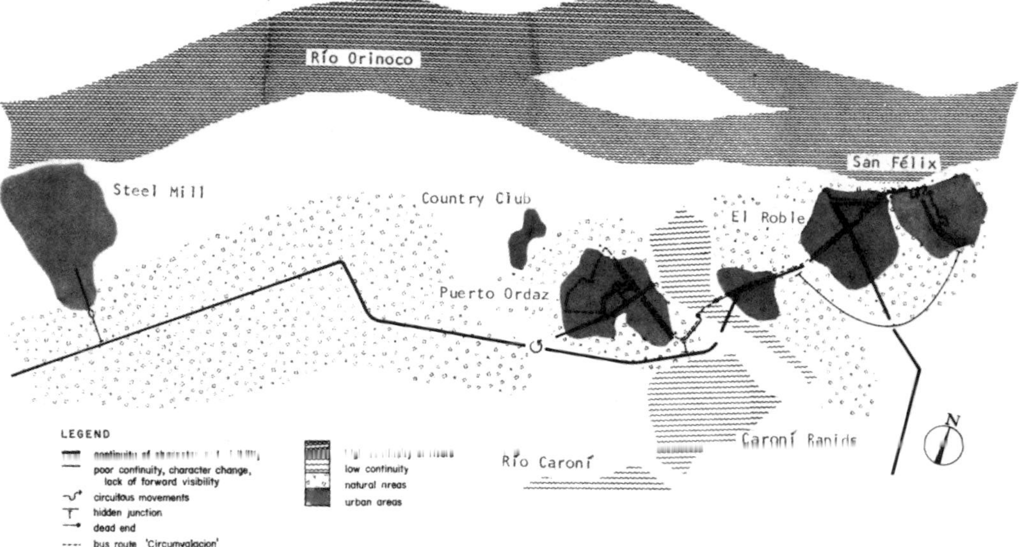

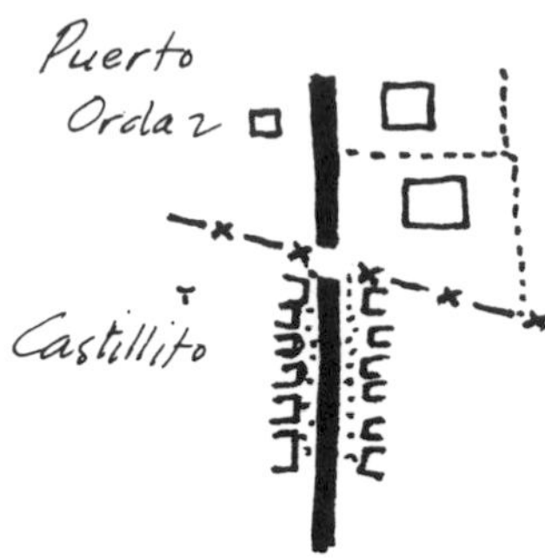

Figure 8.14

Figure 8.15

Figure 8.16

Figure 8.17

city. Continuity of spatial form, building type, view, traffic, vegetation, furniture, or other details builds up the concept of a single, continuous road. If a sufficient number of characteristics change, a character break occurs that may seriously disrupt continuity. The abrupt change in character from Castillito to Puerto Ordaz (figure 8.14), for instance, so disrupted connections between the two communities that 25 percent of the maps showed them in an incorrect spatial relationship despite their direct road connection.

Visible continuity is also a factor. If the road ahead is not visible, the traveler can be subjected to moments of doubt about its future course. Blind curves, hilltops, and humps (figure 8.15) are common sources of structural discontinuity—and of accidents. The western entry into Puerto Ordaz, where the road turned and cut down through the ridge, was one such case; the entry into Castillito from the east was another.

To gain an accurate topological schema of a city, clarity of connections is essential. Confused junctions, where route choices out of an intersection are complex or undifferentiated or where some of the choices are hidden from an entering traveler, can mean missing important routes and may lead to breaks in continuity. Two incongruous intersections in El Roble (figure 8.16), where the most direct routes appeared to be minor choices, created various breaks in subject maps. The link between the main road and the Centro Cívico in Puerto Ordaz, the link from the new Avenida Guayana to Castillito, and the semicircular road to the south of San Félix were all ignored because their entrances were obscure (figure 8.17).

Finally, the use of symbol systems (names, pictures, or numbers) can achieve continuity. The lack of any name for the old east-west road contributed to the disruption of the city, while the new Avenida Guayana promised to make the city more coherent because of its name.

Spatial elements like districts and landmarks can also encourage topological structuring if they are extensive and continuous. The territory of a person's habitual activities will become known by him as a continuous piece of terrain, but the areas of the city that a person covers in detail are usually limited in size.

The continuity of the rivers could have been one of the major structural assets of the city, but since neither was used extensively for public transportation, they were commonly seen only from a distance and fragmentarily. Although everyone knows that rivers are continuous, when there are two rivers in an area, isolated stretches of water might belong to one or the other. Hence, a number of our respondents confused the names of the rivers on their maps. Even so, the Orinoco, by its sheer breadth and simplicity, was a useful structural feature. The Caroní, disrupted by falls, rapids, and meanderings, was more confusing than clarifying. The hills and ridges were large and continuous features, but they were too ambiguous. Slope changes were so gradual that transitions went unnoticed, and our subjects demonstrated little knowledge of their existence.

The visibility of significant features can unify areas of the city. The view of San Félix from the slopes around it and of the slopes from San Félix (figure 8.18) helped to create unity in that area. Surveys were made of such features during the design process. The visibility range of existing landmarks was found to be generally limited; and many of those seen from a distance disappeared on approach. The steel mill in its hollow, the low airport buildings, the thin radio tower, and the unclear shape of the Macagua Dam failed to create an interlocking system. Hence, travel on the major roads was marked by discontinuity and gaps between the presence of major urban focuses.

There did exist, however, many sites that were potentially visible to large areas of the city. Sharp outcrop hills like El Gallo and San Joaquin were scattered through the terrain unnoticed as yet by the inhabitants, but waiting for future landmarks, and the planning group began to exploit these potentialities. The new hospital was later located on the San Félix ridge to be seen from the Caroní Valley, and visibility was a determining factor in the choice of site for the new centers on Alta Vista and Punta Vista. The final plan for the city visualized a linear succession of major focuses, each intervisible with its neighbor (figure 8.33).

Large areas of the city were homogeneous and continuous because of their common social character or because of their common name, both of which appeared to be more important to the inhabitants at this large scale than physical homogeneity. For quite a few, the whole west bank of the Caroní River was thought of as Puerto Ordaz despite its physical and social diversity. The mosaic-type maps depicted settlements like Puerto Ordaz and Castillito in a continuous manner, subdividing them into zones for shopping, schools, and other functions.

A highly structured city from the topological viewpoint will be well connected by sequential and spatial elements continuous in character along which one could move without breaks. Nodal points, boundaries, and junctions between elements will be well connected, allowing good continuity through them

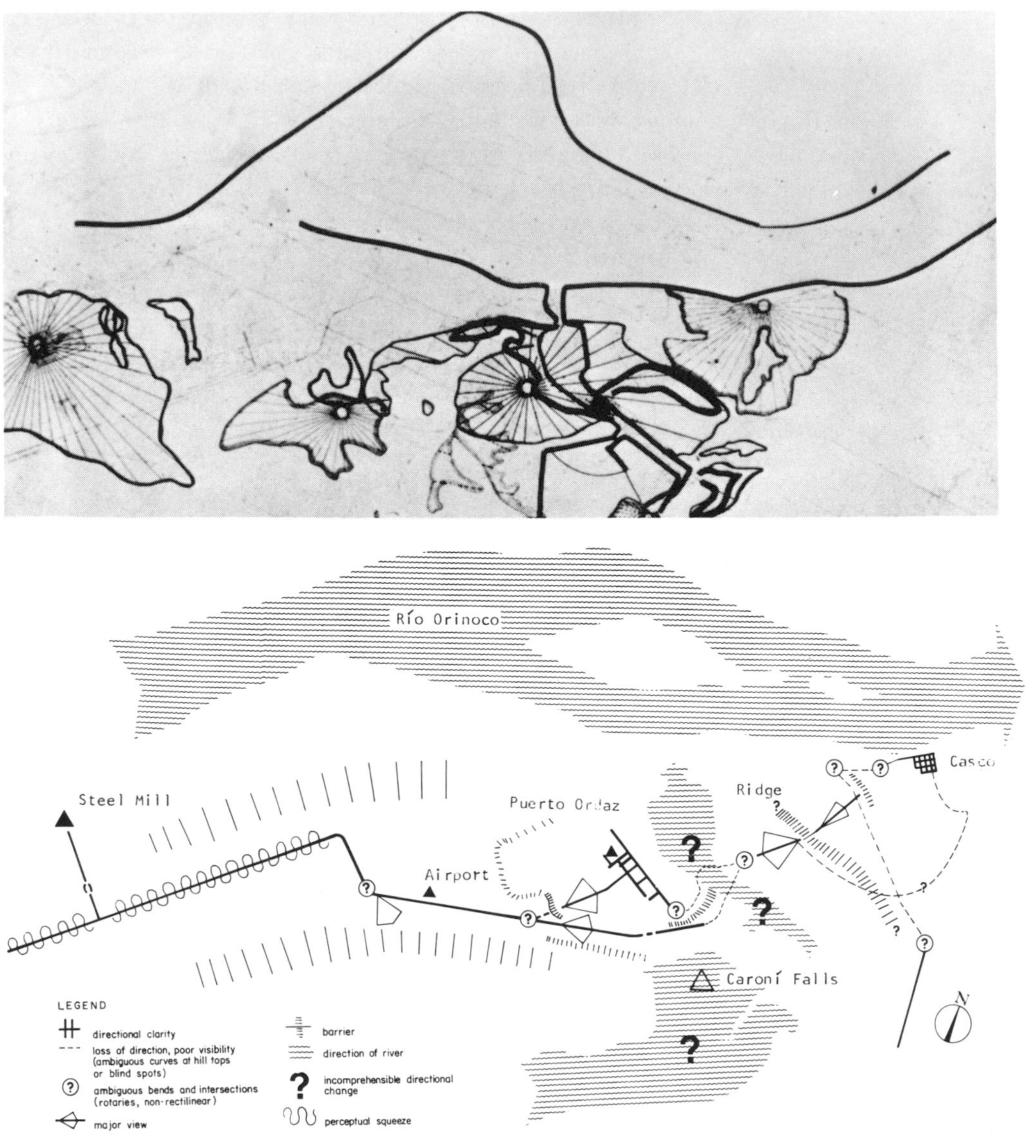

Figure 8.19 Positional structure. The positional structure of the city consisted of islands of directional clarity—Puerto Ordaz, San Félix—and certain axes—parts of the main road, floating in a sea of ambiguity, only partially connected by views across the valley. The approximate east-west orientation of the Orinoco—with the Llanos to the north—was a stabilizing axis for the city. The Caroní, on the other hand, was discontinuous, complex, multidirectional, and mysterious. The two complemented each other. Confinement, barriers, poor visibility, ambiguous curves, nonrectilinear bends and intersections, undifferentiated roads, and ambiguously shaped reference points were the principal problems in determining direction and distance.

Figure 8.18 Visibility range of urban focuses. The centers of Puerto Ordaz and San Félix were on knolls within larger valley bowls, making both of them highly visible from surrounding hills—though not always from the main road. The steel mill set low by the Orinoco was seen only for a short distance on the main road despite its high smokestacks and billowing smoke. The airport, a small building, was seen nearly as well as the steel mill; the new bridge was invisible to most of Puerto Ordaz and was only seen from a sliver of land to the east of the Caroní. The Macagua Dam was invisible from most of the city except from the western ridge.

along major routes. If these elements are well differentiated from one another, so much the better.

Positional Structuring: Direction and Distance

Positional structuring gives the inhabitant a clear sense of the distance and direction of major features, even if he does not know how to move from one to the other or has no general sense of the urban pattern. Positional structuring is dependent primarily on such environmental factors as consistency of direction, clarity of directional change, high visibility, and consistent scaling. It also depends on public maps. Thorough knowledge of maps and mapping techniques is perhaps the most important skill required for this type of structuring, because maps are positionally accurate, even though topologically unclear and silent about character, function, or social structure.

Consider again the major sequential element of Ciudad Guayana, the old east-west road. Where road alignment was consistently straight or bends were rectangular, directions on the subject maps were usually accurate; errors began to appear as soon as directional changes were slow, slight, or otherwise imperceptible (figure 8.20), particularly if there were no views present to correct self-position.

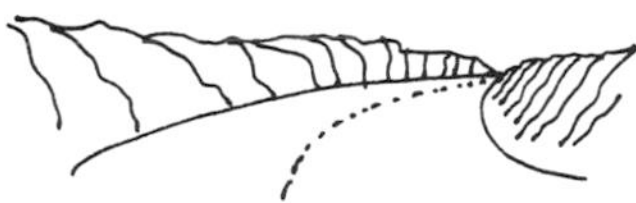

Figure 8.20

The slow curve of the semicircular road to the south of San Félix, for instance, was ignored on most of the drawings. Directional ambiguities at traffic intersections could also set a schema off in the wrong direction, and angles other than right angles were always difficult to assess. Rotaries and cloverleafs are even more of a problem. The new rotary above Puerto Ordaz (figure 8.21), so clear on the plan, was the cause of several structuring errors, despite the view from that point over the whole valley.

Figure 8.21

The marking of changes in direction either by a change in character or by the occurrence of some event was essential; otherwise, they could easily be missed. The curve to the south of Castillito, a very pronounced but unmarked right angle, was noted by less than 50 percent of those who mentioned the road. Bends that occurred in distracting circumstances were also forgotten. For instance, numerous bends occurring at intersections or on hilltops were ignored. Once a change in direction was omitted, the entire conceptual shape of the city could go askew (figure 8.22).

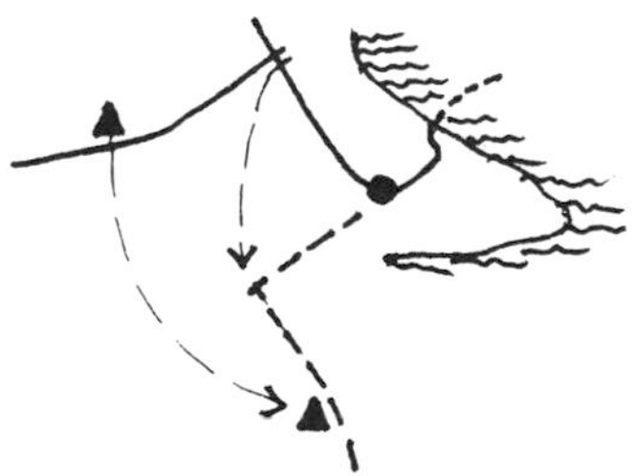

Figure 8.22

Where inhabitants lacked detailed knowledge of the city's structure, they would infer from previous experience or common sense. In conceptualizing the sequential flow of materials through the steel mill (figure 8.23), for instance, they tended

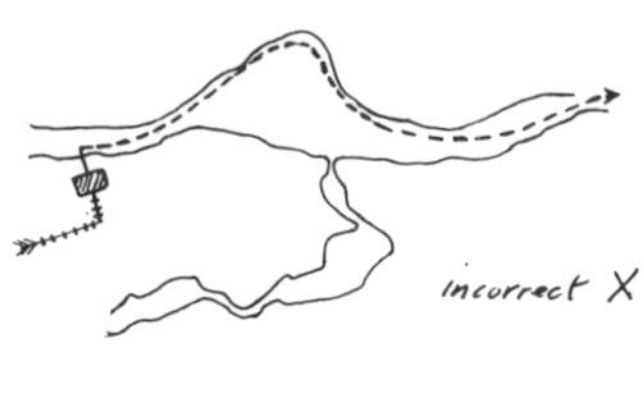

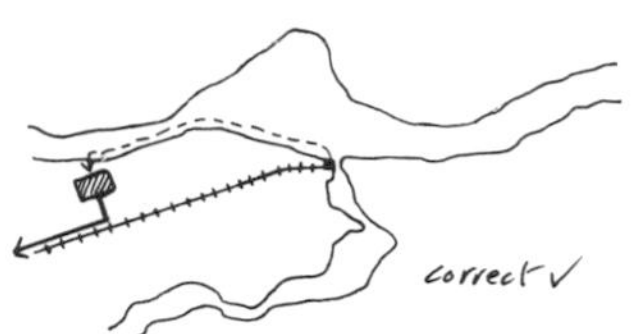

Figure 8.23

to infer a simple east-to-west flow from the mines, through the steel mill, down the river, to the ocean as their positional structure. But in 1964, the actual flow did not follow this pattern at all. The iron ore was transported by railroad to the ports at Puerto Ordaz and Palúa; then, since these were not linked by rail to the steel mill, it was shipped upriver on barges. Furthermore, exports from the steel mill were not carried away by ship, but traveled westward by truck to Ciudad Bolívar, where they were ferried across the Orinoco to be transported by road to other parts of the country. Positionally, the process turned back on itself.

Our respondents incorrectly opted for the more reasonable expectation, ignoring any contrary perceptual evidence. Only 24 percent correctly mentioned ships or barges as conveying raw materials into the mill, and a mere 10 percent accurately described the trucking out of finished products, while 32 percent were partially correct, mentioning ships as well as trucks, and 41 percent were incorrectly convinced that all finished products were exported by boat or rail.

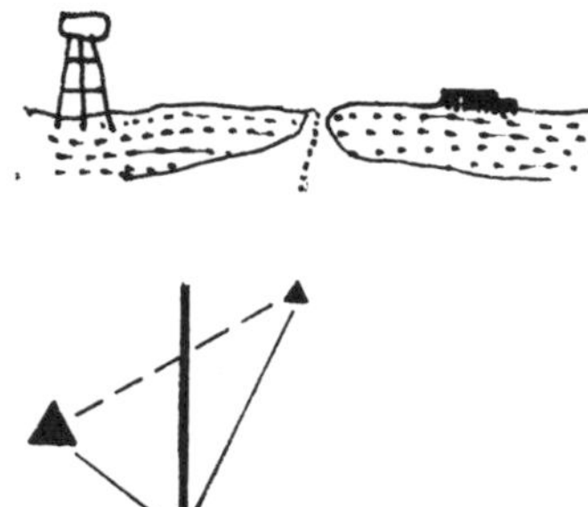

Figure 8.24

Visibility of other city elements and other roads is an invaluable means of placing oneself in the landscape and is a characteristic to which the traveler is highly attentive (Appleyard, Lynch, and Myer 1964). When a known landmark, a river, or a district is seen from a road, the traveler can pinpoint his own probable location by assessing the distance between himself and the landmark (figure 8.24). This cannot be precisely fixed until a second known point is seen or unless the element seen has specific directional differentiation. Panoramic views create a redundancy of fixation points and make it difficult to get lost. When churches face east, or when buildings are clearly oriented to the breeze, views of them fix directions in the viewer's schema. The hilltop views from above Puerto Ordaz and on the San Félix ridge were key points on the circulation system, despite the lack of distinct landmarks and the ambiguous shape of the natural landscape.

The more ambiguous parts of the system were those without views. Traveling westward through the trees from the Caroní Bridge, the road seemed to be directed right out of the city, especially when the Falls appeared on the right, instead of the expected left-hand side (figure 7.7). Was the road going off to the south? At the last moment it curved to the right, past the falls; but temporarily, disorientation was complete.

The range of visibility from the road, then, is a significant structuring device for positional as well as topological structuring. Figure 8.25 shows the area of land covered by views from the old and new east-west roads. More importantly, it shows

Figure 8.25 Visibility from the major east-west road (traveling west to east). This drawing, generated from 360-degree photographs, describes the view field of a traveler on the main road of the city. Shadowed areas represent the foreground views; those enclosed by a dotted line are distant views. The wider views on this trip, from west to east, occur by the Orinoco, while crossing the Caroní, rising up the hill south of Puerto Ordaz, along the plateau west of the airport, and south of the steel mill. Few of the views cover the Orinoco to the north, but many cover the southern view over the Caroní toward the mountains.

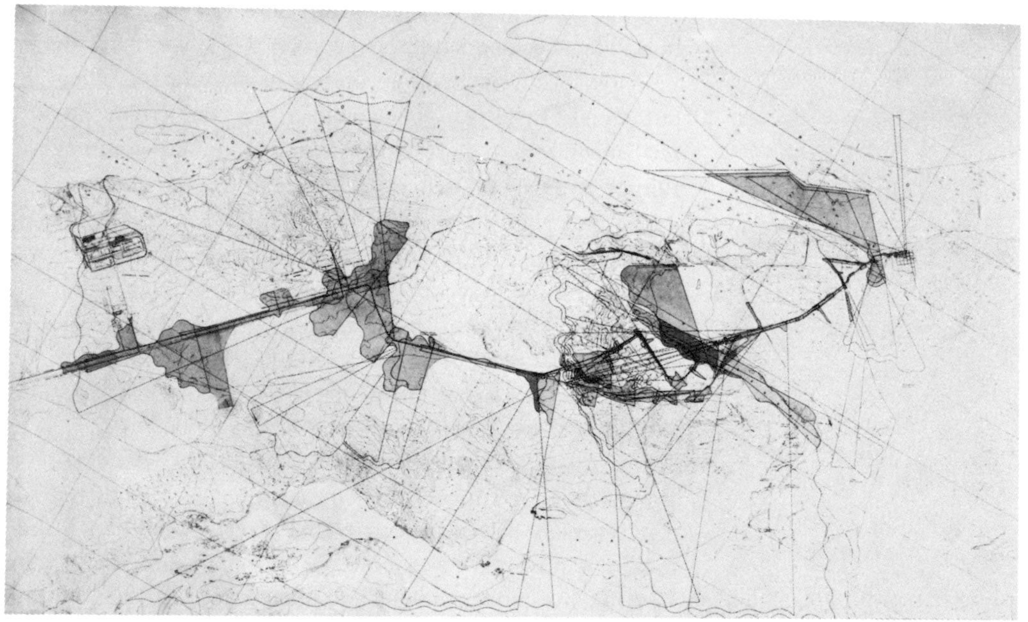

where visibility was poor—a good indicator of where positional problems were likely to occur.

Accurate perceptions of distance were difficult to make, particularly on the uneventful western plateau and on the eastern section between Dalla Costa and El Roble. These sections of road had an insufficient frequency of events by which they could be scaled, and they were consequently compressed in about 20 percent of the maps.

Positional relationships between and within settlements also depended on the systematic directions of streets and intersections within districts and the visible locations of landmarks within these systems. The rectangular plan of San Félix established a clear spatial geometry for those who could infer it. Parts of Castillito also succeeded in achieving this clarity, although both areas floated elastically in the spatial schema of the larger city.

Intervisibility between major residential districts and between highly used centers also increased directional clarity. Views of the Llanos to the north and the Guayana highlands to the south created a stable conceptual setting for the city, but the near environment of meandering rivers and intricate terrain caused considerable confusion. Hence, few subjects were able to achieve accurate relationships between opposite sides of the Caroní River, nor could they accurately trace the course of the river to the south of the city.

The natural pattern of sun and wind and the consistently western direction of the breeze and clouds should have helped orientation in Ciudad Guayana. But only 20 percent of our respondents could locate north correctly on their maps, and a similarly small percentage accurately located the prevailing direction of the breeze. The complexity of the terrain and settlement pattern must have defeated them in their estimation of cardinal points, and the breeze, of course, is always a much more elusive phenomenon.

The influence of inferential structuring on positional orientation is most felt in rectilinear situations. Most cities are built on a rectilinear system, and therefore we have a rectilinear mental model of cities that is confounded by other systems (Bruner 1957a). Hence, many maps "rectangularized" relationships, sometimes quite incorrectly.

The absence of a public map was a serious drawback for those seeking to structure the city positionally. Had there been one, we might have counted a higher percentage of netted and patterned maps. But we should not be too sanguine about the benefits of a public map in a city like Ciudad Guayana, for the usual type of map might be too remote from the inhabitant's experience and too rapidly obsolete to be used effectively by him. We have seen how the designers learned some features, such as details of the shorelines, that were irrelevant to their operational knowledge of the city. Most inhabitants would experience similar difficulty in coordinating a map with their experience unless they were given more experientially descriptive maps, such as annotated aerial photographs or isometric picture plans.

A positionally structured city will therefore contain elements with a clearly directional structure, preferably rectilinear. The elements should be scaled to some regular module, with high levels of intervisibility and simple rectilinear joints between the parts. The whole should be clearly related to the points of the compass and to a public map.

Mixing the Methods

These methods of structuring can be used to describe either the dominant structure of a particular environment or city or the structuring method or style of an urban inhabitant. The three methods do not necessarily lie on a continuum of increasing accuracy. Cities with continuous but viewless street or freeway systems tend to have a topological structure, as do nonrectilinear beaux arts plans like Haussmann's Paris and parts of Washington, D.C. A gridiron street system or an elevated freeway system will be more positional in its structure, especially if there are high hills or landmarks in evidence, and a discontinuous but highly differentiated city like Boston will have a predominantly associational structure. Most cities incorporate aspects of all three types.

These methods were employed more frequently in some map types than in others, but they were frequently intermixed. The fragment and scatter maps, where elements were usually disconnected from each other and unrelated by direction, appeared to be unstructured in any way. But this may have been a limitation of the maps. In traveling about the city, their authors may have concentrated primarily on the nonspatial, nonconnective technique of simply recognizing places and associating them with each other as similar or different images. The chain, branch and loop, mosaic, and link maps, which all exhibited continuity and connections of both sequential and spatial elements, were basically topological in character. The network and pattern maps were usually positional with the parts correctly located in spatial relation to each other. Of these, the network maps were also topologically connected. Other map types, even the scatter maps, were sometimes positionally accurate, but this was rare.

Our map-drawing respondents used a range of techniques, apparently depending on which environmental attributes were available, and on their conceptual abilities, familiarity, travel mode, or general experience. Topological structuring seemed to require the least skill but the most familiarity. Positional structuring, relying on continuous references to surroundings and on mental matching with map images, seemed to demand the highest conceptual skills. Associational patterning required more thoughtful association of characteristics, social patterns, and functions, which, in most cases, would be aided by experience of other cities. The employment of methods was, no doubt, accumulative, with the most skilled and familiar inhabitants able to structure the city in alternative ways.

Summarizing Structural Perception

1. Cities can be understood and structured by either sequential or spatial elements. In the classification presented here, Lynch's paths and nodes are considered sequential elements, and landmarks, districts, and edges are grouped more or less under spatial elements. In Ciudad Guayana the sequential mode was dominant.

2. Respondents used form, visibility, use, and significance patterns to structure the city.

3. Three fundamental methods of relating parts of the city emerge from the map interpretations and the field surveys: the associational method, which depends on the differentiation, association, and patterning of functional, social, or physical character; the topological method, which depends on continuity and juncture of movement and character; and the positional method, which emphasizes spatial placement, direction, and distance.

4. People appeared to structure the city in varyingly schematic ways. Many subjects strove to fit their urban knowledge into a coherent schema. However, given the disjointed nature of the street system, extreme simplification was necessary. Other subjects worked more incrementally, seemingly unable to grasp the larger structure of the city, adding sections of road or area together, or simply setting down disjointed fragments with little regard to overall placement. Schematic maps that attempted to grasp the pattern of the city in some simplified and systematic way were found both at the lowest levels of competence, where they suffered from oversimplicity, and at the highest levels, where maps were laid out in close congruence with the actual urban pattern. The better maps appeared to use a combination of deductive and inductive methods.

5. There was also evidence of inferential structuring. The

European engineer who wrongly predicted the three railroad lines, epitomized this influence. Those who drew a gridiron street system for San Félix were inferring also, probably from much more limited experience. Inferential structuring depends on a person's previous experience of cities and the unconscious personal rules about environmental relationships that develop from that experience. As long as a city structure conforms to that of other cities, the inhabitant knows it will be relatively easy to structure. It is the unique aspects that confound the newcomer. The influence of inferential structuring makes it very difficult to disentangle images derived from direct experience from those based on interpretations of given experience.

Structuring the Future City

Remember that the interviews were made before extensive planning had taken place. The structure of Ciudad Guayana at this time was poorly differentiated and unpatterned; it was discontinuous, directionally ambiguous, unevenly visible, and unscaled. The complexity of the terrain and the numerous unrelated locational decisions were the primary reasons for this.

How much did the city need structuring? The difficulties found in the maps our subjects drew and their expressed concern for better orientational signs and more street names suggest that improvements in the structure of Ciudad Guayana would be welcome. For operational use of the city, the ability to structure it topologically would seem to be the most essential; and for more general knowledge of its social and functional patterns, the ability to differentiate and pattern its parts would be of great benefit. A spatially accurate positional schema may be the least important of all three, although there would be many gains in operational flexibility and environmental mastery if citizens could also structure the city in this way.

Figure 8.26

A well-structured city might also prevent social isolation and encourage contact between different population groups. The danger of an east-west political split could be avoided by achieving social balance both within major settlements and between the two sides of the Caroní (figure 8.26). But the CVG administration was not anxious to have rancho settlements lining the roads between the steel mill, the airport, and the new prestige center on Alta Vista. The image of Ciudad Guayana as a planned and beautiful city was fixed in the minds of the top CVG administration and the Venezuelan public, and it would be an important promotional tool for bringing industry to the city; it must not be threatened by the somewhat disheveled appearance of ranchos. A compromise was reached within the CVG to place low-income self-help housing on the western side of the Caroní, but at a distance of about one mile south of the main road, a location that would not serve the accessibility needs of low-income groups very well.

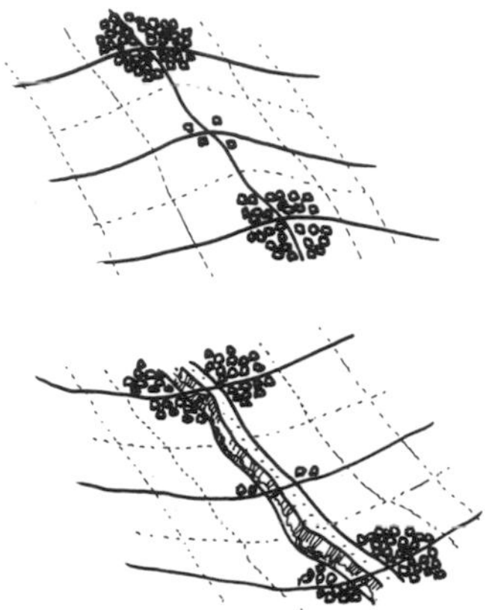

Figure 8.27

The CVG's desire for a clean new city, and the established identity of San Félix, which continued to gather new lower-income growth, made social mixing difficult, and a 1971 visitor to the city reported a "strong sense of two linked cities" (Peattie 1971). Eliminating or playing down barriers between different social groups (figure 8.27) could help. Barriers like major transportation routes, natural ridges and spurs, *quebradas*, and property lines could all be modified by providing centers of activity along or across them.

Finally, a city that is too clearly defined and well connected becomes so predictable that it loses interest, invites no exploration, and becomes regimented. True, the stranger can understand a city like Brasilia within a few hours, but this may not be satisfactory for the inhabitant. Since the desired level of structuring will vary among the population, a city should be structured at different levels and in different ways. For too long, the beaux arts system of structuring cities has been the only coherent method for the planner and urban designer. With their linked networks of boulevards, their geometric patterns, and differentiated *ronds-points*, they incorporated aspects of all three types of structuring. But at the scale of the modern city, the beaux arts system and its megastructural offspring with their small attention to differentiation and association become increasingly monotonous, overbearing, and difficult to "place" oneself in. Their insistent geometrical patterns are rigid and difficult to fit into complex landscapes. The best policy for the planner-designers of Ciudad Guayana was to improve citizens' abilities to structure the city adequately in each of the three ways (figures 8.28-8.34), by spatial or sequential elements on each travel system, yet encourage diversity and spontaneity for it to retain a level of liveliness and urbanity.

Increasing Continuity

With the new Avenida Guayana as the principal east-west linkage through the city, and several of the most significant urban facilities placed alongside or within view of it, a more continuous and differentiated spinal system will be constructed. The effects of this new road on the inhabitants' concepts of the city were already dramatically apparent in the maps they drew the year after a major segment of the road had been opened

Figure 8.28 One early sketch plan for the transportation system. This transportation alternative shows a spinal highway, the Avenida Guayana, with commercial activity alongside, flanked by two freeways, one with views over the Caroní to the south, the other with views to the north over the Orinoco, passing the industrial complex, both terminating in the steel mill to the west: transverse highways slope down to the rivers, in some cases crossing them.

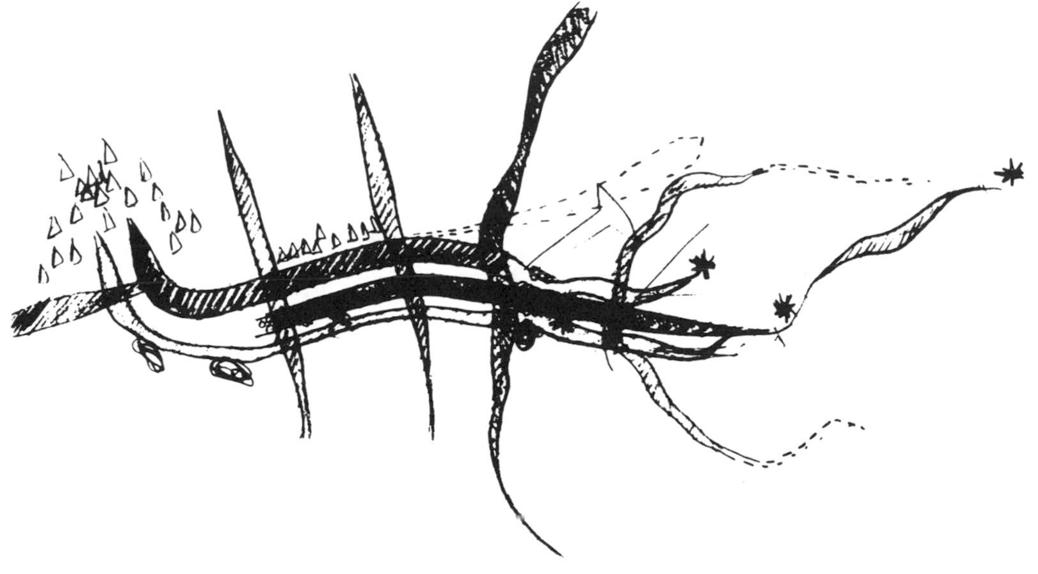

Figure 8.29 Districts.

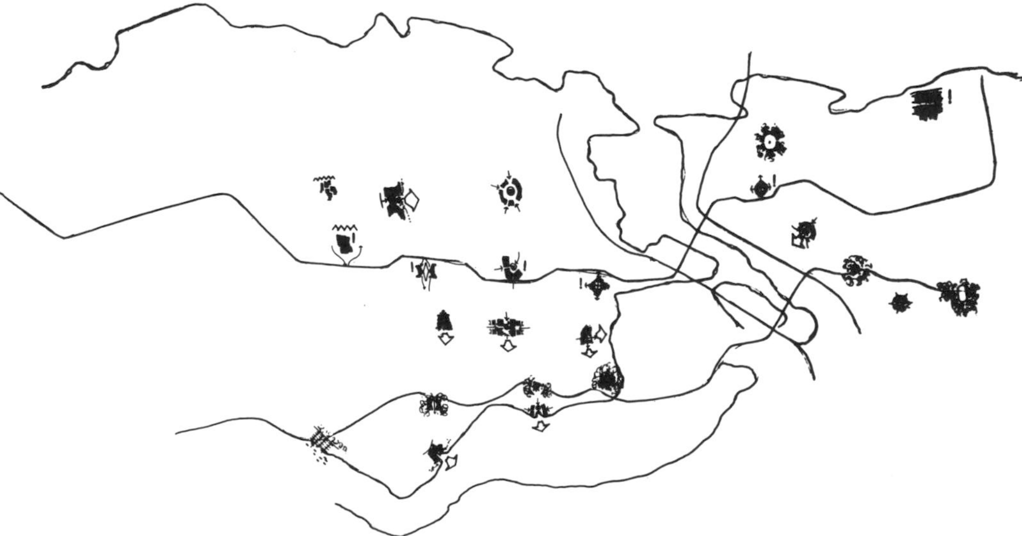

Figure 8.30 Centers.

Figure 8.31 Linkage of spatial elements with main highway.

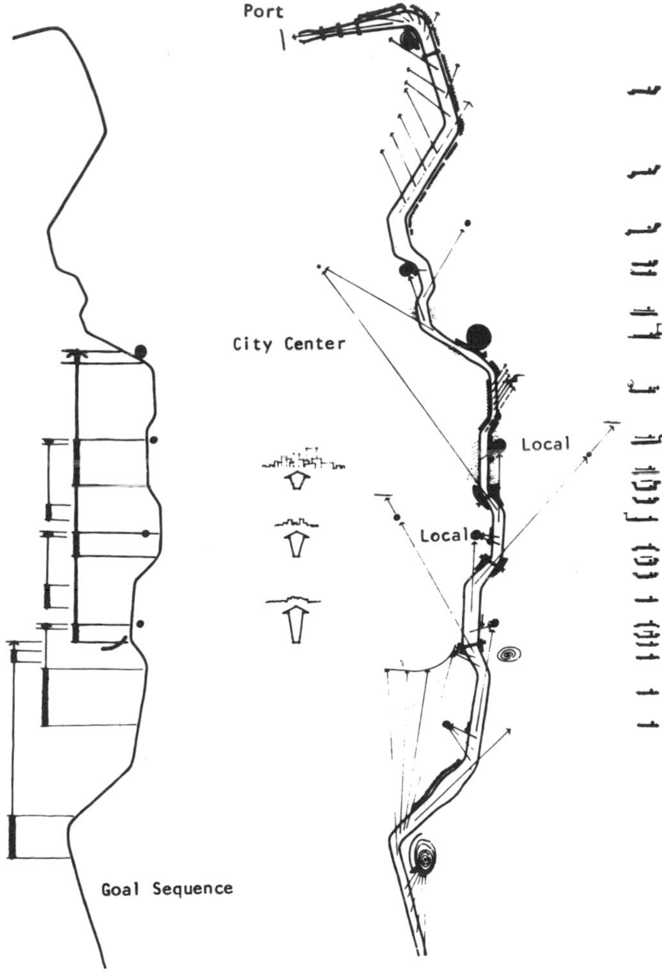

Figures 8.29-8.31 A sample sketch plan. Illustrations from a student sketch plan (G. Kurilko, M.I.T. student, 1962) made early in the project under different economic assumptions serve as an example to show how each urban element can contribute to the structuring of a new city. *Districts* characterized mostly by existing development and the local terrain are not designed to any systematic overall pattern, with the exception of the city center, which in this scheme straddled the Caroní. Local *centers* are patterned so that those nearer the downtown are more enclosed, dense, and formal—those at a distance are more open, low density, and informal. Centers by the rivers are linked with the water by views and by association with fountains and pools. *Landmarks* consisting of industrial plants, bridges, institutions, and the hills, are positioned on the terrain to maintain visible and symbolic connections between the various parts of the city. The final drawing illustrates how such spatial elements might be linked along *the main highway.* The eastern approach passes the steel mill, then swings rhythmically from left to right, taking in views of the Orinoco and Caroní to north and south while approaching on axis successively larger subcenters until the downtown itself appears. This plan is diagrammatic and takes no account of the evolution of the city, but it serves to illustrate how the components of a new city might be characterized, differentiated, and related to one another by a transportation system.

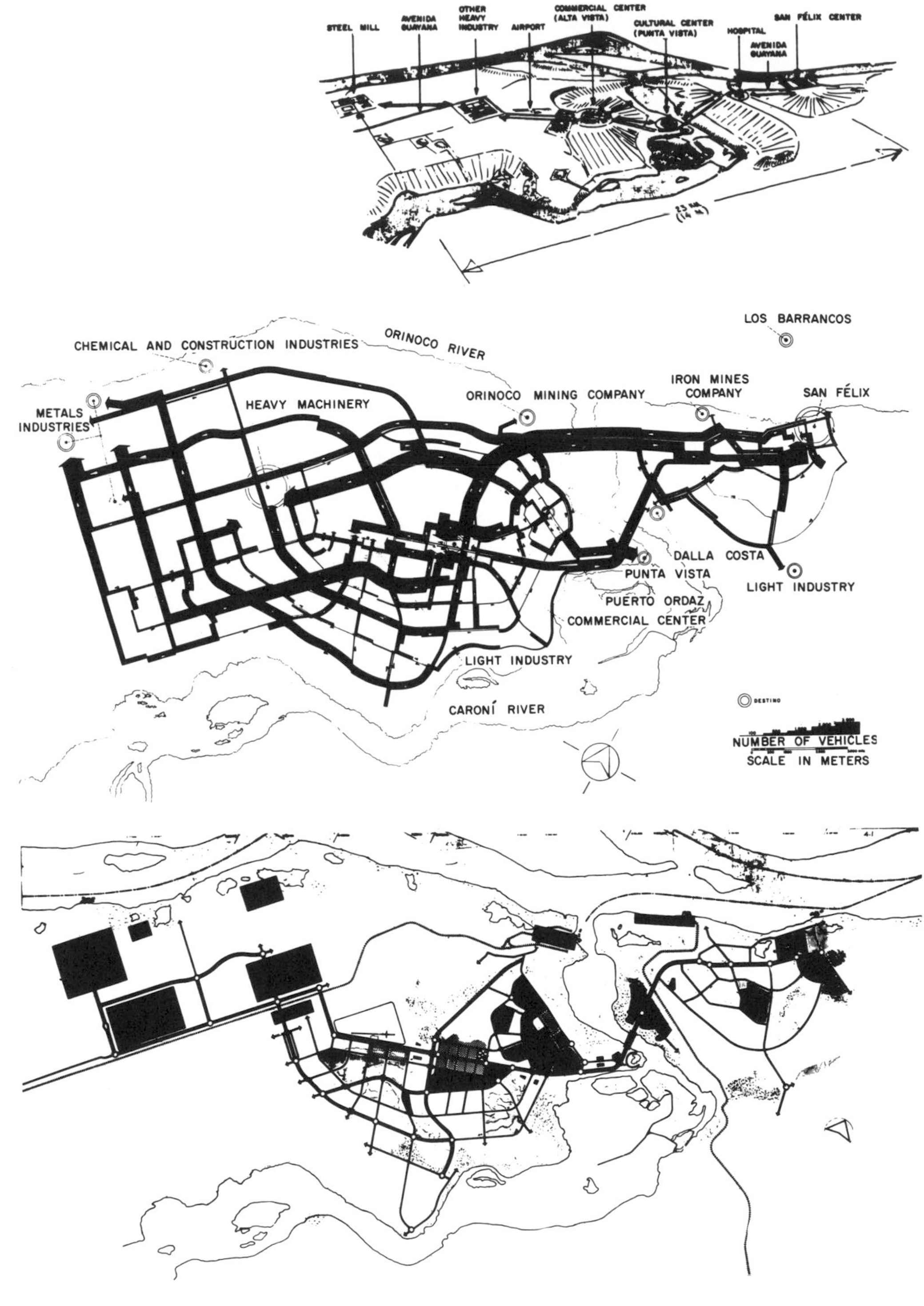
STEEL MILL
AVENIDA GUAYANA
OTHER HEAVY INDUSTRY
AIRPORT
COMMERCIAL CENTER (ALTA VISTA)
CULTURAL CENTER (PUNTA VISTA)
HOSPITAL
AVENIDA GUAYANA
SAN FÉLIX CENTER
LOS BARRANCOS
CHEMICAL AND CONSTRUCTION INDUSTRIES
ORINOCO RIVER
METALS INDUSTRIES
HEAVY MACHINERY
ORINOCO MINING COMPANY
IRON MINES COMPANY
SAN FÉLIX
DALLA COSTA
PUNTA VISTA
LIGHT INDUSTRY
PUERTO ORDAZ
COMMERCIAL CENTER
LIGHT INDUSTRY
CARONÍ RIVER
DESTINO
NUMBER OF VEHICLES
SCALE IN METERS

Figure 8.32 The simplified concept for the city was the intervisibility of the major centers, the steel mill, heavy industrial complex, the commercial center (Alta Vista), the cultural center (Punta Vista), the hospital and San Félix.

Figure 8.33 Evolution of transportation plans. The preliminary 1980 transportation plan was an example of poor topological and positional structuring. A modified 1980 plan brought more topological coherence to the system, but still the Avenida Guayana faded out to the west of Alta Vista, and the gentle curves of the freeway system would create positional difficulties. A final revised 1970 plan (figure 8.34) maintained the continuity of the Avenida Guayana and developed more of a topological grid system for the southwestern development of the city. Even in this plan, however, it is not clear what its associational structure would be like or where views would be experienced, for a plan diagram contains insufficient information by which to evaluate the structure of a system.

Figure 8.34 Land use and transportation plan, 1970. Land uses: industry and ports (black); commerce (crosshatching); residential, high density (black), medium and low density (gray).

(figures 9.10, 9.11). However, continuity of the secondary street system and linkages between Avenida Guayana and the street system will be more difficult.

Directional Consistency

More positional consistency of directions and clear directional changes would greatly improve the structure of this system. If this were not feasible, the preservation of views and the creation of new ones by road location would maintain a general sense of position. More consistent sequences of connections would also aid the city's topological structure.

Differentiation and Association

As it becomes more complex and repetitive, the road system will need more systematic differentiation and patterning both vertically in a hierarchical system and horizontally between roads of similar type (Appleyard 1965; 1968). Without such patterning, associational orientation and local identity will become increasingly difficult.

Once the decisions to locate the industrial, business, administrative, and cultural centers were made, it would be possible to differentiate and relate them and the community centers by function, social pattern, and physical character. This is the least-used method of structuring cities, mostly because land-use and transportation plans contain no vocabulary for physical differentiation.

Maps and Signs

Public maps and coordinated sign systems could enable inhabitants to structure the city in any or all three of the ways, but those who publish and design maps seldom acknowledge plural conceptions of cities. It would be desirable to develop and combine three mapping styles: one simplified topologically (like the famous London underground maps), one positionally accurate (like most maps), and one graphically portraying physical, functional, and social character.[5]

9 CHANGE

Planners and the Future

One quality that distinguishes Ciudad Guayana from many other cities is its rapid rate of change. The simplest aspect of this change is the city's actual and projected rate of population growth. The quoted rate of immigration at the time of the interviews was 1,000 people per month. From approximately 30,000 in 1961, the population had already risen to 70,000 in 1964. The most reliable economic projection at that time forecast a population of 250,000 by 1970 and 600,000 by 1980. Although these figures seem to have been overinflated, between 1960 and 1970 the city nevertheless had a startling 13 percent annual growth rate, and in 1973 the population reported was 169,000. The population is not likely to reach 600,000 by 1980, but a current program to triple the output of the steel mill will encourage continued rapid growth.

The projections of growth were set by the target figures for the industry of Ciudad Guayana, which had to meet its quota of the gross national product by 1980. The planning agency was therefore actively concerned with population increase (especially skilled professionals and technicians) and physical growth. It was also concerned with qualitative change, that is, the urbanization and acculturation of a poorly educated population of mostly rural origin. Both quantitative and qualitative changes were to be carried out simultaneously.

As one of the agents of change, the urban planning group in the CVG visualized the city in the context of future projections. The future fluctuated in and out of focus as economic projections were changed and modified, and as attention shifted between long- and short-range needs. Since there were few records of the existing environment, the city's future sometimes seemed more real than its present. In the first year of operation, the urban design group concentrated on immediate short-range problems, but as the economists began to make predictions about future population size and composition, the future image of the city began to be clarified. When the transportation planners took these figures and ran alternative models for middle- and long-range plans, the layout of the future city came into such clear focus that detailed street patterns for

1980 were worked out (figure 8.34), although the transition between the present and the future was still unclear. Later, when the transportation models stopped running and the uncertainties of the long-range plan became clearer, current pressures began to reassert themselves, and the planning group's attention returned to the immediate future and to development strategy.

The effect of these future images on locational decisions was profound. Take the location of the city center (figure 9.1). Before the CVG took over the planning of Ciudad Guayana, another agency, the Departamento Nacional de Urbanismo had located the center on the eastern ridge toward San Félix. The departamento had no reliable transportation projections and had predicted that the city would grow to only about 150,000 people. As the Joint Center economists began to raise population projections to as much as 600,000 by 1980, and as industrial linkages and transportation factors were established, the future center was moved westward to the Caroní River on the Punta Vista Peninsula. When transportation simulations began to show the points of highest accessibility potential moving steadily through time toward the steel mill, the hypothetical center was again moved, to the Alta Vista site. With the transportation model showing the highest 1980 potential points very close to the steel mill, the Alta Vista site looked like a good middle-range compromise. As we shall see, however, this location was inconceivable to the existing population.

Figure 9.1 The moving center. In 1961, a center had been designed on the San Félix ridge (1). By the end of 1961, it had been moved to the Caroní Crossing (2), where it stayed on the Punta Vista site (3) until a "great debate" in 1963 moved it to the Alta Vista site (4). The far western site (5) was considered at this time but rejected. Finally the center of Puerto Ordaz (6), on Orinoco Mining Company property, became a growing competitor for the center.

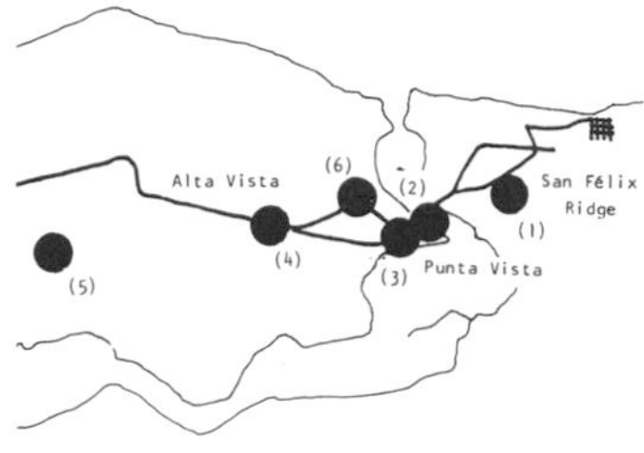

Perceptions of Change

We asked our respondents how they would describe the changes that had taken place both in the city and in their own residential areas. Physical, social, and functional changes were described mostly in quantitative terms, though many noted qualitative improvements. As with the value responses, they emphasized changes in respect to specific facilities.

In table 9.1 the responses to several questions on city change are collected in order to follow the pattern of perceived change through past, recent, and on to expected future change. This pattern is compared with the responses to desired change.

Observed Change

The responses to change over the immediate and more distant past varied very little in the rankings (r_s = .96). As the inhabitants saw it, change had been going on in the same style with the same priorities for several years. The most frequent responses concerned quantitative increases in all fields: more people, more buildings, more construction, more activities, and more shops. These responses did not distinguish between the spread and intensification of development, although both were taking place, but they showed a very clear perception of the city's increasing complexity.

Population growth was the most frequently noted phenomenon (130 and 156 percent). Newcomers were to be found everywhere in the city and probably were seen as competitors for the limited number of jobs available. Increased population, although expected to continue into the future, was not seen as a high-priority need (desired change, 8 percent). Changes in the infrastructure were the most commonly recalled physical changes (120 and 151 percent). The most apparent changes at the time of the interviews, the opening of the new bridge and the diversion of traffic for a new drainage system in Castillito, may well have influenced the responses. Improvements in infrastructure had been long awaited. Only in 1961 did San Félix get paved streets, and the road through El Roble was paved only a few months before the interviews.

It is interesting to compare the perception of district functions described in chapter 4 with those that were seen as changing. While commerce was the most salient activity of the settlements, it was not seen as the dominant activity in change. Despite the invisibility of new housing areas, awareness of new housing was relatively higher (100 percent). Housing was under construction in every settlement, whereas most commercial changes were small in scale.

The relatively small attention given to changes in industry (17 and 26 percent) was remarkable since industry was the primary cause of change in Ciudad Guayana. Industrial construction was slow at the time, but also industrial facilities were outside the city and less noticeable to the inhabitants.

Few respondents noted changes in the physical quality of the environment. San Félix, El Roble, and Castillito were still predominantly indigenous settlements, and the planned parts of the city were, with the exception of Puerto Ordaz, still in the background of development. Some respondents did mention the improvement of indigenous areas, however. The increasing numbers of shops, improved construction, and the glazing of shop fronts in Castillito stimulated comments that this rancho settlement was "in formation" or "in transformation," on the way to becoming a settled and stable community.

The trend from indigenous to planned development brought about a hardening and articulation of the environment from the soft forms of *bajareque* huts and mud paths to the sharp-edged, hard surfaces of concrete blocks, glass, and curbed streets. Clarity replaced ambiguity, and the scale of the environment increased. For instance, the road channel and sidewalk widths of the newer housing areas in Ciudad Guayana conformed to the standard of North American subdivisions, with roads two and three times the width of streets in the barrios. In one new housing development, *two* sidewalks were constructed on *each* side of the main road in an area where walking to the nearest facility would be nearly impossible in tropical heat, a tribute to the influence of the "highest" engineering standards on the design of the city. Houses and other facilities were larger and more spacious; the common multipurpose building types of the indigenous settlements were supplanted in Puerto Ordaz by specific types of building for each particular function.

While the planners might have some qualifications about whether all the various transformations were improvements, the population expressed no criticism. Everything new was welcomed.

Most facilities received no special attention because they were new, for new buildings soon lost their surprise value in this flux (see chapter 5). In one or two cases there were, in fact, signs of a time lag in perception. Obsolete facilities like the old San Félix airport were still recalled, and some apartment buildings obscured by later development in Puerto Ordaz were still seen as outstanding. In general, however, our subjects were current with new developments in the city.

Desired and Predicted Change

In the initial phases of the project, there was concern that change might be too rapid for the inhabitants, but it turned out that the majority (79 percent) wanted the city to grow faster. There were no strong traditions to be broken, and most of the people were voluntary immigrants who had already made a radical change from their previous environments.

Although 97.8 percent of the sample considered the city was changing for the better, their desired changes were very different from those they expected, a strong indication of possible dissatisfaction in the future. Indeed, the rank order correlations between desired and expected change were insignificant ($r_s = .04$), as were those between desired and observed change ($r_s = .10$ and $.24$).

The most-desired facilities were better transportation and utilities services and more community and recreational facilities, followed by housing. Surprisingly, the need for more industry was not seen as a priority by the population, even though this was a primary objective of the planning effort. The people's goals were more immediate and short term—signs of another possible source of future conflict.

Predictions for the future correlated significantly ($r_s = .75$) with the changes observed over the previous years. In other words, predictions were based on past trends, and no surprises were expected. In their predictions of the future, population increase, although not desired, was seen as the most probable type of change, followed by changes in infrastructure (transportation and utilities). Few respondents expected that community services, industry, or recreational facilities would be among the major changes.

When predicting change, many became euphoric, using statements reminiscent of the newspaper headlines: "It will transform itself into a great city"; "It will be the most beautiful city in Venezuela." The elimination of unemployment and ranchos was also forecast. The planners will have to work hard to meet such high hopes.

Differences in Change Perception

Education and Residence Groups

Educational groups responded similarly to the questions on perceived and predicted change, with the exception of slight differences between college-educated and those without education ($r_s = .75, .76$). College-educated subjects emphasized housing, the infrastructure, and the economy as the major past changes, while the less educated pointed to the infrastructure, housing, and the population. The educated also placed more emphasis on administrative changes and recreational facilities. In predicting the future, the college-educated saw housing as the dominant element that would change; the less educated expected population to continue to be the most important.

The two elite residential groups, those from the Country Club and Campo Caroní, were the only ones who correlated less significantly with other groups, or with each other ($r_s = .72$). Again their emphasis was on housing as the major predicted change. Their attention to housing might be explained by their closer affiliation with the planning of physical development. Their greater attention to recreation was similar to their ideal city responses.

One other interesting set of differences between educational groups was the reason given for predicting the growth of the city in a certain direction. While the more educated accounted for their predictions by pointing to available land, the less educated predicted more from the evidence of present construction. This appeared to be one more instance of the concrete present orientation of the latter group and the future planning orientation of the middle class. Indeed, one lawyer from San Félix refused to describe the city as it was, preferring to describe it as it would be.

Age, Sex, and Familiarity

Rank correlations between age and sex groups were all high and significant (r_s's from .90 to .99), but correlations between the new migrants and other groups in predictions about change were less significant (r_s = .62 to .78). The newer migrants predicted new housing, recreational facilities, and beauty slightly more than other groups, who considered population as the most probable predicted change.

Perceived Structural Change

While most changes were incremental additions to the size of the city or gradual transformations of existing areas, structural changes produced radical and sometimes disruptive changes in the perception of the city. The most evident of these were shifts in the use and form of the existing road system as superior channels were opened to use. The kind of problem that may be encountered in the future is illustrated by two changes: one that occurred when an unpaved street system was selectively blacktopped, and another that occurred when part of the new Avenida Guayana was built.

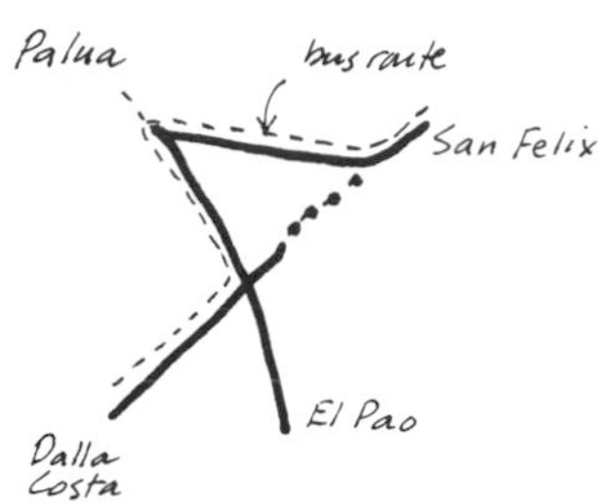

Figure 9.2

For several years the main route from San Félix to Dalla Costa traveled west to the entrance of Palúa (figure 9.2), where it negotiated a sharp bend and took the El Pao road as far as the intersection to Dalla Costa. A circuitous and improbable kind of route, it was nevertheless preferred by nearly all to the direct route through El Roble, which was filled with potholes. A few months before our interviews, the direct road was paved, and we can see in reproductions of the maps the kinds of problems that many people encountered in adjusting to the new situation.

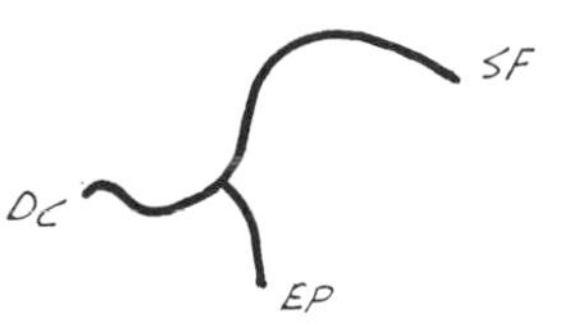

Figure 9.3

There were now two alternative routes, neither of which had clear superiority in both directions. From the west end the direct route was clearly the one to take. From the east end the indirect route was apparently preferable. The route was therefore drawn by some as in figure 9.3 and by others as in figure 9.4. Another group appears to have mixed both concepts, as well as omitting Palúa (figure 9.5). Several did not realize that the El Pao-Dalla Costa intersection, originally approached from the north, was now approached from the east. The ambiguity of the Palúa road (is it a loop or two access roads to Palúa?) further confounded the problem. Some were unable to assemble these concepts (figure 9.6); others remembered them at the last moment (figure 9.7). For many, the direct route had not yet been traversed. By one, it was left as an unconnected finger probing into the community (figure 9.8). Another achieved the connection but did not see it yet as a direct route (figure 9.9). Part of the problem in this instance was that

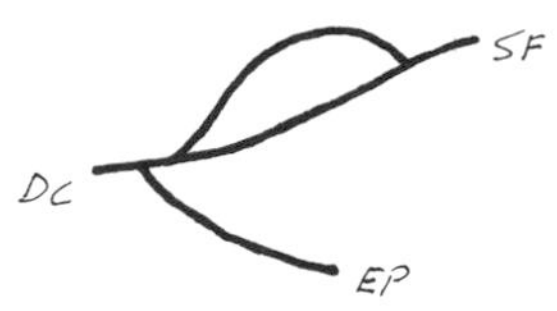

Figure 9.4

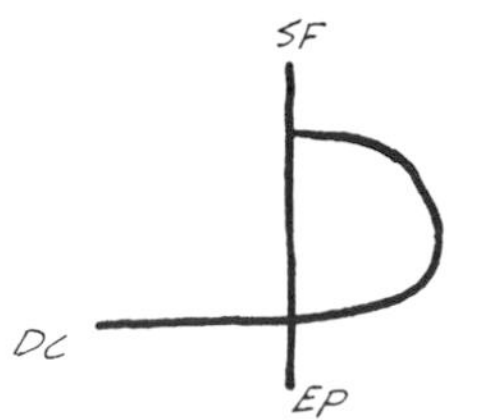

Figure 9.5

Figure 9.6

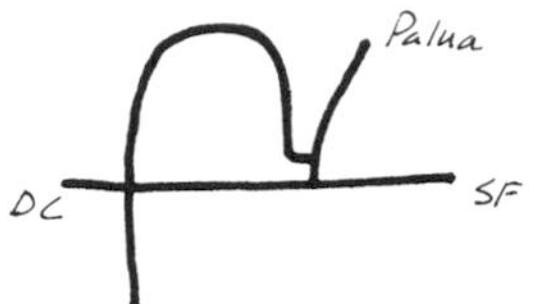

Figure 9.7

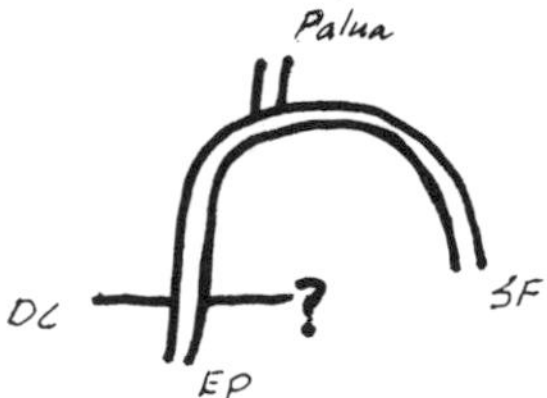

Figure 9.8

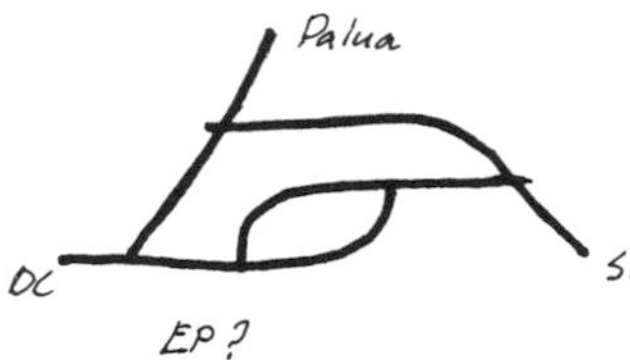

Figure 9.9

the bus, in fear of losing its clientele, continued along the old route, while other traffic began to take the direct route.

With through traffic running along two routes in the community where only one was needed, there was a split in use and attention between the two routes and confusion about which one to take. This reduced the clarity and therefore the identity of El Roble. If the route change had to be made, it should have been more definite.

The construction of the Caroní Bridge and Avenida Guayana provides a more radical case of transformation. While the new bridge dramatically reduced the distance between the two sides of the river, the planning group was also interested in leveling off growth in Puerto Ordaz and Castillito to spur the growth of the Alta Vista Center. Therefore, no link was made between the new road and Castillito.

Many of the interviews were taken during this period, and some of the inhabitants' bewilderment can be seen in their maps. Those interviewed before the bridge opened (figure 9.10) could not imagine where it would link up. Others, interviewed after it opened, assumed that there was a link to Castillito, a reasonable but false expectation. Since the trade of Castillito depended on this link, now turned into a cul-de-sac, the buses made an unscheduled stop on the expressway into the Caroní Park, and travelers walked through the park to pick up the other bus in Castillito. Soon a protest was organized that forced the planning agency to build a road connection. While the initial policy of stimulating westward growth was a reasonable one, the solution was too radical.

The obscure form of the new intersection to Castillito has meant a conceptual bypassing of the community. Interviews taken a year after the bridge opened (figure 9.11) showed both Castillito and Puerto Ordaz as appendages to the Avenida Guayana, with, in several instances, the link to Castillito not even shown. As with the expressway systems in the United States, the cognitive map of the city was transformed in one stroke. The older core of the city, through which all traffic once traveled, has been conceptually reduced and set aside as the cars travel on to other settlements.

These two instances of reaction to structural change, one ambiguous and the other radical, show how the population's expectations were baffled by the planners. To forecast future reactions, we asked our respondents to predict the future spatial pattern of the city.

Predicted Structural Change

The city is planned to grow on the western side of the Caroní toward the steel mill, and the published plans clearly show this

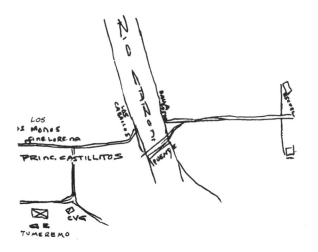

Figure 9.10 Before bridge.

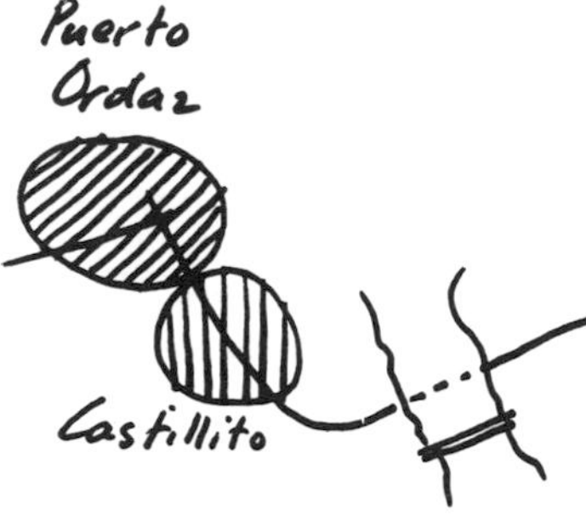

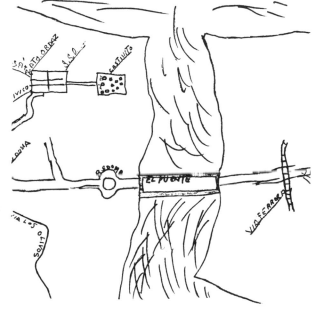

Figure 9.11 After bridge.

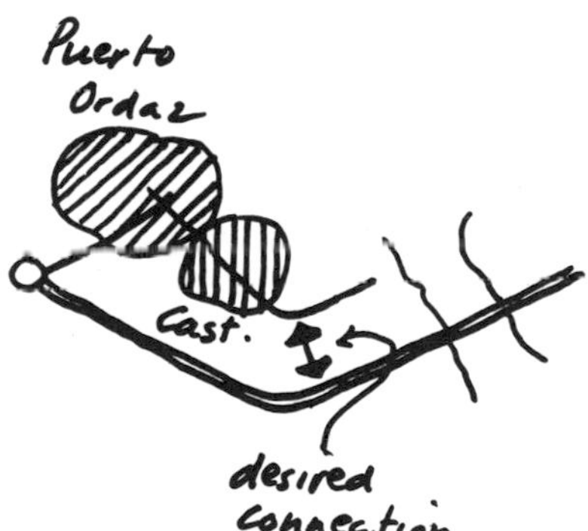

trend (figure 1.3). But at the time of the interviews, no plans had been published. Construction was taking place in all parts of the city, with nearly all the better-quality construction on the western side. The population at the time, however, was still weighted toward the eastern side of the Caroní. When the subjects were asked to predict the future direction of growth, the resulting responses were evenly distributed over all directions, with emphasis (12 to 15 percent each) on north and north-west, south and south-east. For those respondents who gave city zones, the expected areas of growth were also evenly distributed, with a slight emphasis on San Félix and El Roble. The easterly trend in these responses was probably due to the construction of the new subdivision in El Gallo, while the northwesterly trend was perhaps due to the new Banco Obrero housing in Puerto Ordaz.

When asked to give reasons for their predictions, a majority of the respondents pointed to the presence of current construction and housing. Theirs was a short-term future. It was hardly surprising, then, that people in Castillito were still constructing stores when the new bridge was about to cut off their livelihood.

When asked where the future center of the city would be located, responses were similarly distributed and were significantly different. Puerto Ordaz was the preferred location by all those on the west side, and San Félix was favored by those on the east. Even a number of Puerto Ordaz people saw San Félix as a future center, though few in Castillito placed their bets on San Félix. They were apparently too committed to westerly growth. Those in El Roble were split between Puerto Ordaz and San Félix. In contradiction to the planning group's intentions, even in the CVG engineers' camp a majority saw San Félix as the future center. The planned center at Alta Vista was not mentioned in any of the responses. This decision would therefore come as a surprise to the city's inhabitants, who did not recognize the economic importance of access to the western steel mill and future industry. Their view was quite understandable, since the earlier planners also thought the new center should be on the eastern side of the Caroní.

Without knowledge of future plans, visible construction is the only sign of future growth. Expectations depend on extrapolations from existing evidence, one of the clearest examples of the workings of personal inference on city perception. From these responses we get a strong indication of the conceptual inertia of the population when predicting specific locations, an inertia that the planners will have to counteract if they wish to gain support for their changes.

On the other hand, our sample showed amazing faith in the general growth of the city. Fifty-two percent of the group thought Ciudad Guayana might expand at some future date to merge with Ciudad Bolívar forty miles away!

Managing Change

Structural Stability and Ambiguity

The fluidity of the city's form brought with it some advantages. Residential areas were not as segregated as in other Venezuelan cities. There was a certain freedom of location and a chance to speculate where the city might grow. Planned continuance of the open structure might be a wise course. Some theories of economic development have argued that strategies of imbalance and disruption encourage participation, raise aspirations, and spur development (Hirschman 1958). Certainly, the responses of our sample showed that satisfaction was almost unanimous, and hope was high that the city was changing for the better. Yet some people probably suffer from such ambiguity. The older, upper-income groups showed less satisfaction with change. The shopkeepers of Castillito who protested the bypassing of their trade no doubt had ambivalent feelings about it. Perhaps there were hidden strains unrevealed by our interviews.[1] Daniel Lerner predicted dissatisfaction in an early working paper (1961) and argued for a counteracting stability through the creation of strongly identifiable neighborhoods (figure 9.12).

Figure 9.12

Figure 9.13

Much will depend on the policies that evolve for the social pattern. If degrees of social mix, however gross, are accepted as beneficial, then the maintenance of incongruity in the development pattern will be important. Housing areas for different incomes could purposely follow a heterogeneous and disorderly pattern (figure 9.13), as proposed in chapter 7. At the same time, a level of stability could be maintained by clear definition of the transportation and local structure of the city and clear information about future change (Porter 1969).

Programming the Information Structure

As the city grows and complexity increases, the inhabitant must correspondingly increase the scale of his conceptual units if he is to maintain conceptual control over the city. Interestingly, subject maps taken a year after the new Avenida Guayana had been opened treated the city in a simpler way than before and relied more on the larger districts, omitting several important buildings. This raises a significant issue: Which elements should survive each successive transformation of the

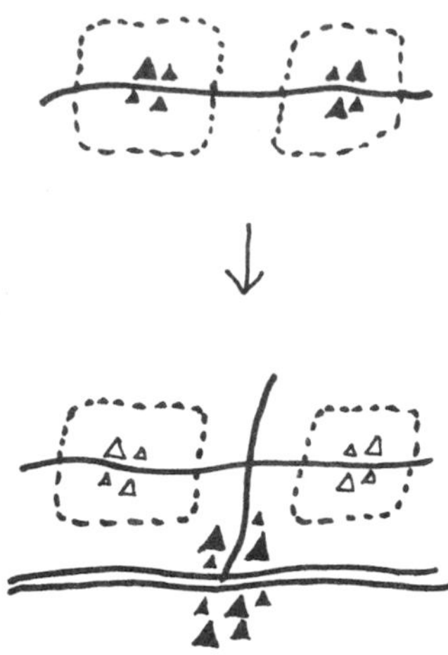

Figure 9.14

city? The communication of a changing functional and social pattern requires an awareness of the dynamics of change and the use of techniques for forecasting future patterns while recalling earlier ones. Cities are often confusing because successive changes are imposed without regard for existing patterns. Facilities and social areas could be programmed to enter and depart from public perception as their past, present, and future relevance changes over time (figure 9.14). For instance, after an initial emphasis on basic utilities and educational and medical facilities, cultural and recreational facilities might begin to play a prominent role throughout the city.

Participating in Change

Another factor in the matrix of satisfaction is the degree to which the population feels it is participating in change. The rancho and self-help housing areas allowed this to happen on a small scale. Those living in the areas of *Mejoramiento Progresivo* still had a relatively free hand in choosing and constructing their houses, and some community action programs did encourage participation in the construction of community facilities, electricity, and water lines. But these opportunities were limited. If this kind of participation is taken away from the inhabitants, feelings of powerlessness may well grow.

Change Information

Information plays a crucial role in maintaining stability during change. Radical change in the spatial structure without forewarning can bring about confusion, disorientation, anxiety, and protest. If changes have to be radical, as with the building of a new circulation system, efforts should at least be made to inform those affected before it takes place.

While the effects of radical change can be ameliorated by information, so can the more subtle effects of ambiguous and slow change. The most serious effects of ambiguous change occur when the change takes place in a person's neighborhood or to his own house, though changes to the structure of travel through the city can also provoke anxiety. Some of this anxiety might be relieved by making changes more definite and more explicitly signaling future change through direct signs and billboards and the physical structure of the environment.

An important role of urban planning and design, then, is not simply the programming of actual change but also the diffusion of information about future change, so that the population can be aware of changes that are taking place in the city and can predict future changes. Such programming will depend on the planner's awareness of the population's values, percep-

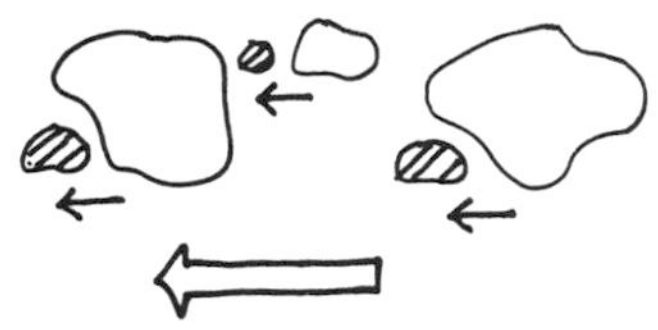

Figure 9.15

tions, and expectations, without which his plans will go astray.

Had the planners been more aware of expectations, for instance, they could have taken steps to prepare the population for westerly development. Since official plans do not get to many people, environmental means could be used to inform them of the future. For example, land for future development could be staked out with fences, plantings, or signs, or all new housing could be placed on the western side of each settlement to shift the citizens' perceptions toward westerly development (figure 9.15).[2]

A publicity office established on the site in 1965 began to disseminate information about plans for the city, and thought was given at that time to the development of an intelligible and useful signing system for various new projects. However, the efforts of this office were directed more toward visiting experts, industrial representatives, and developers than toward those living in the city already.

More planning information would allow people to predict more accurately where they might want to locate. If they understand the rationale of a plan, the inhabitants can also begin to understand the larger-scale implications of various actions. However, there is no point in allowing this to happen unless adequate controls are made to prevent excessive speculation. In the case of the Alta Vista site, public ignorance when the land was being acquired by the CVG allowed some saving of public money, since there was little speculation. Similar situations can occur in conservation areas.

Informing the Planners

Public misperceptions were partly caused by the planners' ignorance of the public mind. Change decisions were being made without proper knowledge of existing attitudes and perceptions. Planners, too, need to be informed.

Changing the Media

For urban planners and designers, one technical difficulty in the planning of change is the difficulty of representing future change in terms that are accurate and comprehensible. The maps describing the future of Ciudad Guayana were little more than snapshots of various stages in its growth (figures 8.33, 8.34). These plans indicated trends in a very inadequate way. Arrows on maps cannot describe the transformations, disruptions, movements, density, and quality of changes that take place in a developing city. Future images should try to predict the alternative consequences of plans (figure 9.16). Self-help rancho areas were planned so that they could be improved over time (figure 9.17), by self-renewal of the ranchos, by the addition of new high-density buildings, and by selective paving of streets and walkways. The social mix might also change in these areas. To describe such changes would require a fairly complex form of time-sequence diagraming or animated movies (figure 9.18). It may be objected that such detailed descriptions of planned and predicted change are unnecessary—but we now know that the influence of paper plans on actual development is considerable. Static and simplistic plans can ossify the development of cities. Once again the media are inadequate.

Figure 9.16 The planners played a risky game in predicting the future. This perspective of the new Alta Vista center predicts symmetrical development on either side of the Avenida Guayana, with buildings of uniform height and construction. Since the main commercial center was to be on the north (left) and lower-income housing on the south side (right), such an evolution would be unlikely.

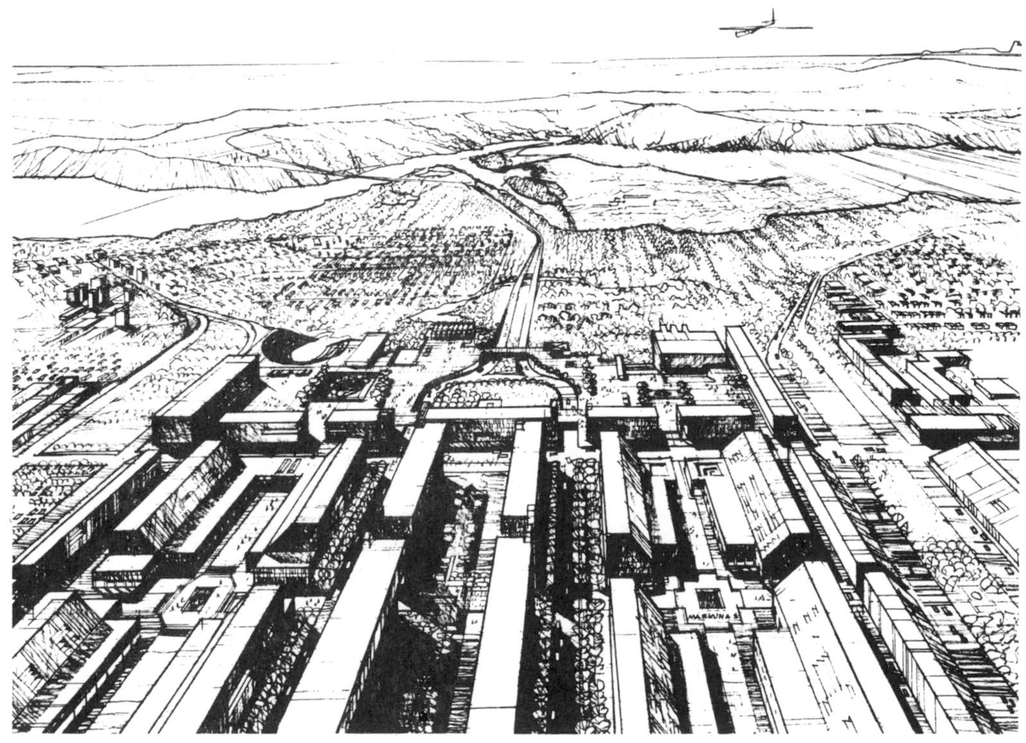

Figure 9.17 Evolution of low-income residential area.

Figure 9.18 An actual record of the development sequence, which shows new growth occurring in all parts of the city during each period of development.

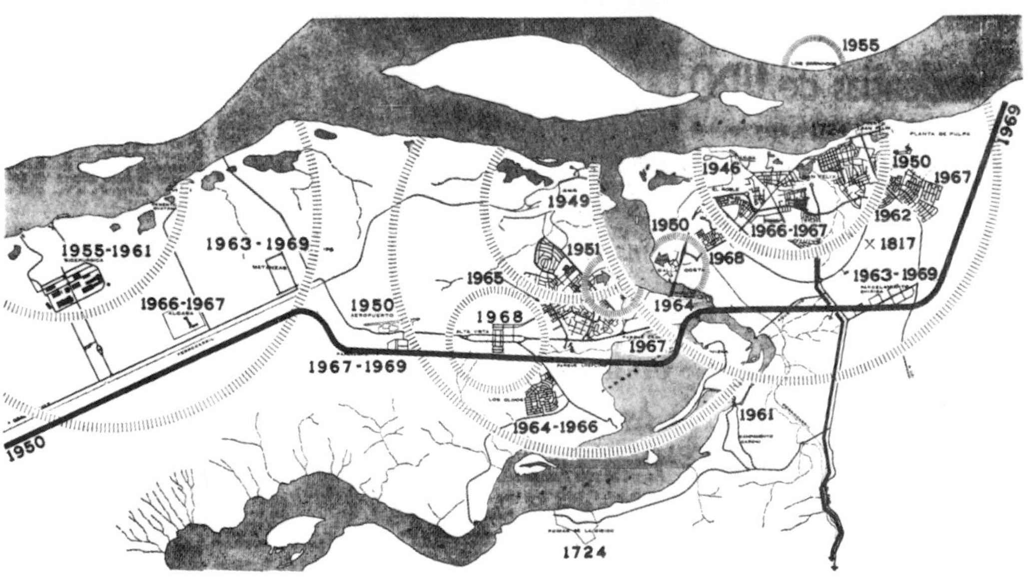

10 MANY CITIES IN ONE

The Personal City

The earlier chapters have described aspects of the inhabitants' perceptions of Ciudad Guayana. Now we shall try to summarize what this means for the nature of urban perception.

Spatial Distribution

A citizen's urban experience takes the form of four concentric zones: (1) an inner zone of personal territory, (2) a zone of regular use and travel, (3) a surrounding zone of visibility, and (4) the vicarious environment of indirect experience and inference. The three inner zones of direct experience are enriched, confused, and sometimes dominated by indirect information sources, the news media, maps, books, and social contacts; but when asked whether they had used, seen, or only heard of certain buildings in the city, respondents placed them in these zones quite easily. More recent studies suggest that people can also define what they see as their personal territory.[1]

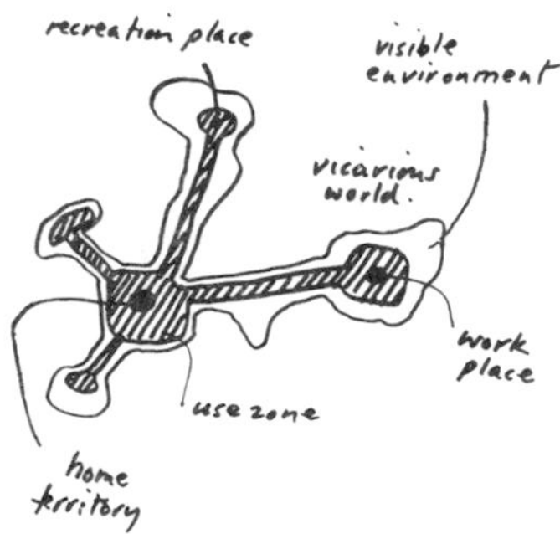

Figure 10.1 The spatial form of urban knowledge.

The typical inhabitant's perception of the city was home based, with "islands of knowledge" around shopping centers, job locations, and places of previous residence. The spatial form of urban knowledge was shaped either like a star or like a constellation of known areas (figure 10.1) connected by tentacles of known territory along the circulation system. Although most of the inhabitants of Ciudad Guayana knew the city extensively, the city they identified with was their local settlement.

Inhabitants of Ciudad Guayana knew rather thoroughly the forms, functions, and meanings of their own residential areas, but they depended more on visible cues to understand what was happening in other areas. In those areas they might seek facilities that were citywide in function, but would usually encounter buildings that were visible and imageable. As the inhabitant moved farther from his home base, he was more likely to depend on the worlds of vision and hearsay to tell what went on in the environment. But the uneven and incongruent pattern of environmental form, visibility, use, and significance breaks up any neat spatial model of urban knowledge.

Modes of Urban Perception

There appear to be three modes of urban perception. We shall call them the *operational, responsive*, and *inferential* modes, depending on the environment, mood, and role being played.

Operationally, the environment is seen as a setting for personal action and behavior. Indeed, we remember many parts of the city only by what we did when we were there, without any environmental image at all. More often elements of the setting are drawn into our concept of the city because they are relevant to personal travel or activities. Hence, seemingly inconsequential items like traffic islands, signs, entrances, and steps are distinctly remembered, because they are essential to the completion of regular tasks, trips, or operations or are visible along the paths of travel to or from the places of activity. The operational environment consists of elements such as goals (Appleyard, Lynch, and Myer 1964), avoidance objects or noxiants (Chein 1954), barriers, and territories (see figure 8.6). Children especially see and learn about the environment through such actions. The doorsteps of houses, cracks in the pavement, places to sit, house numbers, and playground equipment all figure in the foreground of their urban experience. A person's travel mode mediates his environmental perceptions, partly because it changes his travel tasks as he passes through the city.

At other times and in other places people are more responsive to the configuration of the environment. Imageable elements, whether they are brightly colored, uniquely shaped, or of any other distinctive quality, intrude on the operational search patterns of the traveler or catch the gazing eye of the passenger. In moments when tasks are less demanding, when the urban dweller is relaxing, or when he is actively sightseeing as a tourist or explorer in his own city, the environment is perceived more responsively for what it is.

Accepting what is there—the viewpoint of Taoism—is a mode of perception so unusual for Westerners that we must often actively disengage ourselves from the purposes and categories of operational perception before we can perceive the environment as it is (Huxley 1954). "Literal" perception, the term J. J. Gibson gives to this kind of perception, requires "a cautious attentive approach [trying] to jettison meaningful aspects" (Miller 1962).

Trees, sky, lights, billboards, prominent landmarks, and the landscape are frequently perceived in this way, as are colors, textures, sounds, smells, and tactile experiences—the sensuous materials of aesthetic perception (Santayana 1896). Also in this category are various environmental stresses such as noise, fumes, and glare.

Finally, perception is inferential and probabilistic in nature. As we grow up, we develop a generalizable coding system of environmental categories, concepts, and relationships: our personal urban model. When we encounter a new city, we match each new experience against our general expectations: "what is" against "what ought to be." Events are "placed"[2] (Tolman 1951), never-before-seen buildings are identified as belonging to a particular class of building, and functional and social patterns are inferred. Apparently significant places are noted, while those that seem trivial are screened out. Our direct and indirect sources of information are matched with each other. The environment is viewed as a communications medium, and we infer beyond the information given.

Perception in this sense can be seen more as a decision-making process of fitting categories, predicting probabilities, and forming and testing hypotheses (Bruner 1957b); and society has developed and elaborated verbal, numerical, and graphic symbol systems to support this model. The conservative nature of the model is probably essential for our mental stability. It has obvious limitations, however, since it makes difficult the absorption of new experiences and, if the environment is ambiguous or incongruous, can often be a source of error.[3]

As yet, we know rather little about environmental probabilities (Brunswick 1943), either in their objective form or in the common predictions of urban inhabitants. The wider our urban experience and the more conventional the structure of the city, the quicker and more accurate our acquisition of knowledge will be. The items of the environment that occur more frequently will be more accessible in our reference system and will stand a good chance of being identified. Paradoxically, however, the unfamiliar or unusual will also be noticed, just because they differ from our expectations.

Our discourse with the environment, which is, in any case, an intermittent one, is continually shifting between operational, responsive, and inferential modes, between subjective and objective, personal and environmental poles. The tensions between environmentally dominant responsive perceptions and person-dominant operational and inferential perceptions appear to be fundamental to our urban experience. We may travel through the city in an operational frame of mind, checking turns and intersections, and identifying landmarks; then a vista may catch our attention, and we pause to admire it before we note a building with children around it and categorize it as a school. Lowenthal (1967) describes how we compartmentalize urban experience in this way, traveling long distances on recreational trips in an operational frame of mind, ignoring the aesthetic quality—or squalor—of the trip, only to turn on the responsive mode when we arrive at a view of beautiful scenery. Even this response may be triggered more by the inferential perception that the scenery is designated a "park" or "beauty spot" than by pure response.

Structured and Raw Experience

To translate and combine the sources and modes of perception into a coherent and accurate network of knowledge is a formidable task. Indeed, urban knowledge is imperfectly organized and relatively inaccurate. In an effort to organize the flux of environmental experience, we frequently resort to methods that simplify, structure, and stabilize it. The purpose is to reduce cognitive strain. We learn in childhood to develop generalized concepts for classes of events and objects, so that new experiences can be fitted into an existing scheme of experience. In processing visual material, people use such devices as identifying regularities, grouping similar or contiguous events, and emphasizing separation, continuity, closure, parallelism, and symmetry.[4] In situations of changing stimulus, rhythms and cycles are identified (Johanssen 1950). Our limited processing capacities force us to develop strategies that reduce the number of items we have to recall (Miller 1956). The tendency is not entirely one of reduction. Nonexistent features are sometimes imported to make memory more coherent or meaningful. Hence, the process of remembering has been called "reconstructive" rather than "reproductive."[5] In their mental representations of large cities, people often have to schematize drastically to gain any overall comprehension of urban structure, extracting dominant reference points, districts, or even single lines of movement on which to hang their recollections.

Yet there exists no pure and complete processing of information; nowhere is there that clean entity sometimes implied by words like "schema" and "image." Our representations of a city are just as likely to be incremental and disjointed. Fragments of direct experience, more often the results of responsive perception, endure unchanged and unassimilated, while other events are organized into conceptual systems. Sometimes they possess special survival value and become sharpened in recall (Allport and Postman 1945), while others are screened out; but many linger on the edge of memory, half recalled, grasped only with effort. Sometimes these representations remain in conflict. A building passed on the journey to work may be given the wrong name because the name was mentioned in another context. We approach a familiar intersection from a new direction and fail to recognize it. Environmental errors like these occur all the time.

These errors are due partly to the difficulty of organizing a vast amount of discontinuous experience and partly to the fact that we find it unnecessary to organize all experience.[6] This messy characteristic of urban knowledge makes it especially difficult to investigate. At best we can hope only for glimpses of a person's store of recollections, seeking to detect regularities among them and realizing that every item will not fit perfectly into a schema.

Errors made are often harmless orientational mistakes, but occasionally a misunderstanding can mean the loss of an opportunity or the missing of a job and can cause a general feeling of inefficiency. Many people express feelings of guilt when unable to respond to questions about their city. Misinterpretations of the character of other population groups and of conditions in different parts of the city can encourage prejudice and inequity.

The structure of urban knowledge, therefore, is difficult to grasp and full of seemingly contradictory qualities. It can be both concrete yet abstract, schematic yet disjointed, conventional yet imaginative. As a mental counterpart of the environment, it contains elements and attributes that are classed in concepts and categories and structured in spatial systems and systems of meaning; yet, given the formlessness and complexity of most cities, it is also fragmentary, partial, and inaccurate. It is evolutionary in nature and adaptive to all kinds of demands. As anyone who has given interviews will know, the aspects of knowledge revealed will depend on the question.

Different Personal Cities

Given the complexity of learning about cities, it is hardly surprising that people live in different urban worlds. While we did not analyze in depth the urban knowledge of individuals, we did look at various group perceptions of the city. This section will summarize the findings, admittedly limited, of our study, drawing in other research where it seems to be relevant.

From the personal information asked of our respondents, we were able to learn about the general background and particular roles these groups were playing in Ciudad Guayana[7] (see appendix C). The group variables initially examined were education, income, place of residence, time of residence (temporal familiarity), physical mobility (spatial familiarity), age, age of arrival, sex, travel mode, occupation, and urban background. The effects of urban or rural background and age of arrival in the city did not show clear contrasts in the first analysis, so they were dropped.

Education and Social Class

Social class differences were measured by two indices: education and place of residence, which intercorrelated significantly ($r = .30$). Education also correlated with travel mode ($r = .50$), urban background ($r = .34$), and income ($r = .38$).

The population could be seen as comprising three main educational groups: those with some college education (mostly professionals and executives who lived either in the Country Club or in Puerto Ordaz), those with a secondary education (skilled workers, office employees, small businessmen, and students living in Puerto Ordaz, Castillito, El Roble, and San Félix), and those with some primary education or none at all (unskilled workers, service employees, and unemployed living in all parts of the city except Puerto Ordaz, the Country Club, or the Campo Caroní).

The following themes contrasted the perceptions of social groups. Those with primary and secondary education generally had a more complex and extensive knowledge of the city and a predilection for action and imagery rather than schematic perception, for topological rather than positional structuring. They were concerned more with discomforts than aspirations, urban rather than natural interests, satisfaction rather than dissatisfaction. Despite their higher levels of satisfaction, there was no evidence that they were any less achievement- or action-oriented than the middle classes. They ranked educational facilities as a lower priority than did the middle classes, but such facilities were still high on their lists. If attention to churches was any indication, tradition was relatively weak.

The more complex knowledge of the lower-income population was one of the surprising results of our interviews. This was partly due, no doubt, to the number or services they performed in the middle-class areas and to the fact that a large area of the city was lower income. They also displayed high interest in middle-income Puerto Ordaz. In contrast, the educated groups were more ignorant of the city and more status conscious, if confining their attention to their own facilities is evidence. Another survey reported little communication between the lower-income barrios and the middle-class *urbanizaciónes* (MacDonald 1969). Our evidence suggests that the lower groups were interested but the communication was one way—up the social scale.

The spatial location of the upper-income groups contributed to their ignorance, for they lived near industry, avoiding the need to travel through the rest of the city on their journey to work. That the journey to work influences knowledge is supported by the evidence that the skilled industrial workers, many of whom traveled the length of the city to work, achieved very high complexity scores.

The concreteness of lower-class thought was to affect several aspects of their knowledge. Their emphasis on the smaller, more easily grasped conceptual landmarks, their attention to the more vivid attributes of buildings (surfaces, movement, and signs), their greater dependence on visibility, and their enactive modes of structuring the city all pointed to their greater reliance on action and immediate perception than on conceptualization. Similar characteristics have been found in anthropological studies and studies of working-class cognitive styles in the United States (Riessman, Cohen, and Pearl 1964; Irelan 1966).

Because of their more conceptual modes, the highly educated apparently focused their attention on the "skeletal" aspects of buildings, and on political and economic significance more than on use or visibility. While all this enabled them to structure the city better, it may point to a diminished awareness of the immediate environment. Their relatively low complexity scores, their tendency to employ large-scale elements like districts, and their dependence on fewer cues in the identification of buildings suggest that their categorizing abilities were accompanied by some loss of attention to the detailed urban environment.[8]

The less educated attempted to cope with the city's complexity in one of two ways. Most structured it incrementally, by imaginary traveling along the paths of their experience; this made large-scale structuring of street patterns or general relationships difficult. Others, attempting to grasp the whole city, schematized it in a drastic way, drawing the road system as a straight line or referring to the major settlements by circles or names. Neither method of structuring was very accurate. Both were dominantly topological. Errors, reversals, faults, mislocations, and distortions from physical reality were prevalent. They seldom inferred beyond their immediate experience, clinging to the known and concrete world.

The educated were better able to surmount many of these structural problems through superior conceptualization and mapping ability. Their knowledge, though limited, was positionally and topologically more accurate. Schematizing was sufficient but not drastic; inference was more common, even if at times incorrect. Structural explanations were inferred through previous knowledge of urban patterns. Their personal system of urban probabilities appeared to be more developed.

Concreteness affected lower-class values as well as perceptions. Conceptually they tended to move away from immediate problems more than toward desirable ends. They were concerned with the improvement of sanitation and utility services, while the upper-income groups emphasized better education and recreational facilities. The three educational levels also differed in their evaluations of buildings. The least educated reacted in predominantly aesthetic terms, although their definition of beauty appeared to be very broad; those with secondary education emphasized instrumental criteria; and those with college education again reacted aesthetically but to different attributes. We might assume, then, that, with education and industrialization, instrumental values supplant traditional ones, only to be themselves replaced by more refined categories. If true, the implications for design would be far reaching.

Although the North American urban lower class is often characterized by a sense of meaninglessness and anomie (Irelan 1966), this did not typify the responses of the low-income Ciudad Guayana inhabitants. They expressed more satisfaction with the city than did the upper-income groups. Perhaps this is characteristic of a pioneering city where most of the population are voluntary immigrants (Turner 1968). It may also be attributed to the conceptually manageable size of the city. Nevertheless, feelings of powerlessness were reported in another study (Peattie 1968), suggesting the fragility of satisfaction.

The less educated showed a marked preference for urban-oriented rather than natural recreational facilities, as reflected in places they preferred to visit in the city. It seems that they valued gregariousness more than did the educated. Public welfare services and law enforcement agencies also figured more strongly in their perceptions of the city.

Present orientation was a characteristic of nearly all the population, in that few showed any knowledge of current plans, although one-third claimed to have seen some. A large majority were in favor of more rapid change. There was, therefore, a desire for future change but no way of conceiving the future. The result, especially for the less educated, was either a very limited projection from existing conditions or a set of vague generalities about a distant future. In any case, there were no signs of traditionalism, but then we purposely selected a young sample (appendix A).

The physical isolation of the upper-income groups signals a problem that is likely to become more severe as the city grows, for isolation can become easier if the higher-income areas become larger, more self-contained, and farther apart from the rest of the city. Their conceptual skills can also be seen as a possible liability, leading to diminished awareness and concern for the environment.

The less-educated groups suffered from other problems. The difficulties they experienced in putting the city together conceptually indicate the bewilderment they might increasingly experience as the city grows larger and more complicated. Their knowledge of the upper-income areas showed that they were aware of how other groups live; this can be an incentive to achievement if the paths of mobility are kept open, but it promises trouble if aspirations and expectations are frustrated.

Temporal Familiarity: Time of Residence

The newcomer essentially has a learning task—the process of acquiring an understanding of the city. Our results showed a more complex acquisition of knowledge than we had expected. It is possible to identify four phases in the newcomer's learning process: the expectations developed in the prearrival phase; the arrival phase, when preconceptions encounter first impressions; a search phase, when exploration and interest are high; and a settlement phase, when the migrant feels he knows the city and his life pattern becomes more routinized. The length of these phases undoubtedly varies, but respondents in a smaller interview were able to recall both their first impressions and the period after which they felt they knew the city.

Most of those living in the city were migrants, and more than one-half of our respondents had been in the city for less than five years. Of these, only one-third could be considered urbanized (see appendix B), and there was a very low correlation between time of residence (familiarity) and education ($r = .18$). The migrants came from all classes.

There were basically two kinds of migrant: (1) the skilled middle-class, urbanized, long-distance migrant, who came from other regions of Venezuela with employment already offered to him but usually with no local kin; and (2) the poorer immigrant from eastern Venezuela, who came in search of work, often with help from friends or kin. The main reason for migration was employment (MacDonald 1969), and the expectations of nearly all newcomers focused on employment and industry.

No migrant comes to the city without some environmental experience. Even the one who comes from a small village must carry a whole set of expectations and probabilities about this new city. He will be able to recognize indigenous buildings, roads, and the natural environment. Although a steel mill, technical school, or hospital may be strange to him, it would be naive to underestimate the diffusion of mass media even into the remotest village in Venezuela. He may also be familiar with the pattern of the Spanish colonial village, which would enable him to structure parts of the city like San Félix.

The urbanized immigrant will carry with him a far more complex repertoire of environmental probabilities. In an embryonic city like Ciudad Guayana, he may be surprised to find those elemental relationships that his metropolitan background has long ago elaborated and overlaid. He would expect to find paved streets, permanent houses, and segregated housing areas for different income groups; many of these phenomena did not yet exist in Ciudad Guayana.

Expectations may direct first impressions, but they never quite prepare the newcomer for the shock of arrival in a new city. In the arrival phase the events and places that attract the attention of the newcomer are often puzzling. Our newcomers seemed to look for what they expected—the industrial facilities of high economic significance. At the same time, their first impressions were strongly visual, and they noticed the unique features of the city. The two rivers and the new bridge crossing the Caroní, attracted particular attention. One newcomer, a North American girl, interviewed in a pretest, gave all her attention to the landscape—she had not seen tropical vegetation before—and only with difficulty could her interest be directed to the characteristics of the city itself. A North American engineer was struck by the "ranchos," a housing type that was new to his experience. In a similar way, migrants of another type noticed Puerto Ordaz, the new model city, as something unique. It could be that the gas stations, too, received much attention because they were new to the experience of many migrants who saw them as symbols of the affluent urban world to come.

Most of the new migrants already knew someone in the city before they arrived (MacDonald 1969), and a majority of the selected sample said they were shown around at first by friends and relatives. When this happens, the newcomer's information is preselected, of course, and he does not have to learn the city by himself. But it may be difficult for him to see through this preselected screen and understand what is going on until he himself has begun to search.

Even though newcomers were usually taken around, their knowledge did not entirely coincide with what most people thought newcomers should know or would find interesting. Either their guides were not showing them what they believed to be important for newcomers, or the newcomers were not remembering very well, or, most probably, the newcomers' facilities were invisible to them.

As soon as he is on his own, the newcomer really enters the search phase. Interest is high, and knowledge may be rapidly accumulated. Those respondents who had been in the city between six months and one year drew the most complex and detailed maps of any group. Suzanne Keller notes that newcomers to residential areas engage in a period of intensive neighboring in a similar way (1968). These early months are critical. There is evidence that the period of arrival and the age at which a person arrives affect his social contacts throughout his later life in the city (Tilly 1955). During the search period the migrant is making judgments about the city, critically comparing it with his previous residence, gaining impressions that may influence him to stay or leave.

As the migrant begins to understand the city, he gathers information from many sources, through his own explorations, by meeting and talking with others, and by reading the newspapers, listening to the radio, and studying public maps if they are available. The principal task of this period of search is to coordinate the information gained and to fit new information into an accumulating schema. The basic units of mental representation, the landmarks, focuses, streets, and districts are often identified piecemeal, and separate sources of information about the same unit have to be fitted together. A place name will crop up in conversation, and the listener will endeavor to match it with a place already seen, or he will look out for it on his next journey. The planners, for instance, in their field surveys spent a great deal of time identifying their position on the site from their maps. The correlation of perceptual information with knowledge of the city's functioning, social structure, and symbolism is another necessary form of matching. Information from two sources about the same place can and often did remain unintegrated, creating the illusion of two separate places instead of one.

The newcomer's ability to structure the city depended on his physical mobility, travel mode, and intellectual capabilities. The poorer migrant, earthbound, traveling by bus, and without the aid of maps or practice, experienced great difficulty in piecing Ciudad Guayana into an accurate spatial schema. The educated immigrant, often traveling to and from the city by plane, with access to maps, and more experienced in fitting complex environmental information into his own mental map, had a better chance. Schematics and inference further enabled him to master the difficult layout.

Of the small sample of newcomers, the majority could say at

what time they felt they actually knew the city. Many gave three months as the period. In the larger sample, interest continued to grow during the rest of the first year. We do not know their criteria for deciding when they knew the city, but we do know that they were quite often deluded into thinking their knowledge was accurate when it was not.

After settlement into a home, job, shops, and schools, flow patterns begin to stabilize into known paths, and knowledge becomes more firmly anchored and routine and less subject to frequent shifts and extensions. Interest is likely to diminish gradually as routine begins to take over. Places originally visited in search of employment, while looking for a house, or with helpful friends may never be visited again; the city becomes better known but is handled more economically.

After the pretest interviews, it was thought that attention would shift with familiarity from visible and formal attributes to those of social or functional significance. A foreign newcomer talked of the "mud houses and dirty streets" of San Félix, while an older inhabitant spoke of landmarks like "the church, the Consejo Municipal." As knowledge develops, significance deepens; social patterns, historic events, and functional meanings are interpreted through the visible environment. The trend is away from the powerful imagery of the earlier period. But the final correlations did not quite bear this out; the influence of all attributes increased, perhaps because the city was changing so rapidly that its pattern never stabilized. In such a context, the rules of expectation become highly developed, but new situations continually keep physical attributes in the forefront of recognition and recall.

In a stable city the inhabitant may begin to lose interest as he becomes more familiar with it. The newcomer's efforts to minimize surprise make surprise predictable. It takes a rare city to retain that interest. But Ciudad Guayana was changing so rapidly that the older inhabitants seemed to know less than the newer ones. This made for a stimulating environment and probably helped generate the enthusiasm we found in the evaluative responses. It also imposed strains that were evident among a few of the older inhabitants in our sample. Had we inquired among really old inhabitants, we might have found more evidence of this strain.

Age

Since new migrants and more familiar inhabitants were of all ages within the range we studied, there was a low correlation between age and familiarity ($r = .25$).

The teenage group interviewed were all over fourteen and

under twenty years old, and many were still in school. This group demonstrated a higher complexity of knowledge than the older groups. Since correlations between age and education were low ($r = .13$), this higher complexity was probably due either to their greater interest in the city or to their lack of experience in conceptualizing it economically. New to urban experiences and just beginning to encounter the wider world, they reacted like immigrants. They were more susceptible to the visible aspects of the city than other age groups were. They selected plazas, sports stadia, movie theaters, gas stations, and billboards as part of their urban world more than other age groups did.

The twenties to thirties group appeared to be more involved with work and family. Their knowledge of the city was less complex than that of the teenagers. They knew less of the functional pattern, but they were more aware of the forms of buildings and their significance. They paid less attention to schools and more to other facilities affecting family life, such as housing agencies, medical facilities, and parks.

The overthirties were more knowledgeable but followed a pattern similar to that of the middle group. They became interested in schools (probably through their children) and paid greater attention to medical facilities, banks, housing offices, hotels, and the military.

Selection of the more significant facilities by the older groups could be due merely to their selective interests or to their superior competence in penetrating the vagaries of form and visibility. This would support the contention that older people have learned the rules of urban perception more thoroughly than the younger ones. Their lower complexities, paradoxical at first glance, could suggest that their methods were more economical or that their interest had lowered.

Spatial Familiarity and Physical Mobility

The differences between "locals'" and "strangers'" perceptions of a neighborhood were significant. Locals knew their areas well and emphasized features that were locally visible or of local significance, while strangers focused on those parts visible to the outsider or of citywide significance. Locals concentrated more on spatial elements—buildings, districts—to structure a settlement, while strangers relied more on roads. Locals structured their areas more accurately; strangers distorted them.

However, physical mobility necessarily affected the level of spatial familiarity, so that strangers in some parts of the city—the center of San Félix, for instance—knew them almost as well as locals. The physically mobile possessed a more extensive knowledge of the city, though often it was more thinly spread. It happened in Ciudad Guayana that the mobile were not the upper-income groups but the steelworkers, a very different situation from the low mobility of Mexican Americans in Los Angeles, for example (Orleans 1967). Physical mobility appeared to account for many of the differences in perception between both social and occupational groups.

Sex

Sex differences in urban perception seemed to occur because of the contrast in tasks and use of the city. Males possessed a more detailed knowledge of the road system than their female counterparts, and they structured the city slightly more accurately. No pronounced differences in structuring style were discovered, however, although this had been expected.

Males were slightly more form oriented than females and recalled more kinds of facilities, with the exception of churches, supermarkets, and plazas. In evaluations of buildings males emphasized efficiency, location, activity, and size; females concentrated slightly more on beauty and color.

Travel Mode

Although automobile use correlated highly with educational level ($r = .50$), many of the differences between groups could be attributed more directly to travel mode than to cognitive or social differences.

Those who traveled by bus had gained a deep and complex knowledge of the city and used a wider range of attributes than other travel groups. However, they had great difficulty in piecing the city together, a fact that would not be surprising to anyone who traveled the slow and meandering bus system of Ciudad Guayana. Inspection of controlled samples where education was held constant showed that this difficulty was not attributable to lack of education.

Positioned at the other end of the spectrum, the car travelers had developed an ability to structure the street system and sketched more spatially developed maps. Skimming the city, they achieved thin, schematic, structurally coherent, and relatively more accurate mental representations of the road system. Given the speed, scope, and vision of car travel, this is plausible.

Selected Occupations

Occupational differences were analyzed only through the complexity scores and structural styles displayed in subject maps.

Occupational differences appeared to depend primarily on the way in which each group used the city, how mobile they were and where they went, and secondarily on social class and cognitive skill or style differences.

The maps of the more highly educated occupational groups, the business executives and the professionals, were characterized by relative impoverishment of detail, except for the professionals' attention to the road layouts. The business executives tended to produce spatial element maps of a relatively primitive kind. The conclusion is that they were unfamiliar with the city, in many cases living in the isolated Country Club and traveling outside the city to the steel mill or Orinoco Mining plant. The professionals showed more involvement than the business executives.

The skilled workers produced highly complex maps, well developed and of a dominantly sequential character, which fitted with their necessary travel through the city. Office workers and students also produced complex maps. Housewives drew simple primitive chain-type or in some cases scatter maps that demonstrated their strong local orientation. Those in personal services and small businessmen produced similar map types.

The Differentiating Variables

Since there were some significant intercorrelations in the sample, it is difficult to assert with assurance which aspects of individual characteristics were exerting an influence on perception. We may, however, suggest some hypotheses. There appear to be four fundamental reasons why urban perception differs among population types: (1) varying social and environmental needs and dispositions; (2) varying familiarity with the environment; (3) differing cognitive skills, styles, and experience; and (4) the employment of differing media in the processing of environmental information.

Needs and Dispositions

Environmental or social needs and dispositions play a directive role in urban attention patterns. They can be physiological, social, or psychological and may be motivated by necessity, desire, or avoidance. For instance, the necessity of physical survival can direct the search for work, food, shelter, or essential welfare services. Moments of danger may require attention to a traffic circle or a directional sign. Desires for comfort and physical pleasure draw the city dweller to places of agreeable climate, recreation, or entertainment; discomforts may draw to his attention inadequate sanitation systems, traffic congestion, or poor roads. Paradoxically, the places and events that he remembers can be those that give him either the most or the least satisfaction.

Social dispositions strongly color urban perceptions, whether they are drives for social identity, achievement, or status; affiliational needs; or feelings of prejudice, exclusiveness, or powerlessness. The neighborhoods, facilities, attributes, and symbols of other social groups can either draw an outsider's attention or be taboo. An inhabitant's knowledge may be limited to the domain occupied by his own social group, because of group gregariousness or powerlessness in the face of outside hostility. In other cases, the lack of barriers to social and physical mobility may permit a more expansive and dominant disposition toward the city, reflected in wider urban knowledge.

The contrasting psychological motives of curiosity and security seeking may be the reasons some people seek novel and interesting experiences, developing complex and sometimes chaotic representations of the city, while others are content to identify the routine and simple.[9] Certain population groups are likely to be more curious than others. Historically, new migrants have exhibited more adventurous characteristics than those who stayed in their native city.

At a more specific level the life-style and living pattern of each individual will determine much of his attention to facilities and qualities of the city. These attention patterns differ between educational, occupational, age, familiarity, travel, and other groups. A more specific characterization of group life-styles and dispositions will be needed before we can understand the reasons some of the knowledge is acquired.

Familiarity with Environment

One could postulate a classical model of knowledge that increases with familiarity. On first encounter, the physical form of the city would dominate a person's perception, but with repetition its social and functional aspects should take on more importance. With further experience, we should expect an increasing scope, complexity, and depth to a person's environmental knowledge and an increasing awareness of changes in the city's structure. We might also expect loss of the broad perspective and a greater obsession with detail as the city becomes more familiar. As described already, this model of increasing familiarity becomes complicated by other factors, such as previous experience, expectation, and curiosity, which create an early period of intensive search, followed by settlement into a regular routine.

Whether he is a tourist, immigrant, or growing child, the

newcomer belongs to the population group that is perhaps most dependent on the physical environment for perception and knowledge of the city. This may be an extremely significant piece of information for the environmental designer, since it means that this group may be his most dependent and responsive client.

There is no single pattern of migration into cities. In studies of migration to U.S. cities, higher-ranking migrants, who usually come under auspices of work, have managed to accommodate more easily to the new city than low-income migrants, whose occupational life was often completely disrupted (Tilly 1955). A similar pattern was found in Ciudad Guayana (MacDonald 1969), but there seem to be several factors other than job change that affect assimilation of the new city: the migrant's previous urban experience, his information media, and his physical mobility within the city.

Spatial familiarity with the city differentiates a person's perceptions of local and unfamiliar parts of the city. If a citizen travels little, his knowledge should be restricted but intensive; if he travels extensively, it may be broad though superficial. If his travel patterns change, he should learn more of the city than if they remain routine. Spatial familiarity appears to depend on physical mobility and, in turn, on mode of travel, age, income level, and personal characteristics.

Cognitive Abilities or Style

An individual's cognitive abilities or style affect the manner in which he processes encountered environmental information. These abilities depend partly on training and partly on background and character. In developmental psychology and anthropology, considerable attention has been paid to the differences between undeveloped and highly developed cognitive views of the world. It may be useful to paraphrase some of this research here and compare it with educational group contrasts in Ciudad Guayana.

In many preeducated societies, syncretic thinking (the merging of perception, affect, action, and thought) is more common than differentiation and organization into abstract conceptual systems (Werner 1948; Redfield 1953). Perceived objects, for instance, become so embedded in concrete situations that articulation and structuring into larger entities is carried out only with reluctance. Many preeducated peoples possess no general image of their localities, only a multitude of spatial particularities, or words for the various parts. For the natives of West Australia "each twist and turn of a river has a name, but the language does not permit of a single inclusive name for the whole river" (Cassirer 1944). In graphic representations of objects in the environment, chain-type drawings are common. A drawing of a cube, for instance, will be shown as five separate squares, each side drawn separately, so that, seen under different circumstances, the cube may not appear as a single entity. The maps of the less educated in our sample displayed a similar disorientation.

Hierarchical organization or ordering in terms of essential and nonessential elements is also much less common. In primitive narration, a series of events must be recounted in exactly the order they were experienced if the tale is not to be lost, and each event is accorded equal importance. In many primitive societies, spatial orientation depends on the sequential continuum of actions and images. But in others, where paths are treated as self-contained entities and villages are unstructured aggregates, there is no concept of sequential relationships (Lee 1959). Our maps also demonstrated both sequential and spatial types.

Primitive structuring, according to Heinz Werner (1948), is achieved by rigidly learned sequences, arbitrary grouping, or perceptual, enactive, or affective similarities. These methods are similar to the "heaps" and "complexes" with which the child structures the world before he develops superordinate concepts and consistent rules of categorization (Vygotsky 1962). More pertinent even than these analogies are the three stages in the child's conception of space (Piaget and Inhelder 1967): the topological, projective, and Euclidean (see chapter 8).

With better abstracting abilities, the educated individual becomes less dependent on the dominance of the immediate situation and can begin to infer, extending his action and thought beyond the visible field. His awareness of motivation and choice increases, as does his planning behavior, which takes into account the more objective characteristics of things and events. He achieves greater conceptual flexibility, and he increases his ability to roam around his spatial concept of the city.

Differences in cognitive skills and styles have been the subject of extensive research in the fields of cognition, perception, and learning in more civilized countries. Of interest here is the work on conceptual styles and their relation to social setting and primary group structure developed by anthropologist Rosalie Cohen (1969). Cohen maintains that conceptual styles are composites of two cognitive skills: mode of abstraction and field articulation. They are rule sets for the selection and organization of sense data. Dr. Cohen has identified two definite types of cognitive style: analytic and relational. The analytic mode, more common among middle- and upper-class Americans, is stimulus centered, and parts specific, abstracting salient information from a situation in which the parts or attributes have meaning in themselves. The relational mode is self-centered, and only the global aspects of the stimulus have meaning to its users. This mode is more common among those who are reared in shared-function families and social groups—usually low-income. Hence, such people perform poorly on the typically analytic-oriented intelligence tests. These descriptions also relate to work by Levy (1968), summarizing social class differences in consumer behavior and pointing out the difficulties lower-class women have in planning how to shop in the city.

Dr. Cohen points out that relational thinking is also characteristic of creative artists and musicians.[10] Some of these characteristics are very evident in the urban perceptions of ten "writers" reported on by John Gittins (1969), when he took them, together with a group of contrasting "scientists," through Worcester, Massachusetts. The writers' perceptions were more sense filled, incremental, concrete, and complex, and their acquisition of knowledge was a more complex intuitive process. The scientists, who we may assume were more analytic, were more schematic, simple, and abstract in their perceptions, with a learning process characterized by single insightful moments of understanding followed by periods of boredom.

While social background is, no doubt, a primary influence on conceptual style, personality differences, the information media to which they are exposed, and the form of the cities in which people have grown up may be important contributing factors. For instance, gridiron cities may habituate their citizens to the use of numerical systems and devalue the importance of imagery.

Although greater analytic abilities allow an inhabitant to understand the structure of a city more intelligently, he may at the same time lose that immediate awareness of the concrete environment which others experience. That children experience eidetic imagery more frequently than adults supports this contention. The questions that Cohen raises are extremely important for this kind of research and for the planning of cities. While she criticizes the current educational system for neglecting relational thinkers, environmental research runs the risk of discovering only analytical styles. Cities, too, may be planned that neglect the needs and styles of certain types of thinkers.

Media

An array of media, direct and indirect, stands between man and city. Unmediated experience of the environment, dominant in the preindustrialized world, is now quite rare. The most personal and direct media are a man's various forms of apparel and modes of travel; but friends, meetings, maps, movies, radio, television, and newspapers indirectly convey to him a good part of his urban information. We do not know how much.

Modes of travel can cause wide variations in the form and extent of a person's comprehension of the city. The man on foot is action oriented and has free vision but is limited in the scope of his travel; the bus rider is divorced from action, restricted to a side view, and confined to narrow bands of travel; the automobile traveler, more confined in action and vision than the pedestrian, can travel nearly everywhere. These differences did influence each person's mode of representing the city, the extent of his knowledge, and the accuracy of his spatial perception.

The use of maps, aerial photographs, and other media that directly facilitate objective understanding of the spatial city is confined mostly to professionals, although public maps are available in most cities to help orientation. As abstract graphic symbols of reality, maps must be learned and matched with direct experience. They encourage more abstract mental representations of the city and extend knowledge over wider areas, but they are difficult to remember, requiring constant referral. In Ciudad Guayana, there existed no public map, so the influence of specific maps on knowledge was confined to the planners and builders.

Social communications media, the kind and number of people a person meets and their usual topics of conversation, may affect his urban knowledge. A storekeeper, for instance, may spend more time discussing topical city news and directions to various parts of the city than a factory worker. Anyone connected with the physical construction or planning of the city will glean more information about it than others. Many low-income migrants coming to Ciudad Guayana learned about the city through friends or relatives. Most of this knowledge would probably come through verbal (names, building types, and descriptions) rather than visual or spatial information. We did not investigate these social influences in any detail.

Newspapers, radio, and television are likely to keep a citizen more alert to current events and new construction in the city. Even so, it is difficult to gain a clear idea of an urban pattern from a radio or a television program, since they do not usually seek to present information in spatial form. The influence of media on our comprehension of the spatial city has, no doubt, been profound (McLuhan 1965). An appreciation of a world beyond direct experience may have expanded overall urban knowledge while reducing the relative role of direct experience.

The Tenuous Connections between Personal Cities

People in the same city live in different territories, differ in their attention patterns, and have different ways of putting the city together and different hierarchies of significance. There is, therefore, no common image of a large city. Indeed, the anthropologist Lévi-Strauss found that even the inhabitants of small tribal settlements described their settlement in different ways.

> They described, for the most part, a circular village plan in which the two moieties were separated by an imaginary diameter running northwest and southeast. However, several informants vigorously denied that arrangement and outlined another, in which the lodges of the moiety chiefs were in the center rather than on the periphery. (1963, p. 129)

In Ciudad Guayana only the steel mill, the rivers, and the main settlements were mentioned by more than 50 percent of our respondents. And yet few people seem to realize that others see the same city differently. Why is this? There seem to be two reasons. First, people spend most of their lives meeting people like themselves, whether they are neighbors in locally oriented cultures or "metropolites" with similar occupational or cultural interests. Within these groups overlapping personal territories, common sources of information, common attention patterns, similar styles of structuring, and abilities at interpretation reinforce the view that all people see alike.

But there is another reason. We have a common, though minimum, vocabulary of communication with which to describe the urban environment. Place names, street names, and building numbers provide a spatially usable address system, which in most cities is recorded on maps and in telephone books. Hence, there is no need for a common image to be held of a place for its location to be communicated. Some cities, like Tokyo, have no such clear system; cities like Ciudad Guayana are changing too rapidly to have developed such a system; but in most cities this common information base creates a screen that hides the real differences between perceptions.

The Planners' City

The planners were a fairly homogeneous group except for differences in nationality. They were educated, intelligent, sensitive, and informed in a general way but distant from the city.

Although no formal survey of planners' and designers' perceptions was made, they habitually drew both formal and sketchy maps of the city. These maps described the distribution of uses in the broadest categories, density levels, circulation flows, river edges, contours, and, occasionally, plans of buildings. This "plan" world was less complex but more extensive than the inhabitants' knowledge. Only certain functional types, such as schools, hospitals, general commercial uses, and cultural facilities, were selected for their significance. Others deemed important by the inhabitant were neglected. Professional maps described the positional and topological structure of the city but made little mention of character differentiation and patterning. These same maps were almost invariably future oriented. It was indeed difficult to find a record of existing urban conditions in the planning office, partly because of the difficulty of keeping up to date and partly because of a lack of interest on the part of the planning group. The planners' knowledge of the city was not restricted to the language of their maps, but their maps were good indications of their modes of thinking. Language directs thought (Vygotsky 1962), and many decisions were made on the basis of map information.

The planners' knowledge differed from that of the rest of the population in each of the ways in which knowledge is formed. Their dispositions were generally diffuse and future oriented, whereas the inhabitants' dispositions were usually particular, specific, and present oriented. Few of the planning team lived on the site of the city, an increasingly widespread phenomenon throughout the planning world, since projects and cities on remote sites are often planned by teams based in central cities. The city as seen by such nonusers is devoid of personal use or local foreground. The planners' perceptions were oriented more to the supplier than to the user. The planners' cognitive skills had been developed to conceptualize cities in ways that sensitize them to sets of variables different even from those of their educational peers among the public, let alone those of less-educated groups. It was therefore difficult for a planner to see the city with an "innocent eye." His familiarity with it was more like that of an informed visitor than that of an inhabitant. His knowledge was extensive but not deep. He was likely to know his environment well only in areas where new construction was under way and where systematic surveys had been carried out. Finally, the media and language used by the planners to simulate the city biased their view of it.

With all these differences, it should be no surprise that a

conceptual gap existed between the professionals and the population.

Group Environments for Ciudad Guayana

If we can identify the characteristic styles and methods that each population group adopts in perceiving the city, we should be able to suggest policies for shaping a relevant form for the city. The intent is not to bring groups into line with some common model but to raise the effectiveness of each group's relation to the city on its own particular terms. The following are some policies that could be proposed in Ciudad Guayana.

1. To encourage the awareness and interest of the essential middle-income elite of the city and to assure them of stability and security:

a. Plan identifiable residential areas for the upper- and middle-income groups in fine locations but not isolated or inaccessible from other population groups. The size of such areas should be large enough for the resident groups to have a sense of identity but small enough to discourage self-containment. Spatial isolation has not been the principal mode of distinguishing the prestige areas of Venezuelan cities, so it was unfortunate that the trend had begun in Ciudad Guayana. Social status could be satisfied through the quality and character of housing and residential streets, allowing many locations to have social status.

b. Plan lower-income residential areas, with varied kinds of housing in small units to form transitional areas and reduce their monolithic quality. Plan them in contiguity with middle-income areas to encourage acceptable levels of contact depending on the situation.

c. Provide a greater choice of quality environments throughout the city rather than only in elite areas; for example, build parks, recreation areas, and marinas along the rivers, rehabilitate the San Félix waterfront and lagoon, and develop a botanical garden around the Caroní Falls.

d. Create varied routes of bus and automobile travel through the city, passing through or close to different social and functional areas, and activity centers, especially new public facilities.

e. Broaden the chances for overviews of the city by the conservation of viewpoints, directive signs, and viewing plazas, and articulate the parts of the city exposed to such viewpoints.

2. To enable the less educated to structure the city more easily and learn about other social groups, job opportunities, and educational and other facilities:

a. Locate low-income residential areas near major cheap transportation routes and higher-income neighborhoods.

b. Locate the facilities that are significant to these groups on accessible sites exposed to public view, emphasizing physical attributes to which they are sensitive—namely color, signs, and movement. The use of color could be encouraged for several purposes, including coding and differentiating of buildings and various parts of the city.

c. Design the city's layout as a simple basic structure that can be schematized easily without the loss of essential elements. The present linear road system should continue as a basis for structuring the circulation pattern, rather than be disrupted or replaced; but it should be more clearly connected to the main centers and settlements, which could each be developed to enhance their individual characteristics.

d. Route bus services more directly, and coordinate them with the main street system. Locate bus stops at major intersections, and relate terminals to major centers.

e. Coordinate verbal and graphic signs with the buildings, streets, and directions that they signify. Use signs to develop literacy by employing simple, graphic, and verbal languages and to develop knowledge of the city by displaying information concerning investments, social objectives, natural, and other phenomena (M.I.T. students 1963; Wurman 1971; Carr 1971).

3. To help the newcomer learn the city and to maintain the interests and involvement of the long-term inhabitants:

a. Publicity about Ciudad Guayana in other parts of Venezuela should be a coherent part of the city's development program and should disseminate realistic information about the difficulties as well as the benefits of living there. Information on the cost of living and rate of unemployment, for instance, could be given, as well as an up-to-date map.

b. For the new arrival who is trying to learn the city quickly and find the services essential to his settlement, information centers should be located in the most accessible and visible parts of the city, probably at the major road intersections and bus terminals. They should be distinct and well signed, probably with an explanatory map or model of the city displayed outside. Some projects in the city like the new bridge were already explained publicly in this way.

Other facilities, like housing agencies, police, and hotels should also be encouraged to locate in highly accessible and visible positions. It would also be a mistake to construct residential areas for newcomers that were remote from the centers of activity and transportation.

c. More generally, the newcomer will gain from the exposure and distinctness of significant facilities, from articulate signing, and coordination of perceived attributes.

d. The form of the city will be most attractive to the newcomer if it relates in some way to his expectations, so that he can feel secure within its structure. Centers that follow a modified Spanish Colonial pattern would, for instance, be easily understandable for those who came from such towns. On the other hand, the unique qualities of the city, especially the richness of its natural resources, hills, and rivers, could be exposed in such a way that the newcomer and tourist realize that the city has qualities that distinguish it from other cities.

e. For the longer-time inhabitant who has settled into a routine, stability and historic depth will be important. The development and preservation of distinctive sites and places, like old San Félix, the small fishing settlements like La Laja and Acapulco, and the Caroní Falls and rapids, will also be significant for the future richness of the city. The planning of an incremental transportation structure, which "fits" population needs and city form at any one time, could provide more continuity than the initial "jerky" growth pattern.

To keep the long-time inhabitants up-to-date and in touch with development, all new changes should be announced and well signed.

4. To facilitate the urban education of the young and maintain the urban interest of the old:

a. The educational value of the city is important to several groups, particularly young people, newcomers, and those from rural areas. Their enthusiasm should be encouraged. If they wish to innovate and change, they should, within reason, be encouraged to carry it through. This suggests the advantages of a complex and challenging environment, where possibilities and choices are perceived, if not always easily attainable.

For the young the raw fragments of the new road system would be seen as signs of change rather than disruptions of continuity. The young emphasized the bright and sensuous, entertainment and recreation. These might be the best vehicles for opening up broader horizons. Industries and educational and cultural facilities might also emphasize these qualities. Billboards could become a prime means of intercommunication and expression; they could be used to educate and inform people about the city, current entertainment, and events or serve in some cases as outdoor correspondence courses.

5. To acknowledge sex differences in use and understanding of the city:

a. Women, especially housewives, could be encouraged at the very least to participate much more in the planning and improvement of residential areas, for these are generally more important to women than to men.

b. The roads, transportation system, and industry are still primarily male-oriented facilities in Ciudad Guayana. A better transit system would enable females to travel more extensively in the city to be available for employment (when industries are developed that can give them jobs). Locations of low-income residential areas near the major street system would also be helpful for access reasons.

6. To coordinate and improve the knowledge of those who travel by different modes of transportation:

a. The coincidence of bus routes with the major road system, of bus stops with major intersections, and the development of a more direct, less meandering system could enable bus travelers to gain a more coherent knowledge of the system. The buses and bus stops could be clearly formed and signed.

b. Similarly, the road system should be coordinated with a parking and pedestrian system to reduce the conflicts between these subsystems.

7. To extend the knowledge of various occupational groups:

a. Since the skilled workers seem to derive information from their cross-city journey to work, this technique might be used to extend the knowledge of the professionals and executives. The residential areas of these groups could be connected to their work places with routes that pass centers and districts of public importance.

Policies such as these are still very general. One interview cannot find out very much about different population groups. More contacts would be needed to propose sure and specific values.

Six Strategies for Structuring the Plural City

Diverse perceptions of the city pose difficult conceptual as well as policy problems for environmental professionals and public officials. The small planning and design teams that most cities have possess little capacity to cope with this diversity. Yet some strategies for handling the problem must be developed if planners and city governments are to aspire to the professed planning ideal of serving all groups in the population. These policies are, of course, applicable to any planning issue and range beyond the factors discussed in this book.

Plural Participation

One basic strategy is to involve the inhabitants, as well as the public agencies and private developers, in the planning and design of the city. The planning of a new city involves, among other tasks, the responsibility of proposing a basic organization for the city, a plan for its public environment, for the protection of its historical, aesthetic, and natural resources, for the control of environmental exploitation or destruction, and for the provision of a livable environment for all its inhabitants. The more people who can participate in this task, the more segments of the population are likely to be satisfied. The various techniques of community participation are now being discussed in the planning literature, so they will not be discussed here. Community participation, however, does not solve every problem. In planning a new city, much of the future population will not be present, many lower-level decisions will still be made within the planning agency or with only small citizen groups, and both alternative plans and the information base from which they are derived may well be constructed by planners alone.

Identifying Groups

Planners and designers must begin to view the population of a new city as a number of clearly characterized groups, whether they are educational, class, age, occupational, travel, or others. The groups will be better defined when dealing with project and subsystem impact. When dealing with the road system, planners should consider at least the drivers, passengers, bus riders, pedestrians, and neighbors. When designing local residential areas, their concern should be more with housewives, children, and teenagers, and the social class of the population likely to live there. They must also realize that knowledge of the city is home based and that the most involved people in any intervention will be those living closest to it. This may seem obvious, yet in Ciudad Guayana several decisions about road location were made in ignorance of the sensitivities of the people most affected. This concretization of the hitherto anonymous and consequently forgotten "public" could be an important step forward for environmental planning and design.

Priority Populations

Since the public cannot participate in every small decision, professionals should identify which groups are being given priority in decisions when conflicts occur (Mack and Myers 1965). Criteria for priority will probably rest on the numbers of people in a group, their relative involvement in a particular issue; their vulnerability to stress, both objectively and in their own definition; their relative power in the city; and their importance to the city's economic, administrative, or social success. Most important of all may be the identification of hidden or deprived groups who are ignorant or who cannot speak up for themselves. In Ciudad Guayana the needs of the poor were already the subject of attention, but the problems of housewives, for instance, or old people were relatively neglected. The technical and professional personnel in the industrial complex, the political leaders, the poor, the young, and the new migrants were among the priority groups.

Naturally, some of these populations were competing for resources. The lower-income groups are usually those under the most actual stress, yet in Ciudad Guayana, the upper-income groups expressed more dissatisfaction with the city. Since the professional and executive elite were crucial to the economy's success, compromises would have to be worked out to ameliorate the environmental conditions of the *needy*, while providing attractive environments for the *needed.*

Conflict Identification

The most difficult decisions are those that will clearly benefit one group but deprive another, such as whether to emphasize one kind of a transportation system, whether to bypass one part of the city and provide access to another, or even what density to allow in a section of the city. These questions should be identified early in order to develop sufficient information about costs and benefits including impacts on daily lives and perceptions of the city. Thus the public can be informed of the issues and included in negotiations, detailed plans, and decisions.

Choice

The argument is often made that perceptions and life-styles are too complex and create too many conflicts to provide any guidelines for decision making. Admittedly, conflicts are always difficult to resolve, but in many cases environments can provide for different perceptions and desires without conflict. The city should be diverse enough to accommodate these various cognitive and life-styles.

Imaginative Pluralism

Finally, awareness of pluralism can be a source of imaginative planning. The urban vocabularies of each population group could be used to shape the city. Group environments can be created. A city should communicate to the naive and the sophisticated, the poor and the rich, migrants and long-term residents, bus and automobile travelers, the conservative and the adventurous. Simple, straightforward structural patterns can be supported by more complex alternative systems; different levels of communication can be conveyed through the forms of buildings, simple in structure, complex in detail. This ability to structure an entity to be comprehended at different levels and to sustain attention—and affection—after repeated contact is the avowed aim of many works of art. The city being a plural product, should be well suited to its plural inhabitants.

11 THE PUBLIC ENVIRONMENT

Despite the lack of a common image, some parts of the city are held more in common than other parts. These parts we shall call the public environment. The public environment can be defined narrowly by use, those parts commonly used by large numbers of people; by social setting, where people from similar or different backgrounds meet each other; or broadly by common knowledge, known to large numbers of people. In this book we have looked at the publicly known environment—the environment of common knowledge.[1]

The publicly known environment is an arena for communication in the city. Even if people do not meet face to face here, they meet each other's artifacts and products, they "read" the messages, conscious and unconscious, that are sent through this environment. It is a forum, a marketplace, and a stage for communication; it determines the character, image, and self-image of cities (Burchard 1968).

A Paradigm

To show how the public environment relates to the individual inhabitant, consider a hypothetical fragment of city to see how it becomes known.

Environmental knowledge does not begin at any particular point in the man-environment process, so we shall start with the environment itself and its potential for being part of the inhabitant's world. Then we shall identify the environment that is exposed to him or her daily, the environment that is directly used, and the aspects that are of significance from previous and indirect experience. Finally we shall outline the composite urban spatial knowledge gained from his environmental and other experience. At the same time we shall construct the characteristics of public knowledge and the public environment.

Figure 11.1 describes the elements of our inhabitant's distinctive environment that are usually visible to him (generated from figure 11.3). The outer, shaded elements are his potential environment, available to him but not part of his everyday travels. Distinctive features, especially those in the inner, visible core, stand a high probability of capturing his attention and being recalled. These are the imageable features of the city (Lynch 1960): the landmarks (the dam, the conical hill, the lake, the supermarket), defined spaces (the cloverleaf interchange), channels (the river, the elevated freeway), edges (the forest edge), and distinct regions (the white apartments) (see table 11.1). Only parts of districts, boundaries, rivers, and other geographical features may possess such distinctive qualities, and these are all that have been shown. The same features form the potentially distinct environment of the general public, but the pattern of visibility for them changes (figure 11.2) because of different public travel patterns.

In Ciudad Guayana, the distinctive landmarks included billboards, water towers, radio pylons, and a hundred or so buildings, up to very large landmarks like certain hills, the Llovisna Falls, and the steel mill itself. Spatially distinct nodes included the Plaza Bolívar in San Félix, colonial in form, the new plaza in the Centro Cívico of Puerto Ordaz, the traffic circles on the Avenida Guayana, and the new bridge across the Caroní. Some of these, including the Centro Cívico and the bridge, functioned as landmarks from the outside and as spatial reference points when the city was entered. Although most elements of the circulation system were chameleonlike in character, a few channels possessed distinctive and continuous form. They included the Avenida Guayana (a four-lane divided highway), the railroads, and electric power lines; and at the largest scale, the Orinoco and Caroní Rivers, although the physical continuity of the Caroní was frequently interrupted by confusing rapids. Several of these linear elements, especially the rivers, acted simultaneously as defined edges or barriers. The terrain was also sharply divided and bounded by ridges, spurs, and ***quebradas***, but in only a few places (at the north and western edges of San Félix, which were bounded by water, and around the camps of Puerto Ordaz) was there a clear edge to urban development. The landscape, being complex but not dramatic, was generally difficult to grasp as a set of spatial units, although the urban designers made a brave attempt and identified the Caroní and San Félix,"bowls" as major spaces. Urban development was also scattered and amorphous, with the exception of the ***casco*** in San Félix, a distinctive colonial square-block area, and some of the new housing areas on the western side of the Caroní, with their identical house types.

Figure 11.3, depicting the visible environment, shows the range of our inhabitant's vision from his usual paths of action and movement. The areas adjacent to his line of travel, on the axis of his vision or at significant decision points are zones of high visibility. Distinctive elements within this visible zone stand out very much like the features revealed by a car's headlights during a nighttime journey. The effects of visibility fade with distance. These effects are schematically shown by an inner intensive zone and an outer peripheral zone.

Determination of the visible public environment (figure 11.4) will depend on surveys of urban travel patterns and the identification of highly used view points.

In Ciudad Guayana, these features were determined mostly by their visibility from the main road system. Road details like curbs and traffic islands at intersections, small buildings at decision points, small bridges over the railroad lines, and a river edge or the visible side of a housing area were features of this visible system. Several distinctive features (and significant ones) fell outside this range: buildings like the steel mill itself, the hospital, the ports, both plazas (which were invisible from main traffic movement), the railroads, power lines, and rivers (except where crossing the main road), vast areas of the landscape including the Caroní Falls and rapids, and the hinterland of the urban areas, including several new but hidden residential developments.

The inhabitant's used environment (figure 11.5) generates his visual field and covers all those features that are the immediate settings for his activities, social participation, and travel, whether they are local establishments or meeting places, the houses of friends and relatives, his decision points, his regular paths of movement (journey to work), or well-known local territories crisscrossed by his own short journeys.[2] Once in familiar territory, the inhabitant can find his way around without conscious effort, whether the territory is clear or confused. His local territory is often thought of more in the social and action terms of friends and neighbors and frequented paths and places than as a physical form. On our subject maps the entire street system was frequently drawn more as a network of personal paths and decision points than as a system of channels.

The publicly used environment (figure 11.6) depends more on the intensities of flow and densities of activity of the whole population. In our example the possible incongruities between our individual's use of local stores and the public use of facilities have been dramatized to make the point. Thus, for our inhabitant the local school is not directly used but is seen by him as a building of community significance (figure 11.7). From the public viewpoint it is part of the used environment.

This used world is the core of the inhabitant's visible environment, and it is often difficult to make the distinction between his immediate behavior setting and the visible environment. For instance, in this interpretation, a road intersection is defined as the used environment, while a building viewed from it is part of the visible environment.

In Cuidad Guayana, the places of intensive use included the larger industrial plants, commercial, and community facilities. Heavily used outdoor spaces included the plazas, the streets through commercial areas (especially in San Félix and Castillito), and major traffic intersections. The main east-west road was the most heavily trafficked pathway, and the commercial zones again were the most intensely used areas. Certain barriers were primarily barriers to movement. The difference between a ferry and a bridge was a good example. The aggravating delays experienced while waiting for a ferry and the change of vehicular mode made it a memorable use transition. When replaced by the bridge, the river ceased to be a movement barrier but remained for those who crossed it a distinct interlude of water, coolness, and quiet.

The fourth pair of diagrams (figures 11.7 and 11.8) describe the significant environment, the aspects of the city or landscape that are significant for economic, social, political, historical, or aesthetic reasons. The inhabitant learns about this environment from previous experience, from his social communications system, and from the mass media, as well as from personal use. As an environment becomes publicly significant, it usually acquires a name, often a careful choice to connote the proper social status, community function, or economic market. It is then frequently communicated to the inhabitant through the social media in verbal language. Indeed, most people are so used to categorizing the environment verbally that elements with no names, especially larger districts, are more difficult to perceive and recall (Carmichael, Hogan, and Walter 1932). In such cases the inhabitant often infers their presence and configuration from the cues and signs he encounters in his travel about the city, many of which may be inaccurate.

In figures 11.7 and 11.8, elements that are not necessarily visible, distinct, or even used have been mentioned. The inhabitant's own house, club, street, and neighborhood may lack distinguishing qualities to an outsider, but they are significant to the inhabitant from his personal experience. He may picture other parts of town or the local school primarily by social characteristics he has read about in the local newspaper, and he may be particularly conscious of a socially prestigious neighborhood next to his own. For the general public the significant public environment includes economic, political, ecological, historical, and future planned areas, none of which need be physically or visibly evident to the average traveler in the city.

Several elements of Ciudad Guayana were of economic, social, or historical significance. The hydroelectric dam, of fundamental economic importance, was hidden to the south of the city and heavily guarded against visitors. Power lines and railroads, the light industrial park, and the extensive steel mill were all significant, although all except the steel mill were only indirectly or lightly used, and most were invisible to the ordinary inhabitant.

Social significance differentiated many kinds of elements. The socially prestigious Country Club was remote, unseen, and open only to an exclusive few, although it was widely known. Other elements also possessed high social status such as some of the other clubs, a certain street in El Roble that was flanked by larger ***quintas***, and some of the newer and better residential areas. Los Monos, the subject of a recent police raid, was known for different social reasons. The influence of social differentiation was well instanced by the case of the battered fence that separated the Orinoco Mining property from the rancho area of Castillito. Although it could scarcely be seen and offered no barrier to traffic along the road between settlements, those socially "below" it in Castillito mentioned it several times on their maps, an instance of directional perception due to social differences.

Heavily used meeting places like the plazas and main streets were naturally of great social significance. The plazas and their statues were recognized as being historically important, too.

Figures 11.9 and 11.10 (composites of figures 11.1-11.8) illustrate the possible urban knowledge of our inhabitant and of the general public. The diagrams incorporate various elements derived from the earlier maps. For the individual inhabitant, the locally used and significant environment is supplemented by visible and distinctive elements that he encounters in his more frequent travels and items of public significance about which he has learned from his social contacts. There are many omissions: the lake and western hill (neither of which he has visited), the future park, the conservation zone, and the architectural masterpiece (about which he has never heard). Similarly, the elements known by a majority of the public omit several features—the river, the conservation zone, the political boundary—assuming these may not be generally known—but include most of the visible, distinct, and intensively used places and the best-publicized elements of significance.

These diagrams contain the array of elements that subjects

may draw when asked to map the city. They are strictly a plotting of urban knowledge through the selection of attributes and elements, without any graphing of structural and changing relationships of the kind described in chapters 8 and 9. They rest on the assumption, partially confirmed in chapter 4, that the elements of urban knowledge are present in our comprehension of the city because they are either imageable, visible, used, or significant.

In table 11.1 (see appendix A), the various terms used for urban components are hence classified as to whether they are primarily imageable, operational, or significant. Lynch attempted to find terms that covered all aspects of each element's quality. The table suggests other terms that may be used, including some proposed by Clay (1973) in a book on urban elements.

A final and supplemental set of diagrams (figures 11.11, 11.12) has been drawn to depict the valences that accompany urban knowledge. Both inhabitants and the public at large perceive the urban environment in evaluative terms. In this case, given our inhabitant's knowledge of his local area, he may feel positive (+) about his own neighborhood, the freeway he uses, and some of the local natural features, and he may admire the neighboring upper-class neighborhood. But he may evaluate negatively (—) the local supermarket, the dam on the river, the apartment buildings, and lower-class residential area, while feeling neutral or ambivalent (x) about the local gas station and the area surrounding his home neighborhood. Similarly, the public consensus may evaluate the natural areas and the prestige neighborhood positively, the school and part of the freeway negatively, and other areas ambivalently. These evaluations can be made for any number of reasons, such as environmental quality, social problems, conservation, inadequate facilities, or future proposals. Indeed, separate maps could be plotted for each quality, such as levels of public safety, health, natural character, or visual quality (Appleyard and Carp 1974). It is likely, from the evaluations of buildings made in chapter 6, that the best-known parts of an area would receive polarized evaluations; that is, they would be viewed either positively or negatively rather than neutrally.

The Public Environment

The public environment (figure 11.10), known to large numbers of people, is formed when the public patterns of use, travel, and visibility encounter imageable or significant elements in the city. The major circulation system, its principal decision points, and the most intensely used destinations are core components of this environment; but whatever is visible, imageable, or significant within this system may be as well known. The public environment is the structure on which much of a city's image is projected.

The "publicness" of this environment is determined by the number of people who use and know it. In small towns this might be a large majority of the population; in larger cities it will be a smaller percentage and less frequently used. Local or group environments may become more important. Beyond the regularly used public environment lie potential public environments that could become public if use patterns change, if new routes are constructed, or if events occur in them that bring them to the public eye. The natural environment is also a potential public environment, and its protection for future public use or as a vicarious environment possessing an "option value" is of public importance. Definitions of these territories have not as yet been made very specific in cities, and consequently there are clashes over intrusions on the public or local territory.

In monumental cities such as Washington or Brasilia, attempts have been made to produce coherent plans for the public environment, placing significant buildings in prominent locations. But the actual use patterns of these cities have not always conformed to the plans. As in Puerto Ordaz, centers of activity have occurred where people find them most convenient, causing a schism between the planned and actual public environments of each city. Washington's central business district lies "somewhere" to the north of the Mall; Brasilia's main shopping street is off the spinal freeway. The Spanish colonial plazas in some Venezuelan cities have become similarly isolated from their activity centers. Planners of the public environment must either predict well or have flexible plans to maintain a meaningful public environment when use patterns are likely to change its configuration.

But in many new cities the public environment is neglected. Planners seldom define or describe in any detail the public environment in their plans. In most new cities, whether designed on two-dimensional plans or three-dimensional models, the planners rarely if ever describe the configuration and meaning of the city from the viewpoint of those using its public channels or try to predict the inhabitants' perceptions of the city. They usually give much more attention to plan patterns and to the detailed design of residential, industrial, and central areas. Too many new cities present an image of long, empty boulevards, like Chandigarh, or of roads meandering through rustic landscapes, like many English New Towns, with random glimpses of housing developments, shopping centers,

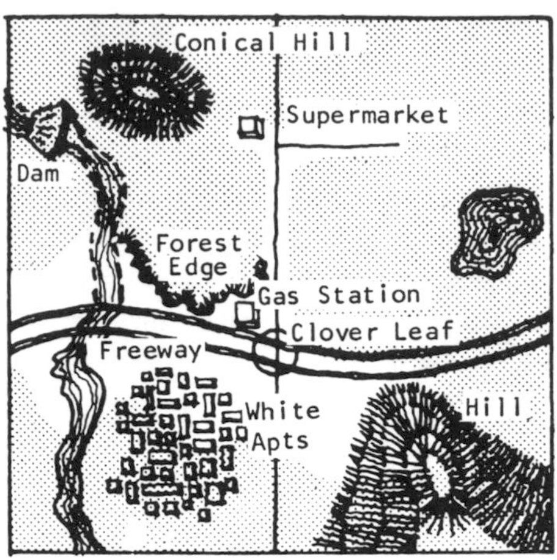

Figure 11.1 Distinctive environment.

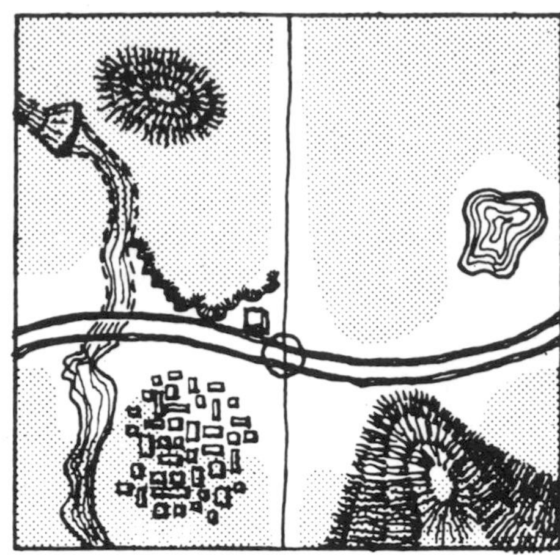

Figure 11.2 Distinctive environment.

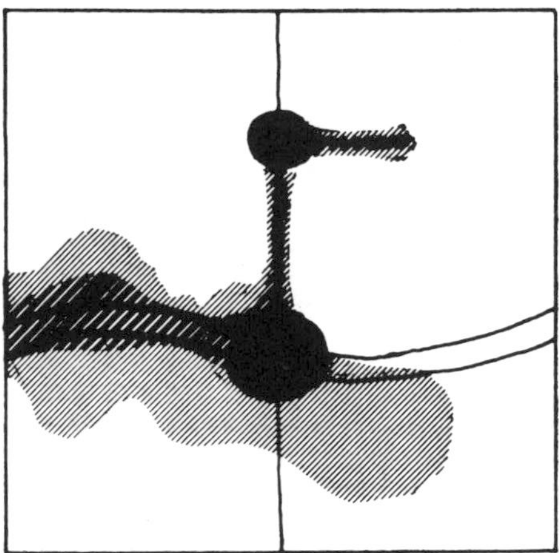

Figure 11.3 Inhabitant's visible environment.

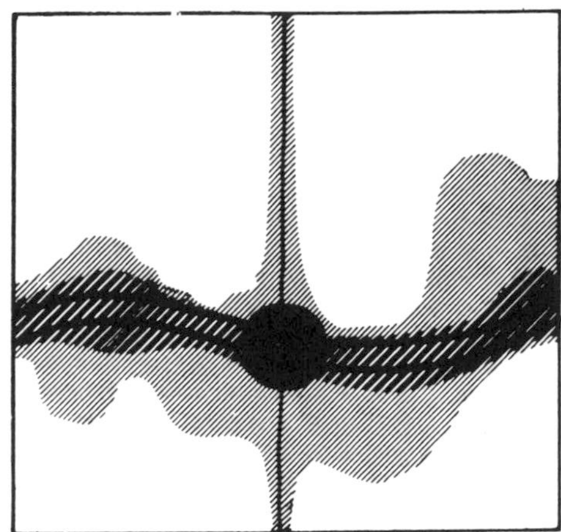

Figure 11.4 Visible public environment.

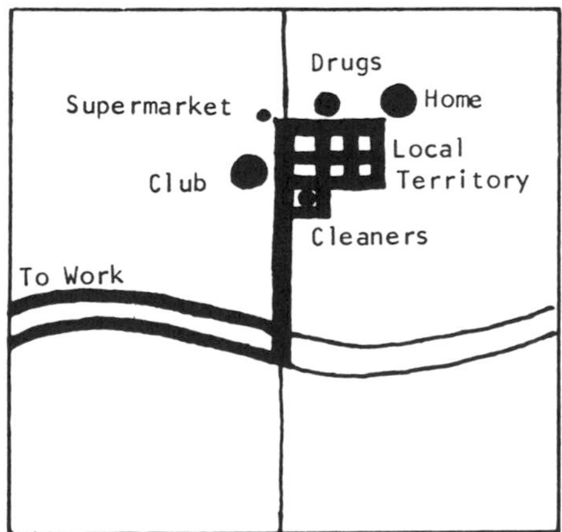

Figure 11.5 Inhabitant's used environment.

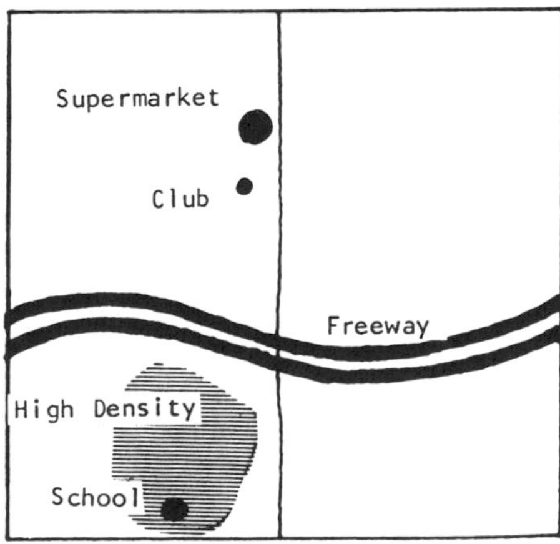

Figure 11.6 Used public environment.

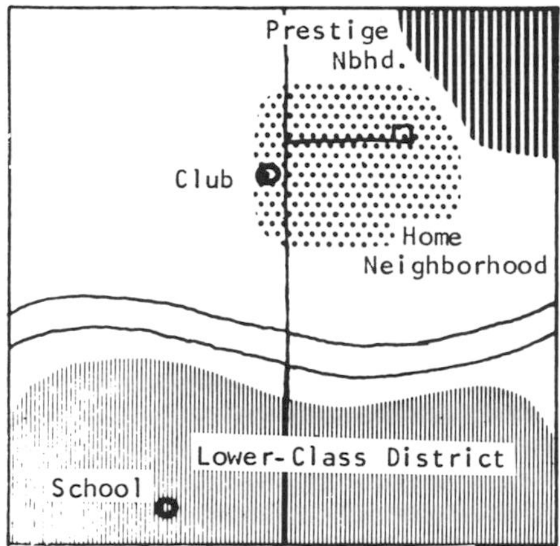

Figure 11.7 Inhabitant's significant environment.

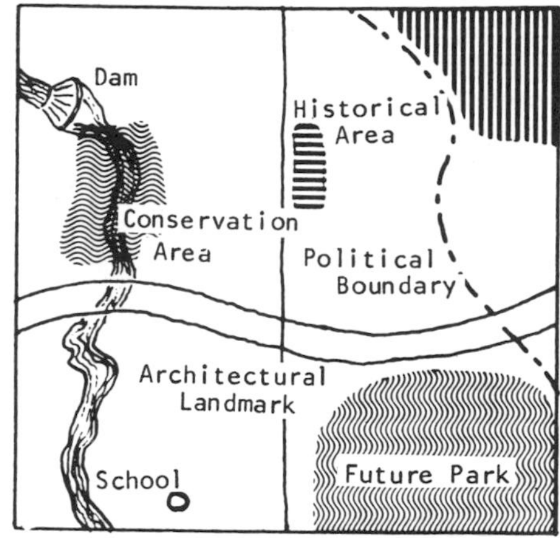

Figure 11.8 Significant public environment.

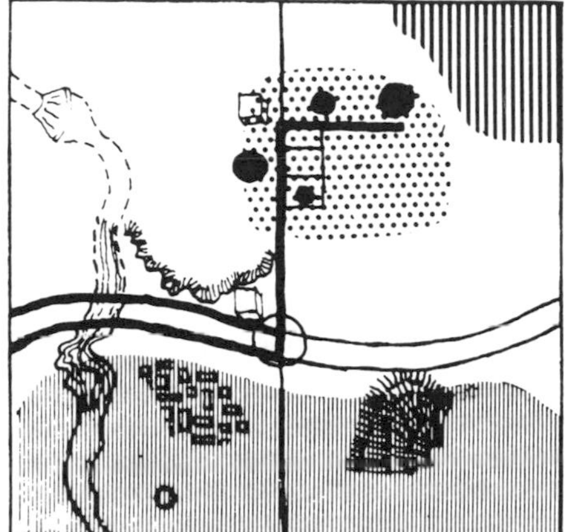

Figure 11.9 Inhabitant's urban knowledge.

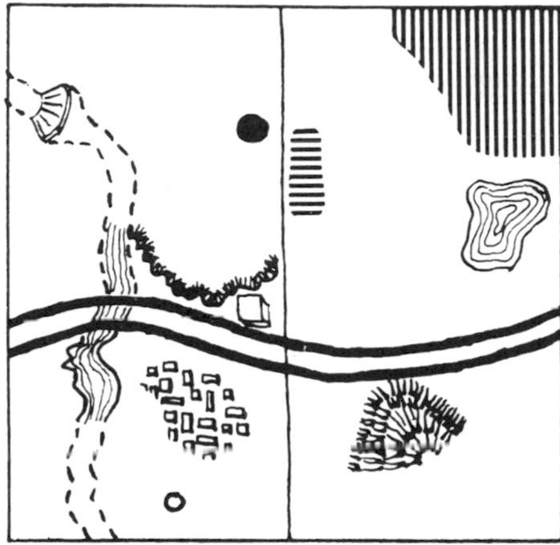

Figure 11.10 Public urban knowledge: the known public environment.

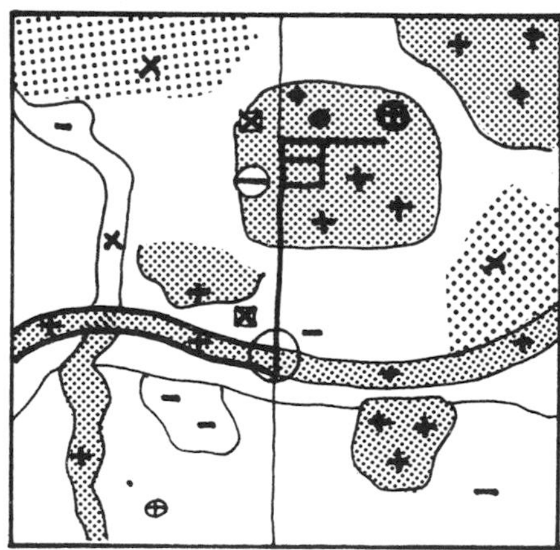

Figure 11.11 Inhabitant's evaluation.

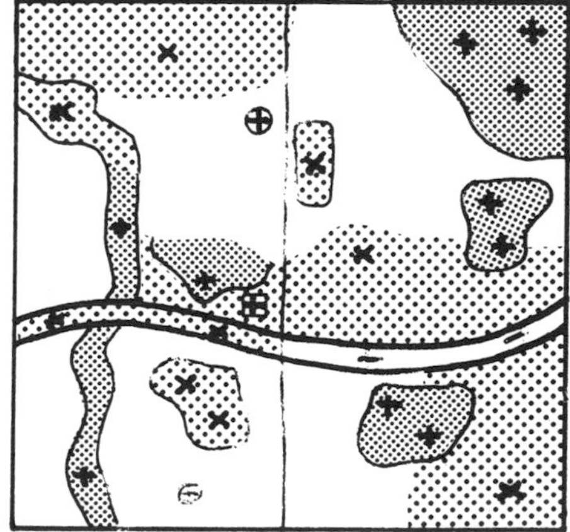

Figure 11.12 Public evaluation.

industrial plants, or institutional buildings. The plans look clear and sensible, but in reality their form and meaning are not apparent.

In existing cities, too, neither planners nor citizens concern themselves in any systematic way with the public environment. The transportation system determines the image of many cities. Commercial enterprises gather around transit terminals and along arterial streets. Public facilities are located on quiet streets in the background. Freeways have sprung loose even from these uses and follow new independent routes, creating new public environments. Until and unless new commerce focuses around the freeway intersections, the public sees the city from its backyard, from industrial sites, from outside the city, by rivers, fields, and hills. The automobile, with its greater mobility, scatters development, and the public environment becomes a wasteland between islands of careful design.

The Public Environment and the Educational City

The primary role of the public environment is one of communication. In recent years this has been almost entirely confined to the transportation of people between different parts of the city. But the public environment can be an arena for all kinds of communication—through images, actions, and symbols. As such it could have a number of desirable qualities.

Richness and Diversity

If the public environment of a city is rich and diverse, it can offer inhabitants and visitors many insights into the various kinds of people, establishments, and activities that exist in their city. Cities with rich public environments invite curiosity, encourage open-mindedness. They are called urbane. Too many new cities lack such interest. They can be visited completely in a few hours, with the feeling that they have been comprehended. A common complaint is made of new cities: they are dull.

This richness is not simply a question of stimulation. From our studies of perceived complexity it is clear that what captured people's attention was the uniqueness of the city's functions, establishments, or physical features. The degrees of difference and levels of uniqueness may therefore be much more meaningful than the actual numbers of different places.

Communicability and Symbolism

The images of a city presented through its public environment can be planned through encouragement and design to inform city users of its functional pattern and its social, economic, and natural structure. The preservation, identification, and exposure of parts of the city belonging to certain social mixes or social groups; the sites of particular trades, industries, or other activities; or places having special natural characteristics can strengthen a sense of place and local identity. The key question is still which aspects should receive priority. It is tempting for cities to present their best face, just like the picture postcards, while hiding the seamier parts. Indeed, it is difficult for cities to resist the powerful and affluent and give communications space to other groups, but some kind of equity must prevail. The public environment of a city should not be a veneer covering its sores, or they may forever be ignored.

Structural Coherence

Relations between different parts of the public environment can be crucial for reasons of accessibility, but they can also affect social and political relationships. Degrees of desirable and acceptable social mix are continuing matters of debate, but there is little doubt that isolation encourages intolerance or at best vague "do-goodism." The public environment, being more communal territory than local environments, has the potential of providing a setting for interaction, even though, with the increasing dominance of the automobile, this environment has also become "privatized." Unless or until this trend is reversed, visible exposure to different groups and functions may be the only way of establishing contacts.

Structuring, we have argued, is not simply automobile or transit access between different parts of the city. How inhabitants put together what they see and experience into a coherent cognitive structure is the crucial issue. If people are ignorant of where places are, good access is useless.

The structure of the public environment depends on the associative character and patterning of its various elements, on its topological continuities and connections, and on its positional referencing through scaled distances and consistent directions, as described in chapter 8. These various devices for conceptually assembling a differentiated spatial structure depend on connective patterns of form, visibility, use, and significance, and of spatial and sequential elements, such as larger-scale routes and districts and widely visible landmarks.

Environments can be overstructured, however. Authoritarian regimes often seek to unify their cities by connecting symbols of power with large-scale boulevards and by insisting on a unified character, while in fragmented and weak political contexts such as the United States, the public environment of cities has little perceptible coherence. The question is one for public debate. How much should the parts of a community relate to one another? What parts should be well related? The interaction matrices used in building design could be developed to include the whole range of urban facilities, social groups, and physical environments. Desirable relations could be stipulated not only on a time-distance basis but also on the bases of similarity of character, visibility, and directness of connection.

Change and Stability

Changes in the public environment occur incrementally through changes in individual buildings and areas and more radically through changes in the transportation system. The building of a new freeway or transit system, the widening of streets, or even changes in one-way street systems can create havoc with the known public environment. Perhaps the most difficult changes to cope with are the ambiguous ones where future change is threatened but its exact timing and nature are unknown. This is more characteristic of cities without plans or in the early stages of planning as in Ciudad Guayana.

The rate and type of changes that occur in the public environment may affect the satisfaction and morale of the public. It may be important for publicly perceived change to occur at about the same rate as real change, that is, to be contemporaneous with the rest of the city. If not, there may be public misperceptions of change. The desired rate of change will vary with public values. In Ciudad Guayana, where the population wants it to change faster, evidence of change in the public environment will be welcomed. In American suburbs, where conservation is presently valued, evidence of stability and continuity in the public environment may be preferred. In situations of stagnation and decay, dramatic changes in the public environment, such as a new transportation system, may be greeted with enthusiasm.

Inventorying the changes in the public environment and the rate of change in relation to the rest of the city could provide useful indicators of its contemporaneity and continuity. The construction of buildings and transport systems probably exert the most powerful changes on the city environment, but changes in traffic levels, rehabilitation, street landscaping, and signs are sometimes equally strong indicators of change.

Conclusion

The public environment will be plurally perceived and must be plural in nature. It should be representative of its city, not simply the monumental facade that it is in some cities or the crowded, polluted, repellant place that it is becoming in most cities. For the public environment to be an arena for communication, it must be attractive enough for people to want to go there—and get out of their cars. The public environment of medieval cities was a place where people actually met each other, a stage where the scenery was recognized and understood. The modern city is in danger of having its population withdraw entirely from its public environment, both for reasons of livability and for lack of interest.

The state of the public environment is likely to become a more definitive focus of attention. However, not until it is defined and cared for by the public itself, rather than by remote authority or professional technicians, is it likely to become an environment meaningful to its citizens—one in which they can have pride.

A

APPENDIX TABLES

Tables

Number

TABLE 2.1

Satisfaction with City, Mean Scale Ratings for Population Groups

Note: Ratings over 5.0 are signs of positive satisfaction; those under 5.0 indicate dissatisfaction.

	Respondents	Means	Standard Deviations
Residence			
Country Club	8	4.25+	1.64
Puerto Ordaz	68	5.35+	2.08
Castillito	66	5.55+	1.97
El Roble	60	5.65+	1.82
San Félix	59	5.91+	2.30
Campo Caroní	10	4.0+	1.34
Education			
Primary	137	5.73*	2.00
Secondary	77	5.48*	2.20
University	28	4.46*	1.57
Age			
Under 20	91	5.93	1.87
21 to 30	67	5.28	2.10
Over 30	114	5.30	2.12
Familiarity			
Under 6 mo.	11	5.27	1.36
6 mo. to 1 yr.	26	6.04	1.91
1 to 5 yr.	109	5.24	2.17
Over 5 yr.	125	5.65	2.01
Travel Mode			
Car	44	5.16	2.47
Por Puesto	36	5.56	2.05
Bus	85	5.88	1.80
Mobility			
Local	103	5.60	2.08
Half City	39	5.36	1.83
Whole City	23	6.13	2.33
Sex			
Male	164	5.44	2.07
Female	107	5.61	2.05

(TABLE 2.1 cont. on next page)

TABLE 2.1 (cont.)

	Respondents	Means	Standard Deviations
Selected Occupations			
Small Business	20	6.05	1.99
Pers. Serv.	17	5.41	2.28
Professionals	14	4.64	2.09
Students	46	5.91	1.85
Unemployed	12	4.83	2.08
Big Business	10	4.50	2.11
Total	272	5.51	2.06

F tests were conducted separately for Residence, Education, Age, Familiarity, Travel Mode, Mobility, Sex, and Selected Occupations.

+ The F test for Residence was 2.37 significant at the .05 level.

* The F test for Education was 5.91 significant at the .01 level.

TABLE 3.1

Perceived and Rated Settlement Complexities

Sources: Perceived complexities and densities are measured by the number of facilities recalled by the total sample in their general maps. Rated complexities were assessed by expert observers through surveys and photo analyses.

	Perceived Complexities			Rated Complexities			
	Perceived Complexity (facilities mentioned)	Settlement Area (hect.)	Perceived Density (facilities/ hect.)	Distinct Form Elements	Singular Form Elements	Intensive Use Elements	Singular Use Elements
Settlement							
Puerto Ordaz	60	294	0.20	30	37	18	58
Castillito	33	120	0.27	6	14	4	15
El Roble	39	400	0.10	16	27	5	30
San Félix	108	348	0.31	22	47	13	79

TABLE 3.2

Perceived Facility and District Complexity Scores (C_{df}) for Each Settlement and Settlement Group.

Source: General Map Responses

Group Complexity measures equal the mean number of districts and facilities mentioned per person in any population group. ( ) Number of respondents in each group.

Residence Groups	Perceived Settlement Complexities: Puerto Ordaz (POC)	Castillito (CC)	El Roble (ERC)	San Félix (SFC)	Perceived Citywide Complexities: C
Puerto Ordaz Residents	2.7 (43)	1.1 (43)	1.7 (43)	1.1 (43)	6.6 (43)
Castillito Residents	2.8 (38)	2.2 (38)	1.5 (38)	3.5 (38)	10.0 (38)
El Roble Residents	0.9 (27)	1.1 (27)	2.1 (27)	2.6 (27)	6.7 (27)
San Félix **Residents**	1.2 (41)	1.3 (41)	3.0 (41)	3.3 (41)	8.8 (41)
TOTAL SAMPLE	2.0 (149)	1.4 (149)	2.1 (149)	2.5 (149)	8.0 (149)

TABLE 3.3

Group Complexity Measures for Whole City

Source: General Map Responses

Group complexity measures represent the mean number of environmental elements (buildings, districts or road units) measured per person in each population group.

	Respondents	Facilities C_f	Districts C_d	Road Units C_r
Residence				
Puerto Ordaz	43	9.4^{o}	2.0	4.4
Castillito	38	13.1^{o}	2.0	4.6
El Roble	27	10.5^{o}	2.1	3.6
San Félix	41	11.4^{o}	2.4	4.6
Education				
None	6	11.0	1.0	6.4
Primary	77	10.9	2.1	4.3
Secondary	56	11.9	2.3	4.4
University	10	7.9	2.2	3.8
Mobility				
Local	93	11.4	2.3	4.2
Half City	35	9.9	1.9	4.7
Whole City	21	11.7	1.8	4.9
Familiarity				
Under 6 mo.	4	10.5	3.3	3.5
6 mos. to 1 yr.	10	14.2	2.6	2.9
1 yr. to 5 yrs.	63	11.1	2.4	4.2
Over 5 yrs.	72	10.7	1.8	4.8
Age				
14 to 20	56	11.3	2.0	4.8^{+}
21 to 30 yrs.	35	10.1	2.6	3.3^{+}
Over 31 yrs.	58	11.5	2.0	4.7^{+}
Travel Mode				
Car	41	10.0	1.8	4.4
Por Puesto	35	12.5	2.2	3.6
Bus	73	11.1	2.3	4.6

(TABLE 3.3 cont. on next page)

TABLE 3.3 (cont.)

	Respondents	Facilities C_f	Districts C_d	Road Units C_r
Sex				
Male	102	11.1	2.0	4.8+
Female	47	11.0	2.5	3.6+
Selected Occupations				
Small Business	19	8.9	1.9	4.4
Personal Service	31	10.8	1.9	3.2
Professionals	8	8.5	3.0	5.0
Students	10	12.6	2.1	4.6
Unemployed	10	8.2	2.4	4.8
Business Executives	28	5.0	2.7	2.7
Office Employees	14	12.4	2.9	3.9
Housewives	6	10.7	2.5	3.6
Skilled Workers	3	13.7	1.4	5.4
TOTAL SAMPLE	149	11.1	2.2	4.4

F-Ratios and Critical F's

F-Ratios	Facilities	Districts	Roads	d.f.	Critical F's (.05)
Residence	2.47°	.41	1.08	3-144	2.67
Education	1.20	.59	1.12	3-144	2.67
Mobility	.83	.84	.91	2-145	3.06
Familiarity	.87	1.34	1.72	3-144	2.67
Age	.64	.94	4.13+	2-145	3.06
Travel Mode	1.61	1.07	1.00	2-145	3.06
Sex	.02	1.46	6.31+	1-146	3.91
Occupation	1.65	.89	1.28	8-120	2.01

°Significant at .10 level.

+Significant at .05 level.

TABLE 4.1

Settlement Attributes (Ranked)

Source: "What is typical or characteristic of ....?" Percentages out of 314 respondents; do not add to 100 since five answers were recorded. Least values not shown on each table.

Mean Responses All Settlements	%	Puerto Ordaz	%	Castillito	%	El Roble	%	San Félix	%
Plazas, Parks	10.8	Plazas, Parks	26	Housing	22	Housing	6	Plazas, Parks	14
Housing	10.3	Housing	10	Trans. Util.	9	Commerce	4	Commerce	11
Commerce	6.3	Production	6	Commerce	7	Plazas, Parks	3	Trans. Util.	7
Trans. Util.	6.0	Commerce	3	Status	5	Comm. Services	3	View	5
Comm. Services	2.3	Comm. Services	3	Pop. Charac.	3	Trans. Util.	2	Comm. Services	4
Production	2.3	Urban Charac.	3	Cleanliness	3	Planning	2	Age	3
Status	2.3	Diversity	3	Bldg. Type	2	Status	1	Street Paving	3
Cleanliness	1.8	Trans. Util.	2	Planning	2	Agency	1	Housing	3
Diversity	1.5	Change	2	St. Charac.	1	Diversity	1	Cleanliness	3
View	1.3	Status	1	Bldg. Comfort	1	Bldg. Type	1	Diversity	2
Pop. Charac.	1.3	Planning	1	Services	1			Pop. Charac.	2
Bldg. Type	1.0			Change	1			Status	2
Urbanity	1.0							St. Charac.	2
Planning	1.0								
Change	1.0								

Spearman Rank Order Correlations (r_s)

	Castillito	El Roble	San Felix
Puerto Ordaz	.37+	.73*	.49*
Castillito		.50*	.40+
El Roble			.43+
San Félix			

*r > .45 significant at the .01 level (N=28)

+r > .32 significant at the .05 level (N=28)

r_s calculated for 28 attributes.

TABLES 4.2A, B, and C

Communication of Functions in the Four Settlements (By Rank)

TABLE 4.2 A

Source: "What are the principal activities of ......?" Percentages out of 303 respondents. Do not add up to 100 since more than one answer was allowed.

Total Respondents = 303

Puerto Ordaz	%	Castillito	%	El Roble	%	San Félix	%
Industry	55	Commerce	67	Commerce	28	Commerce	69
Commerce	38	Employment	13	Employment	17	Industry	20
Employment	22	Industry	7	CVG	7	Education	8
Sport	8	Services	4	Education	7	Sport	3
Social	6	Entertainment	4	Industry	6	Agriculture	3
Entertainment	6	Education	3	Services	5	Public Admin.	2
Culture	4	Construction	3	Construction	4	Private Admin.	2
Education	3	Social	1	Sport	2		
Services	3	Transportation	1	Residence	2		

TABLE 4.2 B

Source: General Map Responses--Elements most frequently mentioned by total sample when mapping each settlement. Percentages out of 168 respondents.

Total Respondents = 168

Puerto Ordaz	%	Castillito	%	El Roble	%	San Félix	%
Centro Cívico	32	Cine Lorena	11	Bomba Phillips	33	Plaza Bolívar	33
Bomba Mobil	27	Esc. Tumeremo	8	Bomba Creole	27	Mercado	32
Hotel Cunucunuma	20	CVG	5	Esc. Técnica	17	Iglesia	18
General Electric	17	Alto Bus	4	Hotel Palúa	14	Seguros Sociales	18
Hospital Urdaz	15	Supersonico	4	CVG	13	Policía	17
Mercado Libre	13	Esc. Fe y Alegría	3	Firestone	13	Cine Park	11
Estadio	13	Cine Rex	3	Col. La Salle	10	Estadio	9
Banco Union	8	Matles Bolívar	2	Cine Bolívar	8	Bomba Creole	8
Policía	7	Farmacia Cast.	2	Matadero	8	Banco Venezuela	8
Blques Banco Obrero	6	Hotel Embajador	2	Club Palúa	5	Liceo	7

TABLE 4.2 C

Source: General Map Response--Elements most frequently mentioned by the local sample when mapping their own settlement.

Local Samples

Puerto Ordaz(43)	%	Castillito(38)	%	El Roble(27)	%	San Félix(41)	%
Civic Center	70	Primary School	57	Gas Station	51	Plaza	69
Hospital	59	CVG	39	CVG	49	Market	63
Market	47	Pharmacy	24	Tech. School	46	Church	59
School	43	Cinema	20	Gas Station	46	Medical	55
Cinema	43	Primary School	17	Cinema	43	Police	53
Gas Station	43	Radio	13	Primary School	32	Primary School	45
Hotel	42	Medical	9	Hotel	30	Consejo	43
Police	40	Hotel	7	Auto Repair	30	P. School	41
Church	36	Chapel	7	Political Hdq.	24	Medical	37
Stadium	36	Bars	7	Primary School	24	Bank	35
Sales Office	36						

TABLE 4.3

District Attributes (Ranked)

Source: "How would you compare .... with ....?" Percentages out of 314 respondents; do not add up to 100 since five answers were recorded. Least values not shown on each table.

Mean Responses All Districts	%	PUERTO ORDAZ Banco Obrero Camp "A"	%	CASTILLITO Mendoza Los Monos	%	EL ROBLE * U.V. 3 U.V. 4	%	SAN FÉLIX La Unidad La Esperanza	%
Bldg. Type	9.1	Bldg. Size	11	Bldg. Type	20	Comm. Services	5	Infrastructure	7
Housing	8.5	Bldg. Type	11	Housing	17	Bldg. Type	2	Housing	6
Admin.	4.5	Housing	7	Pop. Charac.	11	Commerce	2	Bldg. Type	4
Status	3.3	Pop. Status	7	Admin.	9	Topography	1	Comm. Services	4
Bldg. Size	3.3	Admin.	7	Change	9	View	1	Topography	4
Pop. Charac.	3.1	Pop. Natlty.	6	Cleanliness	9	Bldg. Size	1	View	2
Cleanliness	2.6	Bldg. Comfort	5	Planning	6	St. Charac.	1	St. Charac.	2
Comm. Services	2.3	View	2	Quietness	4			Cleanliness	2
Change	2.3			Status	4			Status	2
Infrastructure	2.1							Pop. Charac.	2
Bldg. Comfort	2.0							Admin.	2
View	1.8								
Planning	1.6								
Nationality	1.5								

*Unidades Vecinales 3 and 4.

Spearman Rank Order Correlations (r_s)

	PUERTO ORDAZ		CASTILLITO		EL ROBLE		SAN FÉLIX	
	Banco Obrero	Camp "A"	Mendoza	Los Monos	U.V. 3	U.V. 4	Unidad	La Esperanza
PUERTO ORDAZ								
Banco Obrero		1.00*	.38^{+}	.36^{+}	.55*	.62^{+}	.40^{+}	.41^{+}
Camp "A"			.38^{+}	.36^{+}	.54*	.61^{+}	.40^{+}	.56*
CASTILLITO								
Mendoza				.86*	.30	.33^{+}	.55*	.56*
Los Monos					.32	.34^{+}	.55*	.56*
EL ROBLE								
U.V. 3						.91*	.64*	.65*
U.V. 4							.71*	.72*
SAN FÉLIX								
La Unidad								1.00^{+}
La Esperanza								

*$r_s > .45$ significant at the .01 level.

+$r_s > 32$ significant at the .05 level.

r_s calculated for 28 attributes.

TABLE 5.1

Form Intensity Scales (Verbal Rules)

Note: Form Singularity Scales measured the singularity of each attribute in the scene (Low), in the neighborhood (Medium), and in the city (High).

ATTRIBUTE	Low	Medium	High
Movement	No movement	Potential movement, parked cars, few people	Many people, moving cars, flags waving, water falling
Contour	Blurred boundaries hidden by vegetation attached to other houses	Semidetached corner building	Isolated building with sharp contours
Size	Single-story buildings, houses	Two-story buildings; movie houses	Over two-story buildings; industrial sheds, steel mill, G. Electric
Shape	Simple	Two- or three-block buildings	Complex building divided into several parts
Surface	Plain white	Colored	Brightly contrasted colors and textures
Quality	<u>Bajareque</u> (wattle), mud floors outside, no fences	Modest materials, walls and gardens	Landscaped, fenced, expensive materials, clean conditions
Signs	No signs	Small signs	Large signs readable from a distance

TABLE 5.2

Form Intensity Scales (Graphic Rules)

Attribute	Low	Medium	High
Movement	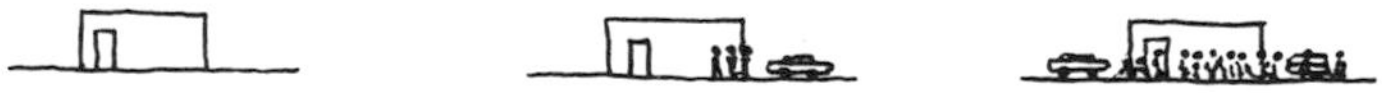		
Contour			
Size	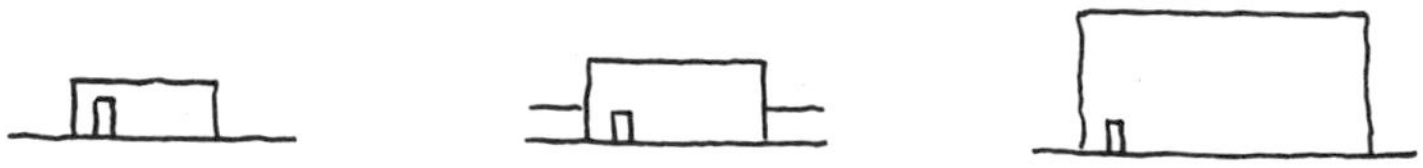		
Shape			
Surface			
Quality			
Signs	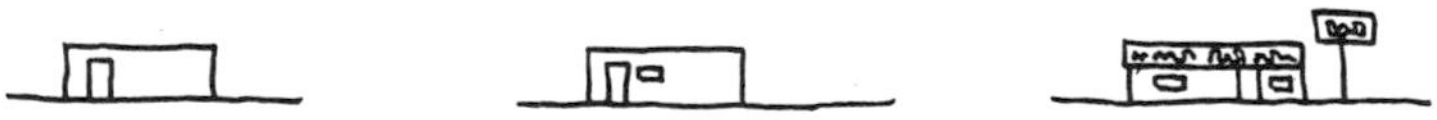		

TABLE 5.3

Visibility Scales

Scale	Low	Medium	High
Viewpoint Intensity	Visible from tertiary roads	Visible from main roads outside urban area, secondary roads in city.	Visible from main east-west road, Puerto Ordaz to San Felix, main pedestrian centers.
Viewpoint Significance	Visible at points of no transition or at decision points on tertiary roads.	Visible at secondary decision points, bends, etc., on major roads or major decision points on secondary roads.	Visible at major decision points, intersections, bus stops, ferry landings on major roads.
Immediacy	Distant objects, poorly seen on main roads, or near objects off axis on secondary and tertiary roads.	Near objects off axis, distant objects on axis on major roads, or axial objects on secondary roads.	Near objects on axis, cutting across line of vision on major roads.

TABLE 5.4

Significance Scales

Scale	Low	Medium	High
Use Intensity	E.g., bars, *abastos*, primary schools	E.g., small supermarkets, small hotels, clinics.	E.g., commercial zones, warehouses, churches, schools, hospitals, bus terminals, etc., banks, steel mill.
Use Singularity	Local singularity, e.g., bar, repair shop.	Community singularity, e.g., primary school, dock, bus terminal.	City singularity, e.g., police station, hospital, C.V.G. office building, cemetery, radio station.
Significance: cultural, political, economic, aesthetic or historical, (*in addition* to use intensity or singularity)	High use and high or low significance, e.g., schools, churches, office buildings.	Medium use and high significance, e.g., factories, police stations.	Low use and high significance, or high use and very high significance, e.g., hydroelectric dam, radio station, statues, steel mill.

TABLE 5.5

Intercorrelations between Expert Ratings of Building Attributes

		FORM														VISIBILITY			SIGNIFICANCE		
ATTRIBUTE		Movement		Contour		Size		Shape		Surface		Quality		Signs		Viewpoint Intensity	Viewpoint Significance	Immediacy	Use Intensity	Use Singularity	Significance
FORM		int.	sing.	int.	sing.	int.	sing.	int.	sing.	int.	sing.	int.	sing.	int.	sing.						
Movement	int.		.55*	.17*	.08	.16*	.12	.23*	.19*	.18*	.14*	.01	.02	-.01	.06	.12	.15*	.20*	.26*	-.05	.04
	sing.			.27*	.13*	.25*	.31*	.32*	.34*	.29*	.31*	.17*	.05	-.24*	-.10	-.08	.08	.10	.32*	.16*	.10
Contour	int.				.53*	.35*	.30*	.13*	.29*	.13*	.16*	.29*	.29*	-.14*	.00	-.22*	.16*	.22*	.11	.22*	.15*
	sing.					.44*	.38*	.21*	.34*	.10	.17*	.31*	.31*	-.22*	-.01	-.17*	.17*	.23*	.02	.32*	.16*
Size	int.						.66*	.37*	.49*	.18*	.17*	.47*	.34*	-.30*	-.06	-.20*	-.06	.09	.14*	.38*	.23*
	sing.							.36*	.44*	.24*	.23*	.32*	.38*	-.32*	-.08	-.14*	.04	.11	.11	.34*	.20*
Shape	int.								.62*	.33*	.40*	.23*	.10	-.13	-.02	-.07	.02	.07	.13	.07	.03
	sing.									.33*	.43*	.31*	.22*	-.17*	-.01	-.11	.06	.09	.09	.24	.13
Surface	int.										.68*	.30*	.14*	.01	-.01	.20*	.12	.22*	.08	.13	-.01
	sing.											.23*	.13	-.08	.06	.13	.20*	.28*	.17*	.20*	.01
Quality	int.												.39*	.00	-.01	-.21*	.09	.06	.21*	.21*	.08
	sing.													-.01	-.04	-.15*	.04	.08	.08	.15*	.11
Signs	int.														.60*	.21*	.08	-.05	.01	-.36*	-.17*
	sing.															.13*	.06	.02	.02	-.12	.01
VISIBILITY																					
Viewpoint Intensity																	.13*	.16*	-.14	-.21*	-.10
Viewpoint Significance																		.47*	.26*	.07	-.01
Immediacy																			.12	.16*	.11
SIGNIFICANCE																					
Use Intensity																				.22*	-.11
Use Singularity																					.27*
Significance																					

*Correlations exceeding .138 are significant beyond the .05 level and are marked (*).

int. = Intensity; sing. = Singularity.

TABLE 5.6

Pearson Product Movement Correlations between Expert Ratings of Building Attributes and Recall Frequencies of Subjects

Attribute		Verbal Recall		Map Recall		Trip Recall	
		int.	sing.	int.	sing.	int.	sing.
Form	Movement	.25+	.34+	.34+	.29+	.35+	.26+
	Contour	.18+	.16	.26+	.30+	.33+	.36+
	Size	.28+	.29+	.25+	.24+	.38+	.35+
	Shape	.22+	.30+	.21+	.23+	.29+	.41+
	Surface	-.08	.14	.19+	.30+	.23+	.43+
	Quality	.17	.09	.15+	.10	.15	.16
	Signs	-.15	-.01	-.06	.06	-.11	.03
Visibility	Viewpoint Intensity	.08		.20+		.18	
	Viewpoint Significance	.13		.39+		.38+	
	Immediacy	.13		.38+		.37+	
Significance	Use Intensity	.32+		.36+		.35+	
	Use Singularity	.22+		.31+		.37+	
	Significance	.08		.07		.05	
Recency		.04		.08		-.12	
Number of buildings in sample		122		188		104	

Correlations exceeding .13 (Map), .17 (Verbal) and .19 (Trip Verbal) are significant at the .05 level.

int. = Intensity; sing. = Singularity

TABLE 5.7

Multiple Correlation Coefficients between Building Attribute Clusters and Recall Frequencies

Attribute Clusters	.05 sig.	Verbal Recall	.05 sig.	Map Recall	.05 sig.	Trip Recall
Form Intensity (7)	.32	.41+	.26	.43+	.35	.56+
Form Singularity (7)	.32	.39+	.26	.44+	.35	.56+
Form Attributes (14)	.42	.49+	.37	.50+	.46	.63+
Visibility Attributes (3)	.22	.15	.18	.47+	.24	.48+
Significance Attributes (3)	.22	.38+	.18	.44+	.24	.45+
Total Attributes (21)	.50	.59+	.43	.67+	.54	.71+
Number of Buildings (d.f.)	122		188		104	

+Correlations significant at .05 level.

TABLE 5.8

Correlations between Building Attributes and Group Recall Frequencies: Local versus All Subjects

Source: General Map Responses

Attributes	Puerto Ordaz		Castillito		El Roble		San Felix	
	All	Local	All	Local	All	Local	All	Local
Number of different buildings mentioned on maps	43	22	30	21	31	16	60	34
.05 Significance	.29	.40	.35	.41	.35	.47	.25	.32
Form Singularity:								
Movement	.33+	.36	.55+	.55+	.11	.09	.38+	.37+
Contour	.19	.49+	.48+	.57+	.32	.34	.27+	-.17
Size	.25	.37	.54+	.60+	-.20	-.10	.42+	.11
Shape	.39+	.25	.39+	.51+	-.02	.08	.24	-.04
Surface	.25	-.17	.22	.27	.47+	.69+	.19	.19
Quality	.01	.02	.37+	.36	.04	-.09	.10	.20
Signs	-.01	.10	.05	-.03	.10	-.22	-.02	-.04
Visibility:								
Viewpt. Intensity	.25	-.16	.05	-.02	.27	.36	.18	.20
Viewpt. Signif-icance	.47+	.27	.63+	.51+	.60+	.61+	.22	-.08
Immediacy	.37+	.16	.46+	.37	.46+	.56+	.26+	.14
Significance:								
Use Intensity	.38+	.41+	.40+	.66+	.54+	.25	.49+	.51+
Singu-larity	.18	.24	.34	.69+	.25	.54+	.45+	.29
Signif-icance	-.00	.00	.11	.06	-.13	-.38	-.10	-.07
Multiple Correlation Coefficients (R)								
Form (14)	.76+	.94+	.84+	.93	.79+	.95	.75+	.77+
Visibility (3)	.51+	.43	.64+	.52	.65+	.69+	.31	.39
Significance (3)	.40+	.49	.41	.72+	.68+	.68+	.58+	.57+
All Attributes (21)	.82+	.95	.92	.96	.88	.99+	.80+	.76

+Correlations significant beyond the .05 level.

TABLE 6.1

Building Attributes Selected by Total Sample in Their Descriptions of the Sixteen Buildings

Source: Appendix C Section D. Percentages calculated using 314 respondents as a base. Up to three answers were recorded for each respondent; therefore percentages do not add up to 100.

Attribute Types	Attributes	Percent
Form (External)	Beauty	9.4
	Size	7.4
	Color	4.4
	Shape	4.4
	Wall Materials	4.3
	Height	3.7
	Arch. Style	3.7
	Extl. Furniture	3.3
	Open Spaces	3.3
	Age	2.2
	Maintenance	1.9
	Entrances	1.5
	Windows	1.1
	Signs	1.0
	Parking	0.5
	Roof	0.4
	Lighting	0.1
Form (Internal)	Rooms	2.5
	Furniture	1.2
	Ventilation	1.0
	Floor	0.1
		57.9
Location		10.0
Significance	Activity Type	7.1
	Efficiency	6.2
	User Intensity	0.6
	Significance	0.6
	User Status	0.4
		14.8
Don't Know		54.6
Totals		137.3

TABLE 6.2

Comparison between Recall and Evaluative Responses to Buildings

Source: "Can you describe...?"
Percentages out of 314 responses. Do not add up to 100 since three responses allowed.
Spearman Rank Order Correlation r_s = .20 (N=16)
(Insignificant at the .01, .05 levels)

Buildings ranked by the total sample able to describe them			Buildings ranked by overall % of positive/negative evaluations		
Building	District	%	Building	District	%
Church	S.F.	76	General Electric	P.O.	+19
Grupo Escolar	S.F.	73	Hotel Cunucunuma	P.O.	+15
General Electric	P.O.	57	Bomba Phillips	E.R.	+11
Bomba Phillips	E.R.	56	Esc. Técnica	E.R.	+ 9
Seguros Sociales	S.F.	56	Esc. Tumeremo	C.	+ 5
Hotel Cunucunuma	P.O.	55	Protestant Church	P.O.	+ 5
Post Office	P.O.	49	Esc. J. A. Ruiz	E.R.	+ 5
Esc. Tumeremo	C.	45	Seguros Sociales	S.F.	+ 4
Esc. Técnica	E.R.	45	Grupo Escolar	S.F.	+ 3
Cine Lorena	C.	43	Consejo Municipal	S.F.	0
Consejo Municipal	S.F.	40	Materiales Bolívar	C.	- 1
Protestant Church	P.O.	36	Cine Bolívar	E.R.	- 3
Cine Bolívar	E.R.	32	Cine Lorena	C.	- 7
Medicatura Rural	C.	27	Medicatura Rural	C.	- 7
Materiales Bolívar	C.	24	Post Office	P.O.	- 8
Esc. J. A. Ruiz	E.R.	13	Church	S.F.	-12

TABLE 6.3

Comparison of Form Attribute Rankings between Selected and Described Buildings. For origins of figures see original tables and text page.

Form Attributes	Selected Buildings (Table 5.6)			Described Buildings
	Map Recall	Verbal Recall	Trip Recall	(Table 6.1)
	r	r	r	percent
Movement	.34	.25	.35	9.2
Contour	.26	.18	.33	10.4
Size	.25	.28	.38	35.2
Shape	.21	.22	.29	23.4
Surface	.19	-.08	.23	15.3
Quality	.15	.17	.15	34.5
Signs	-.06	-.15	-.11	3.6

Spearman Rank Order Correlations (r_s)

	Map Recall	Verbal Recall	Trip Recall	Described Buildings
Selected Buildings				
Map Recall		.79+	.99*	.00
Verbal Recall			.99*	.46
Trip Recall				.88+
Described Buildings				

* $r_s > .89$ significant at the .01 level (N = 7)
+ $r_s > .71$ significant at the .05 level (N = 7)

TABLE 7.1

Characteristics of Ideal City (Ranked)

Source: "Now please imagine an ideal city in which you would like to live. What would be the characteristics of this ideal city?" Percentages do not add up to 100 since five answers were allowed each respondent. Least values not shown.

Total Sample	%	Education None	%	Primary	%	Secondary	%	University	%
Recreation	41	Utilities	32	Utilities	54	Recreation	49	Recreation	34
Utilities	39	Econ. Sec.	19	Recreation	40	Utilities	26	Education	28
Education	25	Med. Serv.	19	Econ. Sec.	27	Education	25	Climate	24
Econ. Sec.	24	Educ. Serv.	19	Education	26	Econ. Sec.	23	Commerce	22
Transptn.	23	Transptn.	16	Transptn.	25	Transptn.	22	Transptn.	22
Med. Serv.	21	Recreation	12	Med. Serv.	24	Med. Serv.	18	Med. Serv.	13
Commerce	14	Commerce	9	Commerce	9	Commerce	18	Econ. Sec.	13
Culture	10	Livg. Cost	6	Culture	9	Soc. Env.	13	Planning	13
Housing	10	Culture	6	Commctns.	8	Culture	13	Progress	13
Climate	8	Housing	6	Housing	7	Housing	12	Utilities	9
Commctns.	8	Cleanlss.	3	Climate	5	Commctn.	12	Culture	9
Soc. Env.	5	Ec. System	3	Sports Flds.	5	Climate	12	Churches	9
		Churches	3	Constrctn.	5				
		Commctns.	3						
		Morality	3						
Respondents	314		32		167		83		32

Spearman Rank Order Correlations (r_s)

	Primary	Secondary	University
None	.74+	.65*	.43+
Primary		.85*	.58*
Secondary			.58*
University			

Residence

Country Club	%	Puerto Ordaz	%	Castillito	%	El Roble	%	San Félix	%	Campo Caroní	%
Commerce	55	Recreation	57	Utilities	42	Utilities	62	Recreation	41	Recreation	60
Education	44	Education	30	Econ. Sec.	36	Transptn.	31	Utilities	29	Education	40
Recreation	33	Transptn.	26	Recreation	29	Recreation	31	Econ. Sec.	27	Climate	20
Climate	33	Utilities	26	Med. Serv.	24	Education	25	Education	24	Commerce	20
Progress	33	Med. Serv.	18	Education	17	Med. Serv.	21	Med. Serv.	21	Med. Serv.	20
Planning	33	Econ. Sec.	15	Transptn.	17	Econ. Sec.	19	Transptn.	19	Churches	20

(Table 7.1 cont. on next page)

Table 7.1 (cont.)

Residence

Country Club	%	Puerto Ordaz	%	Castillito	%	El Roble	%	San Félix	%	Campo Caroní	%
Soc. Env.	33	Culture	12	Commerce	14	Commctns.	11	Culture	9	Housing	20
Churches	22	Climate	12	Housing	8	Housing	10	Commerce	9		
Transptn.	22	Commerce	11	Culture	8	Culture	8	Climate	9		
Constrctn.	22	Tranqulty.	8	Livg. Cost	7	Commerce	8	Commctns.	9		
		Housing	8	Commctns.	7	Cleanlss.	8	Churches	5		
				Soc. Env.	6	Constrctn.	6	Housing	5		
								Soc. Env.	5		
	9		74		74		72		75		10

Spearman Rank Order Correlations (r_s)

	Puerto Ordaz	Castillito	El Roble	San Félix	Campo Caroní
Country Club	$.32^{+}$	.01	.05	.29	.32
Puerto Ordaz		$.63^{*}$	$.67^{*}$	$.76^{*}$	$.55^{+}$
Castillito			$.72^{*}$	$.72^{+}$	$.56^{+}$
El Roble				$.81^{*}$	$.68^{+}$
San Félix					$.73^{+}$
Campo Caroní					

$^{*}r_s > .45$ significant at the .01 level

$^{+}r_s > .32$ significant at the .05 level

r_s calculated for 27 attributes

TABLE 7.2

Characteristics of Worst Imaginable City (Ranked)

Source: "Imagine a city in which it would be very disagreeable to live. What are the characteristics which would make it bad?"
Percentages do not add up to 100 since five answers were allowed each respondent.
Least values on each table not shown.

		Education							
Total Sample	%	None	%	Primary	%	Secondary	%	University	%
Utilities	78	Utilities	62	Utilities	90	Utilities	71	Utilities	55
Transptn.	28	Transptn.	29	Transptn.	28	Transptn.	23	Transptn.	42
Med. Serv.	23	Econ. Scrty.	19	Med. Serv.	28	Med. Serv.	23	Climate	19
Econ. Scrty.	20	Med. Serv.	10	Econ. Scrty.	24	Recreation	21	Recreation	15
Education	16	Education	10	Education	20	Cleanlss.	18	Econ. Scrty.	13
Recreation	15	Housing	6	Recreation	15	Econ. Scrty.	16	Med. Serv.	13
Housing	11	Entertain.	6	Cleanlss.	10	Housing	14	Education	13
Cleanlss.	11	Commerce	6	Commerce	9	Education	13	Tranquility	10
Commerce	7	Cleanlss.	6	Climate	4	Commerce	8	Culture	10
Climate	6	Recreation	6	Econ.	4	Commctns.	7		
Entertain.	5			Entertain.	4	Climate	7		
Commctns.	5			Churches	4	Entertain.	6		
Ec. System	5			Commctns.	4				
Respondent	314		32		167		83		32

Spearman Rank Order Correlations (r_s)

	Primary	Secondary	University
None	.71*	.67*	.47*
Primary		.93*	.54*
Secondary			.49*
University			

(TABLE 7.2 cont. on next page)

TABLE 7.2 (cont.)

Residence											
Country Club	%	Puerto Ordaz	%	Castillito	%	El Roble	%	San Félix	%	Campo Caroní	%
Transptn.	67	Utilities	65	Utilities	70	Utilities	100	Utilities	77	Utilities	80
Climate	44	Transptn.	28	Med. Serv.	24	Transptn.	35	Econ. Scrty.	24	Med. Serv.	30
Recreation	33	Recreation	19	Econ. Scrty.	23	Med. Serv.	24	Transptn.	20	Education	20
Planning	22	Housing	15	Transptn.	22	Education	21	Med. Serv.	19	Econ. Scrty.	20
Culture	22	Med. Serv.	15	Morality	12	Econ. Scrty.	18	Recreation	19	Housing	20
Utilities	22	Econ. Scrty.	13	Recreation	11	Cleanlss.	15	Education	15	Commctns.	20
		Education	13	Entertain.	11	Recreation	14	Cleanlss.	15		
		Climate	7	Housing	9	Housing	10	Morality	11		
		Morality	5	Education	9	Commerce	7	Commerce	8		
		Planning	5	Cleanlss.	8	Commctn.	6	Housing	8		
		Entertain.	5	Commerce	7	Economy	4	Churches	5		
				Economy	7			Climate	5		
				Climate							
Respondents	9		74		72		72		75		10

Spearman Rank Order Correlations (r_s)

	Puerto Ordaz	Castillito	El Roble	San Félix	Campo Caroní
Country Club	.43+	.21	.20	.23	.38+
Puerto Ordaz		.77*	.73*	.65*	.55*
Castillitos			.72*	.69*	.46*
El Roble				.66*	.67*
San Félix					.53*
Campo Caroní					

*$r_s > .45$ significant at .01 level

+$r_s > .32$ significant at .05 level

r_s calculated for 28 attributes

TABLE 7.3

Important Places for a Newcomer

Percentages out of 314 respondents do not add up to 100 since more than one answer was allowed.

Source: A. "What places should a newcomer know?"
B. "Other interesting places a newcomer should know?"

A. Place	Type	%	B. Place	Type	%
CVG	housing office	15.7	Los Saltos	waterfalls	12.8
Matanzas	steel mill	12.8	Matanzas	steel mill	10.5
Centro Cívico	civic center	12.8	Centro Cívico	civic center	8.0
Market San Félix	market	9.6	Plaza Bolívar	square	6.1
Plaza Bolívar	square	9.3	Bridge	bridge	5.8
OMC Offices	employment off.	8.3	Iron Mines Co.	industry	3.8
Police San Félix	police	5.4	Caroní Park	park	3.5
Cine Park	cinema	5.4	Market San Félix	market	3.2
Free Market	market	4.5	Police	police	3.2
OMC	industry	3.5	Church	church	3.2
Cine Rex	cinema	3.2	Seguros Sociales	medical	3.2
			Airport	airport	2.6

TABLE 7.4

Comparative Rankings of Valued and Recalled Elements

Percentages as described in original tables. Percentages under Recalled Element Types are more than 100 because frequency percentages of individual elements of the same type; e.g., bridges, were added together. Least values are not shown.

Valued Elements (see Table 15)		Recalled Elements							
		Types		Individual Facilities					
	%	Map Recall	%	Verbal Recall	%	Map Recall	%	Trip Recall	%
utilities	39	bridges	419	commce/civic	18	steel mill	83	steel mill	86
recreation	36	gas statns.	390	waterfalls	18	bridge	62	airport	61
education	25	hospitals	333	steel mill	17	airport	46	bridge	55
ec. secty.	24	cinemas	219	plaza	16	port	39	gas statn.	38
transpt.	23	schools	214	market	8	water transpt.	34	water transpt.	31
med. serv.	21	plazas	191	bridge	8	gas statn.	33	bridge	30
commce.	14	hotels	178	cinema	7	plaza	33	gas statn.	29
culture	10	water trans.	140	hospital	7	commce/civic	32	plaza	29
housing	10	churches	119	airport	6	market	32	hotel	27
climate	8	wholesale	114	dam	5	bridge	30	bridge	26
communic.	8	stadia	91	port	5	gas statn.	27	tech. sch.	26
soc. environ.	5	drugstores	91	tech. sch.	4	gas statn.	27	quarry	25
		supermkts.	88	park	4	bridge	26	market	24
		police	85	police	4	hotel	20	gas statn.	24
		ad. signs	85	church	4	railroad	19	railroad	22
		banks	81	water trans.	4	church	18	church	20
		tech. sch.	69	stadium	4	hospital	18	railroad	17
		food mfg.	67	hospital	4	quarry	17	police	16
		C.V.G.	66	port	3	police	17	stadium	16

TABLE 7.5

Perception of Selected Functions

Source: General Maps. Figures show aggregate percentages per zone to nearest whole number for all facilities of each type selected from each group of respondents. Comparison should be made between groups rather than between facilities since the facilities varied in numbers. Industry is not shown since the analysis was confined to the main settlement areas.

	Respondents	Adv. Signs.	Banks	Bridges	Churches	Cinemas	Consejo	CVG	Gas Stations	Hospitals	Hotels	Military	Parks	Plazas	Police	Schools	Stadia	Supermarkets
Education[1]		%	%	%	%	%	%	%	%	%	%	%	%	%	%	%	%	%
None	6	50	33	150	13	32	33	100	49	108	9	--	--	100	50	63	--	17
Primary	67	55	22	220	49	69	13	47	111	95	60	54	--	71	29	39	33	22
Secondary	56	53	22	286	48	80	46	18	154	99	49	17	48	80	37	69	63	38
University	10	--	7	167	11	--	--	--	22	33	12	--	122	11	11	13	22	7
Travel Mode[2]																		
Car	41	11	10	216	22	45	29	14	101	80	36	44	49	58	39	61	28	34
Por Puesto	35	18	19	239	29	76	9	25	98	132	29	--	18	79	28	39	59	33
Bus	73	86	27	261	46	78	24	63	120	84	65	23	--	75	32	61	38	22
Age[3]																		
Under 20	56	45	30	239	52	83	42	41	163	78	33	11	17	135	48	46	52	34
21 to 30	35	13	18	290	24	38	33	40	78	85	53	12	39	66	13	39	38	21
Over 30	58	14	31	199	47	74	20	54	88	116	53	25	10	86	33	53	28	17
Sex[4]																		
Male	102	64	27	276	28	77	17	45	122	112	55	23	25	75	37	55	51	25
Female	48	21	18	143	44	54	35	21	72	73	33	25	10	76	29	49	10	25
Familiarity[5]																		
Under 6 mos.	4	--	--	500	--	20	--	33	50	50	--	--	100	--	--	--	--	--
6 mos. to 1 yr.	10	--	10	390	--	38	20	20	138	30	37	--	100	20	15	30	60	42
1 yr. to 5 yrs.	63	28	15	301	20	52	10	29	78	74	37	42	60	62	25	33	36	18
Over 5 yrs.	72	42	24	306	42	37	22	19	88	80	34	24	17	63	23	53	46	22

1 $X^2 = 219.67$, 48 d.f., $P < .001$

2 $X^2 = 138.25$, 32 d.f., $P < .001$

3 $X^2 = 91.32$, 32 d.f., $P < .001$

4 $X^2 = 47.70$, 16 d.f., $P - .001$

5 $X^2 = 99.07$, 48 d.f., $P < .001$

TABLE 8.1

Structural Styles

Sources: General Maps or Local Maps where no General Map was drawn.
Percentages out of 211 respondents who drew maps.

		Local Settlement Maps														Whole City Maps													
		Sequential						Spatial								Sequential						Spatial							
	Respondents with maps	Fragment	Chain	Bent Chain	Branch/Loop	Network	Total	Cluster	Scatter	Mosaic	Link	Pattern		No local map	Total	Fragment	Chain	Bent Chain	Branch/Loop	Network	Total	Cluster	Scatter	Mosaic	Link	Pattern		No city map	Total
Residence																													
Country Club	9	22		11	22	33	88			11			11		99	33	22			22	77	11		11			22		99
Puerto Ordaz	53	6	15	17	19	11	68	9	9	6	8		32		100	9	13	23	17	13	75	9	8	4	2		23	2	101
Castillito	51	4	23	17	19	10	73	2	14		2		18	8	99	10	12	19	23	13	77	4	15				19	2	98
El Roble	38	5	16	24	18	11	74	8	5	5	3		21	5	100	8	13	24	21	11	77	5	11	5		3	24		101
San Félix	50	2	12	14	18	6	52	14	12	6	8	6	46	2	98	2	12	18	24	12	68	6	10	4	2	4	26	6	100
Campo Caroní	10		20			20	40							60	100			30	10	40	80		10	10			20		100
Education																													
None	11	18	18	9	18	9	72	9	9				18	9	99	18	9	9	36	9	81	9	9				18		99
Primary	107	2	19	18	18	6	63	8	11	5	6	3	33	6	102	4	14	24	18	11	71	6	12	5		3	26	4	101
Secondary	67	4	16	15	21	16	72	6	9	4	4		23	3	100	9	9	21	25	16	80	6	7	3	3		19		99
University	26	12	4	19	12	19	66	8	4	4	4		20	15	101	19	15	8	8	23	73	8	12	4			24	4	101
Familiarity																													
Under 6 mos.	7		57	29			86				14		14		100		14	14	43	14	85		14				14	3	102
6 mos. - 1 yr.	14	14	7	14	43		78		14				14	7	99	21	21		36		78		21				21		99
1 yr. - 5 yrs.	91	5	15	16	14	16	66	10	9	2	3	1	25	7	98	8	12	23	14	19	76	5	11	3		1	20	3	99
Over 5 yrs.	99	3	15	16	19	8	61	7	10	7	6	2	32	6	99	7	11	21	21	12	72	8	8	5	2	2	25	2	99
Age																													
Under 20	71	3	19	17	19	11	69	8	7	4	6	1	26	3	98	7	13	22	22	15	79	3	8	3	1	1	16	3	98
21 - 30	52	4	12	21	19	8	64	10	12	2	4		28	10	102	6	15	19	21	12	73	8	13	4			25	2	100
Over 30	88	7	16	14	16	13	66	6	10	6	5	2	29	7	102	10	10	19	17	15	71	8	10	5	1	2	26	2	99
Travel Mode																													
Car	52	4	12	17	21	12	66	10	13	4	4		31	4	101	8	15	12	21	13	69	8	19	2			29	2	100
Por Puesto	43	5	16	21	12	7	61	9	12	12	5	2	38		101	7	9	23	16	7	62	7	14	9	2	2	34	2	98
Bus	95	4	20	17	21	9	71	7	8	1	6	2	24	3	98	5	13	25	24	15	82	5	5	1	1	1	13	3	98
Sex																													
Male	140	3	15	16	22	14	70	7	9	4	4		24	6	100	6	10	18	23	16	73	6	11	4	1	1	23	3	99
Female	71	8	18	17	10	6	59	8	11	4	6	4	33	7	99	11	17	25	13	11	77	6	8	4		3	21	1	99

(TABLE 8.1 cont. on next page)

TABLE 8.1 (cont.)

Occupations Selected																													
Small businessman	17		29	12	29		70	12	12	6			30	--	100		24	12	41		77		18	6			24	--	101
Personal services	10		10	20	20		50	10	20		10		40	10	100	10	20	10	20		50	20	20				40	10	100
Professionals	13	8	8	23	15	15	69	8			15		23	8	100	8	15	15	8	15	61	15	8			8	31	8	100
Students	40		15	18	23	15	71	8	5	5	8	3	29	3	103	3	13	20	23	20	79	3	5	5	3	5	21	--	100
Unemployed	10		10	30	20	10	70		10			10	20	10	100	10	10	10	30	20	80		20				20	--	100
Big business	10				10	30	40	10	10	20		10	50	10	100	20	--	--	10	20	50	20	10	10			40	10	100
Office workers	18	6	17	17	17	6	63	17	11	6			34	6	103	6	11	28	28		73	11	11	6			28	--	101
Housewives	41	10	24	15	7	5	61	7	15	5	5		32	7	100	15	15	29	7	10	76	2	15	5		2	24	2	102
Skilled workers	2	4	15	19	22	22	82	4	4	4	4		16	4	102	4	7	26	19	26	82	7	4	4	4		19	--	101
Total Sample	211	5	17	17	19	12	70	8	10	4	5	1	28	6	104	8	13	21	21	15	78	6	11	4	1	1	23	--	101

TABLE 8.2

Structural Errors

Source: The number of errors for each of nine city zones were recorded from the General Maps. Then the mean number of errors per zone were calculated as a percentage of all those who responded to the General Map, including those from the Country Club and Campo Caroni. Percentages are low because they are in each case one-ninth of the total errors committed.

	Respondents	Zone Faults and Bends per Zone	Zone Reversals per Zone	Zone Mislocations per Zone	Landmark Mislocations per Zone	Road Distortions per Zone	Mean Errors per Zone
Education[1]							
None	4	2.7	--	5.5	1.0	8.0	3.4
Primary	79	5.3	2.2	2.2	3.0	8.9	4.3
Secondary	66	3.1	1.1	1.1	0.5	6.0	2.4
University	18	1.8	--	1.1	--	6.7	1.7
Travel Mode[2]							
Auto	31	6.0	1.7	1.7	0.2	3.5	2.6
Por Puesto	69	4.6	2.5	2.5	1.1	8.3	3.8
Bus	68	3.1	0.4	0.9	0.6	5.4	2.1
Sex[3]							
Male	115	3.3	1.6	1.2	0.6	7.3	2.8
Female	53	3.3	1.0	2.7	1.2	7.6	3.2
Total Sample	168	3.3	1.5	1.7	0.8	7.4	2.9

[1] $\chi^2 = 15.30$, 12 d.f., $P < .30$

[2] $\chi^2 = 14.85$, 8 d.f., $P < .10$

[3] $\chi^2 = 8.48$, 4 d.f., $P < .10$

TABLE 9.1

Perceived, Desired, and Predicted Changes in the City

Sources: 1. "And how has it changed during all the time you have lived here?"
2. "In what way do you find Santo Tome has changed during the last year?"
3. "What do you consider to be the most urgent needs of the city?"
4. "What changes do you expect to see in the city during the next five years?"

Note: Percentages out of 314 respondents do not add up to 100 because up to five answers per respondent were recorded, and categories are aggregates of responses; e.g., if a respondent mentioned two types of community services these would be aggregated.

Rank	1. Observed during Residence	%	2. Observed Last Year	%	3. Desired	%	4. Predicted Next 5 Years	%
1	Population†	130	Population†	156	Infrastructure§	395	Population†	162
2	Infrastructure	120	Infrastructure	151	Commty. Serv.§	232	Infrastructure	78
3	Construction†	57	Housing§	100	Recreation§	92	Construction†	73
4	Housing	45	Construction	90	Housing	67	Economy§	64
5	Economy	39	Economy	73	Commerce§	36	Beauty§	56
6	Commty. Serv.	39	Commty. Serv.	66	Beauty	34	Commty. Serv.	54
7	Industry†	17	Industry†	26	Economy	14	Housing	47
8	Administration§	11	Recreation	17	Population	8	Industry	47
9	Recreation	11	Commerce	15	Industry	4	Administration	42
10	Commerce	11	Physical Beauty	7	Construction	3	Recreation	23

Spearman Rank Order Correlation (r_s)

	Observed Last Year	Desired	Predicted
Observed during Residence	.96*	.10	.75*
Observed Last Year		.24	.73+
Desired			.04
Predicted Next 5 Years			

*r_s .75 significant at the .01 level (N=10)
+r_s .56 significant at the .05 level (N=10)

† ranked highest equal
§ ranked highest among comparable groups

TABLE 11.1

Elements and Attributes of Urban Spatial Structure

Elements	Attributes		
	Imageable	Operational	Significant
Landmarks	Landmarks, buildings, bus stops, hills, billboards, "stacks," (Clay, 1973)	Destinations, goals, noxiants (Chein, 1954) home, work place, local stores	Monuments, civic, community facilities, major construction investments.
Nodes	Plazas, traffic circles, defined places	Events, decision points, intersections, bus stops	Outdoor meeting places, shopping centers
Paths	Channels, boulevards, strips, elevated freeways, rivers, railroad tracks	Paths, routes, journey to work, school, shops, "beats" (Clay, 1973)	Processional ways, historical routes, passegiata
Edges	Edges, walls, river banks, escarpments, "fronts," "breaks," (Clay, 1973)	Barriers to movement, linear obstacles	Social and political boundaries, borders and frontiers, ownership lines
Districts	Valleys, physical districts	Territories, turf, orbits	Social areas, neighborhoods, historical zones

TABLE B.1

Population Sample Distribution

	Total Sample	Country Club	Puerto Ordaz	Castillito	El Roble	San Félix	Campo Caroní
Total	314	9	74	74	72	75	10
Age							
Over 30	140	9	51	25	21	26	8
21-30	75	-	15	18	29	11	2
Under 20	99	-	8	31	22	38	-
Sex							
Male	192	6	50	42	36	51	7
Female	122	3	24	32	36	24	3
Education							
University	32	5	14	3	1	2	7
Secondary	83	2	35	18	8	20	-
Primary	167	2	25	38	49	50	3
None	32	-	-	15	14	3	-
Income							
Over 3000 B's	25	7	7	1	-	1	9
800 to 3000 B's	62	-	27	13	6	16	-
200 to 800 B's	45	-	3	13	12	17	-
Under 200 B's	182	2	37	47	54	41	1
Familiarity							
Over 5 yrs.	144	6	35	20	32	49	2
1-5 yrs.	129	3	31	42	27	18	8
Under 1 yr.	28	-	6	8	9	5	-
Under 3 mos.	13	-	2	4	4	3	-
Urbanity							
Urban	106	4	39	23	14	19	7
Urban-Rural	84	4	15	27	21	16	1
Rural	124	1	20	24	37	40	2
Mobility							
Citywide	39	0	6	14	6	11	2
Half-City	68	1	9	8	27	18	5
Local	207	8	59	52	39	46	3
Travel Mode							
Auto	83	8	41	11	5	15	3
Por Puesto	64	1	13	15	18	14	3
Bus	167	-	20	48	49	46	4

(Table B.1 cont. on next page)

TABLE B.1 (cont.)

	Total Sample	Country Club	Puerto Ordaz	Castill-ito	El Roble	San Félix	Campo Caroní
Occupation							
Sm.Business	28	-	3	10	3	12	-
Service	21	-	2	6	5	8	-
Professional	15	1	8	1	2	1	2
Student	47	-	8	10	11	18	-
Unemployed	15	1	2	4	6	2	-
Lge. Business	9	4	2	2	-	1	-
Office Wkrs.	18	-	8	2	2	5	1
Housewives	82	2	14	23	28	13	2
Skilled Wkrs.	38	1	8	7	14	6	2
Other	41	-	19	9	1	9	3
Nationality							
Venezuelan	244	1	51	62	66	60	4
Latin Amer.	9	1	4	1	-	1	2
British Caribbn.	6	-	3	2	-	1	-
Mediterranean	28	-	6	6	3	10	3
N. American	14	7	6	-	-	1	-
N. European	6	-	4	-	-	1	1
M. East.	1	-	-	1	-	-	-
Other	6	-	-	2	3	1	-

TABLE B.2

Population Group Intercorrelations

314 Respondents

	Residence	Sex	Age	Education	Travel Mode	Familiarity	Age of Arrival	Urbanity	Mobility	Income
Residence		.03	.15*	.30*	.24*	-.12	-.21*	.18*	-.12	.16*
Sex**			.16*	.26*	.13	.12	-.07	.16*	.23*	.61*
Age**				.13	.28*	.25*	.65*	-.22	.07	.44*
Education					.50*	-.08	-.12	.34*	-.05	.38*
Travel Mode**						-.01	-.25*	.19*	-.05	.32*
Familiarity**							.24*	-.06	.15*	.03
Age of Arrival								.17*	-.07	.43*
Urbanity**									-.07	.08
Mobility**										.28*
Income										

* Correlations exceeding .148 are significant at the .05 level.
** Population types analyzed for urban perceptions.

B

APPENDIX THE INTERVIEWS AND FIELD SURVEYS

The Purposive Area Sample Design

To assess the reactions of the inhabitants to different kinds of environment, we chose to stratify the area sample in four main settlements of the city rather than to adopt a citywide frame of reference. These four parts of the city covered the range of settlement type from indigenous to planned, from old to new.

Within these four settlements emphasis was laid on the younger and middle-aged population and on males whose perceptions and decisions might be more critical to the future of the city. To yield enough cases in each district for the analysis within as well as among districts to be possible, 75 subjects (50 males and 25 females) were randomly selected from each residential district, making a total of some 300 cases.

Once all the dwelling units had been located and numbered from a newly created base map, 73 units were randomly selected from the total number of dwellings in each area. A special quota system was established to guide the selection of respondents in each dwelling. One-third of the sample was to be under twenty-one years old, and one-third was to be over thirty-one. These quotas were reasonably met in all settlements except Puerto Ordaz, where, out of the 75 houses visited, only 12 had teenage occupants. For this reason, the age quota had to be modified in Puerto Ordaz, and field-workers were instructed simply to obtain as many interviews with young people as possible.

In addition to the four main sample groups, a small sample of people was selected from the Country Club, a residential suburb for top executives of the Orinoco Mining Company, and another ten people from the CVG engineers' residential enclave at Campo Caroní on the east side of the Caroní River. These small samples were selected for the purpose of getting some perceptions of the leadership groups. Identical procedures for random selection of dwelling units were used. The age quota had to be abandoned here, but a majority of male respondents was attained as originally anticipated.

Original and Substitute Samples

For the total sample, including the two high-income residential areas where only 19 interviews were made, a total of 67 substitutions of the sample dwellings originally scheduled had to be made. This high rate (slightly above 20 percent substitution) in the vast majority of cases was due to the impossibility of fulfilling the age and sex quotas in the selected dwelling units. A considerably smaller percentage was due to temporarily vacant dwellings and to refusals by the selected respondents. All substitutions were drawn following precisely the same selection procedures as in the original sample.

General Characteristics of the Sample

Residence, age, and sex were the bases for the selection of the sample. With 75 persons from each of the main settlements and 10 each from the two elite housing groups, a range of population type and a range of settlement type were sampled. The selection by age resulted in a relatively young overall sample, one-third of whom were teenagers, almost all in their late teens; under one-third of whom were in their twenties; over one-third of whom were over thirty. There were a few who were over fifty years of age. The sample contained more young people in San Félix, more old people in Puerto Ordaz—almost all of whom were from the Country Club and the Campo Caroní. For each individual settlement, and for the total sample, the two-thirds male, one-third female quota was held to more successfully than was the age quota.

Besides place of residence, sex, and age, no other selection of respondents was made. The sample was broken down as in table B.1.

The income figures are complicated by the large number of housewives and students in the sample. Our initial hypotheses that Castillito would represent the low-income bracket and San Félix the mixed-income population were not confirmed by the results. Among the working population, the median monthly income was the same for the inhabitants of San Félix and Castillito, both being about Bs. 600 (Bolívars; U.S. $150) a month. Although the range of income variation in Castillito was from Bs. 25 to Bs. 4,000 a month, in San Félix it was significantly more restricted—only Bs. 60 to Bs. 1,200 a month. On the other hand, the remaining settlements closely conformed to our hypothetical socioeconomic description. El Roble emerged as a working-class community with an active population receiving a median income of Bs. 800 (U.S. $200) a month—within a range of Bs. 100 to Bs. 3,000 a month. And in Puerto Ordaz we found a median monthly income of Bs. 1,250 (U.S. $312) and an income range from Bs. 144 to Bs. 5,500. At the Country Club, the median income was Bs. 11,250 a month (U.S. $2,812) and in the Campo Caroní, Bs. 2,100 a month (U.S. $525), which clearly expresses the privileged position these two communities have in the city.

The educational breakdown followed a somewhat similar pattern. In Puerto Ordaz, 66 percent of the sample had entered or completed a secondary or university education, whereas only 29 percent in Castillito and San Félix and only 12 percent in El Roble had achieved the same level. In the Castillito and El Roble samples, 20 percent in each case had had no education. University graduates in these settlements were to be found primarily in Puerto Ordaz, but seven out of nine respondents in the Country Club had a secondary education or more, and seven out of ten in the Campo Caroní had been to a university.

Practically one-half the population included in the sample had lived in Ciudad Guayana for five years or more. In Castillito, which, like El Roble, was frequently described as a reception area in the city, over two-thirds of respondents had more than a year's residence, but it did contain fewer long-term inhabitants than other settlements. The sample from San Félix, on the other hand, confirmed the expectations associated with its old buildings by containing a greater percentage of long-term inhabitants than any other settlement. Some intracity migration was evident in Castillito, an area where one-fifth the residents had previously lived in San Félix. Each settlement, however, did contain a comparable proportion of new migrants except for the Country Club sample, most of whom had been in the city more than five years. They, of course, were associated with the Orinoco Mining operations.

Over one-third of the sample had a dominantly rural background, just under one-third had a dominantly urban upbringing, and the rest were from mixed backgrounds. The upper-class groups in the Country Club, Puerto Ordaz, and the Campo Caroní were more urban oriented; those in El Roble and San Félix were of dominantly rural background. In general, the long-distance urban migrants came from the more-educated groups (MacDonald 1969). But as a high degree of residential mobility was a common pattern for the majority of respondents, the migrant group was quite heterogeneous with regard to age, sex, and educational level.

Among the other general aspects of the sample, one-half of the respondents used buses as their main mode of transportation, and about one-quarter used either cars or collective taxis (*por puesto*). The relatively high rate of car use is characteristic of Venezuela, although car users are still to be found only among the upper-income and more-educated groups. In our sample, car use was significantly correlated with education ($r = .50$), income ($r = .38$), age ($r = .28$), and urbanity ($r = .19$). Probably as a result of the higher percentage of respondents from the labor force, the overall physical mobility between home and work was not very high. Only one-eighth crossed the Caroní River daily, while two-thirds lived and worked within their own settlements. It should be noted, however, that this measure did not take into account journeys for shopping, entertainment, or any other trips than those for work purposes.

The largest occupational groups in the sample were housewives (25 percent), students, and skilled workers, followed by small businessmen, those in service and office employment, executives, and professionals. The remaining group held "miscellaneous occupations" except for 5 percent who were unemployed. Three-quarters of the sample were Venezuelan-born; the largest minority group, under one-tenth, came from the Mediterranean, while others came principally from the United States (nearly all in the Country Club or Puerto Ordaz), other Latin American countries, the British Caribbean, or the Middle East.

Intercorrelations between Personal Dimensions

Many of the personal dimensions intercorrelated to some degree (table B.2). Education was a better indicator of social class than income, since only a few females interviewed would report income, and income and sex correlated highly ($r = .61$). Education and income correlated significantly ($r = .38$). Since place of residence correlated significantly, though not highly, with education ($r = .30$), it could also be taken as an indicator of social class, but it correlated less with income ($r = .16$).

The age of inhabitants and their age at arrival in the city correlated highly, as would be expected ($r = .65$). Age also correlated with income ($r = .44$), since those in the youngest age group were under twenty years old. Age and education, however, bore each other a negligible relationship ($r = .14$), indicating that the younger generation was as poorly educated as the older generation. We expected a negative correlation, given the increase in educational opportunity, but the figures may have been affected by the fact that the younger category of our sample (under twenty) had not yet had the opportunity to gain a college education. The effect was also minimized because the older generation in the sample contained a high proportion of college-trained respondents from the Country Club and the Campo Caroní.

Familiarity with the city (time of residence) was a relatively independent dimension, even from age (r .25) and age at arrival ($r = .24$), although these were significant. Newcomers were from all age groups. Familiarity did not correlate at all with the urbanity of a person's background ($r = -.06$).

While travel mode correlated highly with education, physical mobility (home-to-work distance) did not ($r = -.05$); neither did physical mobility correlate with travel mode ($r = -.05$). Travel mode therefore had no effect on the distance traveled to work, primarily because of the bus and *por puesto* service to the steel mill and throughout the city.

Interviewing

Forty potential interviewers received one week of training, and from these, ten were finally hired for the fieldwork. Interviewing began in the second week of May 1964 and was completed by the end of June. Each interviewer averaged two interviews a day. They worked without a rigid time schedule, being responsible for a certain number of interviews in each of the sample areas and having to report at least once a day to the central office in San Félix to turn in the work done, obtain necessary substitutions, and revise the completed schedules. The apparently small number of daily interviews per person reflects in some cases the difficulty of finding the selected dwellings and of filling sample quotas and in others the periodical return to the central office to obtain substitutions, a trip that could mean losing half of a working day. In still other cases, mostly in Puerto Ordaz, several appointments with the respondent had to be made before his consent to be interviewed was obtained.

Expert Field Surveys

An essential component of this study, as in Lynch's and the author's previous work, was a field survey by trained observers (Lynch 1960; Appleyard, Lynch, and Myer 1964).

The field surveys in Ciudad Guyana developed the fairly elaborate scaling techniques described in chapter 5, and they assessed the levels of visibility, distinctiveness, use, and functional significance of all buildings and districts in the city. These elements were identified initially from the environmental survey and from inspections of available data on employment from the economists. After the interviews had been completed and processed, all other buildings that were mentioned more than twice on subject maps were also inspected, photographed, and scored. A file of black-and-white photographs was kept of every mentioned building in the city, and the scalings of the building were recorded on the back of each photograph. These photographs were taken from the most common viewpoint of each building. Ratings that could not be made from the photographs, such as relative visibility and color, were made on the site. Photographs were also taken of a "typical" street in each barrio or urbanización. This photo file was indispensable in interpreting the interview results and invaluable as a reference tool. The initial surveys took approximately two weeks of intensive fieldwork. The follow-up surveys took more time, because data processing was carried out in Cambridge, Massachusetts, and communications with the field surveyor in Ciudad Guayana were difficult. All ratings of buildings from the photographs were made by two independent raters, and then differences were resolved through discussion.

Other systematic surveys were made of the trip along the main road of the city. Time-lapse movies, at a rate of approximately four frames per second, were taken on a 16-mm movie camera for the entire length of the city in both directions. Similar movies were taken over the future alignments of the Avenida Guayana and into different residential areas. Tape recordings were made of the trips by both a North American urban designer and a local Venezuelan inhabitant. In addition, 360-degree composite panoramic photographs were constructed at some 50 points along the main road, and plan diagrams of the visible terrain were developed from these photographs. These materials were used in determining many of the reasons underlying the structure of the free-recall maps. Finally, the field surveyors developed their own general maps of what they predicted the inhabitants would show on their maps.

The field survey is useful to the designer for several reasons. First, it makes his variables more explicit. Many analyses of environmental perception produce findings based only on the verbal vocabulary of the ordinary subject, which is useful to the designer in a general but not explicit way. The trained designer, by making his own predictions and evaluations about the environment, is producing explicit hypotheses that can be tested against subject responses. He is forced to develop scales in an environmental nonverbal language.

Coding the Interviews

Although a preliminary coding system was developed for the interview and worked quite well for the personal data, most of the questions asked for open responses. The verbal responses were dealt with in the usual way. A perusal of 25 percent of the responses determined the main coding categories, and all responses were coded, punched, and fed into the computer. Use of the computer was essential to gain information on cross-tabulations.

The coding of subject maps was a lengthy process. Each

building, structure, district, and portion of road, such as a bend or an intersection, was given a number. Coders then systematically read from each map drawn by a respondent, a list of numbers. If a road was mentioned but bends or intersections were missing, the straight segments only would be coded. This explains the segmented nature of the road system on the composite subject maps. The numbers were then punched and given to the computer, and data from the printouts were recorded on maps where all elements were numbered. The graphics of recording followed those used by Lynch (1960). Analyses of structural errors demanded an even more rigorous analysis of the maps. In this case, all distortions from and mismatches with an accurate map of the city were coded. Had the project been timed a few months later, these results could have been recorded much more simply and quickly through a computer graphics program.[1]

C

APPENDIX THE INTERVIEW SCHEDULE

The interview was developed and structured with the assistance of Latin American and North American social scientists. The first interviews were taken by Dr. Lisa Peattie. They were modified, given to the pretest sample, and put in final form.

The interview schedule experimented with several types of questions relevant to perceptions, attitudes, and use of the city. The interview was structured to begin with the most open questions about the respondents' knowledge of the city. First they were asked to draw a map of the whole city and to describe a journey along the main road. A section dealing with perception of change came next, followed by a series of questions about the four local settlements, questions that asked for maps of the local areas and elicited information about the activities, "kinds of people," and other characteristics of each settlement. These were followed by requests for descriptions of four buildings in each settlement. These questions were mostly successful, with the exception of the one on district characteristics, which was not explicit enough, producing responses of a general functional or social nature. If the question asked had been "How would a stranger know he was there?" or "How would you describe its physical characteristics?" the responses might have been more specific and vivid.

The next set of questions, dealing with values and preferences, received rich responses. People appeared to enjoy making judgments. Questions about the functioning of the city were aimed at finding out how much inhabitants knew about such things. These functional questions would have benefited also by comparisons with actual behavior. The final questions were a number of miscellaneous probes into specific items of urban knowledge.

The only difficulties occurred in response to the map questions. Many subjects had never drawn a map before and were either reluctant or unable to attempt one. Consequently, ways were developed to assist them. They were asked to place the steel mill at one side of the map and the settlement of San Félix at the other. If they still could not proceed on their own, they were encouraged to set down the places they had already mentioned in a previous response. In the end, over two-thirds of the sample were able to draw a map of some kind. The difficulties of eliciting maps were worth the effort, for they provided a rich source of data for interpretation.

Interview Schedule (translated from the Spanish)

Personal Data

Questions

1-14. (Personal questions)

General

15a. What do you call this city?

15b. What specific part of this region is called (Ciudad Guayana)?

15c. What do you call the area from San Félix to the steel mill?

16. What area do you call the Zona de Hierro?

17. Now, please think a little about the whole city (Ciudad Guayana). Can you tell me which points or places in the city and its environs you remember best?

18a. In your opinion, which points or places in the city would a person newly arrived need to know to enable him to carry on the normal activities of work, shopping, family life, and recreation? You may name any sites previously mentioned and add new ones.

18b. Are there other things or places in the city and its environs that you would like him to know about? What are they?

19a. Suppose now that here (*interviewer points to one side of the first sheet of the map*) is San Félix, and here (*interviewer points to the edge*) is Matanzas (steel mill); please draw between these a map indicating the points and places in the city that you have just mentioned to me. After that add, please, any other important thing that comes to memory. Try to have all this on one sheet.

19b. Can you show me on this map from which direction the wind comes? (*Make an arrow on the map.*)

19c. And which direction is north? (*Make another arrow indicating the direction.*)

(If the respondent seems unable to begin the map, the interviewer as an example should draw, in green, the first aspect mentioned in question 17. The drawing of the respondent should begin with the black pencil, changing to red if he adds anything in following questions.)

20. Now, would you please describe the road that goes between Matanzas (steel mill) and San Félix, mentioning the appearance, the changes in direction, the views, and all the important or interesting things in the city that you see on the trip.
21. What part of the road seems to you to be the most attractive or most interesting?
22a. And which parts are the most ugly or boring?
22b. From where can you see Los Saltos (Caroní Falls)?
22c. And from where can the Orinoco be seen?
23a. In which parts of the city do you have difficulty finding your way?
23b. Can you tell me why?

Change

24. (*To those who have lived in other towns or cities*) What would you say are the most important differences between the city and the last place where you lived before coming to Ciudad Guayana?
25. (*To all*) The city as a whole can change in many ways. For example, more people can arrive, new activities and places appear, and areas can be transformed. . . .
25a. In what way do you find (Ciudad Guayana) has changed during the last year?
25b. And how has it changed during all the time you have lived here?
26. How do you usually obtain your information about what is happening in the city? By TV, radio, newspapers, by seeing maps, through conversations with friends, or by observations of your own?
27. Considering all the different changes that affect a city as a whole, such as changes in people, in activities and places, in transportation of areas . . .
27a. What changes do you expect to see in the city, during the next five years?
27b. (*If an answer is given to 27a*) Where do you think these changes will occur?
27c. (*To all*) And actually at present, how is (*name the area where the respondent lives*) changing?
27d. In what direction does it seem to you that the city will grow?
27e. Why do you think so?

27f. In your opinion, where will the major center of activities be in the future?
27g. Will the city be larger than Ciudad Bolívar?
27h. Do you think (Ciudad Guayana) can expand to the point of merging with Ciudad Bolívar in the future?
28a. In your opinion, is this city changing for the better or the worse?
28b. Can you explain why?
29a. Sometimes does it seem to you that the city is changing too rapidly, or would you prefer to see it change more rapidly?
29b. Why?
29c. In general, where do the people who have newly arrived in this city live?
30. What do you consider to be the most urgent needs of the city?
31a. Have you seen or heard anything about the official plans for the city?
31b. What have you seen or heard about the plans?
31c. How did you come to know about these plans?

Settlements, Districts, and Buildings

32. Now please think a little about San Félix. What are the things you would say are typical or characteristic of San Félix?
33. And, in your opinion, what kind of people live in San Félix?
34. What would you say are the principal activities in San Félix?
35. By what things would you distinguish Barrio La Esperanza from Barrio Unidad in San Félix?
36. And now, thinking of El Roble, what seems to you to be typical or characteristic of El Roble?
37. And, in your opinion, what kind of people live in El Roble?
38. What would you say are the principal activities of El Roble?
(*Specify.*)
39. By what do you distinguish urbanización UV-3 from that of UV-4 in El Roble?
40. And what are the things that you feel are typical or characteristic of Castillito?
41. What kind of people would you say live in Castillito?
42. What do you think are the major activities in Castillito?
(*Specify.*)
43. What are the things that distinguish Urbanización

Mendoza from Los Monos?

44. And to finish, thinking of Puerto Ordaz, what are the typical or characteristic things of Puerto Ordaz?
45. And what kind of person do you think lives in Puerto Ordaz?
46. What do you feel are the principal activities of Puerto Ordaz?
47. What are the things that distinguish Campo A from Campo B and from the Viviendas of the Banco Obrero in Puerto Ordaz?
    (*Begin with the map and questions of Puerto Ordaz and Castillito for those who live there*)
48. Next I am going to name some areas and ask you to tell me something about them: on this first sheet (*show the sheet of map no. 2*), please make a map of San Félix and El Roble, including schools, the police, hospitals, mercados and shopping areas, churches, places where people meet, the Consejo Municipal, CVG offices, political party offices, and any other site or things that you think important to mention.
49. Now I am going to name several places in this area and ask you to tell me how you distinguish them:

49a. In San Félix, how would you describe Las Seguros Sociales?

49b. How would you describe the Consejo Municipal?

49c. And the church?

49d. What is the appearance of Grupo Escolar San Félix?

50a. In El Roble, how would you recognize the Escuela Técnica?

50b. And how would you know the Cine Bolívar?

50c. And the Bomba Phillips?

50d. How is the Grupo Escolar José Angel Ruiz recognized?

51. On this second sheet (*show the third sheet of the map*), please make a map of Castillito and Puerto Ordaz, including also the schools, hospitals and clinics, churches, places where people meet, mercados and shopping areas, the police, CVG office, political party offices, sports fields, and other sites and things that seem important to mention.
52. Now I shall name some sites in this area and ask you to tell me how you would distinguish them:

52a. In Castillito, can you describe for me the Grupo Escolar Tumeremo?

52b. And how would you recognize the shop Materiales Bolívar?

52c. And the Cine Lorena?

52d. How does the Medicatura Rural look?

53a. In Puerto Ordaz, how would you recognize the General Electric building?

53b. Please describe the post office.

53c. And the Hotel Cunucunuma.

53d. What does the Protestant Church look like?

Values and Preferences

54a. In general, how do you feel about this city? Do you like it, dislike it, or feel indifferent toward it?

54b. Why do you feel this way?

55. Please imagine an ideal city in which you would like to live. What would be the characteristics of this ideal city? (*Specify.*)

56. And imagine a city in which it would be very disagreeable to live. What are the characteristics that make it bad?

57a. Here we have a ladder (*show the drawing*). Suppose at the top of this ladder (*interviewer points*) is your ideal city, and at the bottom of the ladder (*interviewer points*) the worst. Where on this ladder (*interviewer moves his finger up and down quickly*) do you believe is (Ciudad Guayana)? (*Note the number of the rung indicated.*)

57b. How would you compare (Ciudad Guayana) with Ciudad Bolívar? Do you think (Ciudad Guayana) is a better place to live, or worse, or more or less equal?

57c. Why?

58a. And, comparing (Ciudad Guayana) with Caracas, do you believe that (Ciudad Guayana) is a better place to live, or worse, or more or less equal?

58b. Please explain why.

59a. Please name for me the parts of the city that you like to visit.

59b. Why do you like to go there?

60a. Are there places in the city where you prefer not to go or that you dislike very much?

60b. Which places?

60c. Why?

Functions

61. In your opinion, what are the factors that explain the rapid growth of a city in this location?

62. Could you describe for me how the iron ore is transported to (the steel mill)?

63. Where does the iron ore for (the steel mill) come from?

64. And how is the iron transported out of (the steel mill)?

65. Now, I want to ask some questions about places you

know here in (Ciudad Guayana). In your opinion, what are the major recreational areas of the city?

66. Generally, where do people go in the evening and on weekends to enjoy themselves?
67. Where do you believe the major political decisions with respect to the region are made (*places and institutions*)?
68. Please describe a plaza for me (*any*).

Miscellaneous

69. Which parts of the Caroní River do you know? (*Specify.*)
70. And with which parts of the Orinoco are you familiar? (*Specify.*)
71. Can you name for me all the hills that you know in the city (Ciudad Guayana)?
72. Would you like to have access to the falls made easier for everyone, or would you prefer to leave it as it is?
73. What part of the city do you think has the best climate?
74. And which has the worst climate?
75. Do you feel the city should have more signs?
76. What types of signs are most lacking in the city?

D APPENDIX RESEARCH METHODS

Assessing the Public Environment

The state of a city's public environment should be a matter for frequent assessment. Its improvement and development should be of continuing public concern. In future planning operations, the methods used here should be modified depending on the situation, but the parallel methods of interview and field survey are recommended.

As with most planning projects, many more facts needed to be known than could be covered in one interview. Although the interview was long, it still covered only a limited number of issues. In a future planning operation, it would therefore be better to consider more than one set of interviews, even with smaller population samples.

For more organized interviews representatives of different groups could be selected on the basis of predicted differences in their perceptions, attitudes, and behavior. The sample would be selected on the basis of social class, occupation, education, ethnicity (if there were significant ethnic groups), familiarity, age, travel mode, and their information media, and its representativeness of the total population would have to be known. Also selected for separate interviewing would be critical leader groups, such as community leaders, political leaders, developers, business and industrial executives, planners, engineering and design professionals; potentially deprived groups, such as low income, the aged, youth, housewives, and handicapped; and groups vulnerable to particular environmental changes, such as groups near a proposed transportation system.

In the best circumstances, the three aspects of urban behavior—perceptions, attitudes, and use patterns—should be surveyed and interrelated in a systematic way. This study devoted more attention to perception than to attitudes and use patterns. A well-rounded interview might begin with general perceptions of the city through free verbal and map recall. Then more explicit tasks would elicit the features that subjects (1) recall most vividly as images or sensations and (2) deem the most significant—socially, economically, or culturally. These questions may be asked for the city as a whole, for the circulation system, and for certain districts, destinations, buildings, or other places that are either critical issues or are representative of unique characteristics.

Following the perception responses, a series of questions regarding needs and attitudes could usefully be asked. These could begin with general reactions to the city and identification of the most critical issues. The self-anchored scaling technique and comparisons between cities are useful, especially if the question of migration or economic competition is a critical issue as it was in Ciudad Guayana. They could be supplemented with direct questions about the actual choices respondents have made or are likely to make. In most cities the more critical choice level may be in probing attitudes to different parts of the city, comparing districts with each other. But these have to be couched in terms of meaningful and possible choices. In conclusion, questions might focus on attitudes toward various facilities used in everyday life (workplaces, schools, shops, recreational facilities, and the transportation system) and the convenience and appropriateness of their location in the city.

There was concern among some urban designers that the interview should not ask for attitudes toward future alternatives, because "they might not understand them." There also seemed to be some fear that such questions would raise aspirations and create problems for the planning group. There are risks in stimulating large numbers of the population to have an interest in plans for their city, but the gains from frank and early discussion before decisions are probably worth any risk. As it was, the interview was insufficiently future oriented.

If the designers have developed a number of goals for the city, inhabitants could be asked to rate their estimations of importance and the relative success of the urban environment in meeting these goals. If preliminary designs have been developed, responses to these or to alternatives could be asked for. Attitudes toward and knowledge of future changes will convey a useful view of future attitudes and satisfactions. Simulation of future proposals and changes could be a part of such an interview, and, if necessary, trade-offs could be incorporated as part of the procedure (Wilson 1962; Hoinville 1971; Appleyard and Craik 1974).

The personal use patterns of each respondent should be established based on the past and current regularity of his visits to major parts of the city, other cities, and his places of residence, work, shopping, and recreation. Questions about his relative satisfaction with this use pattern could then be asked. From these data, typical use patterns and their success could be characterized.

Correlations between knowledge, attitude, and use could be made to gain insights into each. For instance, attitudes might be associated with use patterns or with patterns of knowledge. Use patterns might be associated with certain attitudes or perceptions.

In many cases it may be necessary to break down this long interview into subinterviews.[1] A citywide and a local interview might be given separately. Also special studies of the circulation system or the open-space system might require separate interviews. Simple methods of polling the population on major issues could also be developed.

Interviews are still a remote means of discovering the inhabitants' views of their city. At the same time, panels of citizen representatives could be formed and community meetings called to discuss issues more openly and vote on the questions. Otherwise, it may be too easy for those who process the interviews to interpret their results in-house and impose their preferred interpretations on the evidence. This may have happened with the interviews reported here, since there was no opportunity to return to the city and check the interpretations. But community meetings alone can be coercive and usually miss the silent mass of the population; so combinations of public meetings, panels, and private interviews would achieve the most rounded awareness of citizen perceptions.

However, to interview large numbers of people is expensive and difficult. Field surveys and the collection of secondary data may be more economical. Traffic flow data, estimates of transit use, and pedestrian flows can identify where people use the outdoor environment (Hassan 1965), and the location of major destinations of high operational significance can be calculated through employee populations, retail sales, or typical trip-generation data for various land-use types.

The operational significance of an urban element in the public environment will depend on the social and spatial realms of its public, and on the relative communication requirements of its operators and users (chapter 7). Its general significance may be social, economic, political, aesthetic, and historical; local, state, or national; present or future. The identification of more generally significant and meaningful locales in the city might be the most difficult to obtain without the help of interviews. However, most cities have guidebooks, public maps, or other publicity that identifies places of historic and other interest. A city's postcards usually show the parts of the city that are valued. In cities more developed than Ciudad Guayana public information systems, such as freeway signs, that provide information about various destinations could be recorded.

The most imageable places—buildings, paths, and districts of the city—can be identified through attributes such as size, isolation, shape, color, texture, visible activity, and singularity (chapter 4). Visibility patterns from different transportation systems can then be separately assessed, with particular attention to main decision and transition points. From automobile routes the cone of vision will be focused ahead, although passengers are freer to look around. Bus and transit systems usually encourage more side vision. Visibility from particular viewing points where the public gathers can also be considered (Steinitz 1968). The relative visibility of the most imageable, used, and significant places can now be calculated in order to map the predicted public environment.

The general significance of the city's public environment and its dominance by various users and political groups can be assessed as suggested in chapter 6. Hence, the relative numbers of exposed commercial, industrial, institutional, public, or recreational establishments might provide a measure of the symbolic profile of a city. The allotment of communications space to various social and interest groups in the public environment could be described and evaluated for the equity of its distribution or its acknowledgment of the public interest. These assessments of diversity, communicability, structure, and change can be carried out in parallel with assessments of other environmental qualities.

One caution should be reiterated. As mentioned in the Introduction, evidence on population perceptions and attitudes should not always define policy. The individual interview may express desires that are not of benefit to the larger society or cost it too much. Desires for single-family houses, several automobiles, and other luxuries may be of this nature. Evidence of individual perceptions may reveal a degree of ignorance that may be limiting opportunities or avoiding responsibilities. In these cases, policies of changing perceptions and expectations may be justified.

In any case, decisions made on behalf of a larger society should not be made by professionals alone but by groups who can represent a larger societal view: political representatives, citizens' committees, and public voters.

Future Research

These surveys are another step in the direction of predicting urban perception and knowledge. More than anything, they require replication in other cities and among other populations.

Beyond replication, there are some other urgent empirical and theoretical needs involving clarification of the relationships between use and knowledge and between knowledge and value. How much spatial use of the city depends on knowledge is still unknown. People make choices on the basis of preference, constraints, and knowledge. How behavior might change if the city were structured to increase knowledge or whether any change in the structure really could affect the level of knowledge are unanswered questions. There should be more investigation into the role of the environment as an information system.

Clearly, we could benefit from a better understanding of people's attitudes toward the large-scale environment, particularly with regard to more general questions like urbanity, diversity, complexity, order, and orientation. Systematic investigations of the ways in which subjects react to ordered and disordered, simple and complex, dense and thinly settled, and static and dynamic urban environments under varying conditions are urgently needed. Even more difficult to measure are latent environmental needs for stability and security, and the phenomenon of environmental adaptation. Reactions to environment, such as perceptions of environment, must fluctuate and vary in time and space. They will be elusive phenomena to pin down, for they involve the many ways in which the human mind copes with the modern world.

NOTES

Introduction

1. Jane Jacobs (1961), Herbert Gans (1968), and more recently Robert Goodman (1972) have attacked planners and architects for ignoring various population groups and what they need from their environment. Gilbert White (1967) describes the conflicts between the professionals' own attitudes, their perceptions of public attitudes, and their perceptions of what public attitudes *ought* to be. Both White and Sewell (1971) point out how different professions perceive environmental problems and solutions through the framework of their own training.

2. Image surveys have been carried out in such widely diverse countries as Lebanon (Gulick 1963), Holland (De Jonge 1962), Mexico (Stea and Wood), Britain (Lee 1963; Goodey 1971, 1974; Gould and White 1974), Thailand, and Italy; and in the United States in the Los Angeles metropolitan area (Orleans 1967), in Minneapolis and Brookline, Massachusetts (Lynch 1965). Many of these have remained unpublished, but according to a brief review by Robert Kates (1970) about 26 cities have been the subject of image surveys.

3. This is evident from the proceedings of the successive EDRA (Environmental Design Research Association) Conferences, from issues of the journal *Environment and Behavior* and reviews of the field by Craik (1969, 1970) and Proshansky, Ittelson, and Rivlin (1970).

Chapter 1

1. Descriptions of these experiences can be found in the essays by Appleyard, Corrada, Penfold, Porter, Rodwin, Von Moltke, and others in *Planning Urban Growth and Regional Development*(Rodwin 1969).

2. "The city is itself fragmentary, a spread-out and often incoherent pattern of streets, open spaces, and clumps of lowrise buildings" (Evenson 1966, p. 4).

3. In contrast, Lucio Costa, the planner of Brasilia refused to visit the site of the city during its development "to be free of the temptation to make changes which might vitiate the purity of the design" (Evenson 1973).

Chapter 3

1. In an unpublished master's thesis Otis reported that upper-income inhabitants in a district of Cambridge, Massachusetts, defined their own neighborhood more stringently and exclusively than did adjacent, low-income neighbors, who defined their neighborhood more generously including the area belonging to the upper-income group (Otis 1964). The life space of upper-income inhabitants in Ciudad Guayana may have resulted from taboos similar to those described by Kurt Lewin in which a child is forbidden to go into certain areas (Lewin 1936). Florence Shelton Ladd found a similar phenomenon with black children in a housing project in Boston, where the all-white neighboring block was left as a blank on their maps (Shelton 1968). For the elite of Ciudad Guayana, as for many North Americans, the low-income areas of the city are unpleasant and dangerous places, to be avoided and forgotten if possible.

2. Examples of this have occurred in the United States in the location and use of schools in desegregation plans. In Boston a new citywide high school campus is to be placed within the borders of Roxbury, a predominantly black area. The location and structure of the campus

and its surrounding area has been the subject of intense interest and controversy.

Chapter 4

1. Form and Stone (1957) identified "style symbolism"—manners, mode of dress, conversational style, and grooming—appearance—gait, posture, and haggardness—and possessions—clothing, cars, and so on—as means of identifying social status in U.S. society. They also found that it was more difficult for people to identify middle-class symbols than those of the upper or lower class.

2. See Redfield and Rojas (1934).

3. Richard Martin, in "The Architecture of Underdevelopment" (1974), identifies *rural, urban*, and *symbolic* phases of neighborhood layout and design in Zambia. The symbolic phase is entered into by the *Apamwamba*, the highly mobile social group that has adopted the values of the colonial elite and prefers houses very much like the *quintas* of Guayana.

4. Projects where people were offered land, utilities, and materials for self-help housing, which was intended to be progressively improved over time.

5. Gans (1968, p. 190), in his recommendations for Columbia New Town, proposed a similar emphasis on block-level homogeneity and community-level heterogeneity. By "block" he meant small groups of houses or apartment buildings as small as four to six houses.

Chapter 5

1. In the development of the scaling systems, the characteristics of all buildings mentioned by the inhabitants were inspected, usually on photographs, and salient attributes were hypothesized. Each building was then scaled, and regressions were run. To maximize prediction, the scaling rules were revised in the light of the results. The scalings passed through three or four iterations of this process during which time new attributes were introduced and others were omitted. The final set of attributes to be correlated still included some that achieved very low correlations. (See Carr and Schissler (1969) for a similar approach.)

The categorizing system faced the usual difficulties of deciding how far to disaggregate. Disaggregation allows for simpler scaling measurements but gives lower individual correlations and makes reaggregation difficult. The case of viewpoint significance was a typical example. Had the scale been completely independent, all decision points even on minor roads would have been accorded a high score. Consequently, correlations would have been very low. Since the scale was combined with viewpoint intensity to give higher scores for decision points on major roads, viewpoint significance received higher correlations, because it had become a partially composite attribute.

2. The role of novelty, incongruity, and surprise in attracting and holding a subject's attention has been noted by many investigators since Berlyne's early studies (Berlyne 1960). In this study we selected the scale of *singularity* as one measure that might incorporate the effects of these variables. It is, in fact, closer to novelty than to incongruity and surprise.

3. The intercorrelations between attributes do suggest some redundancy for predictive purposes. A factor analysis (Harman 1960) could have identified how much they clustered as covariants. However, the present rational clustering of attributes by their conceptual similarities under the headings of form, visibility, and significance is useful to the planner, because these attributes tend to be manipulated separately in the planning of cities.

4. Vernon affirms that contour plays a primary role in the perception of the shape of objects. The perception of contour "depends mainly upon the gradient in brightness between the surface of an object and its background" (Vernon 1962). Contour is also one of the fundamental ways in which children first learn to define objects in drawings (Arnheim 1964).

5. See Lynch (1960, p. 105).

6. An early unpublished study by Lynch, asking people in Cambridge, Massachusetts, to recall a walk past a number of shops, also showed that people seldom recalled the shop signs, although their recall of the goods in the stores was high.

7. Visibility has been measured more accurately in some U.S. studies where more data were available (Hassan 1965; Steinitz 1968). In Hassan's study, elements selected from the earlier Lynch surveys (Lynch 1960) were measured for their visibility. Correlation of visibility with original subject frequencies was very high. No correlation with distinctness or significance was calculated.

8. Attneave has applied some measurement techniques from information theory to visual figures by having subjects predict the successive parts of a hidden figure (Attneave 1954). When they guessed correctly, he scored that part as a low information point; when they guessed incorrectly, it was a high information point. He found that corners, joints, and bends were among the highest information points in the figure. In another test, these elements were selected as the most economical points with which to describe a figure. The study suggests that one could measure environmental information levels anywhere in the city, although the multidimensionality of the task would be formidable.

9. As a matter of interest, the regression formula for predicting building recall from free map recall responses was

A = 2.5 (contour singularity) + 3.1 (movement intensity) + 1.5 (viewpoint intensity) + 2.9 (immediacy) + 1.75 (viewpoint significance) — 2.87 (use intensity + 3.5 (use singularity) — 29.25.

Here A is the best predicted frequency of recall of any building when the mean of all frequencies is 50 and the standard deviation (s.d.) is equal to 10. That is, a building predicted to be on the mean in recall would have a score of 50. The predicted recall score can then be transformed to the recall percentage by standardizing the latter variable to a distribution having mean = 50 and s.d. = 10. The multiple regression equation for A yielded a correlation of .67. The equation employs unstandardized raw scores for the attributes from all three major components: form, visibility, and significance.

10. Multiple regression equations take advantage of all chance relations obtained in an array of data, so that until these coefficients are cross-validated with another sample, we cannot be certain of these relationships. Further, the multiple correlation coefficients still account for less than 50 percent of the variance and therefore cannot be considered to offer a high level of predictability. However, the level of correlation suggests that the attributes under consideration possess predictive qualities that give promise of successful cross-validation in the future.

11. Most links between sex and the form of buildings have been made through the supposed sexual character of buildings and spaces. Urban historians have found this a fine field for speculation. Scully opposes two architectural traditions: one "associated with . . . the female deities of the earth" and another "having to do not with the female engulfment of interior space but with the sculptural challenging evocation" (Scully 1961).

Chapter 6

1. Osgood's semantic differential tests found that the good-bad factor was the one used predominantly by his subjects, and so this strongly evaluative response is not surprising (Osgood, Suci, and Tannebaum 1957).

2. Michelson reported in a survey of housing preferences that his subjects evaluated housing types along different dimensions, such as instrumental, expressive, and individual (Michelson 1966).

Chapter 7

1. Crane's "City Symbolic" (1960) is one of the more interesting early articles on the subject, particularly because of his concept of locational symbolism, which in the terms used here depends on visibility as much as on form.

2. The social realm is similar to that defined by Webber as a nonplace realm (Webber 1964).

3. Florence Kluckholn's estimates of value changes among some American Indians (for instance, in their time orientations, which shifted in a few years from past to present) demonstrated what might well happen in Ciudad Guayana (Kluckholn and Strodtbeck 1961).

4. In a more-developed set of measures this was the basis of Steinitz's study of form-activity congruence in Boston (Steinitz 1968).

5. An earlier study in this field was *Signs in the City*, by a group of M.I.T. students (1963) with Lynch and Appleyard. Subsequently, Steinitz (1968) developed measures for some of these qualities, and Carr developed the policies more completely in *City Signs and Lights* (1971).

6. "Rooted" signs are those whose messages relate to the buildings on which they are placed. "Unrooted" signs, such as billboards, do not (M.I.T. Students 1963).

7. H. Werner once reported an experiment where subjects were asked to draw lines in accord with a given list of emotional states, such as anger and joy; he found a remarkable similarity in the choice of forms (Werner 1948). This is a very controversial question, however, on which Gombrich has written with devastating sarcasm (Gombrich 1960).

8. Such designations were attempted some years ago by Morton Hoppenfeld, then chief of urban design of the National Capital Planning Commission, in an effort to "set" the character of future public buildings in Washington, D.C. (N.C.P.C. 1961).

Chapter 8

1. For another description of the design history of Ciudad Guayana, read "The Evolution of the Linear Form," by Willo Von Moltke (Rodwin 1969), and "Ciudad Guayana: Planning a New City in Venezuela," by Anthony Penfold (1966).

2. A number of common errors were recorded. The spatial relations between nine zones of the city were assessed on each subject map. These relationships were recorded as *faults* where there was a break between zones, and as *bends* where the relationship was spatially distorted. In cases where zones were misplaced on the map or where the positions of two zones had been switched, the errors were coded, respectively, as *mislocations* and zone *reversals. Landmark mislocations* were recorded when a landmark was placed incorrectly in a wrong zone, and spatial *distortions* of the road system within each zone were noted. The most common type of error was the distortion of roads or zones. Of the error types, those that maintained connections between the parts (bends, reversals, and distortions) were solely positional errors; those that disrupted the maps (faults and mislocations) could be termed both topological and positional errors.

3. Anyone familiar with Piaget's writings on the child's conception of space (Piaget and Inhelder 1967) will notice similarities between the methods mentioned here and the *topological, projective*, and *Euclidean* phases of space conception that he claims children pass through. The difference in types occurs because his children were performing small-scale space tasks, where projective techniques such as visual alignment are much easier than in a large-scale urban environment, and where associational techniques are usually unnecessary. For a related designers' viewpoint, see Maki and Goldberg (1962).

4. Ross (1962) in his study of neighborhoods in Boston, found that "*at any distance from the cores of the communities*, working- and lower-class individuals were more likely to 'choose' the working- and lower-class West End label for their area of residence." (Emphasis added.)

5. Some progress in this field is now taking place in the United States with Carr's recent *City Signs and Lights* study (1971), Wurman's *Making the City Observable* (1971), and other projects reported in *Dot Zero*

5 Transportation Graphics (Fall 1968).

Chapter 9

1. Lynch reported that many of the subjects in his Los Angeles interviews felt a sense of loss when well-known landmarks were torn down (Lynch 1960). In a study of environmental change in Boston Svenson also reported that the severest emotional stresses were felt under conditions of ambiguous change (Svenson 1967).

2. In *What Time Is This Place?*, Lynch (1972) suggests several ways in which change can be emphasized through the environment.

Chapter 10

1. In a study of street life in San Francisco (Appleyard and Lintell 1972), people were able to define how much of the environment "belonged" to them.

2. Tolman identified a "placing need" as a fundamental motivation in perception (Tolman 1951).

3. "[W]hen expectations are violated by the environment, the perceiver's behavior can be described as resistance to the recognition of the unexpected or incongruous. . . . Among the perceptual processes which implement this resistance are (1) the dominance of one principle of organization which prevents the appearance of incongruity and (2) a form of 'partial assimilation to expectancy' which we have called compromise" (Bruner and Postman 1949).

4. The Gestalt psychologists pioneered the investigation of environmental schemata, and although Attneave and Hochberg have convincingly suggested that perceptual organization is more a matter of information processing and cognitive economizing than of innate properties of the perceptual machinery, their empirical findings still stand (Wertheimer, 1958; Hochberg and McAlister 1953; Attneave 1954).

5. Bartlett's classic study of memory, *Remembering* (1932), based primarily on the recall of stories, remains one of the most useful and readable analyses of memory processes. Paul's statistical analyses of the same stories substantiates many of Bartlett's earlier findings (Paul 1959).

6. "In the struggle to fit the perceptions to true facts, the consumer is aided by common sense, logic, past experience, and the cooperation of friends and specialists such as foreign correspondents, statisticians, and detectives. He is almost overwhelmed, however, by the powerful influences that distort his perceptions. First, he must act in the present in uncertain anticipation of facts he thinks are waiting for him in the future. Second, his senses cannot possibly cope with the sheer volume of facts in the past, present, and future that are relevant to his purchase. Third, his perceptions may be limited by forgetfulness, limited intelligence, misunderstanding, inattentiveness, blindness, imagination, semantic confusions, insane delusions, or the rigidity of preexisting judgments. Fourth, those who communicate news to him may not only be misled themselves by the influences named; they may also use stereotyped propaganda words, eliminate some of the truth or add some falsehoods, suppress entire messages, or use subterfuge and deception in their messages. So far, one is almost surprised to find any connection at all between true facts and what the consumer perceives." (Clawson 1968).

7. Craik argues that people adopt environmental roles in much the same way that they adopt social roles (Craik 1969). He identifies the "romantic" and "tourist" roles in the landscape. The idea of roles could also apply to "vehicular" or "occupational" roles as long as they demonstrate consistent sets of attitudes and perceptions.

8. In the *Doors of Perception*, Aldous Huxley (1954) described how the taking of mescalin released him from the everyday pressures to see and label the environment in terms of actions. In consequence, the drug made him more highly aware of such common objects as chairs and tables, which he usually took for granted. The conceptual mode of perception may thus separate us from the environment around us.

9. Some years ago there was an interesting controversy with regard to two learning theories. Bruner, a cognitive psychologist, contended that learning began with the identification of "recurrent regularities" (Bruner, Wallach, and Galanter 1959), while the Gibsons (1955) maintained that it began with differentiation. In learning a city, people seem to use both methods.

10. Personal communication from Dr. Cohen, January 1971.

Chapter 11

1. The publicly known environment is user oriented and quite distinct from the publicly owned environment or the "capital web" (Crane 1961), which may or may not be known or used by the general public.

2. Measures of these activity patterns have been attempted (Chapin 1965; Chapin and Hightower 1956; and Buttimer 1972). Buttimer's definitions of three types of socially significant space based on social participation, micro- and macro-services, and three scales of spatial zones (local, intermediate, and diffuse), provide the basis for her use of the Standard Deviation Ellipse as a measure of aggregate activity space orbits of different population groups. It would be interesting to find out how closely this measure compares with the extent and complexity of a group's urban knowledge (chapter 2).

Appendix B

1. As it was, Carl Steinitz, in charge of the map coding on this project, used the techniques of SYMAP in his subsequent dissertation (Steinitz 1968).

Appendix D

1. For examples of this kind of survey, see surveys carried out for the San Francisco Urban Design Plan (San Francisco City Planning Department 1970), and others to evaluate the impacts of the Bay Area Rapid Transit system on residential neighborhoods (Appleyard and Carp, 1974).

GLOSSARY OF VENEZUELAN TERMS

abastos	grocery store
areparia	popular eating place (selling corn cakes)
bajareque	adobe-covered wooden-pole structure
bomba	gas station
barrio	district of indigenous housing
casco	downtown
centro cívico	civic center
consejo municipal	municipal council
cuadra	square
distríto	district
escuela	school
liceo	secondary school
paseo	daily promenade
plaza	square
por puesto	collective taxi running along a set route
quebrada	gully
quinta	villa
río	river
seguros sociales	public health clinic
siderúrgica	steel mill
unidades vecinales	neighborhood units
urbanización	planned subdivision

BIBLIOGRAPHY

Alexander, C. 1965. A City Is Not a Tree. *Architectural Forum* 122, no. 1.

Allport, G. W., and Postman, L. J. 1945. The Basic Psychology of Rumor. *Transactions of the New York Academy of Sciences* 2: 61-81.

Appleyard, D. 1962. The Future Form of Santo Tomé. Unpublished report, Caracas.

_______ . 1965. Motion, Sequence, and the City. In *The Nature and Art of Motion*, ed. G. Kepes. New York: George Braziller.

_______ . 1968. Signs on Urban Highways: Messages, Audiences, and Media. In *Dot Zero 5 Transportation Graphics*, pp. 26-31.

_______ . 1969. City Designers and the Pluralistic City. In *Regional Planning for Development*, ed. L. Rodwin and Associates, pp. 422-452. Cambridge, Mass.: The M.I.T. Press.

_______ , and Carp. F. 1974. The BART Residential Impact Study: A Longitudinal Study of Environmental Impact. In *Improving Environmental Impact Assessment*, ed. T. Dickert. Berkeley: University of California Press.

_______ and Craik, K. 1974. The Berkeley Environmental Simulator: Its Uses in Environmental Impact Assessment. In *Improving Environmental Impact Assessment*, ed. T. Dickert. Berkeley: University of California Press.

_______ , and Lintell, M. 1972. The Environmental Quality of City Streets. *Journal of the American Institute of Planners* 31, no. 2.

_______ , Lynch, K., and Myer, J. R. 1964. *The View From the Road.* Cambridge, Mass.: The M.I.T. Press.

Arnheim, R. 1964. *Art and Visual Perception.* Berkeley and Los Angeles: University of California Press.

Attneave, F. H. 1954. Some Informative Aspects of Visual Perception. *Psychological Review* 61: 183-193.

Barnett, J. 1960. A New Planning Process with Built-in Political Support. *Architectural Record.*

Bartlett, F. C. 1932. *Remembering.* Cambridge: At the University Press.

Berlyne, D. E. 1960. *Conflict, Arousal, and Curiosity.* New York: McGraw-Hill.

Bruner, J. S. 1957a. On Going Beyond the Information Given. In *Contemporary Approaches to Cognition*, pp. 41-69. Cambridge, Mass.: Harvard University Press.

_______ ,1957b. On Perceptual Readiness. *Psychological Review* 64: 123-152.

_______ , and Postman, L. 1949. On the Perception of Incongruity: A Paradigm. *Journal of Personality* 18: 206-223.

_______ , Wallach, M. A., and Galanter, E. H. 1959. The Identification of Recurrent Regularity. *American Journal of Psychology* 72: 200-209.

Brunswick, E. 1943. Organismic Achievement and Environmental Probability. *Psychology Review* 50: 255-272.

Burchard, J. 1968. The Culture of Urban America. In *Environment and Change: The Next Fifty Years*, ed. W. R. Ewald. Bloomington: Indiana University Press.

Buttimer, A. 1972. Social Space and the Planning of Residential Areas. *Environment and Behavior* 4, no. 3.

Carmichael, L., Hogan, H. P., and Walter, A. A. 1932. An Experimental Study of the Effect of Language on the Reproduction of Visually Perceived Forms. *Journal of Experimental Psychology* 15: 73-86.

Carr, S. 1971. *City Signs and Lights.* Boston: Boston Redevelopment and H.U.D.

_______ , and Schissler, D. 1969. The City as a Trip. *Environment and Behavior* 1.1: 7-36.

Cassirer, E. 1944. *An Essay on Man.* New Haven, Conn.: Yale University Press.

Chapin, F. S., Jr. 1965. The Study of Urban Activity Systems. In *Urban Land Use Planning, Urbana*, chap. 6. Urbana: University of Illinois Press.

_______ , and Hightower, H. 1956. Household Activity Patterns and Land Use. *Journal of the American Institute of Planners* 31: 222-231.

Chein, I. 1954. The Environment as a Determinant of Behavior. *Journal of Social Psychology* 39: 115-127.

Clawson, J. 1968. Levin's Psychology and Motives in Marketing. In *Perspectives in Consumer Behavior*, ed. H. Kassarjian and T. S. Robertson. Glenview, Ill.: Scott, Foresman.

Clay, G. 1973. *Close-Up: How to Read the American City.* New York: Praeger.

Cohen, R. A. 1969. Conceptual Styles, Culture Conflict and Non-Verbal Tests of Intelligence. *American Anthropologist* 71, no. 5.

Corrada, R. 1969. The Housing Program. In *Planning Urban Growth and Regional Development*, ed. L. Rodwin and Associates, chap. 12. Cambridge, Mass.: The M.I.T. Press.

Craik, K. 1969. Human Responsiveness to the Landscape. In *Response to Environment.* Student Publication of the School of Design. Raleigh: North Carolina State University.

_______ . 1970. Environmental Psychology. In *New Directions in Psychology* 4, pp. 1-121. New York: Holt, Rinehart and Winston.

Crane, D. A. 1960. The City Symbolic. *Journal of the American Institute of Planners* 26: 289-292.

_______ . 1961. The Public Art of City Building. *The Annals of the American Academy of Political and Social Science* 10: 91-93.

De Jonge, D. 1962. Images of Urban Areas: Their Structures and Psychological Foundations. *Journal of the American Institute of Planners* 28: 266-276.

Dot Zero 5 Transportation Graphics. Fall 1968.

Downs, A. 1969. Creating a Land Development Strategy for Ciudad Guayana. In *Planning Urban Growth and Regional Development*, ed. L. Rodwin and Associates, chap. 10. Cambridge, Mass.: The M.I.T. Press.

Downs, R. M., and Stea, D., eds. 1973. *Image and Environment: Cognitive Mapping and Spatial Behavior.* Chicago: Aldine.

Erikson, E. 1950. *Childhood and Society.* New York: W. W. Norton.

Evenson, N. 1966. *Chandigarh.* Berkeley: University of California Press.

_______. 1973. *Two Brazilian Capitals: Architecture and Urbanism in Rio de Janeiro and Brasilia.* New Haven, Conn.: Yale University Press.

Fawcett, A., and Kise, J. 1962. Alternative Development Plans. Unpublished memo, Caracas.

Form, W. H., and Stone, G. P. 1957. Urbanism, Anonymity and Status Symbolism. *The American Journal of Sociology* 62.

Galbraith, K. 1958. *The Affluent Society.* Cambridge, Mass.: Riverside Press.

Gans, H. J. 1968. *People and Plans.* New York: Basic Books.

Gibson, J. J., and Gibson, E. J. 1955. Perceptual Learning: Differentiation of Enrichment? *Psychological Review* 62.

Gittins, J. S. 1969. Forming Impressions of an Unfamiliar City: A comparative study of aesthetic and scientific knowing. Unpublished Master's thesis, Clark University, Worcester, Mass.

Goering, J. M., and Kalachek, E. M. 1973. Public Transportation and Black Unemployment. *Society*, July, pp. 39-42.

Gombrich, E. H. 1960. On Physiognomic Perception. *Daedalus*, Winter, pp. 228-241.

Goodey, B. 1971. *Perception of the Environment.* Birmingham: University of Birmingham. Centre for Urban and Regional Studies.

_______. 1974. *Images of Place: Essays on Environmental Perception, Communication, and Education.* Birmingham: University of Birmingham. Centre for Urban and Regional Studies.

Goodman, R. 1972. *After the Planners.* New York: Simon and Schuster.

Gould, P., and White, R. 1974. *Mental Maps.* Middlesex: Penguin Books.

Gulick, J. 1963. Images of an Arab City. *Journal of the American Institute of Planners* 29: 179-198.

Harman, H. H. 1960. *Modern Factor Analysis.* Chicago: University of Chicago Press.

Hassan, Y. 1965. *The Movement System as an Organizer of Visual Form.* Unpublished Ph.D. diss., M.I.T., Department of City Planning.

Hirschman, S. O. 1958. *The Strategy of Economic Development.* New Haven, Conn.: Yale University Press.

Hochberg, J. E., and McAlister, E. 1953. A Quantitative Approach to Figural Goodness. *Journal of Experimental Psychology* 46: 361-364.

Hoinville, G. 1971. Evaluating Community Preferences. *Environment and Planning* 3: 33-50.

Huxley, A. 1954. *The Doors of Perception.* New York: Harper and Row.

Irelan, L. 1966. Low Income Outlook on Life. In *Low Income Life Styles.* Welfare Administration, U.S. Government Publication No. 12.

Jacobs, J. 1961. *The Death and Life of Great American Cities.* New York: Random House.

Jacobson, R. 1960. Closing Statement: Linguistics and Poetics. In *Style in Language*, ed. T. Sebeok. Cambridge, Mass.: The M.I.T. Press.

Johanssen, G. 1950. *Configurations in Event Perception.* Uppsala, Sweden: Almqvist and Wiksell.

Kates, R. W. 1970. Human Perceptions of the Environment. Unpublished paper presented at UNESCO Conference on Man's Role in Changing the Environment: Architecture and Urbanism for Growth and Change, Helsinki, Finland.

Keller, S. 1968. *The Urban Neighborhood.* New York: Random House.

Kilpatrick, F. P., and Cantril, H. 1960. Self-Anchoring Scaling: A Measure of Individuals' Unique Reality Worlds. *Journal of Individual Psychology* 16, no. 2.

Kluckholn, F., and Strodtbeck, F. 1961. *Variations in Value Orientations.* Evanston, Ill.: Row, Peterson.

Lansing, J. B., Marans, R. W., and Zehner, R. B. 1970. *Planned Residential Neighborhoods.* Ann Arbor: University of Michigan.

Lee, D. 1959. Codifications of Reality: Lineal and Non-Lineal. In *Freedom and Culture.* Englewood Cliffs, N.J.: Prentice-Hall.

Lee, T. 1963. Psychology and Living Space. *Transactions of the Bartlett Society* 2: 9-36.

Lerner, D. 1961. Unpublished memo, Caracas.

Lévi-Strauss, C. 1963. *Structural Anthropology.* New York: Basic Books.

Levy, S. J. 1968. Social Class and Consumer Behavior. In *Perspectives in Consumer Behavior*, ed. H. Kassarjian and T. S. Robertson. Glenview, Ill.: Scott, Foresman.

Lewin, K. 1936. *Principles of Topological Psychology.* New York: McGraw-Hill.

Lowenthal, D., ed. 1967. *Environmental Perception and Behavior.* Department of Geography Research Paper No. 109. Chicago: University of Chicago.

Lynch, K. 1960. *The Image of the City.* Cambridge, Mass.: The M.I.T. Press.

_______. 1965. *An Analysis of the Visual Form of Brookline.* Community Renewal Program, Brookline, Massachusetts.

_______. 1968. City Design and City Appearance. In *Principles and Practice of Urban Planning*, ed. W. I. Goodman and E. C. Freund, pp. 250-276. Washington, D.C.: International City Managers' Association.

_______. 1972. *What Time Is This Place?* Cambridge, Mass.: The M.I.T. Press.

MacDonald, J. S. 1969. Migration and the Population of Ciudad Guayana. In *Planning Urban Growth and Regional Development*, ed. L. Rodwin and Associates. Cambridge, Mass.: The M.I.T. Press.

McGinn, N. F., and Davis, R. G. 1969. *Build a Mill, Build a City, Build a School: Industrialization, Urbanization, and Education in Ciudad Guayana, Venezuela.* Cambridge, Mass.: The M.I.T. Press.

Mack, R. P., and Myers, S. 1965. Outdoor Recreation. In *Measuring Benefits of Government Investments*, ed. R. Dorfman. Washington, D.C.: The Brookings Institution.

McLuhan, M. 1965. *Understanding Media.* New York: McGraw-Hill.

Maki, F., and Goldberg, J. 1962. Linkage in Collective Form. Unpublished paper prepared at Washington University, St. Louis, Mo.

Martin, R. 1974. The Architecture of Underdevelopment or the Route to Self-Determination in Design. *Architectural Design* 44.

Michelson, W. 1966. Research Note: An Empirical Analysis of Urban Environmental Preferences. *Journal of the American Institute of Planners* 32: 355-360.

Miller, G. A. 1956. The Magic Number Seven Plus or Minus Two. *Psychological Review* 63: 81-97.

_______ . 1962. *Psychology: The Science of Mental Life.* New York: Harper and Row.

Milton Keynes Development Corporation. 1970. *The Plan for Milton Keynes.* Wavendon near Bletchley, Buckinghamshire: Milton Keynes Development Corporation.

M.I.T. Graduate Students of Urban Design. 1963. *Signs in the City.*

Cambridge, Mass.: Department of City and Regional Planning, M.I.T.

National Capital Planning Commission. 1961. *The Nation's Capitol Policies Plan for the Year 2000.* Washington, D.C.

Orinoco Mining Company. 1959. *Orinoco Mining Company.* Puerto Ordaz, Venezuela.

Orleans, P. 1967. Urban Experimentation and Urban Sociology. In *Science, Engineering, and the City*, pp. 103-117. Washington, D.C.: National Academy of Sciences.

Osgood, C. E., Suci, G. J., and Tannenbaum, P. H. 1957. *The Measurement of Meaning.* Bloomington: University of Indiana Press.

Otis, S. A., Jr. 1964. Physical and Social Perception as Factors in Local Area Recognition. Unpublished Master's thesis in City Planning. M.I.T., Cambridge, Mass.

Paul, I. H. 1959. *Studies in Remembering.* New York: International University Press.

Peattie, L. R. 1962. Planning Problems. Unpublished memo, Caracas.

_______ . 1968. *The View from the Barrio.* Ann Arbor: University of Michigan Press.

_______ . 1971. Unpublished report from Ciudad Guayana.

Penfold, A. 1966. Ciudad Guayana: Planning a New City in Venezuela. *Town Planning Review* 35, no. 4.

_______ . 1969. Urban Transportation. In *Planning Urban Growth and Regional Development*, ed. L. Rodwin and Associates. Cambridge, Mass.: The M.I.T. Press.

Piaget, J., and Inhelder, B. 1967. *The Child's Conception of Space.* New York: W. W. Norton. First publication, France, 1948.

Porter, W. 1969. Changing Perspectives in Residential Area Design. In *Planning Urban Growth and Regional Development*, ed. L. Rodwin and Associates. Cambridge, Mass.: The M.I.T. Press.

Proshansky, H., Ittelson, W., and Rivlin, L. 1970. *Environmental Psychology: Man and His Physical Setting.* New York: Holt, Rinehart and Winston.

Redfield, R. 1953. *The Primitive World and Its Transformations.* Ithaca, N.Y.: Cornell University Press.

_______ , and Rohas, A. V. 1934. *Chan Kom: A Maya Village.* Washington, D.C.: Carnegie Institution.

Riessman, F., Cohen, J., and Pearl, A. 1964. Low Income Behavior and Cognitive Style. In *Mental Health of the Poor*, Part 2. Glencoe, Ill.: Free Press.

Rodwin, L., and Associates, 1969. *Planning Urban Growth and Regional Development.* Cambridge, Mass.: The M.I.T. Press.

Ross, H. L. 1962. The Local Community: A Survey Approach. *American Sociological Review* 27: 75-84.

San Francisco City Planning Department. 1970. *Existing Form and Image: Report No. 4.*

Santayana, G. 1896. *The Sense of Beauty.* New York: Scribner.

Scully, V. J., Jr. 1961. Modern Architecture: Toward a Redefinition of Style. In *Reflections on Art*, ed. S. K. Langer. New York: Galaxy Book.

Sewell, W. R. D. 1971. Environmental Perceptions and Attitudes of Engineers and Public Health Officials. *Environment and Behavior* 3, no. 1.

Shelton, F. C. 1968. A Note on "The World Across the Street." *Journal of the Harvard Graduate School of Education.*

Stea, D., and Wood, D. 1971. *Un Atlas Cognitivo: La Geográphica Psicológica de Cuatro Cuidades Mexicanas.* Mexico, D.F.: Instituto Politécnico.

Steinitz, C. 1968. Meaning and the Congruence of Urban Form and Activity. *Journal of the American Institute of Planners* 24: 233-248.

Svenson, E. 1967. Differential Perceptual and Behavioral Response to Change in Urban Spatial Form. Ph.D. diss., M.I.T., Department of City Planning.

Tilly, C. 1955. *Migration to an American City.* Newark: University of Delaware Press.

Toffler, A. 1970. *Future Shock.* New York: Random House.

Tolman, E. C. 1951. A Psychological Model. In *Toward a General Theory of Action*, ed. T. Parsons and E. A. Shils, pp. 279-361. Cambridge, Mass.: Harvard University Press.

Turner, J. F. C. 1968. The Squatter Settlement: The Architecture That Works. *Architectural Design* 38.

Urban Design Division, C.V.G. 1964. *El Sitio.* Unpublished report, Caracas.

Venturi, R., Brown, D. S., and Izenour, S. 1972. *Learning from Las Vegas.* Cambridge, Mass.: The M.I.T. Press.

Vernon, M. D. 1962. *The Psychology of Perception.* London: Pelican.

Von Moltke, W. 1969. The Evolution of the Linear Form. In *Planning Urban Growth and Regional Development*, ed. L. Rodwin and Associates. Cambridge, Mass.: The M.I.T. Press.

Vygotsky, L. S. 1962. *Thought and Language.* Cambridge, Mass.: The M.I.T. Press.

Webber, M. M. 1964. The Urban Place and the Nonplace Urban Realm. In *Explorations into Urban Structure.* Philadelphia: University of Pennsylvania Press.

Werner, H. 1948. *Comparative Psychology of Mental Development.* New York: Science Editions.

Wertheimer, M. 1958. Principles of Perceptual Organization. In *Readings in Perception*, ed. D. C. Beardslee and M. Wertheimer, pp. 115-135. New York: Van Nostrand.

White, G. 1967. Formation and Role of Public Attitudes. In *Environmental Quality in a Growing Economy*, ed. H. Jarrett. Baltimore, Md.: Johns Hopkins Press.

Whorf, B. J. 1956. *Language, Thought, and Reality.* Cambridge, Mass.: The M.I.T. Press.

Wilmott, P. 1962. Housing Density and Housing Design. *Town Planning Review* 33: 124.

Wilson, R. L. 1962. Livability of the City: Attitudes and Urban Development. In *Urban Growth Dynamics*, ed. F. S. Chapin and S. F. Weiss, pp. 359-400. New York: John Wiley.

Wurman, R. S. 1971. *Making the City Observable.* Cambridge, Mass.: The M.I.T. Press.

Index

Publications of the Joint Center for Urban Studies

The Joint Center for Urban Studies, a cooperative venture of the Massachusetts Institute of Technology and Harvard University, was founded in 1959 to organize and encourage research on urban and regional problems. Participants have included scholars from the fields of anthropology, architecture, business, city planning, economics, education, engineering, history, law, philosophy, political science, and sociology.

The findings and conclusions of this book are, as with all Joint Center publications, solely the responsibility of the author.

Published by Harvard University Press

The Intellectual versus the City: From Thomas Jefferson to Frank Lloyd Wright, by Morton and Lucia White, 1962

Streetcar Suburbs: The Process of Growth in Boston, 1870-1900, by Sam B. Warner Jr., 1962

City Politics, by Edward C. Banfield and James Q. Wilson, 1963

Law and Land: Anglo-American Planning Practice, edited by Charles M. Haar, 1964

Location and Land Use: Toward a General Theory of Land Rent, by William Alonso, 1964

Poverty and Progress: Social Mobility in a Nineteenth Century City, by Stephan Thernstrom, 1964

Boston: The Job Ahead, by Martin Meyerson and Edward C. Banfield, 1966

The Myth and Reality of Our Urban Problems, by Raymond Vernon, 1966

Muslim Cities in the Later Middle Ages, by Ira Marvin Lapidus, 1967

The Fragmented Metropolis: Los Angeles, 1850-1930, by Robert M. Fogelson, 1967

Law and Equal Opportunity: A Study of the Massachusetts Commission Against Discrimination, by Leon H. Mayhew, 1968

Varieties of Police Behavior: The Management of Law and Order in Eight Communities, by James Q. Wilson, 1968

The Metropolitan Enigma: Inquiries into the Nature and Dimensions of America's "Urban Crisis," edited by James Q. Wilson, revised edition, 1968

Traffic and The Police: Variations in Law-Enforcement Policy, by John A. Gardiner, 1969

The Influence of Federal Grants: Public Assistance in Massachusetts, by Martha Derthick, 1970

The Arts in Boston, by Bernard Taper, 1970

Families Against the City: Middle Class Homes of Industrial Chicago, 1872-1890, by Richard Sennett, 1970

The Political Economy of Urban Schools, by Martin T. Katzman, 1971

Origins of the Urban School: Public Education in Massachusetts, 1870-1915, by Marvin Lazerson, 1971

The Other Bostonians: Poverty and Progress in the American Metropolis, 1880-1970, by Stephan Thernstrom, 1973

Published by the MIT Press

The Image of the City, by Kevin Lynch, 1960

Housing and Economic Progress: A Study of the Housing Experiences of Boston's Middle-Income Families, by Lloyd Rodwin, 1961

The Historian and the City, edited by Oscar Handlin and John Burchard, 1963

The Federal Bulldozer: A Critical Analysis of Urban Renewal, 1949-1962, by Martin Anderson, 1964

The Future of Old Neighborhoods: Rebuilding for a Changing Population, by Bernard J. Frieden, 1964

Man's Struggle for Shelter in an Urbanizing World, by Charles Abrams, 1964

The View from the Road, by Donald Appleyard, Kevin Lynch, and John R. Myer, 1964

The Public Library and the City, edited by Ralph W. Conant, 1965

Regional Development Policy: A Case Study of Venezuela, by John Friedmann, 1966

Urban Renewal: The Record and the Controversy, edited by James Q. Wilson, 1966

Transport Technology for Developing Regions: A Study of Road Transportation in Venezuela, by Richard M. Soberman, 1966

Computer Methods in the Analysis of Large-Scale Social Systems, edited by James M. Beshers, 1968

Planning Urban Growth and Regional Development: The Experience of the Guayana Program of Venezuela, by Lloyd Rodwin and Associates, 1969

Build a Mill, Build a City, Build a School: Industrialization, Urbanization, and Education in Ciudad Guayana, by Noel F. McGinn and Russell G. Davis, 1969

Land-Use Controls in the United States, by John Delafons, second edition, 1969

Beyond the Melting Pot: The Negroes, Puerto Ricans, Jews, Italians, and Irish of New York City, by Nathan Glazer and Daniel Patrick Moynihan, revised edition, 1970

Bargaining: Monopoly Power versus Union Power, by George de Menil, 1971

Housing the Urban Poor: A Critical Evaluation of Federal Housing Policy, by Arthur P. Solomon, 1974

The Politics of Neglect: Urban Aid from Model Cities to Revenue Sharing, by Bernard J. Frieden and Marshall Kaplan, 1975

Planning a Pluralist City: Conflicting Realities in Ciudad Guayana, by Donald Appleyard, 1976

The Joint Center also publishes monographs and reports.